Forecasting Financial Markets

WILEY

SERIES IN
FINANCIAL ECONOMICS
AND QUANTITATIVE ANALYSIS

Series Editor: Stephen Hall, *London Business School, UK*

Editorial Board: Robert F. Engle, *University of California, USA*
John Flemming, *European Bank, UK*
Lawrence R. Klein, *University of Pennsylvania, USA*
Helmut Lütkepohl, *Humboldt University, Germany*

Forecasting Financial Markets

Exchange Rates, Interest Rates and Asset Management

Edited by Christian Dunis

Chemical Bank, London

John Wiley & Sons

Chichester · New York · Brisbane · Toronto · Singapore

Chapters 2, 9, 10 and 13 were originally published in the *Working Papers in Financial Economics*,
Chemical Bank. Chapter 8 was originally published in the *Journal of Banking and Finance* and
Chapter 4 originally published in the *European Journal of Finance*.

Other Wiley Editorial Offices

John Wiley & Sons, Inc., 605 Third Avenue,
New York, NY 10158-0012, USA

Jacaranda Wiley Ltd, 33 Park Road, Milton,
Queensland 4064, Australia

John Wiley & Sons (Canada) Ltd, 22 Worcester Road,
Rexdale, Ontario M9W 1L1, Canada

John Wiley & Sons (Asia) Pte Ltd, 2 Clementi Loop #02-01,
Jin Xing Distripark, Singapore 129809

Library of Congress Cataloging-in-Publication Data

Forecasting financial markets : exchange rates, interest
and asset management / edited by Christian Dunis.
        p.   cm. — (Series in financial economics and quantitative
analysis)
    Includes bibliographical references and index.
    ISBN 0-471-96653-3 (alk. paper)
    1. Capital market—Mathematical models. 2. Foreign exchange
market—Mathematical models. I. Dunis, Christian. II. Series.
HG4523.F67 1996
332′.0414—dc20   96-22532
                                                            CIP

British Library Cataloguing in Publication Data

A catalogue record for this book is available from the British Library

ISBN 0-471-96653-3

Typeset in 10/12pt Times by Keytec Typesetting Ltd, Bridport, Dorset.
Printed and bound in Great Britain by Biddles Ltd, Guildford.
This book is printed on acid-free paper responsibly manufactured from sustainable forestation,
for which at least two trees are planted for each one used for paper production.

Contents

List of Contributors

EMMANUEL ACAR
Banque Nationale de Paris, London Branch, London, England.

DIRK-EMMA BAESTAENS
Erasmus University, Rotterdam, Dept of Finance, Rotterdam, The Netherlands.

ANDREW N. BURGESS
Department of Decision Science, London Business School, London, England.

MICHEL M. DACOROGNA
Olsen & Associates, Research Institute for Applied Economics, Zürich, Switzerland.

RICHARD DALLAWAY
Fusion Systems Ltd, London, England.

JÉRÔME DRUNAT
IREFI, University of Paris XII, France.

GILLES DUFRÉNOT
ERUDITE, University of Paris XII, France.

CHRISTIAN L. DUNIS
Quantitative Research and Trading, Chemical Bank, London, England.

CHRISTIAN JOST
Olsen & Associates, Research Institute for Applied Economics, Zürich, Switzerland.

ANDRÉ KELLER
Université UVHC, Valenciennes, France.

SWEE LEONG
Quantitative Research and Trading, Chemical Bank, London, England.

PIERRE LEQUEX
Banque Nationale de Paris, London Branch, London, England.

ANDREA LORASCHI
SIGE Consulenza SIM S.p.A., Milan, Italy.

AARON H. W. LOW
Department of Finance and Banking, School of Management, National University of Singapore, Singapore.

ALLAN M. MALZ
Markets Group, Federal Reserve Bank of New York, New York, NY, USA.

LAURENT MATHIEU
MODEM, University of Paris X, France.

MANUEL MORENO
Departamento de Economia de la Empresa Universidad Carlos III de Madrid, Madrid, Spain.

ULRICH A. MÜLLER
Olsen & Associates, Research Institute for Applied Economics, Zürich, Switzerland.

JAYARAM MUTHUSWAMY
Department of Finance and Banking, School of Management, National University of Singapore, Singapore.

IAN NABNEY
Aston University, Birmingham, England.

RICHARD B. OLSEN
Olsen & Associates, Research Institute for Applied Economics, Zürich, Switzerland.

J. IGNACIO PEÑA
Departamento de Economia de la Empresa Universidad Carlos III de Madrid, Madrid, Spain.

OLIVER V. PICTET
Olsen & Associates, Research Institute for Applied Economics, Zürich, Switzerland.

WENDY REDSHAW
Summit Financial Systems Limited, London, England.

A. N. REFENES
Department of Decision Science, London Business School, London, England.

STEPHEN J. TAYLOR
Department of Accounting and Finance, Lancaster University, Lancaster, England.

ANDREA G. B. TETTAMANZI
Universita degli Studi di Milano, Dipartimento di Scienze dell'Informazione, Milan, Italy.

W. M. VAN DEN BERG
Erasmus University, Rotterdam, Dept of Finance, Rotterdam, The Netherlands.

H. VAUDREY
Erasmus University Rotterdam, Dept of Finance, Rotterdam, The Netherlands.

J. ROBERT WARD
Olsen & Associates, Research Institute for Applied Economics, Zürich, Switzerland.

XINZHONG XU
Department of Accounting and Finance, University of Manchester, Manchester, England.

BIN ZHOU
Sloan School of Management, Massachusetts Institute of Technology, Cambridge MA, USA.

About the Contributors

EMMANUEL ACAR

Emmanuel Acar is one of the two portfolio managers of managed accounts at Banque Nationale de Paris in London. He joined the BNP proprietary trading desk in July 1990. Since then, he has been active in the development of proprietary trading models and portfolio management methods. He has experience in quantitative strategies, having done his Ph.D. on the stochastic properties of trading rules. Mr Acar is a member of the Forex Association, the European Managed Futures Association and the Managed Futures Association.

DIRK-EMMA BAESTAENS

Currently Assistant Professor of Finance at the Finance Department, Erasmus University Rotterdam. Studied law and applied economics and graduated from the Manchester Business School with a Ph.D. in business economics. Teaches extensively at the Rotterdam School of Management as well as the Rochester-Nijenrode Executive MBA programmes. Co-author of *Neural Network Solutions for Trading in Financial Markets*, Financial Times–Pitman Publishing.

ANDREW NEIL BURGESS

Andrew Neil Burgess is a research fellow at the NeuroForecasting Unit of London Business School working on applications of advanced decision technologies to problems in finance and marketing. At Thorn-EMI Central Research Laboratories he worked in the European ESPRIT Project HANSA.

Over the past seven years, he has been actively researching in the areas of neural networks and fielded live applications of both database marketing and financial trading. Other activities include lecturing and consulting in the USA, South Africa, Europe and the UK.

MICHEL M. DACOROGNA

Michel M. Dacorogna is one of the founding members of Olsen & Associates (O&A), a research institute in applied economics. He has devoted the past few years to an extensive research and development project involving a real-time, value-added information system in the field of applied economics. His main research interest is the application of computer science and numerical analysis to dynamic systems in various fields in order to gain insight into the behaviour of such systems. In addition to his research duties at O&A, Dr Dacorogna has assumed a leadership role in organizing the first international conference on high frequency data in finance. Dr Dacorogna received his Ph.D. and M.Sc. in physics from the University of Geneva. Prior to joining O&A, he was a postdoctorate in the solid state theory group at the University of California at Berkeley.

RICHARD DALLAWAY

Richard Dallaway received a first class honours degree in computing and artificial intelligence from the University of Sussex. For his doctoral thesis at Sussex he used neural computing to model the dynamic behaviour of natural systems, namely children and adults learning and solving arithmetic problems.

Richard joined Logica in 1993 as a software engineer and consultant, working on a variety of machine learning projects. He now works on visualisation, web and database projects for Fusion Systems Ltd, a City-based consultancy.

JÉRÔME DRUNAT

Jérôme Drunat is a senior researcher with the IREFI Research Group of Paris XII University. He is currently working on the effects of nonlinear dynamics in the field of finance. Recently published papers discuss applications of ARCH family models to a variety of high frequency data.

GILLES DUFRÉNOT

Gilles Dufrénot is a senior research scientist with the ERUDITE Research Group of Paris XII University where he received his Ph.D. in economics. His research encompasses nonlinear econometrics and chaotic dynamics applied to macroeconomics and finance. Recently published papers examine the application of bispectral analysis to macroeconomic time series.

CHRISTIAN L. DUNIS

Christian L. Dunis is the Head of Quantitative Research and Trading (QRT) at Chemical Bank. He is a Vice-President with Chemical's Global Trading Division based in London. He is responsible for developing the bank's quantitative research capabilities and managing the development of computer models for generating proprietary trading revenues.

C.L. Dunis holds a Diploma in Higher Studies in economics and international finance and a Ph.D. in economics from the University of Paris. He is a member of the Securities and Futures Authority in London, of the French Association of Corporate Treasurers (AFTE) in Paris and of the International Institute of Forecasters (USA).

He is the organiser, with Imperial College, of an annual international conference held in London on 'Forecasting Financial Markets: Advances for Exchange Rates, Interest Rates and Asset Management'.

He is the editor of Chemical's *Working Papers in Financial Economics*, a quarterly bulletin open to academics, and a member of the editorial board of *The European Journal of Finance*. He is also the co-author of *Exchange Rate Forecasting* published by Woodhead-Faulkner in 1989 and the co-editor and co-author of *Nonlinear Modelling of High Frequency Financial Time Series* to be published in 1997 by John Wiley & Sons.

CHRISTIAN JOST

Christian Jost graduated in mathematics at the University of Zürich in 1993. His minor subjects were biology and computer science. He worked at Olsen & Associates as a part-timer during his studies and as a junior researcher. During his stay he particularly explored the behaviour of trading models under varying market hours. Currently he is working on a Ph.D. thesis in theoretical ecology (predation theory applied to aquatic communities) in Paris.

ANDRÉ KELLER

André Keller received his Ph.D. in economics from the University of Paris. He is a Professor of Economics at the University of Valenciennes where he teaches microeconomics and time series analysis.

Dr Keller's research experience centres on building and analysing large size econometric models, as well as forecasting. Since 1985, his research interests have mostly concentrated on time series modelling with an application to the foreign exchange market.

SWEE LEONG

Swee Leong, is a quantitative analyst in the Quantitative Research and Trading Group at Chemical Bank, London. He holds a B.Sc. in applied mathematics (first class hons.) and a Ph.D. in aeronautical engineering, both from the University of London. He is responsible for the detailed specifications of the trading models used by QRT. Dr Leong joined Chemical in 1993. He has extensive experience of quantitative models, having previously worked in similar positions in the City.

PIERRE LEQUEUX

Pierre Lequeux is one of the two portfolio managers of the managed accounts at Banque Nationale de Paris in London. He joined the Banque Nationale de Paris London Branch in 1987. Mr Lequeux is a graduate in international trade and holds a diploma of the Forex Association. He joined the BNP proprietary desk in 1991 as a dealer after gaining experience on the treasury and corporate desks. Then as senior dealer, he became active in the research and development of trading models and portfolio risk management techniques. Mr Lequeux is a member of the Forex Association, the European Managed Futures Association and the Managed Futures Association.

ANDREA LORASCHI

Andrea Loraschi received a degree in political economy from the Bocconi University of Milan in 1991 with a major in monetary and financial economics. He has worked for two financial institutions before joining SIGE Consulenza SIM (Milan), the mutual fund advisory company of the IMI Group. In SIGE Consulenza, he is responsible for the team which provides quantitative support to the investment decisions, both on the asset allocation and the portfolio selection level. He also co-manages the Japanese equities portfolio.

AARON H. W. LOW

Dr Low is a lecturer in finance and banking with the Faculty of Business Administration at the National University of Singapore. Dr Low graduated with an honours degree in engineering from NUS and a C.Phil. and Ph.D. in Finance from UCLA. He has taught graduate business finance courses at

UCLA, Stanford and Peperdine universities, and published in the *Review of Futures Markets*, and *Research in Finance*. Prior to joining NUS, Dr Low worked with IBM. His research interests are primarily in derivatives, securities pricing, and market microstructure.

ALLAN MALZ

Allan Malz is an economist at the Federal Reserve Bank of New York with responsibility for introducing new market monitoring and analytical techniques to the foreign exchange and open market operations desks. He previously was a trader on the New York Fed's foreign exchange desk and an economist in the Research Department. Mr Malz has a doctorate in economics from Columbia University and a master's degree in economics from the University of Munich.

LAURENT MATHIEU

Laurent Mathieu is a senior research scientist with the MODEM Research Group of Paris X University. He has written several articles on parametric models for nonlinear time series. His current work centres around the construction of chaotic and nonlinear stochastic models for financial time series.

MANUEL A. MORENO

Manuel A. Moreno is a Ph.D. student at the Business Economics Department of the Universidad Carlos III de Madrid. He holds a BS degree in mathematics from the Universidad Complutense.

ULRICH A. MÜLLER

Throughout his studies and professional career, Dr Müller has worked in Zürich while changing his working fields several times. He did his undergraduate studies in solid-state physics, became a teaching assistant at the ETH (Swiss Federal Institute of Technology), and wrote his Ph.D. thesis on thermoacoustic oscillations which won the Georg A. Fischer prize. He made quantitative risk analyses at an engineering company and became self-employed.

In 1985, he was a founding member of Olsen & Associates (O&A). Quantitative finance was the new field to which he applied his skills in mathematics and programming. Large research and development projects have taught him to work in a team with his colleagues. He is the co-author of most of O&A's scientific publications, among them the recent paper on the HARCH model which describes prices as generated by many market actors with different time horizons. He has given invited talks at conferences and in academic institutions.

JAYARAM MUTHUSWAMY

Dr Muthuswamy is currently a senior lecturer in finance and banking with the Faculty of Business Administration at the National University of Singapore. Dr Muthuswamy holds an undergraduate degree in economics and statistics from the London School of Economics, an MBA in finance from the Wharton School, an MS in statistics from Stanford University, and a Ph.D. in Finance from the University of Chicago. He has published in the *Journal of Finance*, *The Review of Futures Markets*, and *Research in Finance*. Dr Muthuswamy previously taught at Duke University's Business School in the United States. He has also been a foreign exchange trader, as well as a staff economist with the Development Bank of Singapore. Prior to joining academia, he was a treasurer with the Development Bank of Singapore. Dr Muthuswamy's research interests are in asset pricing theory, the pricing of derivative securities, the micro-structural theory of finance, as well as econometrics.

IAN NABNEY

After completing a BA in mathematics at Oxford, and a Ph.D. in mathematics at Cambridge, Ian Nabney joined Logica Cambridge Ltd in 1989. He has been active in neural network research and deployment for over five years. During his time at Logica, he developed applications using neural networks, rule induction and other statistical techniques, in a wide range of applications, including financial time series analysis, system identification and control, image analysis and marketing, and was the system architect for a rule induction based data exploration toolkit. He joined the Neural Computing Research Group at Aston University as a lecturer in January 1995. He has 17 publications, principally in neural networks and rule induction, and is the chair of the scientific programme committee for the Neural Computing Applications Forum.

RICHARD B. OLSEN

After completing his studies at the University of Zürich (law) and Oxford (economics), Dr Olsen worked for two years at a private bank in Zürich, initially as legal counsel, then as a financial analyst, and finally as a foreign exchange dealer. During the course of his studies, Dr Olsen had developed a

number of theories on financial markets, theories which he then saw supported by the behaviour of foreign exchange practitioners, who seemed to understand certain elements of those theories intuitively. Thus motivated, he founded Olsen & Associates, a private research institute, in August of 1985. There, Dr Olsen and his staff developed a real-time information system providing decision support to foreign exchange dealers.

J. IGNACIO PEÑA

J. Ignacio Peña is Titular Professor of Finance at the Universidad Carlos III de Madrid. He has previously held teaching and research positions at the Universidad Autonoma de Madrid and at the University of Chicago. He has published numerous articles in finance, economics and econometrics journals as well as in professional volumes. His papers cover topics such as mergers and takeovers, market efficiency, option pricing and international financial integration. He is associate editor of *The European Journal of Finance*.

OLIVIER V. PICTET

After completing his undergraduate studies in architecture and physics, Dr Pictet got his Ph.D. in solid-state physics from the University of Geneva. In addition, he followed a one-year postdoctoral course in artificial intelligence at the Swiss Federal Institute of Technology in Lausanne. His main research interest is the application of numerical analysis and computer science to solve complex problems in various fields.

He joined Olsen & Associates in 1987 to become one of its research group members. Working on large research and development projects, like the O&A's real-time value-added information system, he gained a wide experience in applied economics and high-quality software development. During the last years, he played a leadership role in the implementation of a powerful research environment for developing trading models in finance.

WENDY REDSHAW

After graduating in mathematics from Imperial College in 1987, Wendy joined Logica where she worked for over eight years. Her role during that time involved the design, development and management of a variety of projects, primarily in the finance sector. Her early involvement with knowledge based systems covered many different projects. As a result of her work, she wrote a paper on 'Expert Systems in Business' which won the Logica Publications Prize. Following a period advising in the area of risk management and the use of advanced technologies, Wendy moved across to manage the early stages of the joint project with Chemical Bank which forms the basis of Chapter 10. She then took up a management position at Barclays Network Services, being responsible for the piloting of distributed UNIX software applications for Barclays nationwide.

Early in 1995, she moved to Summit Financial Systems, a risk management and financial analytics company, as a project manager.

APOSTOLOS-PAUL REFENES

Apostolos-Paul Refenes has written over 70 papers and edited 2 books on the subject of neural computing and financial engineering applications. His previous appointments include University College London, University of Athens and the DTI, as well as consultancy for both government and private organisations in Europe, the USA and Japan. Currently, he is Associate Professor of Decision Science and Director of the NeuroForecasting Programme at the London Business School. His research interests focus on neural networks, financial engineering applications, portfolio managemement/ asset allocation and term structure models.

STEPHEN TAYLOR

Stephen Taylor is a Professor of Finance at Lancaster University, England, where he teaches international finance and financial econometrics. He has also taught at universities in Austria, Belgium, Hong Kong, Australia and New Zealand. His numerous publications include the research text *Modelling Financial Time Series* (Wiley), in which he presented the first description of stochastic volatility models. Recent volatility papers have appeared in *Mathematical Finance* and the *Journal of Financial and Quantitative Analysis*. BA (Cambridge), MA, Ph.D. (Lancaster).

ANDREA G. B. TETTAMANZI

Andrea G. B. Tettamanzi received a master's degree in computer science from the University of Milan in 1991 and a Ph.D. in computational mathematics and operations research from the same institution in 1995. From 1994 to 1995 he was with the Computer Science Division of the University of California, Berkeley, as a visiting scholar. In 1995, he established Genetica—Advanced Software Architectures S.r.l. (a consulting firm in computer science applications) in Milan. His current areas of interest are evolutionary algorithms, fuzzy logic and soft computing and is the author of several scholarly publications in that field.

WILLEM-MAX VAN DEN BERGH

Currently Associate Professor of Finance at the Finance Department, Erasmus University Rotterdam. Developer of simulation models on currency and exchange risk management in cooperation with ABN AMRO Bank. Co-author of *Neural Network Solutions for Trading in Financial Markets*, Financial Times–Pitman Publishing.

HERVÉ VAUDREY

Hervé Vaudrey is a research assistant at the Faculty of Economics Department of Finance, Erasmus University Rotterdam. He graduated as an engineer from Ecole Supérieure de Physique Chimie Industrielles de Paris. He holds a DEA of Cognitive Science from the University Paris VI.

His interests include: handwritten character recognition and stock price forecasting with neural networks.

ROBERT WARD

Robert Ward studied general engineering and computer science at the University of Cambridge, England, where he gained BA and MA degrees.

After working as a research assistant providing software support to the Energy Research Group at the Cavendish Laboratories in Cambridge (1979–1980), he moved to Vienna, Austria, where he was a staff member of the International Institute for Applied Systems Analysis (1980–1985). Here he developed the db++ relational database management system. He then found himself employed by Ascom AG, Berne, Switzerland (1985–1988), where he was involved in many projects developing real-time software as well as establishing a centre of Unix 'know how' and software expertise within Ascom. Since joining O&A in 1988, he has worked as software engineer and manager in both the O&A Software and Research groups. He is currently joint manager of the Software group and is heavily involved in redesigning the O&A software systems to take advantage of modern engineering techniques.

GARY XU

Gary Xu is a lecturer in accounting and finance at the University of Manchester, England. He teaches investment analysis and capital market theory. His main research interests include volatility modelling and forecasting, the efficiency of financial futures and options markets, and empirical tests of asset pricing models. He has published in a number of leading academic journals including the *Journal of Banking and Finance*, the *Journal of Financial and Quantitative Analysis*, and the *Review of Futures Markets*. B.Sc. (Peking), MBA (Aston), Ph.D. (Lancaster).

BIN ZHOU

Dr Zhou is an Assistant Professor at the Sloan School of Management, Massachusetts Institute of Technology. He holds a Ph.D. in statistics from the University of California at Berkeley. His research focuses on developing statistical methodology and theory for analysing ultra high-frequency financial time series. He introduced a concept of observation noise in modelling high-frequency data and a concept of f-consistency in evaluating parameter estimation. Dr Zhou also developed a real-time foreign exchange rate forecasting system using the devolatilisation methodology he developed earlier. The system can also be extended to many other financial markets.

Series Preface

This series aims to publish books which give authoritative accounts of major new topics in financial economics and general quantitative analysis. The coverage of the series includes both macro and micro economics and its aim is to be of interest to practitioners and policy-makers as well as the wider academic community.

The development of new techniques and ideas in econometrics has been rapid in recent years and these developments are now being applied to a wide range of areas and markets. Our hope is that this series will provide a rapid and effective means of communicating these ideas to a wide international audience and that in turn this will contribute to the growth of knowledge, the exchange of scientific information and techniques and the development of cooperation in the field of economics.

Stephen Hall
London Business School, UK

Preface

Forecasting Financial Markets is based on the International Conference of the same name organised in London in 1994 and 1995 by Chemical Bank's Quantitative Research & Trading Group, and Imperial College.

Since its inception in 1994, the Conference has grown in scope and stature year by year. Following the 'call for papers', over 30 articles were submitted in 1994, over 50 in 1995 and over 80 in 1996! The number of papers actually presented has also surged, from 18 in 1994 to 51 in 1996, with the participation of prestigious academic and research institutions from all over the world including major central banks and quantitative fund managers.

The interest in *Forecasting Financial Markets* certainly shows the growing belief, not only among market practitioners but also in the world of academia, that most markets are not perfectly efficient in so far as prices of financial assets do not immediately and fully reflect new information.

More fundamentally, the interest in financial markets and the possibility to forecast their course, at least to some degree, seems to be linked to the growing recognition, among economists and policy-makers, of the increasing impact of financial variables on the real economy and, thus, on economic policy in general.

Until the late 1970s, excess demand was always accommodated with extra credit and, ultimately, some extra inflation. But the realisation of the dangers of inflation after the two oil shocks of 1973 and 1979 has led to economic policies which have had price stability as their main priority. Combined with the liberalisation and the globalisation of world financial markets during the 1980s, this change in policy priorities has provoked a higher volatility in interest rates. And precisely because the fight against inflation had become paramount and more successful, increases in the nominal interest rate translated in fact into real interest rate rises, with negative consequences upon the level of economic activity and employment.

Accordingly, since the early 1980s, the key economic adjustment variable has switched from inflation to the interest rate. Because of the links of all interest rate markets via the exchange rate, the higher volatility of interest rates has spilled over to all other assets, helped by the liberalisation and the globalisation of world asset markets. This instability has increased uncertainty, pushing creditors to ask for higher risk premia, a move that has been reinforced by the apparently irresistible rise in indebtedness.

It is this increased uncertainty which has sparked the development of new hedging tools and has been behind the exponential rise of derivative markets since the late 1980s and early 1990s. Whether these new markets have reduced volatility levels by opening new opportunities for risk diversification or whether, on the contrary, they have contributed to the rise in global instability in the financial markets remains an open question at this stage, but numerous recent events, such as the Procter & Gamble/Bankers Trust case in February 1994, the fall of Barings in February 1995 and the demise of the US subsidiary of Daiwa in October 1995, have clearly demonstrated the necessity for commercial and industrial companies and financial institutions (and their regulators) to closely monitor their risk positions.

At the same time when uncertainty was increasing, empirical evidence has emerged during the past decade that pockets of predictability do exist in financial markets. Academics have developed new mathematical and statistical tools to help predict future price moves. Combined with extensive data banks (and also higher frequency data banks) and the greater availability of powerful computers, these new techniques which rely heavily on the analysis of nonlinearities now make it possible to devise systems that can help take and manage risk positions in the different asset markets. They are increasingly used by major trading institutions and fund managers and there is also an increasing interest from some large corporates.

Today's financial markets are characterised by a large number of participants, with a different appetite for risk, a different time horizon, different motivations and reactions to unexpected news. In the circumstances, it would come as a surprise if all these complex interactions were to average out in a linear fashion. Furthermore, the introduction of nonlinearities in the modelling approach should allow one to explain some price moves that previously seemed random, without resorting to stochastic mechanisms.

Not surprisingly, the 'Forecasting Financial Markets' Conference revolves around all the major themes of today's state of the art financial research while always keeping a strong emphasis on empirical applications so as not to lose the practitioner's perspective.

In total, 48 papers channelled into 6 mainstream sessions were presented during the 1994 and the 1995 Chemical Bank/Imperial College 'Forecasting Financial Markets' Conference. This is approximately equivalent to four books of the same size as this volume! Clearly, a choice needed to be made and it could only be done on the basis of a subjective appraisal of the most novel themes investigated in the Conference.

Accordingly, I have selected three main themes for this book: *Modelling with High Frequency Data*, *The Informational Content of Volatility Markets* and *Applications of Neural Networks and Genetic Algorithms*.

1 MODELLING WITH HIGH FREQUENCY DATA

Not so long ago the assumption that price changes in financial markets were unpredictable was still one of the undiscussed pillars of finance. True, the seminal work of Mandelbrot (1963) gave a first blow to the well-established theory of a Gaussian distribution of financial asset returns and underlined the presence of volatility clusters in these time series.

Almost 20 years later, Engle (1982) formalised this latter idea with the Autoregressive Conditional Heteroskedastic or ARCH model: basically, this model states that the variance of asset returns in any given period directly depends on a constant and the previous period's squared random component of the return. This model was later generalised by Bollerslev (1986) and Taylor (1986) to give the Generalised Autoregressive Conditional Heteroskedastic or GARCH model: in this case, the variance of asset returns in any given period directly depends on a constant, the previous period's squared random component of the return and the previous period's variance. In other words, financial theory had recognised that the variance of asset returns was indeed predictable, if not the returns themselves which remained independently and identically distributed or i.i.d.

Still, one had to wait until the 1990s, with easier accessibility to financial data banks and greater computer power, to have a thorough demonstration of the benefits of technical trading rules and, consequently, of the possibility to forecast not only the variance but also the mean of financial asset returns: among others, let us note the contributions of Dunis and Feeny (1989), Neftçi (1991), Brock *et al.* (1992), Taylor and Allen (1992) and Levich and Thomas (1993).

This latter research area paved the way for papers whose aim was precisely to demonstrate that price changes themselves were predictable when models and time frequencies adequate for financial markets were chosen: among the contributions concentrating on frequencies from intraday down to the week, and without being exhaustive, one can note again Taylor (1986), but also LeBaron (1992), Dacorogna *et al.* (1992, 1993), Pictet *et al.* (1992), Moody and Wu (1995) and Dunis (1996).

Clearly, there has been a growing recognition that the introduction of nonlinearities in the modelling approach could allow one to explain certain price moves that seemed previously random. At the same time that it enabled the testing of new categories of models, and particularly nonlinear models, the access to higher frequency data banks has made it possible to explore the *microstructure* of financial markets.

The annual 'Forecasting Financial Markets' Conference has certainly also contributed to this effort, as well as the Conference on 'Microstructure of Foreign

Exchange Markets' held in Perugia in July 1994 and the Conference on 'High Frequency Data in Finance' held in Zürich in March 1995.

The five chapters of this first section have been presented at the 'Forecasting Financial Markets' Conference either in 1994 or in 1995 and represent therefore a contribution to this endeavour. They are respectively:

1. 'Information Flows in High Frequency Exchange Rates' by A. Low and J. Muthuswamy: this chapter is a thorough investigation of the empirical features of the foreign exchange market studied at a five-minute sampling interval. It presents a practical analysis of the *microstructure* of the currency market which aims at studying the *effects of news* on price and spread dynamics. The chapter gives more insight about several other aspects of high frequency exchange rates such as *intraday seasonality* and, as expected, it shows that news activity increases the conditional volatility of both spreads and returns. An interesting finding is that news activity also increases the *level* of spreads contrary to traditional theory which would rather assume that, once news is released and uncertainty lifted spread levels should narrow.
2. 'Stochastic or Chaotic Dynamics in High Frequency Exchange Rates?' by J. Drunat, G. Dufrénot, C. Dunis and L. Mathieu: this chapter investigates which is the best modelling strategy for exchange rates sampled at 10-minute, 30-minute and 60-minute frequencies. The chapter uses a linearity test based on a *frequency* domain approach to see whether these time series conform to linear or nonlinear processes. Stochastic and deterministic nonlinearities are further discriminated by estimating stochastic models that allow for nonlinearities in the *mean* of the series and by testing for chaotic dynamics. In contradiction with previous work on daily data, the assumption that high frequency exchange rates are best described by low dimensional chaotic systems is clearly rejected.
3. 'Forecasting Foreign Exchange Rates Subject to De-volatilization' by B. Zhou: this chapter presents a new approach to the problem of heteroskedasticity of financial time series. It suggests to analyse a *homoskedastic subsequence* of the data, i.e. to 'de-volatilize' the time series. This procedure reduces the noise effect as well as the level of heteroskedasticity and it produces a return series which is quasi-normally distributed. It also allows for a *volatility-varying* sampling frequency, with more data being collected when the market is more active and less when it shows a greater level of inertia. The use of the distribution characteristics of the 'de-volatilized' return series helps to detect short-term trends early and to forecast the market's evolution accordingly.
4. 'Heterogeneous Real-Time Trading Strategies in the Foreign Exchange Market' by M. M. Dacorogna, U. A. Müller, C. Jost, O. V. Pictet, R. B. Olsen and J. R. Ward: this chapter presents a set of profitable trading models developed for different geographical locations from an underlying tick by tick data bank. It shows that the profitability of a given intraday trading algorithm can vary significantly depending on the *working hours* it is tested with. In particular, it

demonstrates that the best choice of working hours is usually when the markets for a given asset are most active. This is in contrast with the traditional 'efficient market' hypothesis which relates the possibility of excess returns to inefficiencies (and therefore, among others, periods of illiquid markets) and confirms the *heterogeneous* nature of the foreign exchange market.

5. 'Dynamic Strategies: A Correlation Study' by E. Acar and P. Lequeux: this chapter investigates the correlation properties between rates of return generated by dynamic trading strategies applied to daily data for exchange rates and futures prices for stock indices, government bonds and commodities. In particular, it shows that correlations between the same trading rule applied to several different assets are positive but lower in absolute terms than correlations between the underlying markets. It also demonstrates that strategies based on daily data but triggered at *different times of the day* may be an alternative to the use of intraday data. This introduces a non-synchronous trading problem which is dealt with by establishing the correlation coefficient between identical trading strategies applied to the same market but triggered at different times of the day.

2 THE INFORMATIONAL CONTENT OF VOLATILITY MARKETS

This section concentrates on the informational efficiency of the options markets and investigates whether these markets can help forecast the underlying financial markets. True, options markets are still often viewed by many as markets which are only concerned with the pricing of the volatility of the assets underlying the option contract. Nevertheless, in recent years, microstructure theory in finance has been preoccupied with issues such as the informational content of traded volumes and the informational content of price movements in so-called 'allied' markets such as the options markets (see O'Hara (1995)). Accordingly, this section is focused on what information, if any, can be derived from the options market to help forecast either the mean or the variance of financial time series. It presents four chapters which are respectively:

1. 'Using Option Prices to Estimate Realignment Probabilities in the European Monetary System' by A. Malz: this chapter describes a procedure for deriving the market's expectations of future exchange rate changes not from interest rate differentials as is generally the case, but from currency option prices. Using daily data, this chapter shows how 'risk reversals', i.e. the combinations of an out-of-the money call with an out-of-the-money put, could be used to retrieve the realignment probabilities of the French franc and pound sterling in 1992 and 1993. This is done by estimating the parameters of a *jump–diffusion model* of exchange rate behaviour from option prices. These parameters are then employed to calculate the *ex ante probability distribution* of both the French franc and pound sterling and thus their realignment probability.

2. 'On the Term Structure of Interbank Interest Rates: Jump–Diffusion Processes and Option Pricing' by M. Moreno and J. Ignacio Peña: this chapter shows how different assumptions about the effects of information arrival on interest rate changes imply different stochastic processes and hence different partial equilibrium conditions. The chapter assumes that a *combined jump–diffusion process* is generating the daily Spanish interbank rate, which in turn allows the authors to relate the jumps with known interventions by the monetary authorities. It shows that the interest rate behaviour during the review period is better explained by the combined process than by a pure diffusion model. Additionally, it demonstrates that, if the informational content of the jumps is not taken into account, there is a *systematic underpricing* of both bond and call option prices.

3. 'Conditional Volatility and Informational Efficiency of the PHLX Currency Options Market' by X. Xu and S. J. Taylor: this chapter investigates the relative performance of implied and historical volatility predictors in forecasting future volatility. The accuracy of the volatility forecast implied by option prices is taken as a measure of the *information content of option prices* and is tested for four currency options quoted on the Philadelphia Stock Exchange, using daily data from 1985 to 1991. The authors also use ARCH models to check whether the series of historical currency returns contain any additional information to that derived from option prices. By showing that their implied volatility forecasts significantly outperform the forecasts derived from past returns, be it the historical volatility forecast or the ARCH-generated forecast, they attest to the informational efficiency of the PHLX currency option market.

4. 'Efficiency Tests with Overlapping Data: An Application to the Currency Options Market' by C. Dunis and A. Keller: this chapter presents the results of an empirical study into the efficiency of the over-the-counter currency options market, using daily data from September 1989 to September 1993 for six exchange rate implied volatilities. The methodology relates the historical volatility to the implied volatility of an option on the underlying asset at a specified prior time and then proceeds to test obvious hypotheses about the values of the coefficients. The authors employ *panel regression* to address the problem of overlapping data. They also use volatility data directly quoted on the market in order to avoid the *biases* which may occur when 'backing out' volatility from specific option pricing models. In general, the evidence rejects the hypothesis that the currency options market is efficient and suggests that implied volatility is not the best predictor of future exchange rate volatility.

3 APPLICATIONS OF NEURAL NETWORKS AND GENETIC ALGORITHMS

As mentioned earlier, today's financial markets are characterised by a large number of participants, with a different appetite for risk, a different time horizon, different motivations and reactions to unexpected news. It seems therefore unlikely that all these complex interactions could average out in a linear fashion and it should come as no surprise that, with the development of greater computer power along with the better accessibility of more extensive data banks, researchers have become more keen to explore techniques particularly suited for the study of nonlinear behaviour, such as neural networks and genetic algorithms. This last section is consequently dedicated to the application of neural networks and genetic algorithms to the analysis and forecasting of financial markets. It contains four chapters, which are respectively:

1. 'Leading Edge Forecasting Techniques for Exchange Rate Prediction' by I. Nabney, C. Dunis, R. Dallaway, S. Leong and W. Redshaw: this chapter describes how, from an underlying tick by tick data bank, modern machine learning techniques can be used in conjunction with statistical methods to forecast short-term exchange rate movements and produce models suitable for use in trading. The chapter compares the results achieved by *rule induction*, which is a method of extracting rules from data, and *neural networks*, which are a powerful and general method for nonlinear modelling and shows how they can be used in a complementary fashion. It stresses some of the problems the authors encountered with these modelling techniques. As forecasting accuracy is not a sufficient condition for economic performance, the results are also evaluated by means of a trading strategy.

2. 'Market Inefficiencies, Technical Trading and Neural Networks' by D. J. E. Baestaens, W. M. van den Berg and H. Vaudrey: this chapter uses Unilever's daily stock price from January 1973 to March 1992 to show that adaptive nonlinear systems can be trained to perform *technical analysis* with a minimum of assumptions. The authors aim at demonstrating that the pattern recognition capabilities of neural networks make them particularly well suited for technical analysis: the computation of technical indicators such as moving averages and relative strength indices is seen as a method of pattern recognition. As neural networks have in principle the capacity to *classify* such patterns, it is deemed that they should consequently help to predict the corresponding return profile. The proposed model achieves a satisfactory forecasting accuracy, but further research is still required as this is not sufficient to ensure a profitable trading strategy.

3. 'The Use of Error Feedback Terms in Neural Network Modelling of Financial Time Series' by A. N. Burgess and A. N. Refenes: this chapter investigates the use of *error feedback terms* as a means of reducing the impact of non-stationarity in a time series and of modelling more accurately processes which are at least partly 'moving average' in nature. The authors demonstrate that the performance of both linear and nonlinear models is considerably improved by the use of error feedback terms. Using daily data from January 1987 to March 1992, they apply the methodology to the modelling of the dynamic effects of

nonlinear cointegration between the German DAX index and the French CAC40 index, and overlay a trading strategy on the results of their models. The neural network model with three error feedback terms significantly outperforms its linear counterpart, which suggest that the cointegration relationship is a nonlinear one.

4. 'An Evolutionary Algorithm for Portfolio Selection within a Downside Framework' by A. Loraschi and A. Tettamanzi: this chapter presents an application of genetic algorithms to portfolio asset allocation that enables one to use non-standard indices of risk. The authors focus on the *downside part of the distribution of returns* rather than on the variance, as the chance of incurring a loss is deemed to represent more appropriately what is the essence of risk for an investor. The asset allocation problem is then formulated as a two-objective optimisation problem where the expected return is maximised at the same time when a downside risk measure is minimised. This problem is successfully solved by a genetic algorithm using a parametric fitness function that accounts for different potential trade-offs between risk and expected return.

Having gone through the reasons that have led me to select the three themes of this book and briefly presented each article, I cannot conclude this preface without thanking again all its contributors, and also R. Baggaley of John Wiley & Sons who persuaded me to edit it, T. Maibaum, the Director of the Department of Computing at Imperial College who has enthusiastically supported the 'Forecasting Financial Markets' Conference, and his colleagues at Imperial College, B. Rustem and A. Jones.

I also wish to thank my colleagues of the Quantitative Research & Trading Group at Chemical Bank, S. Leong, M. Gavridis, A. Harris, P. Nacaskul and R. Atekpe, as without their help the Conference and thus the book would not have existed. Special thanks go to M. Gavridis who has helped me to revise several chapters, and to my wife and daughters who have had to put up with my bad mood on several occasions while I was preparing and revising the final manuscript.

Christian L. Dunis
London

REFERENCES

Bollerslev, T. (1986), 'Generalized Autoregressive Conditional Heteroskedasticity', *Journal of Econometrics*, **31**, 307–327.

Brock, W., Lakonishok, J. and LeBaron, B. (1992), 'Simple Technical Trading Rules and the Stochastic Properties of Stock Returns', *The Journal of Finance*, **47**, 1731–1764.

Dacorogna, M.M., Gauvreau, C.L., Müller, U.A., Olsen, R.B. and Pictet, O.V. (1992), 'Short Term Forecasting Models of Foreign Exchange Rates', Technical Report MMD.1992-05-12, Olsen & Associates, Zürich.

Dacorogna, M.M., Müller, U.A., Nagler, R.J., Olsen, R.B. and Pictet, O.V. (1993), 'A Geographical Model for the Daily and Weekly Seasonal Volatility in the FX Market', *Journal of International Money and Finance*, **12**, 413–438.

Dunis, C. (1996), 'The Economic Value of Neural Network Systems for Exchange Rate Forecasting', *Neural Network World*, **6**, 43–55.

Dunis, C. and Feeny, M. (1989), *Exchange Rate Forecasting*, Woodhead-Faulkner, Cambridge (particularly Chapter 5, 165–205).

Engle, R.F. (1982), 'Autoregressive Conditional Heteroskedasticity with Estimates of U.K. Inflation', *Econometrica*, **50**, 987–1008.

LeBaron, B. (1992), 'Forecast Improvements Using a Volatility Index', *Journal of Applied Econometrics*, **7**, 137–149.

Levich, R.M. and Thomas, L.R. (1993), 'The Significance of Technical Trading-Rule Profits in the Foreign Exchange Rate Market: A Bootstrap Approach', *Journal of International Money and Finance*, **12**, 451–474.

Mandelbrot, B.B. (1963), 'The Variation of Certain Speculative Prices', *Journal of Business*, **36**, 394–419.

Moody, J. and Wu, L. (1995), 'Statistical Analysis and Forecasting of High Frequency Exchange Rates', Research Paper, Computer Science Department, Oregon Graduate Institute of Science & Technology.

Neftçi, S.N. (1991), 'Naive Trading Rules in Financial Markets and Wiener–Kolmogorov Prediction Theory: A Study of 'Technical Analysis'', *Journal of Business*, **64**, 549–571.

O'Hara, M. (1995), *Market Microstructure Theory*, Blackwell Business, London.

Pictet, O.V., Dacorogna, M.M., Olsen, R.B. and Ward, J.R. (1992), 'Real-Time Trading Models for Foreign Exchange Rates', *Neural Network World*, **2**, 713–744.

Taylor, M.P. and Allen, H. (1992), 'The Use of Technical Analysis in the Foreign Exchange Market', *Journal of International Money and Finance*, **11**, 304–314.

Taylor, S.J. (1986), *Modelling Financial Time Series*, John Wiley & Sons, Chichester.

PART I
Modelling with High Frequency Data

1
Information Flows in High Frequency Exchange Rates

AARON H. W. LOW and
JAYARAM MUTHUSWAMY

1.1 INTRODUCTION

While the growth on theoretical research in market microstructure has been impressive, much work remains to be done on empirical testing. Intraday data on securities and exchange rates provides a rich testing ground for the study of microstructural effects of information flows on prices and trading activity. In this chapter, we study the effects of public information (publicly released news announcements) on the dynamics of quote returns and spread behavior of three major exchange rates.

It is important to understand the dynamics of market microstructure and the process by which prices and bid–ask quotes react to news. Such analyses have key public and institutional policy implications for different trading processes as well as better understanding of trading and information cycles crucial for improving market efficiency.

In this chapter, we document some interesting results. We find strong long-term cyclical serial dependencies in squared returns, as well as short-term autocorrelation in returns. In lead/lag analysis, we find some evidence showing faster price adjustment in exchange rates with higher volume. The relatively more active USD/JPY rate leads the DEM/JPY rate while the most active USD/DEM rate leads the DEM/JPY rate. The two most active rates, the

Forecasting Financial Markets: Exchange Rates, Interest Rates and Asset Management. Edited by Christian Dunis. © 1996 John Wiley & Sons Ltd.

USD/JPY and USD/DEM rates, exhibit a tendency to absorb news very quickly, and show weak cross-correlations in the immediate lag terms.

French and Roll (1986) and Ross (1989) argue that information will be reflected in returns volatility. Most studies use this result to relate the high variability of opening returns to the accumulation of overnight news as well as to support the empirical evidence that trading day variances exceed that of nontrading days. Using exchange rate data, which provides continuous trading and thus much less bias from opening and closing effects, our regressions show that news activity is indeed positively related to the conditional variability of returns. In addition, news announcements are found to arrive in clusters and cause an increase in returns volatility.

One somewhat surprising result in this chapter is the finding that news activity increases bid–ask spreads. Using news proxies, Bollerslev and Domowitz (1993) find no consistent relationships between news arrivals and exchange rate spreads. In this instance, our result is new. Classic finance theory predicts that once information is released, resolution of uncertainty will imply that bid–ask spreads (which are measures of informational asymmetry) should narrow. We find the opposite result. One possible reason could be that most of the news items do not have the same attributes as major market news such as money supply, trade balance or interest rate announcements. Such major news events are normally easy to read since they occur at fixed and known dates and traders are fully informed about market expectations. For such news, market reaction will be quick. This is reported by Berry and Howe (1994). But what about the rest (and majority) of the news? These tend to be unpredictable and, worse yet, there may not be readily available information on market expectations. If this were the case, then it will be difficult for prices to adjust immediately and a delayed reaction process will occur.

The structure of this chapter is as follows. The next section gives a detailed description of the high frequency database that this chapter is concerned with. Section 1.3 presents the findings of an exploratory analysis for the data. In section 1.4, we conduct formal econometric tests designed to reveal the nature of information flows in exchange rate markets, while section 1.5 reports the lead/lag structures of all three exchange rate series. Section 1.6 reports conditional variances in quote returns and spreads as well as the effect of exogenous news activity on volatility. We conclude with section 1.7.

1.2 DATA

We use the currency exchange rates and news data from the high frequency database supplied by Olsen & Associates (O&A)[1] of Zurich. The exchange rate database consists of real-time (GMT) stamped (to the nearest second) bid and ask quotes for three major exchange rates, namely the US dollar/German Deutsche Mark (USD/DEM), US dollar/Japanese Yen (USD/JPY), and the cross-rate Japanese Yen/German Deutsche Mark (DEM/JPY). Observations are for the one-year period from 1 October 1992 to 30 September 1993, including weekends. Each bid–ask quote record also includes the name and location (country and city) of the originating bank or institution that submitted the quote. Outliers or errors in the bid–ask quotes are identified with filter flags.

The news data set comprises a single line text of the headline from a news item. This is extracted from the Money Market Headline News that reports global financial and other headline news 24 hours every day. Date and time records are also registered to the nearest second GMT and corresponds to the same period for the exchange rate series.

The volume of activity allows us to use five-minute sampling intervals (without too many missing observations) for the majority of our analyses. The use of five-minute returns yields 105 120 observations for each price and news item series, a very sizeable data set for study indeed.

To reduce potential biases in measuring returns, we compute returns using closing quotes. This is especially important for our variance ratios tests. For example, the use of transactions prices will induce a spurious bias (of $s^2/2$ where $s =$ spread) in the observed variance of the returns process. Variance ratios, consequently, will also be biased (see Jones *et al.* 1994 for the bias in variance ratios). The use of closing quotes may also have problems. These problems could arise for instance if there are many trades taking place within the bid–ask quotes, but these quotes do not change after the trades have taken place. If this is indeed the case, quote returns will suffer a positive serial correlation bias. Fortunately, this is more of a problem for stock data. The advantage in currency data lies in the greater intensity of quotes and trade activity compared to equity markets. Indeed, our tests reveal the strong presence of negative serial correlation as reported in the ensuing sections.

1.3 PRELIMINARY DATA ANALYSIS

In view of the complex nature of the high frequency data (HFD), it was deemed prudent to perform an exploratory data analysis, in order to gain a overall perspective and feel for the data.

In view of the powerful seasonalities associated with the HFD—especially for the weekends, it was considered appropriate to perform the proposed econometric tests (next two sections) additionally on a *reduced* data set that involved the omission of weekends.[2] Whereas the full data set for five-minute intervals engendered a total of 105 120 time series observations, the reduced data set contained only 75 168 observations for five-minute returns. In the following sections (especially section 1.4), some of the econometric tests have been performed on both data sets so as to assess the effects of the presence of large strings of zero returns, on data analytic procedures. We will, henceforth, refer to the reduced data set simply as the reduced data set.

1.3.1 Summary Statistics

The summary statistics shown in Table 1.1 are based on five-minute sampling of quotes. We confirm the recent appreciation of the yen against both the dollar and Deutsche Mark and appreciation of the dollar against the Deutsche Mark.[3] Removing the weekends increases this trending effect for all three rates. Standard deviations are increased due to the additional volatility during the week. Exclusion of the weekends also reduces the kurtosis of the returns distribution.

We examine two measures of spreads. The latest spread takes the last bid–ask quote to arrive over a five-minute interval. The USD/DEM rate gives the lowest spread, whereas the USD/JPY has the highest. This ordering is also the case when we use the best bid and best ask over the five-minute interval as the other measure. Weekend quotes are consistently higher than weekday quotes and this is readily apparent when we compare across both spreads. It is quite remarkable that the kurtosis of the USD/DEM rate is much lower than that of the other two rates. For example, when weekends are excluded, the best spread has a kurtosis of only 0.966. This is quite remarkable considering the well-documented presence of fat tails in intraday financial returns and spreads.

Figure 1.1 shows the average number of news releases over the Money Market Headline News feed in real time over a five-minute interval. Each headline has a time stamp to the nearest second. Public information arrival is distinctly cyclical over the trading day with the greatest news items from 0730 hours GMT to 1600 hours GMT, corresponding to the duration of the European working day. Weekday and weekend figures are shown separately with much more news transmitted over weekdays than on weekends.[4] It is interesting to note that the average frequency of news releases differs by time zones and does not exhibit much difference across each weekday. Asia–Pacific's time zone has the least news items averaging 0.6 headline over five minutes.

Figure 1.2 shows the average number of arrivals of bid–ask quotes over a five-minute interval for each day of the week. This activity is negligible over the weekends and for reasons of clarity, is omitted from the figure. The USD/DEM exchange rate registers the greatest quote arrivals with a total of 1 472 241 bid–ask quotes for the entire year or an average of 4034 per day.

Table 1.1 Summary statistics

	Mean	Standard Deviation	Skewness	Kurtosis
Returns[a]				
USD/JPY	−0.0117	4.297	0.1764	28.9
DEM/JPY	−0.0257	3.945	−0.4947	23.4
USD/DEM	0.0127	4.204	0.1639	28.5
Returns excluding weekends[a]				
USD/JPY	−0.0147	5.004	0.1130	20.17
DEM/JPY	−0.0356	4.603	−0.4265	16.26
USD/DEM	0.0189	4.898	0.1560	19.92
Latest spread[b]				
USD/JPY	0.0727	0.0520	6.536	53.23
DEM/JPY	0.0581	0.0239	7.011	172.9
USD/DEM	0.0553	0.0313	5.430	40.26
Latest spread excluding weekends[a]				
USD/JPY	0.0662	0.0273	8.195	219.5
DEM/JPY	0.0537	0.0214	7.199	187.0
USD/DEM	0.0501	0.0163	0.826	15.55
Best spread[b]				
USD/JPY	0.0525	0.0530	5.782	45.75
DEM/JPY	0.0491	0.0272	4.994	107.8
USD/DEM	0.0376	0.0351	4.478	30.59
Best spread excluding weekends[a]				
USD/JPY	0.0395	0.0283	7.339	184.3
DEM/JPY	0.0423	0.0237	5.537	130.0
USD/DEM	0.0271	0.0187	1.061	0.966
Average interval of last trade (sec)				
USD/JPY	48.44	61.74	2.033	3.971
DEM/JPY	82.55	72.55	1.132	0.5138
USD/DEM	26.44	55.27	3.523	12.89

Note:
Prices are constructed from the average of the latest quotes, $1/2(\text{Bid} + \text{Ask})$, to arrive over a five-minute interval. Returns are taken from differences of log prices multiplied by 100, $R_t = 100 \times \ln(P_t/P_{t-1})$. The observations are from 1 October 1992 to 30 September 1993. Latest spread is taken to be the last bid–ask spread that arrives over the interval. Best spread is taken to be the best bid and best ask over the five-minute interval.
[a]Means and standard deviations are multiplied by 100.
[b]Best bid and best ask over the fine minute interval.

Correspondingly, the USD/JPY rate is the second most active with an annual rate of 570 814 quote arrivals and daily rate of 1564. Not surprisingly, the DEM/JPY is the most thinly traded of the three rates with numbers of 158 979 and 436 respectively.

It is interesting to examine the intraday arrival patterns of each rate. There

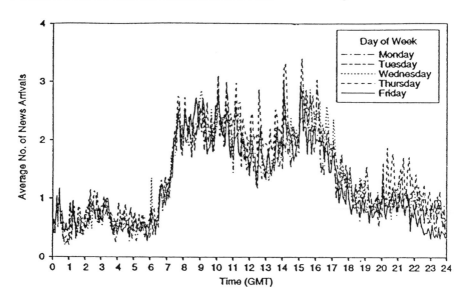

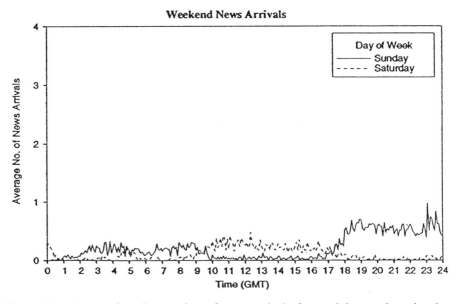

Figure 1.1 Average intraday number of news arrivals for weekdays and weekends. The plots show the average number of news arrivals within a five-minute interval over a normal trading day. Daily observations for the period Thursday, 1 October 1992 to Thursday, 30 September 1993 are used. News arrivals are time stamped to the nearest second using a 24-hour GMT time

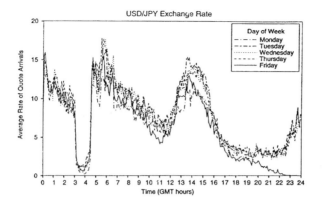

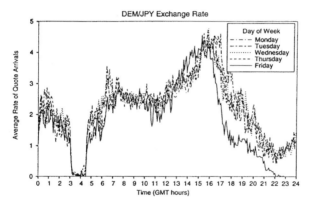

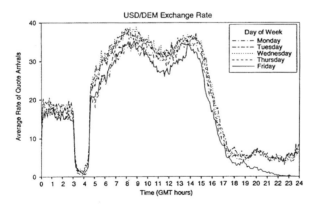

Figure 1.2 Average intraday number of quote arrivals for USD/JPY, DEM/JPY and USD/DEM exchange rates. The plots show the average number of quote arrivals within a five-minute interval. Daily observations for Thursday, 1 October 1992 to Thursday, 30 September 1993 are used, with weekends excluded

seems to be a general pattern for all rates with the greatest activity during the Asia–Pacific time (APT), Europe (GMT) and New York time (EST) trading zones. This pattern corresponds to the pattern of news observations in Figure 1.1. Trading starts to pick up just prior to 0000 hours GMT time (0900 hours Tokyo time).[5] There is very little trading activity during the Asia–Pacific lunchtime break around 0300–0430 hours GMT. Quote arrivals pick up again after lunch and continue until Europe (Zurich, Frankfurt, London) opens at around 0700 hours GMT. New York starts at around 1200 hours GMT (0800 hours EST) and trading increases together with the other (Europe) banking center. Quote arrivals start to taper off just prior to New York noon time which is when London begins to wind down at 1600 hours GMT.

The USD/DEM exchange rate is most active during European early mornings (Asia–Pacific late afternoons) and New York early mornings (Europe late afternoons) with a smaller plateau during Asia–Pacific's early morning. Even with the overlapping nature of the three major time zones, there seems to be evidence of the U-shaped patterns documented in Foster and Viswanathan (1993). This is easy to identify since the U-shape is nothing more than a spike at the opening and closing of a market. This is most pronounced in the USD/JPY rate with three spikes coinciding with Asia–Pacific's morning and afternoon open as well as Europe's close. The effect of Europe's open is attenuated for the USD/JPY rate, but can be seen for the USD/DEM and DEM/JPY rate. The most evident effect is Europe's close where the spike is seen for all three rates. This is consistent with Bollerslev and Domowitz (1993) where they find a U-shape pattern in quote activity only in the European markets and not in the US market.

1.3.2 Returns

To avoid potential staleness of prices, we compute prices based on the average of the latest bid and ask quote over a five-minute interval, that is, $P_t = (Bid + Ask)/2$. Returns are computed from log differences multiplied by 100. For returns, we use the latest bid–ask spread as a proxy for true price instead of the best bid–ask quote given the data set. The O&A foreign exchange rate database gives quote arrivals but not the true bid–ask schedule that would allow for reconstruction of the true best bid and best ask at any specific time.[6] Typically, the best bid and best ask is determined from all arriving quotes over a sampling time interval and used as a proxy for the best market bid–ask for the interval. This is reasonable if market prices respond slowly to news announcements or if quotes do not arrive quickly enough. However, there is evidence that this may not be so. News activity and market reaction in the highly liquid currency markets indicate that exchange rates respond very quickly to news releases. Ederington and Lee (1993) find that the bulk of price adjustments in foreign exchange futures markets to major public macroeconomic news occurs within the first minute.[7]

Figure 1.3 shows the unconditional standard deviations of the log returns over 261 trading days excluding weekends. The same consistency across all traded currencies is apparent with the DEM/JPY rate exhibiting slightly lower volatility especially during the APT lunchtime break and after the close of the European trading day. Some U-shaped patterns in the volatility of returns can be seen. Market opening spikes are more readily discernible. The first U-shape starts around 0000 hours GMT (0900 hours APT) and ends around 0800 hours GMT (1700 hours APT). The second U-shape starts around 0800 hours GMT and ends around 1500 hours GMT which is roughly the start and end of European trading hours. There is a spike at 1200–1300 hours GMT (0800–0900 hours EST) indicating the start of trading on Wall Street.

It is difficult to identify any spike to mark the tail end of New York trading. This is not altogether surprising. Wood *et al.* (1985) also find that the tail end

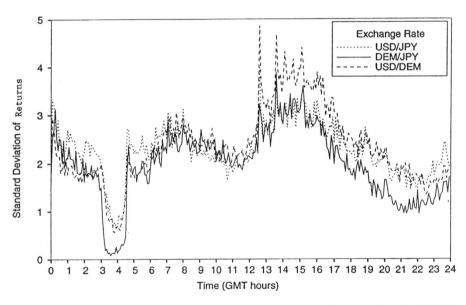

Figure 1.3 Average intraday standard deviation of returns for USD/JPY, DEM/JPY and USD/DEM exchange rates. The figure shows the average standard deviation of returns for all three currencies within a five-minute interval for each exchange rate over a normal trading day. Returns are computed from log differences of average of the latest bid–ask quote. Daily observations, excluding weekends, for the period Thursday, 1 October 1992 to Thursday, 30 September 1993 are used, totalling 261 days. Quote arrivals are time stamped to the nearest second using a 24-hour GMT time

(close of trading day) of the U-shape in volatility is not as strong as the start of a trading day. However, using half-hourly standard deviation on a minute-by-minute basis, Hsieh and Kleidon (1994) are able to magnify volatility effects and find high variation in returns during the individual open and close of both the New York and London markets. They find no evidence of spillover in volatility from the New York opening onto London late afternoon trading. Since typical market microstructure information models predict that informed traders usually enter the market during the open and close to explain the U-shape, this will imply that more information is generated during the New York open. If this is indeed relevant information, we should observe a simultaneous (or even lagged) increase in volatility in the London market when New York opens. This is not apparent in the data when we isolate activity on both markets. Also, Figure 1.1 does not indicate any unusual increase in news activity around the New York open. Like Hsieh and Kleidon, this simple observation does not lend support to the Admati and Pfeiderer (1988) type of asymmetric information model.[8]

1.3.3 Relative Spreads

The dynamics of spreads in currency markets are different from those of equity markets. The centralized order-driven specialist market system of the New York Stock Exchange (NYSE) contrasts sharply with the decentralized quote-driven dealer market system of currency trading. There is no predetermined minimum tick size with currency quotations yielding a smoother continuous distribution. The NYSE and other stock exchanges have defined opening and closing periods, whereas trading in foreign exchange takes place round the clock seven days a week. In addition, currency markets are often influenced by an additional player—the central banker, with each currency rate being affected by at least two central banks.

Quotations on foreign exchange are typically placed by participating banks acting as market makers. The major cities dealing in these global currencies are London, New York, Zurich, Tokyo and Hong Kong. It is difficult to obtain actual data on transaction prices and contracted volume since there is no governing exchange or institution in the over-the-counter (OTC) spot market.

Spreads in the spot currency markets are typically very tight due to the heavy liquidity. The summary statistics in Table 1.1 reveal that the relative spreads for the latest quote range from 0.0488% for the USD/DEM to 0.0646% for the USD/JPY rate. These may very well overstate the true bid–ask since some transactions are privately negotiated and usually completed within the current best posted bid–ask. Bessembinder (1994) finds that currency spreads in the forward markets are about twice that of the spot markets. Amihud and Mendelson (1986) report that average spreads on the

NYSE decile portfolios typically range from 0.5 to 3.2%, or about 50 times greater. Stoll (1989) shows that OTC decile firms post average spreads ranging from 1.2 to 6.9%, or about 100 times as much.

As is the case with intraday data, distributions for spreads exhibit fat tails. Kurtosis for our sample data range from 20.3 for the USD/DEM to 184.2 for the USD/JPY and 183.0 for the DEM/JPY rate. This may be attributed to the larger variation in quote arrivals and activity for the more thinly traded USD/JPY and DEM/JPY rates compared to the USD/DEM rate.

To examine the dynamics of the bid–ask spread, we construct two bid–ask series. The first bid–ask series as mentioned in the previous section is extracted from the latest bid–ask quote that arrives over the five-minute sampling interval. The second takes the best bid and best ask from all quotes that arrive over the same five-minute interval. Figure 1.4 shows that the dynamics of both spreads follow similar intraday patterns. Spreads are typically largest during the APT lunchtime break and after Europe's close. This is only logical considering the reduction in trading and quote activity for all rates.

Quote activity can be seen to generate the obvious patterns shown in Figure 1.4. One interesting trend that arises for all three rates is the narrowing of the differences of the two spreads around the APT lunchtime break as well as after New York's close. This is consistent with the less frequent quote arrivals over the same periods shown in Figure 1.2. Heavy quote activity in the USD/DEM rate reduces the average best bid–ask spread to as much as a third of the average quote bid–ask spread, whereas the best bid–ask tracks the average bid–ask quite closely for the more thinly traded DEM/JPY rate. We also find that spreads typically increase over the weekends as well as late on Fridays when the markets prepare for the large drop in trading over the weekend (see Bessembinder 1994).

1.4 INFORMATION FLOWS

Having conducted the preliminary data analyses of the full high frequency data set, we now proceed to examine the nature of information flows using this data. In this section, we employ a number of statistical techniques to accomplish the examination of informational flows within a global financial system. The next section begins the formal econometric analysis by examining sample autocorrelations for varying holding period returns. Section 1.4.2 uses the variance ratio to glean some insights into the temporal aggregation properties of intraday returns. Section 1.4.3 examines the structure of temporally aggregated *contemporaneous* correlations betwen the various return series.

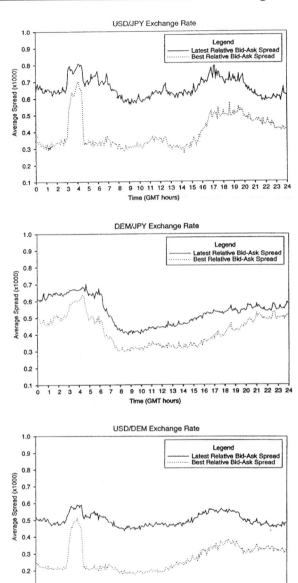

Figure 1.4 Average intraday spreads for USD/JPY, DEM/JPY and USD/DEM exchange rates. The plots show average relative bid–ask spreads using daily observations, excluding weekends, from Thursday, 1 October 1992 to Thursday, 30 September 1993. The first spread uses the latest pair of bid–ask quote. The second spread uses the best bid and best ask over the five-minute interval. All spreads are multiplied by 100

1.4.1 Autocorrelation Tests

The use of autocorrelation tests is quite standard practice in empirical financial research. Typically, if the equilibrium expected return for an asset is constant through time, statistically small sample autocorrelations are indicative of market efficiency (see Fama 1976, for the formal theory of market efficiency). For the small horizons being used in the time series of high frequency returns, the assumption of an *approximately* constant expected return might appear to be reasonable (see e.g. Miller *et al.* 1994). However, the graphical evidence presented in the previous section also serves to warn of the existence of strong time-varying seasonal patterns in the returns series that may lead to a violation of the constant expected return assumption—thereby necessitating the need to be conservative in any statements about market efficiency.

Section 1.4.1.1 examines autocorrelation patterns of five-minute returns while section 1.4.1.2 looks at autocorrelation patterns of squared five-minute returns.

1.4.1.1 Autocorrelations of Five-minute Returns

Figure 1.5 shows a plot of the sample autocorrelation function of five-minute returns for the USD/JPY exchange rate series, based on the full data set of 105 120 observations. Plots for the DEM/JPY and the USD/DEM series are not shown since they are essentially similar in structure.

With the exception of the first-lag autocorrelation for five-minute returns (with an effective sample size of 105 119), the majority of the autocorrelations are not overwhelmingly significant.[9] With $\hat{\rho}_1 = -0.124$, the first-lag auto-correlation is overwhelmingly significant, being more than 20 times its standard error! However, most of this is attributable to bid–ask bounce arising from the very high sampling frequency.[10] Indeed, the second lag autocorrelation is -0.0165 with a significance of only 2.675 standard errors. Overall, the autocorrelations seem to indicate a random series with little predictable power beyond the first lag. It can therefore be reasonably well characterized as a moving average (MA)(1) process.

We next examine the autocorrelations of squared returns.

1.4.1.2 Autocorrelations of Squared Five-minute Returns

The motivation behind examining the sample autocorrelations of squared returns lies in the fact that the squared return provides a sufficient statistic for the variance of the process. Indeed, if the actual return series (x_t say) is white noise, it is unlikely that x_t^2 will not also be so.

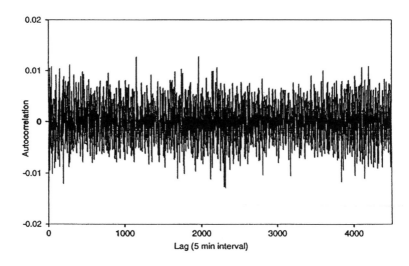

Figure 1.5 Sample autocorrelations for five-minute returns of the USD/JPY exchange rate using the full high frequency data set. The plots above show the sample autocorrelations for the five minute returns of the USD/JPY exchange rate series, plotted against the lag. The full data set is used with 105 120 observations for the USD/JPY time series

Figure 1.6 shows sample autocorrelations for the square of the USD/JPY series using five-minute returns. The results are truly surprising.[11] First, the first-lag autocorrelation at 0.2166 is a massive 35 standard errors! Second, a large fraction of the autocorrelations up to 4500 lags remain significant—some (not counting $\hat{\rho}_1$) being overwhelmingly so. Third, there is a very strong tendency for there to be a repeat of the autocorrelation cycle after approximately 2000 lags corresponding to about 10 000 minutes on a 24-hour clock—or about a week—a perfectly intuitive lag spike.

The autocorrelation structures for the square of the five-minute returns for the DEM/JPY and USD/DEM series exhibit basically the same behavior as that for the USD/JPY series, and therefore require no additional elaboration.

1.4.1.3 Implications of the Autocorrelation Tests

It is very clear from the fixed horizon autocorrelation tests of five-minute returns as well as the squared five-minute returns, that significant serial dependencies—possibly nonlinear in nature, exist in high frequency returns data. The fact that squared five-minute returns are not white noise and contain

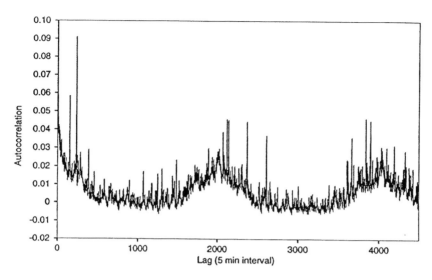

Figure 1.6 Sample autocorrelations for five-minute squared returns of the USD/JPY exchange rate using the full high frequency data set. The plots above show the sample autocorrelations for the squared five-minute returns of the USD/JPY exchange rate series, plotted against the lag. The full data set is used ($n = 105\,120$)

strong cyclical components while raw returns follow a straight MA(1) process suggests the definite possibility that subtle nonlinearities may be present.

We therefore conclude that the five-minute exchange rate returns are significantly heteroskedastic in the sense that strong serial correlations in variances are present. We deal with this finding more completely via the use of formal autoregressive conditional heteroskedastic (ARCH) models in section 1.5.

1.4.2 Variance Ratio Tests

The basic concept underlying the variance ratio test is simple. If an asset price process follows a homoskedastic random walk (with i.i.d. increments), then the variance of an n period return is n times that of a single period return. This idea is similar to the fact that the variance of a standard Brownian motion is linear in the elapsed time interval.

Variance ratio tests have been frequently employed by economists to test for the random walk property of asset prices and even macroeconomic variables—such as consumption and GNP (see e.g. Cochrane 1988, Lo and MacKinlay 1988, and Porterba and Summers 1988). In the case of high frequency returns, the variance ratio test can be an extremely useful diagnostic since it is capable of showing up not only nonlinear serial dependencies in high frequency data in an elegant manner, but also the presence of microstructural frictions.

Figures 1.7 and 1.8 show plots of the sample variance ratios for the USD/JPY, DEM/JPY, and USD/DEM exchange rates for increasing horizon lengths in multiples of five minutes, for both the full as well as the reduced high frequency data sets.

It is quite clear from Figures 1.7 and 1.8 that for both the full and the reduced data sets, the observed variance ratios are curvilinear in horizon length. For instance, the variance of the 2000-minute return for the USD/JPY *unreduced* series is only 238.9 times that of the five-minute return—instead of the 400-fold multiple that it should be if the variances grew perfectly linearly. Indeed, for all three series and for both the full as well as the reduced data sets, the $n > 1$ horizon returns were consistently less than n times the single (five-minute) period return.

It is interesting to note that the variance ratios for the reduced set (Figure 1.8) demonstrate greater linear growth than the unreduced set. For comparison the variance of the 2000-minute return for the USD/JPY reduced series is 252.4 times that of the five-minute return—compared with 238.9 for the case

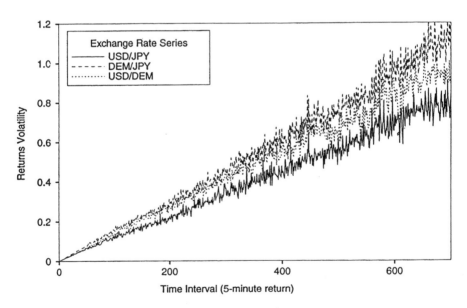

Figure 1.7 Sample variances for returns of the USD/JPY, DEM/JPY and USD/DEM exchange rates for varying holding periods using the full high frequency data set. The plots above show the sample variances for the returns of the USD/JPY, DEM/JPY and USD/DEM exchange rate series, plotted against the holding period (in five-minute intervals). The variances are computed using the standard moments estimator, and the holding period ranges from 5 minutes to 3525 minutes—the latter corresponding to 705 five-minute return intervals

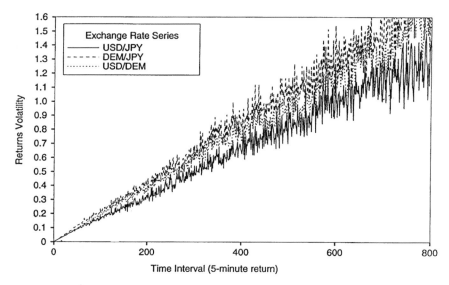

Figure 1.8 Sample variances for returns of the USD/JPY, DEM/JPY and USD/DEM exchange rates for varying holding periods using the reduced high frequency data set. The plots above show the sample variances for the returns of the USD/JPY, DEM/JPY and USD/DEM exchange rate series, plotted against the holding period (in five-minute periods). The variances are computed using the standard moments estimator, and the holding periods range from 5 minutes to 4450 minutes—the latter corresponding to 890 five-minute return intervals

of the unreduced set. This suggests that the effect of having very thin trading sessions—such as weekends and public holidays, is to induce a downward bias for the variance ratio statistic.

Also of interest is the fact that for very short horizons (less than 200 minutes), the variance ratios grow more rapidly than at larger horizons—suggesting that serial dependencies are more likely to exist at longer lags.[12] This is consistent with the earlier finding that strong long lag autocorrelations are present in the squared returns. The complex serial dependencies are the cause for the nonlinear growth of n period variances. If the series were genuinely random, variances should compound additively.

We next turn to the analysis of contemporaneous correlations between returns.

1.4.3 Contemporaneous Correlation Structure

In principle, returns of the three exchange rate series—USD/JPY, USD/DEM, and DEM/JPY—should be strongly contemporaneously correlated[13]—this being because of the common informational shocks affecting the three currencies. However, the empirical observation of the correlations may be affected by the high frequency returns sampling process. Indeed, Epps (1979) shows that as the sampling interval is progressively shrunk, the otherwise significant contemporaneous correlation between stock price returns is reduced to white noise. Epps does not quite give the precise cause of this attenuation of the contemporaneous correlation. In more recent work, Low *et al.* (1994) attribute this systematic destruction of the sample correlation of *very* high frequency data to nonsynchronicities in the recording process (see Cohen *et al.* 1979, Lo and MacKinlay 1990, Muthuswamy 1990, and Scholes and Williams 1976, 1977, for detailed expositions of the effects of nonsynchronicities on measured returns).

Figure 1.9 shows plots of the observed contemporaneous correlations for varying holding periods, for the full high frequency data set. A corresponding analysis for the reduced data set (without weekends), not shown here, exhibits a very similar pattern. This is interesting on several counts. First, the Epps-effect comes through clearly in both plots—at very high sampling frequencies when the returns are observed at intervals less than 15 minutes, the

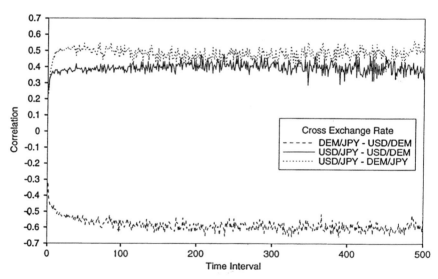

Figure 1.9 Observed correlations between returns for the USD/JPY, DEM/JPY and USD/DEM exchange rates for varying holding period returns using the full high frequency data set. The plots above show the observed correlations between the returns of the USD/JPY, DEM/JPY and USD/DEM exchange rates. The correlations are based on the standard moments estimator, and computed using the full high frequency data set. The holding period of the returns ranges from 5 minutes to 2900 minutes—for instance with a time interval of 200, the horizon is effectively 200 × 5 or 1000 minutes

contemporaneous correlations rapidly decay to zero. The Epps-effect is less pronounced for reduced data—suggesting that large strings of zero returns, like the case for the full data set, can cause further corruption of any correlation signal present. Second, once a certain horizon length is reached (on the order of four hours), the correlations tend to remain fairly stable.[14] Third, magnitudinally (in absolute terms so as to avoid the 'numeraire' problem in the USD/JPY–DEM/JPY case), the three returns have about the same correlation strength.

1.5 LEAD/LAG STRUCTURES

We now examine the lead/lag structure of the three pairs of exchange rates using the cross-correlation function. We find evidence that the more actively traded USD/DEM and USD/JPY rates lead the less active DEM/JPY rate. Market microstructure theory postulates that greater trading activity generates higher liquidity and information trading.[15] This implies of course that the USD/DEM and USD/JPY rates tend to adjust and reflect information faster than the DEM/JPY rate.

Table 1.2 reports the lead/lag cross-correlations for ±5 leads and lags between the USD/JPY–DEM/JPY, DEM/JPY–USD/DEM, and USD/JPY–USD/DEM pairs of five-minute exchange rate returns. The result shows that with the exception of the contemporaneous (zero) and possibly first three lags, the serial cross-correlations fade to (statistical) insignificance quite rapidly. For instance, for the USD/JPY–DEM/JPY pair, the contemporaneous correlation is 0.233 or approximately 75.16 standard errors. By contrast, the −1 lag cross-correlation—or the case of the USD/JPY exchange rate return *lagging* the DEM/JPY exchange rate return by five minutes, is only 0.023 or about 7.42 standard errors. Also, the +1 lead cross-correlation—or the case of the USD/JPY return *leading* the DEM/JPY return by five minutes, is 0.100 or about 32.26 standard errors. In addition, the +2 lag cross-correlation is still quite significant at 8.39 standard errors. However, beyond the first three or four leads and lags, the higher order cross-correlations are generally insignificant.

Note that the signs for cross-correlations of the USD/JPY–DEM/JPY and for the USD/JPY–USD/DEM rates are positive while the cross-correlation of the DEM/JPY–USD/DEM rate is negative. This arises from the common denominator currency used for the cross-correlation. For example, take the case of the cross USD/JPY–DEM/JPY rate. If there is bad news about Japan's economy hitting the markets, then both the USD/JPY and DEM/JPY will rise. Our cross-correlation coefficients show which rates tend to rise first. On the other hand, for the DEM/JPY–USD/DEM rate, the denominator currency is not common. Along the same line, suppose that the market receives bad news

Table 1.2 Cross-correlations between USD/JPY, DEM/JPY, USD/DEM exchange rates based on five-minute returns

Lag–Lead	USD/JPY–DEM/JPY	DEM/JPY–USD/DEM	USD/JPY–USD/DEM
−5	−0.007	−0.000	−0.003
	(−2.25)	(0.00)	(−0.97)
−4	0.007	−0.000	−0.010
	(2.25)	(0.00)	(−3.23)
−3	0.013	0.012	−0.013
	(4.19)	(3.87)	(−4.19)
−2	0.009	−0.013	−0.007
	(2.90)	(−4.19)	(−2.25)
−1	0.023	−0.133	0.036
	(7.42)	(−42.90)	(11.61)
0	0.233	−0.326	0.256
	(75.16)	(−105.16)	(82.58)
+1	0.100	−0.009	0.030
	(32.26)	(−2.90)	(9.68)
+2	0.026	0.021	−0.012
	(8.39)	(6.77)	(−3.87)
+3	0.008	0.019	−0.005
	(2.58)	(6.13)	(−1.61)
+4	0.007	0.012	−0.004
	(2.25)	(3.87)	(−1.29)
+5	0.001	0.001	−0.001
	(0.32)	(0.32)	(−0.32)

Note:
Cross-correlations between the USD/JPY, DEM/JPY, USD/DEM exchange rates are shown for up to five lead–lags based on five-minute returns. Numbers in parentheses denote *t*-statistics under the null that the two series are serially and contemporally uncorrelated, for a sample size of 75 168 observations.

about the German economy. Then the DEM/JPY will fall and USD/DEM will rise, moving in opposite directions. In this case, we note in Table 1.2 the tendency for the USD/JPY return to lead the DEM/JPY return more than the converse.

Although not reported in Table 1.2, we also computed sample cross-correlations for much longer leads and lags. In general, most of the longer lead/lag cross-correlations exhibited virtually no statistical significance—with the exception of a few random cases that probably occurred by chance and chance alone.

1.6 NEWS AND CONDITIONAL VOLATILITY

The autocorrelation structure present in the second order moments (see section 1.4) as well as the obvious cyclical variation of the intraday standard deviations shown in Figure 1.3 for all three exchange rate series indicate some form of heteroskedasticity in the second moments. This is readily apparent in returns and we also find evidence of such variation in spread behavior as well. In this section, we use the directly observable news announcements as an exogenous variable and find that it is very significant as an explanatory factor for influencing volatility in returns. We also find that it generally reduces the spread as well as increases the volatility in spreads.

1.6.1 Conditional Volatility of Returns

It is well documented that exchange rate volatility exhibits strong autocorrelation. Baillie and Bollerslev (1989) find that this autocorrelated structure is well represented by a generalised autoregressive conditional heteroskedastic GARCH(1,1) process. In particular, Bollerslev and Domowitz (1993) report that exogenous market activity has a significant lagged effect on return volatility. They use the number of quote arrivals, best bid–ask spreads, as well as the time between trades as proxies for news or market activity. Fortunately, our database provides directly observable news announcements that are direct determinants of market activity. This gives a cleaner regression result.

To examine how news activity affects the conditional variance of returns, we use the following Garch specification:

$$100\Delta \log P_t = \mu + \epsilon_t + \theta \epsilon_{t-1} \tag{1}$$

$$\sigma_t^2 = \omega + \alpha \epsilon_{t-1}^2 + \beta \sigma_{t-1}^2 + \delta(\text{News})_t \tag{2}$$

$$\epsilon_t | \Psi_{t-1} \sim N(0, \sigma_t^2) \tag{3}$$

Serial dependence in returns is captured by the MA(1) specification in the conditional mean, while the GARCH(1,1) process tracks the conditional volatility in returns. We use comtemporaneous news as the determinant of conditional volatility since currency markets react very quickly to news announcements.[16] We feel this is further justified since the number of quote arrivals far outnumbers the number of news announcements.[17] The residuals conditional on past information are assumed to be normally distributed.

The results are very interesting. Table 1.3 reports the significance of the GARCH representation for returns volatility. We find significant negative autocorrelation for all exchange rates, with the most negative θ's for the USD/JPY rate and lowest θ's for the DEM/JPY rate which could be suggestive of market overreactions in heavily traded assets. All parameters in the conditional variance term are significant, indicating strong support for the MA(1)–GARCH(1,1) model. Consistent with Bollerslev and Domowitz (1993), we also find evidence of an IGARCH or Integrated GARCH model, with the coefficients $\alpha + \beta$ approaching one for all three exchange rate series.

Table 1.3 GARCH maximum likelihood estimates of volatility for USD/JPY, DEM/JPY, USD/DEM exchange rates

	USD/JPY	DEM/JPY	USD/DEM
μ^a	0.0448	−0.1833	0.0282
	(0.1126)	(0.1370)	(0.1084)
θ	−0.1755	−0.0116	−0.1287
	(0.0043)	(0.0044)	(0.0042)
ω^a	0.0809	0.0885	0.0561
	(0.0021)	(0.0024)	(0.0016)
α	0.1346	0.0915	0.1680
	(0.0024)	(0.0020)	(0.0029)
β	0.8456	0.8708	0.8274
	(0.0024)	(0.0025)	(0.0026)
Log L^b	129646.4	131984.0	132418.0
$Q(12)^c$	50.65	19.73	74.28
$\rho(1)^d$	0.021	0.010	0.016
$\rho(2)$	−0.004	0.004	−0.009
$\rho(3)$	−0.007	−0.007	−0.010

Notes:
Prices are constructed from the average of the latest bid–ask quotes 1/2(Bid + Ask), to arrive continuously over a five-minute sampling interval for the three exchange rate series. Returns generated are taken from differences of log prices multiplied by 100, $R_t = 100 \times \ln(P_t/P_{t-1})$. The observations are time stamped to the nearest second for the period 1 October 1992 to 30 September 1993. Weekends are excluded from this series for a total of 75 168 observations, with returns being noncumulative over the weekends. The maximum likelihood estimates are obtained from the following model:

$$100\Delta \log P_t = \mu + \epsilon_t + \theta\epsilon_{t-1}$$
$$\sigma_t^2 = \omega + \alpha\epsilon_{t-1}^2 + \beta\sigma_{t-1}^2$$
$$\epsilon_t | \Psi_{t-1} \sim N(0, \sigma_t^2)$$

[a] Estimated coefficients and standard errors are multiplied by 10^3.
[b] Log L is the value of the maximized Gaussian log likelihood function.
[c] $Q(12)$ denotes the Box–Pierce–Ljung portmanteau test statistics of the standardized residuals $\hat{\epsilon}_t\hat{\sigma}_t^{-1}$.
[d] $\rho(i)$ denotes the autocorrelation at lag i of the standardized residuals $\hat{\epsilon}_t\hat{\sigma}_t^{-1}$.

Past studies (see Bollerslev and Domowitz 1993 and Jones *et al.* 1994) have not been able to find any effect of unobservable news activity (using the intensity of quote arrivals per unit time) on conditional volatility. Using directly observable news headlines in Table 1.4 we find a strong relationship between volatility and contemporaneous news activity for all exchange rates. The coefficients are greatest for the USD/DEM rate and weakest for the DEM/JPY rate, further suggesting that news has a stronger predictive power for the volatility of more heavily traded rates.

Table 1.4 GARCH maximum likelihood estimates of volatility for USD/JPY, DEM/JPY, USD/DEM exchange rates with contemporaneous exogenous news activity

	USD/JPY	DEM/JPY	USD/DEM
μ^a	0.0454	−0.1813	0.0227
	(0.1116)	(0.1367)	(0.1085)
θ	−0.1762	−0.0113	−0.1305
	(0.0043)	(0.0044)	(0.0042)
ω^b	0.6456	0.8526	0.4721
	(0.0218)	(0.0265)	(0.0174)
α	0.1422	0.0966	0.1679
	(0.0027)	(0.0022)	(0.0031)
β	0.8277	0.8519	0.8052
	(0.0027)	(0.0030)	(0.0031)
δ^b	0.3194	0.2407	0.3796
	(0.0177)	(0.0182)	(0.0201)
Log L^c	129781.6	132066.3	132653.4
$Q(12)^d$	48.46	18.48	78.00
$\rho(1)^e$	0.021	0.009	0.017
$\rho(2)$	−0.003	0.003	−0.010
$\rho(3)$	−0.006	−0.007	−0.010

Note:
Prices are constructed from the average of the latest bid–ask quotes $1/2(\text{Bid} + \text{Ask})$, to arrive continuously over a five-minute sampling interval for the three exchange rate series. Returns generated are taken from differences of log prices multiplied by 100, $R_t = 100 \times \ln(P_t/P_{t-1})$. The observations are time stamped to the nearest second for the period 1 October 1992 to 30 September 1993. Weekends are excluded from this series for a total of 75 168 observations, with returns being noncumulative over the weekends. The news variable denotes the total number of headline news announcements from Money Market Headline News. The maximum likelihood estimates are obtained from the following model:

$$100\Delta \log P_t = \mu + \epsilon_t + \theta\epsilon_{t-1}$$
$$\sigma_t^2 = \omega + \alpha\epsilon_{t-1}^2 + \beta\sigma_{t-1}^2 + \delta(\text{News})_t$$
$$\epsilon_t|\Psi_{t-1} \sim N(0, \sigma_t^2)$$

[a]Estimated coefficients and standard errors are multiplied by 10^3.
[b]Estimated coefficients and standard errors are multiplied by 10^4.
[c]Log L is the value of the maximized Gaussian log likelihood function.
[d]$Q(12)$ denotes Box–Pierce–Ljung portmanteau statistics of standardized residuals $\hat{\epsilon}_t\hat{\sigma}_t^{-1}$.
[e]$\rho(i)$ denotes the autocorrelation at lag i of standardized residuals $\hat{\epsilon}_t\hat{\sigma}_t^{-1}$.

1.6.2 Conditional Volatility of Spreads

To obtain a feel for the spread dynamics, we examine the spread volatility and the manner by which news activity drives the conditional variance term. Table 1.5 reports the regression coefficients of the relative spread with exogenous

Table 1.5 Maximum likelihood estimates of relative bid–ask spreads for USD/JPY, DEM/JPY, USD/DEM exchange rates with contemporaneous exogenous news activity

	USD/JPY	DEM/JPY	USD/DEM
μ^a	0.6668	0.5241	0.5102
	(0.0014)	(0.0009)	(0.0008)
γ^b	−0.6191	−1.0085	−0.5424
	(0.0700)	(0.0400)	(0.0408)
θ	0.2274	0.4107	0.2088
	(0.0042)	(0.0039)	(0.0037)
ω^c	0.5148	0.0461	0.0156
	(0.0156)	(0.0013)	(0.0008)
α	0.1103	0.1753	0.1096
	(0.0087)	(0.0045)	(0.0039)
β	0.0888	0.7123	0.8235
	(0.0252)	(0.0060)	(0.0064)
δ^d	0.1120	−0.0400	0.0138
	(0.0238)	(0.0038)	(0.0027)
Log L^e	515930.7	548768.3	553450.1

Note:
Bid–ask relative spreads are constructed from the average of the latest bid–ask quotes, 1/2(Ask − Bid)/(Ask + Bid), to arrive continuously over a five-minute sampling interval for the three exchange rate series. The observations are time stamped to the nearest second for the period 1 October 1992 to 30 September 1993. Weekends are excluded from this series for a total of 75 168 observations. Truncation of weekend data is clean without summing the total number of news releases over the weekend for the first observation of the week. The news variable denotes the total number of headline news announcements from Money Market Headline News recorded over the same contemporaneous five-minute interval for the same period. The maximum likelihood estimates are obtained from the following model:

$$(\text{Spread})_t = \mu + \gamma(\text{News})_t + \epsilon_t + \theta\epsilon_{t-1}$$
$$\sigma_t^2 = \omega + \alpha\epsilon_{t-1}^2 + \beta\sigma_{t-1}^2 + \delta(\text{News})_t$$
$$\epsilon_t|\Psi_{t-1} \sim N(0, \sigma_t^2)$$

[a]Estimated coefficients and standard errors are multiplied by 10^3.
[b]Estimated coefficients and standard errors are multiplied by 10^5.
[c]Estimated coefficients and standard errors are multiplied by 10^7.
[d]Estimated coefficients and standard errors are multiplied by 10^8.
[e]Log L is the value of the maximized Gaussian log likelihood function.

news in the mean and variance terms. As expected, there is high positive autocorrelation in the spreads though the effect of news on the variance term is not consistent for all three rates. We caution that this may not be the most useful analysis for the study of spreads. In preliminary analysis, we find unit roots in the spreads of all three exchange rates. This is consistent with Madhavan (1992) and Bollerslev and Domowitz (1993). Instead of relative spreads, we now use the first differences in the log of the relative spread. The role of news is now formally modelled in the context of a heteroskedastic specification:

$$\Delta \log (\text{Spread})_t = \mu + \gamma(\text{News})_t + \epsilon_t + \theta\epsilon_{t-1} \tag{4}$$

$$\sigma_t^2 = \omega + \alpha\epsilon_{t-1}^2 + \beta\sigma_{t-1}^2 + \delta(\text{News})_t \tag{5}$$

$$\epsilon_t|\Psi_{t-1} \sim N(0, \sigma_t^2) \tag{6}$$

Bollerslev and Domowitz (1993) find that this GARCH specification does reasonably well for changes in spreads. Table 1.6 confirms the significance of the MA(1)–GARCH(1,1) model. All terms except the constant of the means

Table 1.6 Maximum likelihood estimates of changes in relative bid–ask spreads for USD/JPY, DEM/JPY, USD/DEM exchange rates

	USD/JPY	DEM/JPY	USD/DEM
μ^a	−0.0175	−0.1069	−0.0554
	(0.0133)	(0.0209)	(0.1087)
θ	−0.8857	−0.7603	−0.8994
	(0.0016)	(0.0026)	(0.0015)
ω^a	0.6450	0.5917	0.3895
	(0.0296)	(0.0159)	(0.0181)
α	0.0954	0.1418	0.0883
	(0.0027)	(0.0028)	(0.0024)
β	0.8530	0.7924	0.8759
	(0.0044)	(0.0038)	(0.0035)
Log L^b	−25405.4	−6328.2	−19915.3
$Q(12)^c$	552.15	943.76	260.1
$\rho(1)^d$	0.072	0.077	0.051
$\rho(2)$	0.017	−0.012	0.010
$\rho(3)$	−0.002	−0.033	0.007

Note:
Bid–ask relative spreads are constructed from the average of the latest bid–ask quotes, $1/2(\text{Ask} - \text{Bid})/(\text{Ask} + \text{Bid})$, to arrive continuously over a five-minute sampling interval for the three exchange rate series. The observations are time stamped to the nearest second for the period 1 October 1992 to 30 September 1993. Weekends are excluded from this series for a total of 75 168 observations. The maximum likelihood estimates are obtained from the following model:

$$\Delta \log (\text{Spread})_t = \mu + \epsilon_t + \theta\epsilon_{t-1}$$

$$\sigma_t^2 = \omega + \alpha\epsilon_{t-1}^2 + \beta\sigma_{t-1}^2$$

$$\epsilon_t|\Psi_{t-1} \sim N(0, \sigma_t^2)$$

[a] Estimated coefficients and standard errors are multiplied by 10^2.
[b] Log L is the value of the maximized Gaussian log likelihood function.
[c] $Q(12)$ denotes the Box–Pierce–Ljung portmanteau test statistics of the standardized residuals $\hat{\epsilon}_t\hat{\sigma}_t^{-1}$.
[d] $\rho(i)$ denotes the autocorrelation at lag i of the standardized residuals $\hat{\epsilon}_t\hat{\sigma}_t^{-1}$.

are significant. The changes in spreads are seen to be highly negatively serially correlated, a pattern similar to that of the returns. These results are also reported by Bollerslev and Domowitz (1993).[18]

Table 1.7 documents the effects of exogenous news activity on the means

Table 1.7 Maximum likelihood estimates of changes in relative bid–ask spreads for USD/JPY, DEM/JPY, USD/DEM exchange rates with news activity

	USD/JPY	DEM/JPY	USD/DEM
μ^a	−0.1740	−0.1926	−0.2292
	(0.0257)	(0.0345)	(0.0207)
γ^a	0.1180	0.0725	0.1384
	(0.0175)	(0.0257)	(0.0143)
θ	−0.8860	−0.7617	−0.9014
	(0.0016)	(0.0025)	(0.0015)
ω^a	0.6010	0.4647	0.3938
	(0.0285)	(0.0148)	(0.0189)
α	0.0990	0.1493	0.0937
	(0.0028)	(0.0031)	(0.0026)
β	0.8465	0.7543	0.8643
	(0.0046)	(0.0046)	(0.0040)
δ^a	0.0618	0.2830	0.0477
	(0.0112)	(0.0118)	(0.0091)
Log L^b	−25365.7	−5935.4	−19855.1
$Q(12)^c$	563.2	1006.9	275.6
$\rho(1)^d$	0.072	0.084	0.053
$\rho(2)$	0.022	−0.007	0.011
$\rho(3)$	0.001	−0.030	0.008

Note:

Bid–ask relative spreads are constructed from the average of the latest bid–ask quotes, 1/2(Ask − Bid)/(Ask + Bid), to arrive continuously over a five-minute sampling interval for the three exchange rate series. The observations are time stamped to the nearest second for the period 1 October 1992 to 30 September 1993. Weekends are excluded from this series for a total of 75 168 observations. Truncation of weekend data is clean without summing the total number of news releases over the weekend for the first observation of the week. The news variable denotes the total number of headline news announcements from Money Market Headline News recorded over the same contemporaneous five-minute interval for the same period. The maximum likelihood estimates are obtained from the following model:

$$\Delta \log(\text{Spread})_t = \mu + \gamma(\text{News})_t + \epsilon_t + \theta\epsilon_{t-1}$$
$$\sigma_t^2 = \omega + \alpha\epsilon_{t-1}^2 + \beta\sigma_{t-1}^2 + \delta(\text{News})_t$$
$$\epsilon_t|\Psi_{t-1} \sim N(0, \sigma_t^2)$$

[a]Estimated coefficients and standard errors are multiplied by 10^2.
[b]Log L is the value of the maximized Gaussian log likelihood function.
[c]$Q(12)$ is the Box–Pierce–Ljung portmanteau test statistics of standardized residuals $\hat{\epsilon}_t\hat{\sigma}_t^{-1}$.
[d]$\rho(i)$ denotes the autocorrelation at lag i of the standardized residuals $\hat{\epsilon}_t\hat{\sigma}_t^{-1}$.

and variances of spread changes. Once again, there is the presence of strong negative serial correlation in the means. What is important is that our results show evidence of the pronounced influence of actual news announcements on spread changes. Intensity of news activity appears to have significantly positive effects on the conditional variance of all three rates. This is not surprising in view and is consistent with Bollerslev and Domowitz (1993).

If prices adjust quickly to news, then we should observe a decrease in spreads. This is not seen to be the case. Significant positive coefficients in the mean terms, shown in Table 1.7, imply that an increase in contemporaneous news activity increases spreads. Using proxies for news activity, Bollerslev and Domowitz (1993) report mixed results for the effects of news on spread changes. One possible reason for their finding could be related to the argument of Hsieh and Kleidon (1994). If volume of trading (especially at the open and close of the trading day) does not exactly reflect new information reaching the market, then the use of variables such as news arrivals and duration will not provide for a direct measure of news activity.

Of course, this result could also well suggest that prices take a longer time to adjust, and that when news arrives, this could indicate uncertainty about how the market will interpret and react. To see if there is indeed a lag effect, we ran the model using lagged news instead. Our results, which are not reported here, are remarkably similar to the coefficients reported above for contemporaneous news. For example, using the intensity of news with one-period lag, we found the γ term to be 0.1218, 0.071 and 0.1427 (all multiplied by 100) for the USD/JPY, DEM/JPY and USD/DEM rates respectively. This suggests that spreads increase with news activity. To determine if there is a potential for any bias in using spreads from the latest bid–ask quotes, we applied the same heteroskedastic representation on another spread measure— this time using the best bid–ask quote as described previously. The results are again strikingly similar. For example in this case our γ's[19] turn out to be 0.4077 (t-stat. of 9.6), 0.0830 (t-stat. of 2.4) and 0.4307 (t-stat. of 11.26) for the USD/JPY, DEM/JPY and USD/DEM rates respectively.

1.7 CONCLUSION

We find strong evidence of the effects of public information on quote returns volatility and spread changes. News activity directly increases conditional volatility in both spreads and returns as expected. It is interesting to note the consistent daily cyclical nature of frequency of news releases and quote arrivals across all trading days and across different markets. Sharp increases in trading activity at the beginning and end of each market trading day, however, does not seem to coincide with the level of news activity. If market volatility at the open and end of the trading day is indeed generated by informed traders, then this should spill over into other markets that are simultaneously open. Like Hsieh and Kleidon (1994), we do not find evidence of this spillover effect.

ACKNOWLEDGEMENTS

This paper was first presented at the 1995 International Conference on Forecasting Financial Markets, London, and the 1995 HFDF I International Conference, Zurich. We acknowledge with thanks, Olsen and Associates of Zurich, Switzerland, for their help in making available to us their unique high frequency data set. We also thank participants from both the HFDF-I and Forecasting Financial Markets conferences for helpful comments. Any errors are due to us alone.

ENDNOTES

1. O&A is a research institute which provides real-time forecasts, historical analysis and trading advice for various foreign exchange rates.
2. We did not omit holidays since there are only a few holidays that are considered common to all financial markets.
3. The yen has been enjoying low inflation and strong macroeconomic performance with respect to the Japanese balance of payments, whereas Germany is still fighting high inflation due to reunification.
4. Using the North American feed from Reuter's News Service, Berry and Howe (1994) also found that the majority of public news observations in the USA starts at 0800 hours New York time and ends at 1900 hours during the week. Their data revealed that weekend news averaged to about 6% of weekday news.
5. Official trading hours in Japan are 0900–1200 hours and 1430–1530 hours Tokyo time though actual trading activity is widely acknowledged to start before and end after the official period. This will soon change to accommodate increased trading hours.
6. There is no cancellation of quotes on the data set.
7. Though they use tick-by-tick data of transactions prices instead of bid–ask quotes, the speed of news diffusion should be roughly equal for either series. It must be noted that their findings are restricted to the futures markets and our generalization of their results to cash markets is only a conjecture on our part.
8. Hsieh and Kleidon (1994) conjecture the U-shape in spreads and volatility to two different effects: when markets open, traders post quotes to try to get a 'feel' for the new trading day. This period of learning quickly passes and the market then settles down. Then at the closing of the market trading day, these traders would then try to unwind their inventory positions, which creates another flurry of quote or trading activity, thereby completing the U-shape.
9. In view of the very large sample size, one must be on guard for a possible manifestation of Lindley's paradox.
10. See Wood et al. (1985) for a more complete discussion of high frequency sampling induced negative autocorrelation.
11. We are not at all the first to document this finding—see for example the papers by Müller et al. (1990) and Dacorogna et al. (1993).

12. This is not quite so evident from the plots but is clear from the numerical variance ratios.
13. Actually, two of the three pairwise correlations will be positive while the third (in this case the USD/JPY–DEM/JPY pair) will be negatively correlated—but this being artificially so only because of a 'numeraire' effect.
14. As the horizon becomes very large, instability sets in again—but this time only because the sample size diminishes enough that the estimator's standard error becomes too large.
15. See Lo and MacKinlay (1988). Empirical work on equity markets find consistent evidence that large stocks lead small stocks. This could arise from the fact that large stocks are more heavily traded and have a greater analyst following, thus implying that large stocks or portfolios are better researched.
16. This contrasts with Bollerslev and Domowitz (1993) who use a one-period lagged market activity proxy to reduce spurious effects between the proxies and measured returns.
17. Quote arrivals for the USD/DEM rate is approximately 20 times the number of news releases while the USD/JPY and DEM/JPY rates are approximately eight and two times respectively. Suppose currency prices adjust within the first minute of news announcements, as reported by Ederington and Lee (1993). Then, based on the number of quote arrivals, the price effect of any news release would have been well reflected by the latest bid–ask quote.
18. It is likely that the negative serial correlation is an artifact of an error correction mechanism (ECM) arising from the cointegration of the bid and ask prices. We are also aware of the warning by Miller *et al.* (1994) of spread differences to exhibit very strong but entirely spurious mean reverting behavior.
19. All multiplied by 100. To compare with Bollerslev and Domowitz (1993), we use news arrivals with a one-period lag.

REFERENCES

Admati, A. and Pfleiderer, P. (1988), 'A Theory of Intraday Patterns: Volume and Price Variability', *Review of Financial Studies*, **1**, 3–40.

Amihud, Y. and Mendelson, H. (1986), 'Asset pricing and the Bid-Ask Spread', *Journal of Financial Economics*, **17**, 223–249.

Baillie, R. and Bollerslev, T. (1989), 'The Message in Daily Exchange Rates: A Conditional Variance Tale', *Journal of Business and Economic Statistics*, **7**, 297–305.

Berry, T. and Howe, K. (1994), 'Public Information Arrival', *Journal of Finance*, **49**, 1331–1345.

Bessembinder, H. (1994), 'Bid–Ask Spreads in the Interbank Foreign Exchange Markets', *Journal of Financial Economics*, **35**, 317–348.

Bollerslev, T. and Domowitz, I. (1993), 'Trading Patterns and Prices in the Interbank Foreign Exchange Markets', *Journal of Finance*, **48**, 1421–1443.

Cochrane, J. (1988), 'How Big Is the Random Walk Component in GNP?' *Journal of Political Economy*, **96**, 893–920.

Cohen, K. *et al.* (1979), 'The Returns Generation Process, Returns Variance, and the Effect of Thinness in Securities Markets', *Journal of Finance*, **33**, 149–167.

Dacorogna, M.M. *et al.* (1993), 'A Geographical Model for the Daily and Weekly

Seasonal Volatility in the Foreign Exchange Market', *Journal of International Money and Finance*, **12**, 439–448.

Dimson, E. (1979), 'Risk Measurement When Shares Are Subject to Infrequent Trading', *Journal of Financial Economics*, **7**, 197–226.

Ederington, L. and Lee, J.H. (1993), 'How Markets Process Information: News Releases and volatility', *Journal of Finance*, **48**, 1161–1191.

Epps, T.W. (1979), Comovements in Stock Prices in the Very Short Run', *Journal of the American Statistical Association*, **74**, (366), Applications Section, 291–298.

Fama, E. (1976), *Foundations of Finance*, Basic Books, New York.

Fama, E. and French, K. (1988), 'Permanent and Temporary Components of Stock Prices', *Journal of Political Economy*, **96**, 246–273.

Foster, D. and Viswanattian, D. (1993), 'Variations in Trading Volume, Return Volatility and Trading Costs: Evident on Recent Price Formation Models', *Journal of Finance*, **48**, 187–211.

French, K. and Roll, R. (1986), 'Stock Return Variances: The Arrival of Information and the Reaction of Traders', *Journal of Financial Economics*, **17**, 5–26.

Harvey, C. and Huang, R. (1991), 'Volatility in the Foreign Currency Futures Market', *Review of Financial Studies*, **4**, 543–569.

Hsieh, D. and Kleidon, A. (1994), 'Bid–Ask Spreads in Foreign Exchange Markets: Implications for Models of Asymmetric Information', Working paper, Duke University, Durham, NC.

Jones, C., Kaul, G. and Lipson, M. (1994), 'Information, Trading, and Volatility', *Journal of Financial Economics*, **36**, 127–154.

Lo, A. and MacKinlay, A.C. (1988), 'Stock Prices do not Follow Random Walks: Evidence from a simple specification test', *Review of Financial Studies*, **1**, 41–66.

Lo, Andrew, and MacKinlay, A. Craig (1990), 'An Econometric Analysis of Infrequent Trading', *Journal of Econometrics*, **45**, 181–211.

Low, A. *et al.* (1994), 'The Correlation Structure of Asset Returns', Working paper, National University of Singapore.

Madhaven, A. (1992), 'Trading Mechanisms in Securities Markets', *Journal of Finance*, **47**, 607–641.

Miller, M., Muthuswamy, J. and Whaley, R. (1994), 'Mean Reversion of Standard & Poor's Index Basis Changes: Arbitrage-induced or Statistical Illusion?', *Journal of Finance*, **2**, 479–513.

Müller, U.A. *et al.* (1990), 'Statistical Study of Foreign Exchange Rates, Empirical Evidence of a Price Change Scaling Law, and Intraday Analysis', *Journal of Banking and Finance*, **14**, 1189–1208.

Muthuswamy, J. (1990), 'Nonsynchronous Trading and the Index Autocorrelation Problem', Ph.D. Dissertation, Graduate School of Business, University of Chicago.

Porterba, J. and Summers, L. (1988), 'Mean Reversion in Stock Returns: Evidence and Implications', *Journal of Financial Economics*, **22**, 27–50.

Ross, S. (1989), 'Information and Volatility: The No-arbitrage Martingale Approach to Timing and Resolution Irrelevancy', *Journal of Finance*, **44**, 1–17.

Scholes, M. and Williams, J. (1976), 'Estimating Betas from Daily Data', Working paper, Graduate School of Business, University of Chicago.

Scholes, M. and Williams, J. (1977), 'Estimating Betas from Non-synchronous Data', *Journal of Financial Economics*, **5**, 309–327.

Stoll, H.R. (1989), 'Inferring the Components of the Bid–Ask Spread: Theory and Empirical Tests', *Journal of Finance*, **44**, 115–134.

Wood, R.A. *et al.* (1985), An Investigation of Transactions Data for NYSE Stocks', *Journal of Finance*, **3**, 723–741.

2
Stochastic or Chaotic Dynamics in High Frequency Exchange Rates?

JERÔME DRUNAT, GILLES
DUFRÉNOT, CHRISTIAN DUNIS
and LAURENT MATHIEU

2.1 INTRODUCTION

An emerging body of research has emphasised the role of nonlinearities in providing information about foreign exchange volatility (Diebold and Pauly 1988, Hsieh 1988, 1991, LeBaron 1992). Empirical studies have also shown that exchange rate logarithmic returns may be generated by regime-switching models (Hamilton 1989) and bilinear processes (Maravall 1983).

These approaches are quite well adapted for providing an explanation of the 'dormant' fluctuations of exchange rates over some periods, suddenly interrupted by 'burst' phenomena during other periods. Recent econometric advances have further investigated the chaotic behaviour of foreign currencies. Medio (1992) and Tan (1995), among others, provide support for the view that exchange rates may sometimes be drawn by low-dimensional chaotic systems.

Our study can be regarded as a continuation of previous work. We give further insights into nonlinear model fitting of foreign currencies by looking at the results one obtains when confronted with high frequency data. In section 2.2, we present the data sources and briefly review some summary statistics. This leads us to show that our series are drawn from asymmetric

This chapter previously appeared under the same title in *Working Papers in Financial Economics*, No. 6, June 1995, pp 1–7. © 1995 Chemical Bank. Reproduced with permission.

and leptokurtic distributions. The assumption that exchange rates are drawn from a non-normal distribution raises the question as to whether they conform to linear or nonlinear processes.

To provide an answer to this question, section 2.3 presents the methodology employed. We try to discriminate between a linear and nonlinear specification, thereby applying a test for linearity suggested by Hinich (1982). We find strong evidence for the presence of nonlinearities in some series. We further discriminate between *stochastic* and *deterministic* nonlinearities. This is done by estimating *stochastic models* that allow for nonlinearities in the mean of the series. Finally, we also test for *chaotic dynamics*.

2.2 DATA SOURCES AND PRELIMINARY STATISTICS

We have selected three exchange rates for our study: US dollar/Deutsche Mark (USD/DEM), US dollar/French franc (USD/FRF) and Deutsche Mark/ French franc (DEM/FRF). Our empirical investigation covers the period 2 January 1993 to 31 December 1993 and we use Chemical Bank's database, selecting 10-minute, 30-minute and 60-minute frequencies.

To investigate the statistical properties of our series we have computed their logarithmic returns. This transformation implies that the data are mean-stationary as well as variance-stationary. The first differences relate the original series to their variability, while taking logarithms may induce homoskedastic distributions. In addition, computing the logarithmic rates of change (in percentages) avoids problems arising from Jensen's inequality.[1]

Since we use high frequency data, it is convenient to assume that the behaviour of our exchange rates may change substantially over time. This has led us to split the raw data into 12 samples corresponding to the 12 months of the year.

The study of some preliminary statistics, namely the mean, variance, skewness and kurtosis of the rates of returns, appears to be an essential step when investigating their nonlinear and chaotic structure. The main feature is the non-normality for all our series as evidenced by the high kurtosis and the skewness, which rarely denotes symmetry (for more details, please refer to Drunat *et al.* 1995). It is noteworthy that the period of the DEM/FRF crisis in the summer of 1993 exacerbated these characteristics by showing huge kurtosis and pronounced asymmetry.

Our findings are different from those obtained previously for daily exchange rates (see Friedman and Vandersteel 1982, Hsieh 1988). Indeed, many authors have found symmetric distributions for foreign currencies. This difference could be due to the fact that they use series that have far fewer data points than ours.

The rejection of the Gaussianity assumption has an economic implication. It implies that the mean–variance analysis (which bears upon the assumption that returns are normally distributed) is not an optimal strategy for an agent who wishes to invest in currencies when one considers 10-, 30- or 60-minute time intervals.

Furthermore, rejecting the normality assumption will also have statistical implications. One major reason for requiring a Gaussian distribution is to allow for linear representations of a time series. This is due to the Wold decomposition theorem which stipulates that any stochastic process, weakly stationary, can be expressed as a linear combination of uncorrelated variables.

Still, being confronted with a non-normal process raises the question as to whether or not the underlying model is linear.

2.3   LINEAR AND NONLINEAR DYNAMICS

We have just noted that our data are non-Gaussian. This could be due to the fact that (i) exchange rates conform to stochastic linear models, or that (ii) nonlinear stochastic dynamics can resemble the time paths of our exchange rate series, or that (iii) low-order nonlinear deterministic models (for instance chaotic models) account for the observed dynamics despite the fact that our series do contain measurement errors. We shall try to distinguish between these three possibilities.

2.3.1   Testing for Linearity

The formal ideas involved in testing for linearity refer to polyspectral analysis. A thorough review of the literature on this topic is beyond the scope of this chapter, but the reader may refer to Priestley (1989) for a comprehensive review or to Drunat et al. (1995) for an introductory presentation. This section will only deal with a few theoretical considerations that are required to understand our results.

Let us assume that x_t is a weakly stationary time series. Its p-order cumulant and polyspectral density function are respectively defined by

$$C(k_1, \ldots, k_{(p-1)}) = E\left[(x_t - \hat{x}) \prod_{\tau=k_1}^{k_{(p-1)}} (x_{t+\tau} - \hat{x})\right] \qquad (1)$$

and

$$p(\theta_1, \ldots, \theta_n) = \left(\frac{1}{2\pi}\right)^{p-1} \sum_{k_1=-\infty}^{+\infty} \cdots \sum_{k_{(p-1)}=-\infty}^{+\infty} C(k_1, \ldots, k_{p-1}) \exp\left(-i \sum_{j=1}^{n} \theta_j\right)$$

$$(2)$$

where $\hat{x}$ is the mean of the time series and $n = p - 1$; $k_1, \ldots, k_{p-1}$ are $(p - 1)$ lags; we also have $-\pi < \theta_j < \pi$. If $p - 1 = 2$, then $j = 1, 2$. In that case, the expressions given above are respectively the third-order cumulant and the bispectral density function of x_t. Bispectral estimates can be used to test for linearity by testing that the normalised bispectrum

$$\hat{V}(\theta_1, \theta_2) = \frac{|\hat{P}(\theta_1, \theta_2)|^2}{\hat{P}(\theta_1)\hat{P}(\theta_2)P(\theta_1 + \theta_2)} \tag{3}$$

is constant at all frequencies within a region usually defined as the triangular set:

$$\{0 < \theta_1 < 1/2, \theta_2 < \theta_2, 2\theta_1 + \theta_2 < 1\} \tag{4}$$

$\hat{P}(\theta_1, \theta_2)$ is a consistent estimator of the bispectrum:

$$\hat{P}(\theta_1, \theta_2) = \left(\frac{1}{S}\right)^2 \sum_{\nu_1=(S-1)}^{\theta_1(S-1)} \sum_{\nu_2=(\theta_2-1)S}^{\theta_2 S-1} H(\nu_1, \nu_2) \tag{5}$$

$$H(\nu_1, \nu_2) = \frac{1}{T}\Psi(\nu_1)\Psi(\nu_2)\Psi^c(\nu_1 + \nu_2) \tag{6}$$

where $\Psi(\nu_1)$ is the Fourier transform of the series and $\Psi^c(\nu_1)$ its complex conjugate. Equation (5) is obtained by considering frequency pairs within a domain of S^2 points defined by

$$D = \{(2\nu_1 - 1)S/2, (2\nu_2 - 1)S/2, 1 \leqslant \nu_1 \leqslant \nu_2\} \tag{7}$$

$$\nu_1 \leqslant (T/2S - T/2 + 3/4) \tag{8}$$

As shown by Ashley and Patterson (1989), $V(\theta_i, \theta_j)$ is the square of the skewness. The joint test that all estimates are constant can be conducted using the statistic $2|\hat{P}(\theta_1, \theta_2)|^2$ which is distributed as $\chi_\eta^2(2)$ under the null hypothesis that the series follows a linear process; η is a centrality parameter which varies with each frequency pair. The null hypothesis that a series is linear is rejected when the sample distribution exceeds that given by the theoretical distribution.

Using Monte Carlo simulations, Ashley et al. (1986) have shown that the best measure of dispersion was given by the empirical eightieth percentile, noted $b_{0.8}$, which is asymptotically distributed as a normal law $N(b_{0.8}, \sigma_{0.8})$, where $\sigma_{0.8}$ is estimated by

$$\sigma_{0.8} = (1/P)0.8(1 - 0.8)f^{-1}b_{0.8} \tag{9}$$

P is the number of squares of the domain of definition and f is the density function of $\chi_\eta^2(2)$. Testing for the linearity of our series therefore implies calculating the Q statistic:

$$Q = b_{0.8}/\sigma_{0.8} \tag{10}$$

Table 2.1 reports this Q statistic for our USD/DEM, USD/FRF and DEM/FRF exchange rates. The hypothesis of linearity is rejected at the 5% confidence level when the statistic exceeds 1.96 (and 1.64 at the 10% confidence level), which is the threshold value corresponding to a normal law with zero mean and unit variance.

First, as can be seen in Table 2.1, nonlinear processes seem to characterise the higher frequency data. Second, the results for the 30-minute series differ depending on the exchange rate. Nonlinear processes seem to characterise the DEM/FRF data, while the nonlinearity hypothesis is justified only for half the series in the case of the USD/DEM and USD/FRF.

Table 2.1 Linearity test

(60-minute)

Rate	January	February	March	April	May	June
USD/DEM	−0.82	1.11	1.47	1.26	0.79	0.28
USD/FRF	0.07	1.23	2.78	−1.37	−0.48	−0.53
DEM/FRF	1.31	4.94	0.65	2.32	1.19	4.70

Rate	July	August	September	October	November	December
USD/DEM	−1.27	2.00	−1.23	0.80	1.96	0.58
USD/FRF	1.14	3.11	−0.15	0.95	0.99	0.46
DEM/FRF	2.92	1.86	1.46	−0.12	2.72	2.42

(30-minute)

Rate	January	February	March	April	May	June
USD/DEM	−1.28	1.69	1.69	2.03	4.69	1.22
USD/FRF	1.53	0.63	1.11	1.45	1.94	1.06
DEM/FRF	4.6	1.69	3.68	2.27	5.13	3.25

Rate	July	August	September	October	November	December
USD/DEM	1.98	3.09	2.09	0.88	4.28	1.08
USD/FRF	2.52	1.00	3.51	3.22	1.82	−0.25
DEM/FRF	3.64	4.15	2.56	1.33	1.80	2.49

(10-minute)

Rate	January	February	March	April	May	June
USD/DEM	2.47	3.39	5.15	6.62	4.11	4.56
USD/FRF	5.32	2.93	5.30	4.80	8.20	3.68
DEM/FRF	3.01	6.79	6.35	5.19	5.83	3.61

Rate	July	August	September	October	November	December
USD/DEM	3.54	6.08	5.36	4.93	7.12	6.94
USD/FRF	4.78	5.47	7.11	5.33	3.95	6.94
DEM/FRF	6.51	5.45	6.35	6.87	5.63	9.24

Globally, for the majority of the series, time aggregation 'smoothes' nonlinearities inherent to 10- or even 30-minute exchange rate data. This result is similar to that obtained by Drunat *et al.* (1994) for daily and weekly exchange rates. The transformation of high frequency data that include nonlinearities (especially those series with a 10- or 30-minute interval) into low frequency exchange rates (i.e. hourly data) often succeeds in producing linear structures. When this is not the case, the nonlinear structure of high frequency exchange rates is not identical to that of lower frequency series.

We also observe that whenever a series with a frequency higher than one hour appears to be linear, this linearity is not necessarily preserved for hourly data. This implies that 'disaggregated' linear models of exchange rates do not necessarily produce 'aggregated' linear models.[2]

In evaluating the nonlinear dynamics of exchange rates, some authors have argued that the equations governing their evolution may switch over time. Hamilton (1989) and Engel and Hamilton (1990) have proposed a *regime-switching model* for the US dollar. Others have also suggested the existence of 'jump' or 'burst' phenomena in exchange rates. Maravall (1983) provides such an example by applying a *bilinear model* to the Spanish currency. There has also been a growing interest on the part of international economists for adopting models where exchange rates depend nonlinearly on economic fundamentals (see Flood *et al.* 1990 for instance).

For our exchange rates, we will concentrate on exponential autoregressive (EXPAR) models.

2.3.2 Estimating EXPAR Models

Exponential autoregressive models are needed to describe certain types of behaviour in financial data. They first exhibit jump phenomena, thereby mimicking successions of periods during which exchange rates are 'dormant', but occasionally interrupted by periods of 'burst'. They can also capture other characteristics of nonlinear dynamics such as limit-cycle behaviour, i.e. self-sustained periodic cycles. These features occur in natural sciences (see the pioneering work of van der Pol 1927). However, as pointed out by Mills (1991), EXPAR models have so far found no applications for economic and financial data. It therefore remains to be seen whether they are useful for the modelling of economic and financial time series.

Our work can be regarded as an attempt to answer this question, even though we limit our attention to high frequency exchange rates. We will start by briefly discussing the form of the model.[3] The standard EXPAR model is defined as follows:

$$r_t = \sum_{i=1}^{P} \{\phi_i + \pi_i \exp(kr_{t-1}^2)\} r_{t-1} + u_t \tag{11}$$

where r_t refers to the logarithmic return, μ_t is a white noise with a mean equal to zero and a constant variance, k is a real parameter bounded by 0 and $+\infty$. The maximum lag P is determined by using Akaike's information criterion (AIC).

Clearly, for large $|r_{t-1}|$ values, equation (1) behaves like a linear model, while the degree of nonlinearity, so to speak, is increased for small values of $|r_{t-1}|$. EXPAR models are therefore capable of behaving just like threshold autoregressive (TAR) models, but, unlike TAR models, their coefficients change smoothly between their two extreme values.

As there is no economic theory that allows one to choose appropriate values for the parameter k, the choice is determined empirically.

The estimation of such a model consists of two stages: (i) least-squares methods are used to estimate the values of the coefficients (for a fixed value of k); this is best done by minimising the sum of squared residuals; (ii) once the coefficients have been estimated, we have to find an optimal value for k. The above procedure is repeated and the values of k should be chosen such that the exponential terms vary between 0 and 1. The optimal k is then selected by using the AIC.

But applying these procedures to our exchange rates is not easy and the EXPAR specification is problematic. We have first used ordinary least squares, as suggested by Priestley (1989, p. 88). Still, our estimations were not efficient as their residuals were autocorrelated.

To overcome this problem, we had to use a two-step procedure: (i) we have first used instrumental variables to conduct our least-squares regressions in order to get efficient estimations; (ii) also, we have used the approach proposed by Hatanaka (1974) to remove the autocorrelation from the residuals.

We just report some of our results here. As argued above, EXPAR models can exhibit several types of dynamics. In particular, we have found evidence of the existence of limit-cycle behaviour, a feature which seems quite interesting and is evidenced by the V-statistics in Table 2.1. Indeed, a sufficient condition for the existence of limit cycles is given by

$$V = \left[\left(1 - \sum_i \phi_i \right) \Big/ \sum_i \pi_i \right] > 1 \quad \text{or} \quad < 0 \qquad (12)$$

We therefore provide a few examples that illustrate our most significant results.[4]

Table 2.2 also reports the maximum lag chosen for a few of our series, the order of the significant lag values and the root mean squared error (RMSE). We have also reported the regression results for the three 60-minute series.[5]

As can be seen, many coefficients are small, but their inclusion substantially reduces the residual variance. We can further observe from the Durbin-h statistic that the serial correlation has been removed from the

Table 2.2 Summary statistics for some EXPAR models

		Month	Maximum lag	Significant coefficients	V	RMSE
60-minute	USD/DEM	November	8	$(2)^a$	12.4862	4.88E-5
	USD/FRF	January	8	(1)	16.30437	2.801E-4
	DEM/FRF	July	7	(2,3)	9.05748	4.753E-5
30-minute	USD/DEM	May	8	$(4)^b$	7.03308	3.243E-5
	USD/FRF	December	8	(3,5)	3.7677	1.854E-4
	DEM/FRF	April	7	(1)	69.8805	1.605E-6
10-minute	USD/DEM	November	10	(2,7)	2.505787	1.188E-5
	USD/FRF	July	10	(1,4,7,8)	1.61387	1.932E-4
	DEM/FRF	April	10	(1,6)	31.5263	8.8705E-7

USD/DEM EXPAR model (60-minute)—November

ϕ_1	ϕ_2	ϕ_3	ϕ_4	ϕ_5	ϕ_6	ϕ_7
−0.44E-4	0.98E-4	0.18E-4	0.14E-4	−0.47E-5	0.38E-5	0.58E-5
(−0.827)	(1.844)	(0.335)	(0.266)	(−0.089)	(0.072)	(0.110)

ϕ_8	π_1	π_2	π_3	π_4	π_5	π_6
0.48E-4	0.055	0.080	0.06118	0.049	0.1163	0.21713
(0.833)	(0.055)	(7.412)	(5.364)	(5.364)	(4.202)	(6.872)

π_7	π_8	Durbin-h	Ljung–Box	k	RSS	—
0.16201	0.25847	0.04748	81.3345	0.5	9.32E-7	—
(8.499)	(7.712)	(0.962)	(0.873)			

USD/FRF EXPAR model (60-minute)—January

ϕ_1	ϕ_2	ϕ_3	ϕ_4	ϕ_5	ϕ_6	ϕ_7
0.54E-3	0.73E-4	−0.69E-5	0.107E-3	−0.128E-3	0.206E-4	−0.16E-4
(3.2740)	(0.44)	(−0.041)	(0.6530)	(−0.779)	(0.1242)	(−0.098)

ϕ_8	π_1	π_2	π_3	π_4	π_5	π_6
0.18E-3	0.0613	0.0996	0.1858	0.0343	0.124	0.284
(1.1445)	(7.242)	(6.224)	(9.132)	(3.015)	(5.57)	(11.52)

π_7	π_8	Durbin-h	Ljung–Box	k	RSS	—
0.057	0.157	−0.7678	80.1813	0.5	0.33E-4	—
(4.151)	(7.43)	(0.4425)	(0.917)			

Table 2.2   Continued

DEM/FRF EXPAR model (60-minute)—July

ϕ_1	ϕ_2	ϕ_3	ϕ_4	ϕ_5	ϕ_6	ϕ_7
0.12E-3	−0.17E-3	−0.14E-3	0.55E-4	−0.60E-4	−0.75E-4	0.46E-4
(1.842)	(−2.511)	(−2.055)	(0.807)	(−0.850)	(−1.057)	(0.656)
ϕ_8	π_1	π_2	π_3	π_4	π_5	π_6
—	0.004	0.094	0.1104	−0.0685	0.4256	0.2577
—	(0.379)	(5.622)	(4.837)	(−3.025)	(12.137)	(6.857)
π_7	π_8	Durbin-h	Ljung–Box	k	RSS	—
0.177	—	0.533229	106.17	0.5	8.49E-4	—
(5.55)	—	(0.5938)	(0.2462)			—

[a]This coefficient was significant at the 10% confidence level.
[b]This coefficient was significant at the 10% confidence level.

residuals as the probability to reject wrongly the null hypothesis of no serial correlation is higher than 5% in all three cases. Similarly, the Ljung–Box statistics show that there is no serial correlation of order 2 or above.

Furthermore, all our exchange rates are explained by EXPAR models whose maximum lag is at least equal to 7. It does not necessarily imply that our data incorporate long memory behaviour. Indeed, for all our results, we have rarely selected a model for which the highest significant coefficient ϕ_i is greater than 4.

We can also see differences between our exchange rates, according to their frequency. Most of the time, EXPAR models with a maximum lag equal to 10 turned out to be well adapted for 10-minute returns. The value of the maximum lag decreased for 30- and 60-minute exchange rate returns.

Our results yield important insights into the presence of limit cycles. We have previously seen that our data exhibit asymmetric behaviour. Accordingly, while our models are suited for detecting cyclic phenomena, these cycles may be regarded as being asymmetric.

Asymmetric cycles suggest the presence of *hysteresis*, a feature which can be interpreted as follows: if logarithmic returns have been stable until a given period, then their dependence on previous levels is reinforced; but if they have been rising, then their dependence is reduced and the risk of larger errors associated with forecasts of future returns therefore increases.

Generally, EXPAR models manage to capture consistently the dynamics of our exchange rate data. Still, a careful reader may be troubled by the use of stochastic models, which form the substance of our analysis so far. This hypothesis is traditionally supported by two ideas: (i) measurement errors may be present in exchange rate series, and (ii) explanatory variables may have been omitted in the statistical models.

The assumption of stochasticity can nevertheless be relaxed and, accordingly, we consider the implication of a *nonlinear deterministic analysis*, i.e. the possibility of chaotic dynamics.

2.3.3 Are Exchange Rates Chaotic?

The methodology to discriminate stochastic from deterministic processes was suggested by Brock *et al.* (1987) who devised a statistical procedure which tests the null hypothesis that a time series is identically independently distributed (i.i.d.).

As has been pointed out by several authors, such as Ashley and Patterson (1989) and Hsieh (1991) the independence of the path of a variable from its history does not necessarily imply that it conforms to a white noise process. On this particular issue, alternative explanations have to be examined: chaos, non-stationarity or conditional heteroskedasticity can be responsible for the rejection of i.i.d. Consequently, appropriate tests must be used, which allow for the detection of a direct evidence of chaotic behaviour. The basic framework to be used is the *correlation dimension* and the *Lyapunov exponent*. To compute these statistics, we first need to pre-whiten the data. As a result, all linear dependencies are removed from the original series.

Because we are using empirical data, the law of motion which produces the dynamics of the series is unknown. So, how shall we know that there exists a chaotic system that produces the time paths of our series? A solution has been proposed by Takens (1981). The author has suggested con-structing an observer function. More specifically, we must form *m*-histories as follows:

$$r_t^1 = r_t$$

$$r_t^2 = (r_t, r_{t-1}) \qquad (13)$$

$$r_t^m = (r_t, r_{t-1}, \ldots, r_{t-m+1})$$

where *m* is the *embedding dimension* and r_t^m an *m*-history. The justification of this approach is that there exists a relationship (a diffeomorphism) between the *m*-histories and the data-generating process, i.e. the former re-creates the dynamics of the original logarithmic returns (noted here by r_t). Furthermore, Takens has shown that *m* must be larger or equal to $(2n + 1)$, where *n* is the true, but unknown, dimension of the system that has generated the raw data. Once this is done, it becomes possible to compute the correlation dimension.

There are several ways to define the dimension of a set. However, we will henceforth consider the calculation of dimension proposed by Grassberger and Procaccia (1983).

First, one defines the correlation integral, which calculates the average fraction of pairs (r^τ_t, r^θ_t) that are close to each other, within a radius:

$$C_m(T, \varepsilon) = \frac{2}{n(n-1)} \sum_{1 \leq \tau \leq \theta \leq T} \left(\prod_{l=0}^{m-1} I_\varepsilon(r_{\tau+l}, r_{\theta+l}) \right) \qquad (14)$$

One assumes that there exists n distinct pairs of m-length trajectories, which can be generated from the original returns T denotes the number of total observations of the original series $I_\varepsilon(x, y)$ is the Heaviside function taking the value of 1 if the distance, induced by the selected norm, between x and y is larger or equal to ε and 0 if it is less than ε (the norm that we have chosen here is the sup- or max-norm).

The correlation dimension is related to the correlation integral and is defined as follows:

$$\nu_m = \lim_{T \to \infty} \lim_{\varepsilon \to 0} \frac{\ln [c_m(T, \varepsilon)]}{\ln (\varepsilon)} \qquad (15)$$

We now calculate the slope of $\ln [C_m(T, \varepsilon)]$ versus $\ln (\varepsilon)$ and then examine how it varies with m. This leads to the following conclusion: (i) if the quantity ν_m does not increase with m, then the data are consistent with *chaotic* behaviour; (ii) if it does not saturate, then the dynamics of the exchange rates may be regarded as *stochastic*.

When adopting this approach, two practical problems emerge. First, we have to select appropriately a 'coarse' grid of embedding dimensions m. Brock *et al.* (1991) have shown from Monte Carlo simulations that, when confronted with a finite amount of data, the values of m must be chosen such that $T > 200m$. For our exchange rate series, we have used embedding dimensions of 2, 5 and 10. Second, to measure the ability of the previous procedures to detect chaotic dynamics, ε must be constrained and set between 0.5 and 2 standard deviations of the series.

Table 2.3 shows the estimated dimension only for the 10-minute exchange rate series, as the other series do not contain enough data points to obtain efficient estimates. One can see, irrespective of the month considered, that the correlation dimension increases with the embedding dimension, thereby suggesting the *predominance of underlying stochastic processes*. Moreover, the dimension appears to be relatively low, between 1 and 2 (except a few cases where it reaches 3), the numbers being smaller for the DEM/FRF and larger for the USD/DEM.

The above results are reinforced when one studies the dependence to initial conditions. There is a close connection between the dimensionof a chaotic system attractor and the time variation of the motion, as characterised by Lyapunov exponents. In a chaotic state the greatest Lyapunov exponent is positive, thereby indicating divergence of trajectories. It implies that an initial

Table 2.3   Correlation dimension (10-minute)—$\varepsilon/\sigma = 0.5$

m	Rate	January	February	March	April	May	June
	USD/DEM	0.70	0.60	0.60	0.56	0.62	0.57
2	USD/FRF	0.60	0.60	0.50	0.50	0.55	0.57
	DEM/FRF	0.44	0.47	0.43	0.48	0.46	0.42
	USD/DEM	1.60	1.33	1.30	1.20	1.30	1.30
5	USD/FRF	1.16	1.34	1.10	1.01	1.11	1.25
	DEM/FRF	0.86	0.88	0.84	0.94	0.85	0.84
	USD/DEM	2.45	2.20	2.10	2.00	2.20	2.33
10	USD/FRF	1.61	2.12	1.74	1.60	1.75	2.21
	DEM/FRF	1.35	1.30	1.27	1.47	1.24	1.27
m	Rate	July	August	September	October	November	December
	USD/DEM	0.54	0.54	0.51	0.54	0.51	0.63
2	USD/FRF	0.53	0.47	0.44	0.40	0.48	0.54
	DEM/FRF	0.32	0.43	0.52	0.52	0.60	0.47
	USD/DEM	1.18	1.16	1.11	1.10	1.10	1.30
5	USD/FRF	1.05	0.92	0.88	0.86	0.97	1.02
	DEM/FRF	0.60	0.80	1.00	1.03	1.13	0.87
	USD/DEM	1.84	2.02	1.71	1.92	1.91	2.20
10	USD/FRF	1.55	1.40	1.30	1.43	1.50	1.50
	DEM/FRF	0.90	1.21	1.52	1.63	1.75	1.28

state may be known with a high (but finite) degree of precision, but the ability to predict later states diminishes because of the divergence of the trajectories. The Lyapunov exponents therefore constitute a quantity for characterising the rate of divergence of two initial points.

Formally, for an n-dimensional system there exists n exponents, each noted λ_i, $i = 1, \ldots, n$. Customarily, they are ranked from the largest to the smallest. All of them can be calculated by evaluating the dimension of the system that has generated the logarithmic returns.

For simplicity, we consider a system of n first-order difference equations which we shall write in compact notation as follows:

$$r_{t+1} = f(r_t), \quad r \in R^n \qquad (16)$$

Let us further define two initial points r_0 and r_0', with $\varepsilon_0 = M(r_0, r_0')$ which is a Euclidean measure of distance between the two points. After the linearisation of the system, the distance between the corresponding t points belonging to the trajectory will be defined by

$$\varepsilon_n = \left(\prod_{i=0}^{n-1} J(r_i) \right) \varepsilon_0 \qquad (17)$$

where $J(r_i)$ is the Jacobian matrix evaluated at r_i. The expression in brackets represents the product of n Jacobian matrices evaluated along an orbit. It is noteworthy that the product of the n Jacobian matrices equals the Jacobian matrix of the whole system. Its dimension is $n \times n$, and thereby it possesses n eigenvalues. By denoting them as μ_i and ordering them from the largest to the smallest, we define the Lyapunov exponents of the system as

$$\lambda_i = \lim_{T \to \infty} (1/T) \log_2 |\mu_i|, \qquad i = 1, \ldots, n \qquad (18)$$

When all Lyapunov exponents are negative on an attractor, it means that the attractor is negative. A limit cycle must involve a $\lambda_i = 0$. A two-torus, i.e. a two-frequency quasi-periodic attractor, can emerge if two Lyapunov exponents are equal to zero.

Many algorithms have been constructed to estimate the entire Lyapunov spectrum efficiently (see Dechert and Gençay 1990, 1992), or only the largest (see Wolf et al. 1985, Nychka et al. 1992). The algorithm that we employ is due to Wolf et al. (1985) and has now become standard use.[6]

Table 2.4 gives the estimates for the Lyapunov exponents for the 10-minute exchange rate series. These results are consistent with those obtained previously for the correlation dimension. Where there seems to be a chaotic regime, Lyapunov exponents are *positive*. Conversely, *negative* Lyapunov exponents seem to indicate the presence of stable behaviour.

Table 2.4   Lyapunov exponents[a]

	Rate	January	February	March	April	May	June
	USD/DEM	−0.09(1)	−0.03(1)	−0.10(1)	−0.05(1)	−0.13(1)	0.03(1)
		0.01(2)	0.01(2)	−0.01(2)	−0.01(2)	0.01(2)	−0.01(2)
10-	USD/FRF	0.03(1)	−0.07(1)	−0.10(1)	−0.08(1)	−0.13(1)	−0.15(1)
minute		0.01(2)	0.01(2)	−0.01(2)	0.02(2)	0.00(2)	−0.01(2)
	DEM/FRF	−0.08(1)	−0.15(1)	0.02(1)	0.05(1)	−0.01(1)	0.02(1)
		−0.15(2)	—	−0.17(2)	0.01(2)	−0.20(2)	—

	Rate	July	August	September	October	November	December
	USD/DEM	−0.15(1)	−0.08(1)	−0.05(1)	−0.10(1)	−0.07(1)	−0.09(1)
		0.01(2)	0.01(2)	0.02(2)	0.02(2)	−0.01(2)	0.15(2)
10-	USD/FRF	−0.12(1)	−0.08(1)	−0.12(1)	−0.08(1)	0.01(1)	−0.05(1)
minute		0.02(2)	0.01(2)	—	—	—	—
	DEM/FRF	0.15(1)	−0.15(1)	0.005(1)	−0.015(1)	−0.10(1)	−0.06(1)
		—	—	−0.01(2)	−0.01(2)	−0.12(2)	−0.10(2)

[a]System dimension induced by the correlation dimension given in parentheses.

In calculating the Lyapunov exponents we have been confronted with some of the difficulties that we met with the computation of the correlation dimension. For instance, for the USD/FRF and an attractor of 1, the Lyapunov exponent is 0.03 in January, a very small positive value for which it is impossible to calculate the statistical significance and thus derive any firm conclusion. Furthermore, we only present our results for the 10-minute exchange rate series, as we did not have enough data points at the 30- and 60-minute frequencies.

We have calculated either one or two values for the Lyapunov exponents, according to the system dimension induced by the correlation dimension. For instance, the dimension for the DEM/FRF for January is between 0.44 and 1.35. Thus, one could conclude that the attractor is either 1 or 2. Globally, most of our series possess negative Lyapunov exponents, indicating the *stability of the underlying process.*

The interpretation for the USD/DEM exchange rate appears particularly difficult: true, the sign of the Lyapunov exponent in dimension 1 is systematically opposed to the one in dimension 2!

2.4   CONCLUSION

The aim of this chapter was to extend new methods already adopted to study the behaviour of daily and weekly exchange rates to high frequency data. This has led us to several conclusions.

First, our time series appear to be both asymmetric and leptokurtic. This feature seems consistent with the results which are traditionally obtained for daily and weekly exchange rates.

Second, it is apparent that these series do not conform to white noise processes. However, as stressed by Hsieh (1991), one should treat such a conclusion cautiously, since the higher the frequency of the data, the higher the probability of detecting spurious serial dependence in exchange rates reflecting mostly market microstructure.

Third, allowing for serial dependence raises the question as to whether one is confronted with linear or nonlinear processes. We have seen that nonlinear stochastic models are capable of capturing the dynamics of our series. Furthermore, we have also indicated the possibility of using a class of nonlinear stochastic models, namely EXPAR models, that help in detecting limit cycles as limit behaviour in our exchange rate series.

Finally, the assumption that high frequency exchange rates can be described by low-dimension chaotic systems has clearly been rejected. This is in contradiction with previous work on daily data that had shown a strong evidence of chaos.

ACKNOWLEDGEMENTS

We are grateful to Chemical Bank's Quantitative Research & Trading Group for providing us with the data used in this study. We would also like to thank D. Patterson for providing us with his program to compute bi-spectrum estimates. The responsibility for any remaining errors rests with the authors.

ENDNOTES

1. Jensen's inequality states that if h is a convex function, then $E[h(X)] \geq h(E[X])$. Accordingly, with $h = 1/X$, this implies that the results of any analysis will differ depending on whether one uses *direct* or *indirect* quotes, i.e. for instance, whether one uses the number of USD per DEM or the number of DEM per USD.
2. We are talking about time aggregation.
3. For a more exhaustive review, the reader may refer to Ozaki and Haggan (1981).
4. Complete results are available from the authors upon request.
5. For each coefficient we have reported the Student-t statistic in parentheses. We have also provided the significance level for both the Durbin-h and Ljung–Box statistics.
6. Other algorithms provide a relatively easy way of calculating the Lyapunov exponents, but they either have a positive bias (Kurths and Herzel 1987) or do not perform satisfactorily with a limited number of observations (Brown *et al.* 1991).

REFERENCES

Ashley, R.A., Hinich, M.J. and Patterson, D.M. (1986), 'A Diagnostic Test for Dependence in Time Series Fitting Errors', *Journal of Time Series Analysis*, **7**(3), pp. 165–178.

Ashley, R.A. and Patterson, D.M. (1989), 'Linear versus Nonlinear Macroeconomics: A Statistical Test', *International Economic Review*, **30**(3), pp. 685–704.

Brock, W.A., Dechert, W.D. and Scheinkman, J.A. (1987), 'A Test for Independence Based on the Correlation Dimension', University of Wisconsin, Working Paper No. 8702.

Brock, W.A., Hsieh, D.A. and LeBaron, B. (1991), *Nonlinear Dynamics, Chaos and Instability*, MIT Press, Cambridge, Massachusetts.

Brown, R., Bryant, P. and Abarbanel, D.I. (1991), 'Computing the Lyapunov Spectrum of a Dynamical System from an Observed Time Series', *Physical Review A*, No. 43, pp. 2787–2806.

Dechert, W.D. and Gençay, R. (1990), 'Estimating Lyapunov Exponents with Multilayer Feedforward Network Learning', Department of Economics, University of Houston.

Dechert, W.D. and Gençay, R. (1992), 'Lyapunov Exponents as a Nonparametric Diagnostic for Stability Analysis', *Journal of Applied Econometrics*, **7**, pp. S41–S61.

Diebold, F.X. (1986), 'Testing for Serial Correlation in the Presence of ARCH', unpublished manuscript, University of Pennsylvania.

Diebold, F.X. and Pauly, P. (1988), 'Endogenous Risk in a Rational Expectations Portfolio Balance Model of Deutschmark/Dollar Rate', *European Economic Review*, No. 32, pp. 27–54.

Drunat, J., Dufrénot, G. and Mathieu, L. (1995), 'Nonlinear and Chaotic Dynamics in High Frequency Exchange Rates', Chemical Bank and Imperial College International Conference 'Forecasting Financial Markets: Advances for Exchange Rates, Interest Rates and Asset Management', London, 22–24 March 1995.

Drunat, J., Dufrénot, G., Mathieu, L. and Dunis, C. (1994), 'Testing for Normality and Linearity in Exchange Rates: A Frequency Domain Approach', *Working Papers in Financial Economics*, Chemical Bank, No. 4, pp. 1–5.

Engel, C. and Hamilton, J.D. (1990), 'Long Swings in the Dollar: Are They in the Data and Do Markets Know it?', *American Economic Review*, No. 80, pp. 689–713.

Flood, R.P., Rose, A.K. and Mathieson, D.J. (1990), 'An Empirical Exploration of Exchange Rate Target Zones', NBER Working Paper, No. 3543.

Friedman, D. and Vandersteel, S. (1982), 'Short-Run Fluctuations in Foreign Exchange Rates', *Journal of International Economics*, No. 13, pp. 171–186.

Grassberger, P. and Procaccia, I. (1983), 'Measuring the Strangeness of Strange Attractors', *Physica 9D*, pp. 189–208.

Hamilton, J.D. (1989), 'A New Approach to the Economic Analysis of Nonstationary Time Series and the Business Cycle', *Econometrica*, No. 57, pp. 307–317.

Hatanaka, M. (1974), 'An Efficient Two-Step Estimator for the Dynamic Adjustment Model with Autoregressive Errors', *Journal of Econometrics*, **2**, pp. 199–220.

Hinich, M.J. (1982), 'Testing for Gaussianity and Linearity of a Stationary Time Series', *Journal of Time Series Analysis*, 3(1), pp. 169–176.

Hsieh, D.A. (1988), 'The Statistical Properties of Daily Exchange Rates: 1974–1983', *Journal of International Economics*, No. 24, pp. 129–145.

Hsieh, D.A. (1991), 'Chaos and Nonlinear Dynamics: Application to Financial Markets', *The Journal of Finance*, 46(6), pp. 1839–1877.

Kurths, J. and Herzel, H. (1987), 'An Attractor in a Solar Time Series', *Physica D*, No. 25, pp. 165–172.

LeBaron, B. (1992), 'Forecast Improvements Using a Volatility Index', *Journal of Applied Econometrics*, No. 7, pp. 137–149.

Maravall, A. (1983), 'An Application of Nonlinear Time Series Forecasting', *Journal of Business and Economic Statistics*, No. 3, pp. 350–355.

Medio, A. (1992), *Chaotic Dynamics, Theory and Application to Economics*, Cambridge University Press, New York.

Mills, T.C. (1991), 'Nonlinear Time Series Models in Economics', *Journal of Economic Survey*, 5(3), pp. 214–242.

Nychka, D., Ellner, S., Gallant, A.R. and McCaffrey, D. (1992), 'Finding Chaos in Noisy Systems', *Journal of the Royal Statistical Society*, **B4**, pp. 202–216.

Ozaki, T. and Haggan, V. (1981), 'Modelling Nonlinear Random Vibrations Using an Amplitude-Dependent Autoregressive Time Series Model', *Biometrika*, No. 68, pp. 189–196.

Priestley, M.B. (1989), *Non-Linear and Non-Stationary Time Series Analysis*, Academic Press Limited, London.

Takens, F. (1981), 'Detecting Strange Attractors in Turbulence', in Rand, D. and Young, I. (eds), *Dynamical Systems and Turbulence*, Springer-Verlag, Berlin, pp. 366–381.

Tan, P.Y. (1995), 'Using Neural Networks to Model Chaotic Properties in Currency Exchange Markets', *Working Papers in Financial Economics*, Chemical Bank, No. 5, pp. 8–15.

Van der Pol, B. (1927), 'Forced Oscillations in a System with Non-Linear Resistance', *Philosophical Magazine*, No. 3, pp. 65–80.
Wolf, A., Swift, J.B., Swinney, H.L. and Vastano, J.A. (1985), 'Determining Lyapunov Exponents from a Time Series', *Physica D*, No. 16, pp. 285–317.

3
Forecasting Foreign Exchange Rates Subject to De-volatilization

— BIN ZHOU —

3.1 INTRODUCTION

Empirical studies have shown little success at forecasting foreign exchange rates using structural and time series models (Meese and Rogoff 1983a, b). One of the obstacles to effective modeling and forecasting of exchange rates is heteroscedasticity (changing variance). The autoregressive conditional heteroscedastic (ARCH) model addresses heteroscedasticity by estimating the conditional variance from historical data and has been used in modeling many financial time series (see Engle 1982 and Bollerslev 1986). However, forecasting exchange rates remains difficult. The recent availability of high frequency data has created new possibilities for forecasting exchange rates.

High frequency data, such as minute-by-minute or tick-by-tick data, have recently received attention from Goodhart and Figliuoli (1991) and Zhou (1992). As reported in Zhou's paper, high frequency data behave differently from low frequency data and they have a significant noise component. Zhou suggested the following process for high frequency exchange rates:

$$S(t) = d(t) + B(\tau(t)) + \epsilon_t \tag{1}$$

where $S(t)$ is the logarithm of the price at time t, $B(\cdot)$ is standard Brownian

Forecasting Financial Markets: Exchange Rates, Interest Rates and Asset Management. Edited by Christian Dunis. © 1996 John Wiley & Sons Ltd.

motion, $d(\cdot)$ is a drift, $\tau(\cdot)$ is a positive increment function, ϵ_t is a random noise with mean zero, independent of the Brownian motion $B(\cdot)$. Here $\tau(t)$ is called *cumulative volatility* and an increment of $\tau(b) - \tau(a)$ is called the *volatility* in period $[a, b]$. The return $X(s, t) = S(t) - S(s)$ then has the following structure:

$$X(s, t) = \mu(s, t) + \sigma(s, t)Z_t + \epsilon_t - \epsilon_s \tag{2}$$

where Z_t is a standard normal random variable and $\sigma(s, t) = \tau(t) - \tau(s)$. Returns of high frequency data are often negatively autocorrelated due to the noise. This autocorrelation decreases as the frequency decreases.

This article presents a new approach to heteroscedasticity of financial time series. In section 3.2, we introduce a de-volatilization procedure, which takes a homoscedastic subsequence from high frequency data. In section 3.3, we test the de-volatilization procedure by examining various properties of de-volatilized exchange rates. Finally, in section 3.4, we construct a forecasting procedure from the de-volatilized time series.

3.2 DE-VOLATILIZATION

One of most significant characteristics of a financial time series is heteroscedasticity. Heteroscedasticity tends to become more severe as sampling frequency increases. This poses a great difficulty in modeling financial time series. One obvious shortcoming of equally spaced time series is that information is insufficient at highly volatile time intervals and is redundant at other times. A time series with more data at highly volatile times and less data at other times is desirable. Unfortunately no financial time series are recorded in this manner. However, availability of high frequency data allows us to sample a subsequence that has adjacent points with equal volatility apart. We call such a procedure *de-volatilization*. The subsequence produced by the procedure is called a de-volatilized time series or *dv-series* and differences of successive measurement of dv-series are called *dv-returns*.

To carry out the de-volatilization procedure, we need to estimate the volatility process $\tau(t)$ first. Given high frequency data, $\{S(t_i)\}$, Zhou (1992) has proposed an estimator of the volatility increment $\tau(b) - \tau(a)$ for any given period $[a, b]$ by

$$\widehat{\tau(b) - \tau(a)} = \frac{1}{k} \sum_{t_i \in [a, b]} [X^2(t_{i-k}, t_i) + 2X(t_{i-k}, t_i)X(t_{i-2k}, t_{i-k})], \tag{3}$$

where $X(s, t) = S(t) - S(s)$, and k is a constant. This volatility estimator is almost unbiased. For a given volatility estimator, we have the following de-volatilization procedure.

Algorithm 1 (De-volatilization)

Suppose that $\{S(t_i)\}$ is a series of observations from process (1). This algorithm takes a subsequence from the series and forms a dv-series, denoted as r_τ. The return of the dv-series has approximately the same volatility.

1. Set the initial value $r_0 = S(t_0)$;
2. Suppose that we have obtained an element of a dv-series at time t_m, i.e. $r_\tau = S(t_m)$;
3. Estimate the volatility increment $V(t_{m+i}, t_m) = \tau(t_{m+i}) - \tau(t_m)$ by equation (3) for $i = 1, \ldots$, until the increment $V(t_{m+i}, t_m)$ exceeds the level v, a predetermined constant. Let

$$k = \min\{i; \tau(t_{m+i}) - \tau(t_m) \geqslant v \text{ and } |S(t_{m+i}) - S(t_{m+i-1})| < \sqrt{v}\} \quad (4)$$

   and $r_{\tau+1} = S(t_{m+k})$ is the next element in the dv-series.
4. Repeat step 3 until the end of series $\{S(t_i)\}$.

Since high frequency exchange rates are characterized by excessive noise, we add an extra condition in equation (4) to make the dv-series less sensitive to this. Often, we see that the price jumps back and forth due to noise. When the first jump comes, it may significantly bias the volatility estimate. Waiting for the next data point can minimize the impact of noise on the dv-series.

The de-volatilization procedure is easy to carry out because of the dynamic structure of the volatility estimator. The parameter v can be arbitrarily chosen to meet the different needs of a variety of analyses. However, it should be large enough so that the volatility estimate is acceptable. The noise ratio $\text{Var}(\epsilon_{t_i})/v$ should also be small enough so that the noise ϵ_t in the dv-series can be neglected.

The 1990 tick-by-tick Deutsche Mark/US dollar (DM/$) exchange rates are used to test our de-volatilization procedure. The same data set has also been used in Zhou (1992). It has more than 2.1 million observations. Annual volatility is estimated as $0.010\,349$, and average noise level $\text{Var}(\epsilon) \approx 2.6\text{e-8}$. Based on these figures, we choose $v = 3\text{e-6}$. This gives us an average of 600

Table 3.1 Summary statistics of the returns: dv-series and bi-hourly series

	Dv-series	Bi-hourly
No. Obs.	3324	3268
Mean	−3.209e-5	−3.333e-5
Variance	3.578e-6	3.292e-6
Median	0.000	0.000
Skewness	−0.001	−0.394
Kurtosis	2.974	7.809

data points to estimate the volatility between two dv-series data points, and it is more than 100 times the noise level. The k in equation (3) is chosen to be 6 as in Zhou (1992). The basic statistics of the returns of the dv-series are listed in Table 3.1. The statistics of bi-hourly series are also given in Table 3.1 for comparison. The variance of dv-returns is always a little larger than v. Both dv-series and bi-hourly series and their returns are plotted in Figures 3.1 and 3.2.

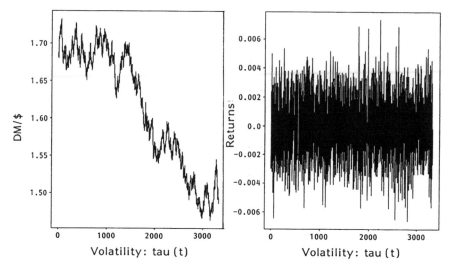

Figure 3.1 De-volatilized DM/$ and its returns (1990)

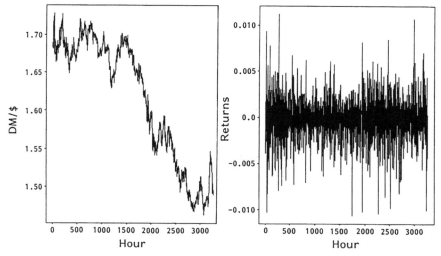

Figure 3.2 Bi-hourly DM/$ and its returns (1990)

3.3 HOMOSCEDASTICITY OF DV-SERIES

Under the assumption that the process (1) is a good approximation of exchange rates, the dv-series should be homoscedastic and dv-returns should be normally distributed. To visually inspect these properties, we plot the month-by-month sample variance and sample kurtosis of the dv-returns in Figure 3.3. Statistics for bi-hourly returns are also shown for comparison. Figure 3.4 shows Q–Q normal plots of both dv-returns and bi-hourly returns.

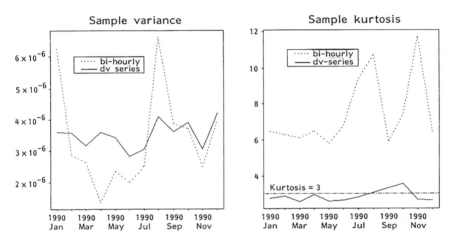

Figure 3.3   Monthly sample variance and sample kurtosis

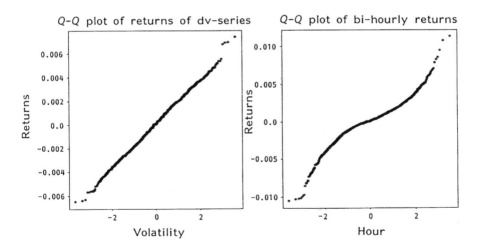

Figure 3.4 Q–Q normal plots

Compared to bi-hourly returns, dv-returns are much closer to homoscedastic; monthly kurtoses are much closer to 3 and the Q–Q plot is close to a straight line. Therefore we can conclude that the heteroscedasticity of the exchange rates has been largely removed.

To test the normality of dv-returns, we use both the classic Kolmogorov–Smirnov (KS) test and the well-known SW test introduced by Shapiro and Wilk (1965). The SW test statistic is calculated by using a computer program developed by Royston (1982a, b). The test statistics are given in Table 3.2. The p-value was calculated by computer simulation on 1000 replications for each sample size. The dv-returns of January and February show marginal significance in the KS test and the dv-returns of June show marginal significance in the SW test. However, both tests conclusively (at the 1% level) reject the normality hypothesis for every month of bi-hourly returns.

When we look at the dv-returns of an entire year, the normality is rejected by the KS test. However, it is not rejected by the SW test, which is considered more powerful than the KS test in many cases. The rejection of normality of a series with more than 3000 observations is not surprising, since no one believes that the return of an exchange rate follows exactly a normal distribution. De-volatilization only produces a series with approximately equally spaced volatility. The normality should be rejected by some tests for a large n. However, the test results indicate that normal distribution is not a bad approximation of the distribution of the dv-returns. A small deviation from the normality assumption may indicate that the market is not a random walk and that there may be a forecastable component in exchange rates.

To test for homoscedasticity, we use the Chi-square test, which can be traced back to as early as 1937 (Bartlett 1937, Ostle and Mensing 1975). It is

Table 3.2 Testing normality of dv-returns

Month	Size	Kurtosis	KS	SW
Jan.	527	2.741	0.986[a]	0.985
Feb.	228	2.846	1.033[a]	0.980
Mar.	232	2.522	0.886	0.979
Apr.	143	2.928	0.544	0.983
May	226	2.559	0.691	0.976
June	161	2.631	0.703	0.967[a]
July	249	2.792	0.592	0.976
Aug.	371	3.060	0.607	0.987
Sept.	343	3.335	0.877	0.991
Oct.	334	3.543	0.760	0.989
Nov.	245	2.646	0.837	0.981
Dec.	253	2.619	0.731	0.981
1990	3323	2.974	1.422[b]	0.990

[a]Significant at 5%.
[b]Significant at 1%.

designed to test the null hypothesis of k independent normal populations having the same variance. The test statistic is

$$\chi^2 = 2.3026 \left[\log_{10} s^2 \sum_{i=1}^{k} (n_i - 1) - \sum_{i=1}^{k} (n_i - 1) \log_{10} s_i^2 \right] \tag{5}$$

where s_i^2 and n_i are the sample variance and size of ith sample and s^2 is the pooled variance defined as

$$s^2 = \frac{\sum_{i=1}^{k} (n_i - 1) s_i^2}{\sum_{i=1}^{k} (n_i - 1)} \tag{6}$$

Under the assumption that data are normal and the variances are equal for all samples, χ^2 has approximately a Chi-square distribution with $k - 1$ degrees of freedom.

Dividing the dv-returns into 12 monthly groups, we have

$$\chi^2_{dv}(11) = 22.35 \ (p = 0.022)$$

From the hourly series, which we also divide into 12 monthly subgroups, we have

$$\chi^2_{hourly}(11) = 273.43 \ (p = 0.000)$$

Clearly, heteroscedasticity exists in the hourly series. However, it is significantly reduced in the dv-series.

Like many other financial time series recorded in calendar time, the bi-hourly exchange rate shows autocorrelation in its squared or absolute returns. From our assumption of exchange rates (equation 1), this correlation comes from the autocorrelation of volatilities. Therefore, autocorrelation in its squared returns or its absolute returns should also be removed in dv-returns. The Box–Pierce Q-statistic in equation (7) is chosen to test for autocorrelation:

$$Q_m = n \sum_{i=1}^{m} r_i^2 \tag{7}$$

where r_i is the sample autocorrelation of the time series with lag i, and n is the size of the data; Q_m is approximately $\chi^2(m)$. By choosing $m = 10$, we calculated the Box–Pierce Q-statistics for both dv-returns and the bi-hourly returns. The statistics with their p-values are listed in Table 3.3. These results show that the autocorrelations of returns, squared returns and absolute returns for the dv-series are small.

Table 3.3 Testing autocorrelation of dv-series returns

Q_{10}	X_i	(p)	X_i^2	(p)	$|X_i|$	(p)
Dv-series	19.44	(0.04)	16.75	(0.08)	20.70	(0.02)
Bi-hourly series	13.68	(0.19)	85.14	(0.00)	169.42	(0.00)

In conclusion, the de-volatilization procedure produced a near homo-scedastic dv-series of the exchange rate. The distribution of dv-returns is much closer to a normal distribution than that of bi-hourly returns. These results indicate that forecasting foreign exchange rates is difficult. We do not expect any traditional time series forecast models to be successful here. In the next section, we propose a new forecasting procedure that utilizes the advantages of dv-series.

3.4 FORECASTING FOREIGN EXCHANGE RATES AFTER DE-VOLATILIZATION

Since the noise ϵ_τ in the dv-series is negligible, dv-returns can be written as

$$x_\tau = s_\tau - s_{\tau-1} = \mu_\tau + \sigma Z_\tau,$$

where σ^2 is the variance of the return, μ_τ is the trend (which is often small), and σ^2 is a constant. For 1990 DM/\$ dv-returns obtained in section 3.3, $\sigma^2 = 3.578\text{e-}6$. When there is no trend, the return of dv-series ranges from -1.96σ to 1.96σ. However, when the market receives external information, a significant change occurs in drift and the return is likely to be out of the -1.96σ to 1.96σ band. We say that an 'event' has occurred whenever a dv-return falls outside this -1.96σ to 1.96σ band. If the market is not pure random walk, a trend may be formed after the event. To test this hypothesis, we calculate the correlation between the price changes during the event and those after the event. Let E be the index set of all events,

$$E = \{\tau, |x_\tau| > 1.96\sigma\}$$

Correlation coefficients

$$r_k = \frac{\sum_{\tau \in E} x_\tau(x_{\tau+1} + \ldots + x_{\tau+k})}{\left(\sum_{\tau \in E} x_\tau^2 \sum_{\tau \in E} (x_{\tau+1} + \ldots + x_{\tau+k})^2\right)^{1/2}}$$

are calculated and listed in Table 3.4. There are in total 147 'events' in 1990. By examining Table 3.4, we find that there is a positive correlation between

Table 3.4   Correlation of price changes during and after the 'events'

k	r_k	k	r_k	k	r_k	k	r_k
1	−0.028	6	0.165[a]	11	0.148	16	0.097
2	0.039	7	0.134	12	0.125	17	0.056
3	0.119	8	0.178[a]	13	0.111	18	0.049
4	0.182[a]	9	0.144	14	0.126	19	0.032
5	0.180[a]	10	0.150	15	0.084	20	0.016

[a]Indicates significant at 5% level.

the initial movement of the price during the event and the trend after the events. The trend lasts only a few steps. Therefore it is difficult to analyze using daily data. To further test the forecastability of exchange rates, we propose a simple forecasting procedure.

Algorithm 2 (Forecasting Procedure I)

Given a dv-series $\{s_\tau, \tau = 0, \ldots, n\}$, this procedure generates forecasting signals $\delta_\tau \in \{-1, 0, 1\}$ corresponding to downward, flat and upward trends.

- Initialize all δ_τ to 0, $\tau = 1, \ldots, n$;
- If $|s_\tau - s_{\tau-1}| > 1.96\sigma$

$$\delta_{\tau+i} = \text{sign}(s_\tau - s_{\tau-1}), \ i = 1, \ldots, k, \text{ and } \tau + i < n;$$

This forecast overrides any previous forecast.

To evaluate the forecast, we use the following criteria:

$$CI = \sum \delta_\tau \, \text{sign}(x_\tau) \tag{8}$$

$$CII = \sum \delta_\tau x_\tau \tag{9}$$

where CI is the difference between the number of right and wrong predictions and CII is the total return assuming no transaction costs. The larger they are the better. If dv-returns are independent mean zero random noises, the forecast signal δ_τ depends only on returns x_i, $i < \tau$ and both CI and CII have approximately normal distribution with

$$E[CI] = 0 \quad \text{and} \quad \text{Var}(CI) = np,$$

and

$$E[CII] = 0 \quad \text{and} \quad \text{Var}(CII) = np\sigma^2.$$

where n is the number of nonzero returns and p is the percentage of nonzero forecast signals among these returns.

The only parameter in the procedure is the integer k, the length of the trend. The σ is predetermined by the de-volatilization procedure and is subject to previous optimization. Table 3.4 suggests that k lies in the interval 3 to 14. To illustrate, we list forecasting results of 1990 DM/\$ for all $k = 1, \ldots, 15$ in Table 3.5. When $k = 5$, both CI and CII are significantly greater than zero at the 5% level.

Although this is a nonparametric procedure, it is analyzed using the 1990 data retrospectively. It is more convincing to forecast a succeeding year of exchange rates. We obtained 1991 DM/\$ tick-by-tick data from J. P. Morgan. Using exactly the same de-volatilization and forecasting procedures, we show forecast results of 1991 DM/\$ in Table 3.6. For 1991, CI and CII are not only significant at $k = 5$, but at many other levels of k as well.

Table 3.5 Forecasting 1990 DM/\$ by forecasting procedure I

k	CI	CI/SE	CII	CII/SE	np
1	0	0.00	−0.018	−0.83	132
2	13	0.80	0.012	0.40	265
3	40	2.02	0.048	1.28	392
4	58	2.56	0.084	1.95	514
5	65	2.58	0.105	2.20	635
6	48	1.75	0.068	1.32	750
7	47	1.61	0.056	1.01	857
8	48	1.55	0.079	1.34	962
9	48	1.47	0.071	1.15	1062
10	53	1.56	0.089	1.38	1161
11	66	1.86	0.108	1.61	1256
12	80	2.18	0.110	1.59	1344
13	69	1.83	0.090	1.26	1427
14	64	1.65	0.095	1.30	1508
15	51	1.28	0.074	0.99	1589

Table 3.6 Forecasting 1991 DM/\$ by forecasting procedure I

k	CI	CI/SE	CII	CII/SE	np
1	21	1.39	0.029	1.01	229
2	39	1.85	0.067	1.68	445
3	30	1.18	0.049	1.02	648
4	54	1.87	0.098	1.79	834
5	54	1.70	0.135	2.25	1012
6	70	2.04	0.166	2.56	1180
7	66	1.81	0.180	2.61	1336
8	61	1.58	0.170	2.33	1489
9	65	1.61	0.190	2.48	1633
10	65	1.54	0.175	2.20	1773
11	66	1.51	0.171	2.07	1906
12	54	1.20	0.157	1.84	2028
13	56	1.21	0.160	1.83	2136
14	82	1.73	0.240	2.68	2240
15	76	1.57	0.247	2.70	2340

We conclude that the exchange rate often forms a trend after the 'event' and this trend is forecastable. The forecasting result is very encouraging. However, profits are very slim if we take account of the bid–offer spread. Using the following simple trading program with $k = 5$ and bid-offer spread 0.05% of the price, we have a profit of 2.1% for 1990 and a profit of 2.6% for 1991. Further improvement is necessary to make the forecast more profitable.

Algorithm 3 (Trading Program)

This program assumes that a fixed number of US dollars are traded at each position.

- At time τ, suppose that no position is held:
  1. If $\delta_{\tau+1} = 1$, take a long position;
  2. If $\delta_{\tau+1} = -1$, take a short position.
- At time τ, suppose that one position is held.
  1. If $\delta_{\tau+1}\delta_\tau > 0$, keep the same position;
  2. If $\delta_{\tau+1}\delta_\tau = 0$, square the position;
  3. If $\delta_{\tau+1}\delta_\tau < 0$, reverse the position.
- If one position bought at time τ_0 and sold at time τ_1:

$$\text{profit} = \left[\frac{\delta_{\tau_0}(\exp(s_{\tau_1}) - \exp(s_{\tau_0}))}{\exp(s_{\tau_0})} - 0.0005\right] \times 100\%. \tag{10}$$

Recent stock market studies suggest that price has less autocorrelation during periods of large volume or large volatility (LeBaron 1990, Campbell *et al.* 1992). If this is also true for currency exchange markets, an event occurring during a period of extremely high volatility may not form a future trend. We therefore modify our forecasting procedure as follows.

Algorithm 4 (Forecasting Procedure II)

Given a dv-series $\{s_\tau, \tau = 0, \ldots, n\}$, this procedure generates forecasting signals $\delta_\tau \in \{-1, 0, 1\}$ corresponding to downward, flat and upward trends. Let $t(\tau)$ be the time (in seconds) that price s_τ is recorded and $\bar{v}_{\text{hr}}$ be the average hourly volatility,

- Initialize all δ_τ to 0, $\tau = 1, \ldots, n$;
- If $|s_\tau - s_{\tau-1}| > 1.96\sigma$, and
  1. if $\sigma^2/[t(\tau) - t(\tau - 1)] < a\bar{v}_{\text{hr}}/3600$,
  $$\delta_{\tau+i} = \text{sign}(s_\tau - s_{\tau-1}), \quad i = 1, \ldots, k, \text{ and } \tau + i < n;$$
  2. if $\sigma^2/[t(\tau) - t(\tau - 1)] \geq a\bar{v}_{\text{hr}}/3600$, set all nonzero $\delta_{\tau+i}$, $i > 0$, to be zero.
  This forecast overrides any previous forecast.

Empirical results show that forecast procedure II increases not only the values of *CI* and *CII*, but the profitability as well. The results of forecasting with $\alpha = 5$ are listed in Tables 3.7 and 3.8. The choice of $\alpha = 5$ in the forecasting procedure is arbitrary. Results for α between 4 and 6 are very

Table 3.7 Forecasting 1990 DM/$ by forecasting procedure II

k	CI	CI/SE	CII	CII/SE	Profit (%)	PP–LP	PT/TT (%)
1	6	0.59	0.001	0.04	−5.57	54–48	1.8
2	16	1.11	0.028	1.03	−2.75	59–48	4.8
3	41	2.34	0.069	2.09	1.51	59–43	7.1
4	55	2.73	0.099	2.59	4.51	68–37	9.8
5	72	3.21	0.141	3.32	8.86	65–37	12.8
6	61	2.49	0.117	2.53	6.52	62–39	16.1
7	63	2.40	0.117	2.37	6.64	58–41	19.6
8	64	2.30	0.134	2.55	8.44	58–37	22.0
9	64	2.18	0.125	2.26	7.56	56–42	24.2
10	67	2.18	0.139	2.39	9.03	55–40	26.7
11	68	2.13	0.142	2.35	9.49	55–37	28.7
12	82	2.47	0.143	2.29	9.69	54–38	31.1
13	73	2.13	0.129	2.00	8.38	51–38	33.5
14	71	2.02	0.136	2.04	9.09	53–36	35.5
15	58	1.60	0.117	1.71	7.27	48–40	37.9

PP–LP: profit positions–loss positions.
PT/TT: position time/total time of the year × 100%.

Table 3.8 Forecasting 1991 DM/$ by forecasting procedure II

k	CI	CI/SE	CII	CII/SE	Profit (%)	PP–LP	PT/TT (%)
1	20	1.70	0.025	1.12	−4.76	78–57	1.6
2	40	2.43	0.073	2.33	0.33	79–57	4.4
3	33	1.66	0.073	1.92	0.52	74–53	6.2
4	62	2.73	0.121	2.81	5.53	73–55	7.8
5	76	3.02	0.173	3.62	10.82	79–48	13.2
6	85	3.10	0.194	3.74	13.07	80–45	15.5
7	90	3.07	0.226	4.06	16.34	78–46	18.3
8	93	2.98	0.238	4.04	17.63	82–41	20.6
9	96	2.93	0.260	4.20	19.98	73–46	22.7
10	89	2.59	0.245	3.77	18.62	73–46	25.5
11	84	2.35	0.223	3.30	16.48	72–44	28.6
12	64	1.73	0.179	2.56	12.17	69–47	31.4
13	67	1.75	0.198	2.73	14.03	68–46	33.3
14	67	1.70	0.219	2.93	16.29	69–42	34.5
15	73	1.80	0.236	3.08	18.25	62–47	36.3

PP–LP: profit positions–loss positions.
PT/TT: position time/total time of the year × 100%.

similar. For $4 \leqslant k \leqslant 11$, *CI* and *CII* for both 1990 and 1991 are significant at the 5% level. Both years show sizeable profits. For $k = 10$, there is 9.03% profit in 1990 with only 26.7% of total time in the market and 18.62% profit in 1991 with only 25.5% of total time in the market. In Figures 3.5 and 3.6, we show: (i) the dv-series; (ii) the forecast signal δ_τ and (iii) the cumulative profit/loss curve.

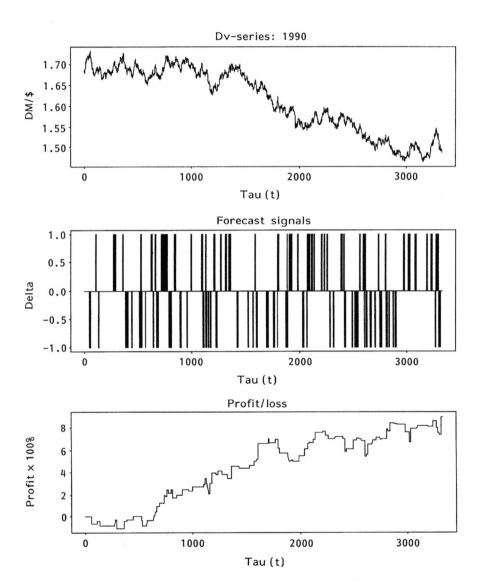

Figure 3.5 Forecast 1990 DM/$ by procedure II ($k = 10$)

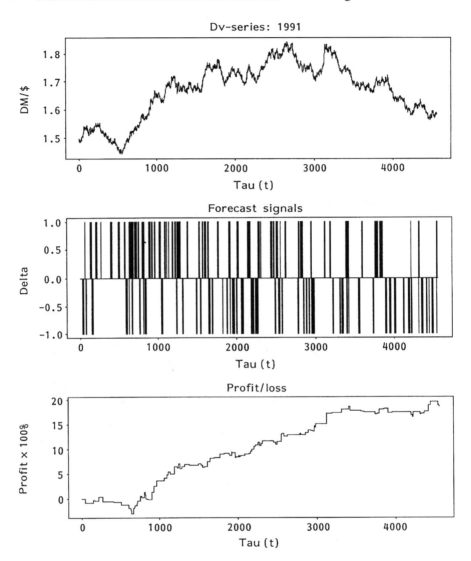

Figure 3.6 Forecast 1991 DM/$ by procedure II ($k = 10$)

There is another interesting result: most profits are from 'events' that happened in the European and the US markets. The 'events' in other markets are merely noises. Dividing the 24-hour market into four sections: Europe only (3:00a.m. EST/EDT–8:00a.m. EST/EDT), Europe and US (8:00a.m. EST/EDT–12:00a.m. EST/EDT), US only (12:00p.m. EST/EDT–5:00p.m. EST/EDT) and Asia/other (5:00p.m. EST/EDT–3:00a.m. EST/EDT next day),

Table 3.9 Distribution of events and profits in different sections of the market ($k = 10$)

Year		Europe only 3a.m.–8a.m. EST/EDT	Europe and USA 8a.m.–12a.m. EST/EDT	USA only 12a.m.–5p.m. EST/EDT	Asia/other 5p.m.–3a.m. EST/EDT
1990	PP–LP	8–10	24–10	15–9	20–13
	Profit	−2.21%	7.80%	4.84%	1.01%
1991	PP–LP	26–16	29–18	13–10	15–13
	Profit	7.98%	8.38%	1.53%	−0.97%

we calculate possible profits from the 'events' in different sections of the market (Table 3.9). The numbers may not add up to the total in Tables 3.7 and 3.8 because a position taken in one section may hold in the next section of the market.

The largest number of 'events' occur during the period when both European and American markets are open, although this section of the market only lasts four hours. Profit distribution in different sections of the market is consistent with our expectation that only news from European or US markets is relevant to the DM/$ exchange rates. These results indicate the correlation between the 'events' in our forecasting procedure and real news events in the market.

3.5 CONCLUSION

We believe that foreign exchange markets do not follow a pure random walk. They contain many small trends. These trends last only a day or two and occur in random directions. Consequently precise forecasting of daily exchange rates is extremely difficult.

De-volatilization is an efficient way to use high frequency data. It not only reduces the noise effect in the data, but reduces heteroscedasticity as well. The de-volatilization procedure takes more observations in an active market and helps to detect trends early. It corresponds closely to the way sophisticated traders 'look' at exchange markets. The procedure can be used in any market with high frequency observations.

BIBLIOGRAPHY

Baillie, Richard T. and McMahon, Patrick C. (1989), *The Foreign Exchange Market*, Cambridge University Press, Cambridge.

Baringhaus, L., Danschke, R. and Henze, N. (1989), 'Recent and Classical Tests for Normality: A Comparative Study', *Communications in Statistics*, **18**, 363–379.

Bartlett, M.S. (1937), 'Some Examples of Statistical Methods of Research in Agriculture and Applied Biology', *Journal of the Royal Statistical Society* (Suppl.), **4**, 137.

Bollerslev, T. (1986), 'Generalised Autoregressive Conditional Heteroskedasticity', *Journal of Econometrics*, **31**, 307–328.

Calderon-Rossel, Jorge and Ben-Horim, Moshe (1982), 'The Behavior of Foreign Exchange Rates', *Journal of International Business Studies*, **13**, 99–111.

Campbell, John Y., Grossman, Sanford J. and Wang, Jiang (1992), 'Trading Volume and Serial Correlation in Stock Returns', NBER Working Paper No. 4193, Washington.

Clark, P.K. (1973), 'A Subordinate Stochastic Process Model with Finite Variance for Speculative Price', *Econometrica*, **41**, 135–155.

Conover, W.J. (1980), *Practical Nonparametric Statistics*, 2nd edn, Wiley, New York.

Diebold, Francis X. (1988), *Empirical Modeling of Exchange Rate Dynamics*, Springer-Verlag, New York.

Diebold, Francis X., Lee, C.W.J. and Im, J. (1985), 'A New Approach to the Detection and Treatment of Heteroskedasticity in the Market Model', Working Paper, University of Pennsylvania.

Engle, R.F. (1982), 'Autoregressive Conditional Heteroskedasticity with Estimates of the Variance of UK Inflation', *Econometrica*, **50**, 987–1008.

Evans, M.A. and King, M.L. (1985), 'A Point Optimal Test for Heteroscedasticity Disturbances', *Journal of Econometrics*, **27**, 163–178.

Friedman, Daniel and Vandersteel, Stoddard (1982), 'Short-run Fluctuation in Foreign Exchange Rates', *Journal of International Economics*, **13**, 171–186.

Gilchrist, Warren (1976), *Statistical Forecasting*, Wiley, London.

Godfrey, L.G. (1978), 'Testing against General Autoregressive and Moving Average Error models When the Regressions Include Lagged Dependent Variables', *Econometrica*, **46**, 1293–1302.

Goodhart, C.A. and Figliuoli, L. (1991), 'Every Minute Counts in Financial Markets', *Journal of International Money and Finance*, **10**, 23–52.

Harvey, Andrew C. (1981), *The Econometric Analysis of Time Series*, Wiley, New York.

Harvey, Andrew C. (1989), *Forecasting, Structural Series Models and the Kalman Filter*, Cambridge University Press, Cambridge.

Hsieh, David A. (1988), 'The Statistical Properties of Daily Foreign Exchange Rates: 1974–1983', *Journal of International Economics*, **24**, 129–145.

Hsieh, David A. (1989), 'Testing for Nonlinear Dependence in Daily Foreign Exchange Rates', *Journal of Business*, **62**, 339–368.

Knoke, J.D. (1977), 'Testing for Randomness against Autocorrelation: Alternative Tests', *Biometrika*, **64**, 523–529.

LeBaron, Blake (1990), 'Some Relations between Volatility and Serial Correlations in Stock Market Returns', Working Paper, Social Systems Research Institute, University of Wisconsin.

Lehmann, E.L. (1983), *Theory of Point Estimation*, Wiley, New York.

Mandelbrot, B. and Taylor, H. (1969), 'On the Distribution of Stock Price Differences', *Operations Research*, **15**, 1057–1062.

Meese, R.A. and Rogoff, K. (1983a), 'Empirical Exchange Rate Models of the Seventies: Do They Fit out of Sample?', *Journal of International Economics*, **14**, 3–24.

Meese, R.A. and Rogoff, K. (1983b), 'The out of Sample Failure of Empirical Exchange Rate Models: Sampling Error or Misspecification?', in J. Frenkel (ed.), *Exchange Rates and International Microeconomics*, University of Chicago Press, Chicago, 67–112.

Murphy, John J. (1986), *Technical Analysis of the Futures Markets: A Comprehensive Guide to Trading Methods and Applications*, New York Institute of Finance, New York.

Ostle, B. and Mensing, R.W. (1975), *Statistics in Research: Basic Concepts and Techniques for Research Workers*, 3rd edn, Iowa State University Press, Ames.

Royston, J.P. (1982a), 'An Extension of Shapiro and Wilk's W Test for Normality to Large Samples', *Applied Statistics*, **31**, 115–124.

Royston, J.P. (1982b), 'The W Test for Normality', *Applied Statistics*, **31**, 176–180.

Shapiro, S.S. and Wilk, M.B. (1965), 'An Analysis of Variance Test for Normality', *Biometrika*, **52**, 591–611.

Stock, James H. (1988), 'Estimating Continuous-time Processes Subject to Time Deformation', *Journal of the American Statistical Association*, **83**, 77–85.

Taylor, Stephen (1986), *Modelling Financial Time Series*, Wiley, Chichester.

Zhou, Bin (1992), 'High Frequency Data and Volatility in Foreign Exchange Rates', MIT Sloan School Working Paper 3485-92.

4

Heterogeneous Real-time Trading Strategies in the Foreign Exchange Market

MICHEL M. DACOROGNA,
ULRICH A. MÜLLER,
CHRISTIAN JOST, OLIVIER V. PICTET,
RICHARD B. OLSEN and J. ROBERT WARD

4.1 INTRODUCTION

In a recent paper (Müller *et al.* 1993), we proposed the heterogeneous market hypothesis. This hypothesis regards the foreign exchange (FX) market as composed of agents with different dealing constraints and thus heterogeneous expectations. The FX market is worldwide, but the dealers differ in their geographical locations (time zones), working hours, time horizons, home currencies, access to information, transaction costs, and other institutional constraints. The variety of time horizons is large: from intra-day dealers, who close their positions every evening, to long-term investors and central banks. Depending on these constraints and goals, the different market participants need different investment strategies. Moreover, these strategies do not simply aim at profit maximization but rather at maximization of a utility function derived from a specific risk profile. Each market component has its own risk profile. We argue in Müller *et al.* (1993) that the reason for the excess return found by many authors using simple trading strategies does not lie in inefficiencies but rather in the structure of the market. A market composed of

This chapter previously appeared under the same title in the *European Journal of Finance* Vol 1 No 4 pp 383–403. © 1995 European Journal of Finance. Reproduced with permission.

different types of agents who dynamically adjust to new information presents properties that depart from a random walk. Some of the empirical properties supporting this hypothesis are presented in Müller *et al.* (1993).

The idea of this chapter is to use some trading models developed at Olsen & Associates (O&A) as a tool to study the market structure. These models act like filters that concentrate on typical price movements and give us information about the market itself. The hypothesis of a heterogeneous market leads to three conjectures, for which our study presents some evidence:

1. In a heterogeneous market, there is no particular trading strategy that is systematically better than all the others. Excess return can be gained for different trading profiles, so various ways of assessing the risk and return of trading models are needed.
2. The different geographical components of the FX market have different business hours according to different time zones and, on the assumption of the heterogeneous market hypothesis, different strategies. Therefore, there are disruptions in the market behaviors from one geographical component to the next. Trading models which do not explicitly analyze the geographical components can avoid these disruptions only by restricting their active hours to the normal business hours of one geographical market. For such models, trading 24 hours a day does not pay.
3. The most profitable models actively trade when many agents are active in the market (liquid periods) and do not trade at other times of the day and on weekends. The heterogeneous market hypothesis attributes the profitability of trading models to the simultaneous presence of hetero-geneous agents, whereas the classical efficient market hypothesis relates this profitability to inefficiencies. (This would imply that the illiquid periods of the market are the most favorable for excess returns.) If our conjecture is right, the optimal daily trading time interval should depend on the traded FX rate rather than the model type. Trading will be most profitable when the main markets for a particular rate are active.

Realistic intra-day trading strategies can be studied only if high frequency data is available. Olsen & Associates have collected and analyzed a large quantity of FX quotes by market makers around the clock. Based on this data, a set of real-time intra-day trading models has been developed (Pictet *et al.* 1992). These models give explicit trading recommendations under realistic constraints. They are only allowed to trade during the opening hours of a market, depending on the time zone and local holidays, and fully account for transaction costs. This information can be specified separately for each market, so that every O&A trading model algorithm can run for various geographical markets (see Pictet *et al.* 1992). The consistent profitability of these models, running real-time over the past few years, undoubtedly demonstrates the success of these trading strategies and, therefore, the presence of structures undetected until recently.

Three trading models based on different algorithms are used in this study. The performance of these models is analyzed against changing market conditions, trading intervals, opening and closing times, and market holidays.

Recently, the skepticism among academics toward the possibility of developing profitable trading models has decreased with the publication of many papers that document profitable trading strategies in financial markets even when including transaction costs. Some of the papers that recently came to this conclusion are: Brock *et al.* 1992, LeBaron 1992, Taylor and Allen 1992, Surajaras and Sweeney 1992, Levich and Thomas 1993, Acar *et al.* 1993). This list is by no means exhaustive, but it shows the renewed interest in this topic. In one of the cited papers (LeBaron 1992), the models are used in a way similar to ours to explore the presence of nonlinearities in the FX market.

In the assumption of a heterogeneous market, there is no trading strategy that is absolutely better than others. The answer to this question will depend on the trading and risk profile of the investor. This is confirmed by the existence of many different types of portfolio and investment strategies in the financial markets. It is also why we use in this study different trading model algorithms and we believe that these new type of investment strategy will not change fundamentally the heterogeneous composition of financial markets.

The rest of the present chapter deals with the following: section 4.2 presents the O&A trading model structure and the high frequency data; section 4.3 discusses different performance measures for trading models and introduces a risk-sensitive measure; section 4.4 briefly describes the three different algorithms and presents various performance results over a long sample; section 4.5 discusses results for a set of different geographical markets; in section 4.6, the study is extended to longer and shorter trading periods and a systematic variation of the opening and closing hours, and section 4.7, finally, presents the conclusion of these studies.

4.2 THE TRADING MODELS AND THE DATA

Consistent with the heterogeneous trading hypothesis, a clear distinction should be made between a price change forecast and an actual trading recommendation. A trading recommendation naturally includes some kind of a price change forecast, but it must also account for the specific constraints of the dealer or user of the respective trading model. A trading model must take its past trading history into account while a price forecast is not biased by a position in which the trading model might be. A trading model thus goes beyond predicting a price change: it must decide if and at what time a certain action has to be taken.

Our trading models offer a real-time analysis of FX-rate movements and generate explicit trading recommendations. These models are based on the continuous collection and treatment of FX quotes by market makers around the clock.

Our models imitate the trading conditions of the real FX market as closely as possible. They do not deal directly but instead instruct human FX dealers to make specific trades. In order to imitate real-world trading accurately, they take transaction costs into account in their return computation, generally avoid trading outside market working hours and avoid trading too frequently. In short, these models act realistically in a manner that a human dealer can easily follow.

Imitating the real world requires a system that collects all available price quotes and reacts to each FX-rate movements in real time. For our trading models we have mainly used Reuters data, but other high frequency data suppliers provide similar information in their FX quotes. Using software developed in-house, we collect, validate and store price quotes in our database for future use. A full description of this data and its filtering is given in Müller *et al.* (1990) and Dacorogna *et al.* (1993). The tick frequency has been varying since the beginning of our data collection. Currently it is approximately 5000 ticks per business day for USD–DEM, approximately 3000 for the other major rates (USD–JPY, USD–CHF and GBP–USD), and around 1500 for the minor rates (USD–FRF, USD–NLG and USD–ITL).[1] Altogether, our database currently contains more than 12 million ticks for USD–DEM.

Every trading model is associated with a local market that is identified with a corresponding geographical region. In turn, this is associated with generally accepted office hours and public holidays. The local market is defined to be open at any time during office house provided it is neither a weekend nor a public holiday. Our trading models presently support the Zurich, London, Frankfurt, Vienna and New York markets and it is straightforward to extend this set. Typical opening hours for a model are between 8:00 and 17:30 local time, the exact times depending on the particular local market.

The overall structure and data flow of an O&A trading model are depicted in Figure 4.1. Except for closing an open position if the price hits a stop-loss limit, a model may not deal[2] outside opening hours or during holidays.

Indicator computations providing an analysis of past price movements form a central part of an O&A trading model. (A detailed description of the indicators is given in Pictet *et al.* 1992.) The indicators are mapped into actual trading positions by applying various rules. For instance, a model may enter a long position if an indicator exceeds a certain threshold. Other rules determine whether a deal may be made at all. Among various factors, these rules determine the timing of the recommendation.

A complete trading model thus consists of a set of indicator computations combined with a collection of rules. The former are functions of the price

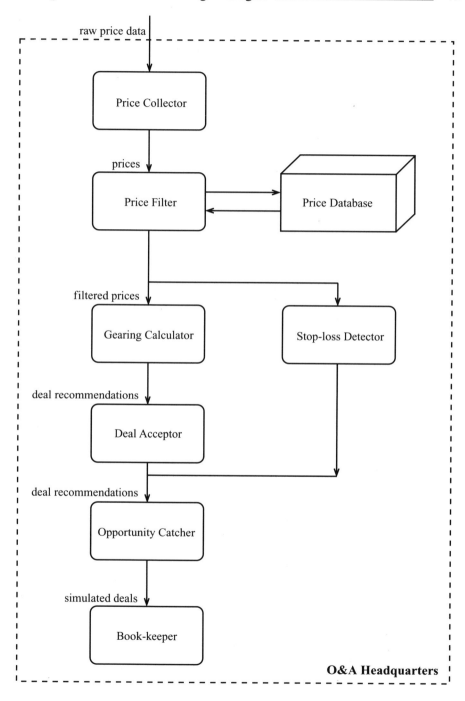

Figure 4.1 Data flow of prices and deal recommendations within a trading model

history. The latter determine the applicability of the indicator computations to generating trading recommendations. The model gives a recommendation not only for the direction but also for the amount of the exposure. The possible exposures (gearings) are $\pm\frac{1}{2}$ or ± 1.

4.3   TRADING MODEL PERFORMANCE MEASURES

There are many aspects to the trading model performance; therefore, different quantities have to be computed to assess the quality of a model. In this section we describe some of the important variables that need to be watched for deciding if a model is good or not. We also introduce a risk-sensitive measure which will be the basic quantity used in further sections to analyze the behavior of the models.

In the trading room, people seldom take a full exposure at once. The traders like to build their position in steps (gearing steps). In such cases, it is useful to introduce an auxiliary variable, the average price $\bar{p}$ paid for achieving the current exposure (gearing). This variable simplifies the computation of the return of a position built in steps. After a new deal with index i, the average price depends on the type of transaction as follows:

$$\bar{p}_i \equiv \begin{cases} \text{undefined} & \text{if } g_i = 0 \\ p_i & \text{if } g_i g_{i-1} < 0 \vee g_{i-1} = 0 \\ g_i \left[\dfrac{g_i - g_{i-1}}{p_i} + \dfrac{g_{i-1}}{p_{i-1}} \right]^{-1} & \text{if } |g_i| > |g_{i-1}| \wedge g_i g_{i-1} > 0 \\ \bar{p}_{i-1} & \text{if } |g_i| < |g_{i-1}| \wedge g_i g_{i-1} > 0 \end{cases} \tag{1}$$

where g_{i-1} and g_i are the previous and current gearings respectively, p_i is the current transaction price, and $\bar{p}_{i-1}$ the average price before the deal. In the initial case, when the current gearing is neutral, the average price $\bar{p}$ is not yet defined. If we start from a neutral position $g_{i-1} = 0$ or reverse a position $g_i g_{i-1} < 0$, the price to build the position is simply the current price p_i. If the new position is built on top of a previous position, then we need to compute the average price paid from the price paid for each fraction of the full position. If the new position is just unfolding part of the previous position, then the average price paid for the position does not change. It is simply either profit taking or stop-loss.

The average price $\bar{p}$ is needed to compute a quantity central to a trading model, the *return* of a deal:

$$r_i \equiv (g_{i-1} - g_i')\left(\frac{p_i}{\bar{p}_{i-1}} - 1\right) \qquad (2)$$

where the gearing g_i' is equal to 0 if the model takes an opposite position ($g_i g_{i-1} < 0$) and g_i otherwise. There are deals with no return: those starting from a neutral gearing, $g_{i-1} = 0$, and those increasing the absolute value of the gearing while keeping its sign. In these cases, equation (2) does not apply (whereas equation (1) applies to all deals).

The above equations both allow the computation of a set of other quantities that are important for the performance evaluation of the trading models:

- The *current return*, r_c that is, the unrealized return of a transaction when the current position is off the equilibrium ($g_i \neq 0$). If p_c is the current market price required for going back to neutral, generalizing equation (2) yields the current return

$$r_c \equiv g_i\left(\frac{p_c}{\bar{p}_i} - 1\right) \qquad (3)$$

- The *total return*, R_T, which is a measure of the overall success of a trading model over a period T, equal to

$$R_T \equiv \sum_{j=1}^{n} r_j \qquad (4)$$

where n is the total number of transactions that generated a return during the period T and j is the jth transaction that generated a return. The total return expresses the amount of profit made by a trader always investing up to his initial capital or credit limit in his home currency.
- The *cumulated return*, C_T, which is another measure of the overall success of a trading model, expressing the amount of profit made by a trader always reinvesting up to his current capital including gains or losses:

$$C_T \equiv \prod_{j=1}^{n} (1 + r_j) - 1 \qquad (5)$$

This quantity is slightly more erratic than the total return and cannot be expected to increase linearly with time.
- The *maximum drawdown*, D_T, over a certain period $T = t_E - t_0$, which is defined as

$$D_T \equiv \max(R_{t_a} - R_{t_b} | t_0 \leqslant t_a \leqslant t_b \leqslant t_E) \qquad (6)$$

where R_{t_a} and R_{t_b} are the total returns of the periods from t_0 to t_a and t_b respectively.
- The *profit over loss ratio*, P/L, which gives an idea of the type of strategy used by the model and is defined as

$$\frac{P_T}{L_T} \equiv \frac{N_T(r_j|r_j > 0)}{N_T(r_j|r_j < 0)} \qquad (7)$$

where N_T is a function that gives the number of elements of a particular set of variables under certain conditions during a period T.
- The *dealing frequency*, F_T, which is the average number of transactions per week over the test period.

Choosing the best parameters for a trading model is always a problem. Usually, they are chosen through optimization on past data, but optimizing a trading model with minimum overfitting is a difficult task. Overfitting means building the model to fit a set of past data (termed the *in-sample* data) so well that it is no longer of general value: instead of modeling the principles underlying the price movement, it models the specific price moves observed during a particular time period. Such a model usually exhibits a totally different behavior or may fail to perform *out-of-sample*, that is, with data that was not used for the optimization process. To avoid overfitting during optimization, we need a good measure of trading model performance and robust optimization and testing procedures. A strict division of the available historical data into in and out-of-sample sets is essential to achieve robustness of the results. To minimize the risk of overfitting in the in-sample period and also to be able to compare different trading models, we have developed a risk-sensitive performance measure to evaluate the profit of the models against the risk incurred by the investor.

We need a measure of trading model performance that accounts for the following:

- a high total return
- a smooth, almost linear increase of the total return over time
- a small clustering of losses
- no bias toward low frequency trading models

A measure frequently used by practitioners to evaluate portfolio models is the Sharpe ratio (Burke 1993). Unfortunately, this measure neglects the risk due to unrealized losses while the model is in a position and thus introduces a bias in favor of models with a low dealing frequency. Furthermore, the Sharpe ratio is numerically unstable for small variances of returns and cannot consider the clustering of profit and loss trades. This measure clearly does not meet our requirements.

As a basis of our risk-sensitive performance measure, a new trading model return variable $\tilde{R}$ is defined to be the sum of the total return R (equation (4)) and the unrealized current return r_c (equation (3)). The variable $\tilde{R}$ is more continuous over time than R and reflects the additional risk due to unrealized returns. Its change over a test time interval Δt is termed $X_{\Delta t}$:

$$X_{\Delta t} = \tilde{R}(t) - \tilde{R}(t - \Delta t), \text{ where } \tilde{R}(t) = R(t) + r_{\mathrm{c}}(t) \tag{8}$$

where t expresses the time of the measurement and becomes the main variable of the above functions. We can make N independent observations of $X_{\Delta t}$ within the total test period T, where

$$\Delta t = \frac{T}{N} \tag{9}$$

A risk-sensitive measure of trading model performance comparable to the average return can be deduced from the utility function formalism of Keeney and Raiffa (1976). We assume that the variable $X_{\Delta t}$ is stochastic and follows a Gaussian random walk about its mean value $\bar{X}_{\Delta t}$ and that the risk aversion C is constant with respect to $X_{\Delta t}$. The resulting utility $u(X_{\Delta t})$ of an observation is $-\exp(-CX_{\Delta t})$, with an expectation value of $\bar{u} = u(\bar{X}_{\Delta t}) \exp(C^2 \sigma_{\Delta t}^2 / 2)$, where $\sigma_{\Delta t}^2$ is the variance of $X_{\Delta t}$. This expectation of the utility can be transformed back to a variable termed the *effective return*: $X_{\mathrm{eff}, \Delta t} = -\log(-\bar{u})/C$. The following definition is obtained:

$$X_{\mathrm{eff}, \Delta t} = \bar{X}_{\Delta t} - \frac{C\sigma_{\Delta t}^2}{2} \tag{10}$$

The risk term $C\sigma_{\Delta t}^2 / 2$ can be regarded as a risk premium deducted from the original return. The variance is computed from the sample:

$$\sigma_{\Delta t}^2 = \frac{N}{N-1} (\overline{X_{\Delta t}^2} - \bar{X}_{\Delta t}^2) \tag{11}$$

For a particular time horizon Δt, the variable $X_{\mathrm{eff}, \Delta t}$ is our new measure of trading model performance including risk. Unlike the Sharpe ratio, this measure is numerically stable and can differentiate between two trading models with a straight line behavior ($\sigma_{\Delta t}^2 = 0$) by choosing the one with the better average return.

The measure $X_{\mathrm{eff}, \Delta t}$ still depends on the size of the time interval Δt. It is hard to compare $X_{\mathrm{eff}, \Delta t}$ values for different intervals. The usual way to enable such comparison is through annualization: multiplication by the annualization factor, $A_{\Delta t} = 1 \text{ year}/\Delta t$,

$$X_{\mathrm{eff, ann}, \Delta t} = A_{\Delta t} X_{\mathrm{eff}, \Delta t} = \bar{X} - \frac{C}{2} A_{\Delta t} \sigma_{\Delta t}^2 \tag{12}$$

where $\bar{X}$ is the annualized return, no longer dependent on Δt. In the second term of the last form of equation (12), we find the factor $A_{\Delta t} \sigma_{\Delta t}^2$. This factor has a constant expectation, independent of Δt, if the return function $\tilde{R}(t)$ is assumed to follow a Gaussian random walk in addition to a linear drift. For such a return function (our reference case), we introduce the condition that the expectation of $X_{\mathrm{eff, ann}, \Delta t}$ must not be biased by the choice of Δt. This condition is fulfilled only if the risk aversion C is constant, that is, independent of Δt. Annualized effective returns $X_{\text{eff, ann}, \Delta t}$, computed for different intervals Δt by equation (12) with a constant C value, can therefore be directly compared.

This measure, though annualized by equation (12), still has a risk term associated with Δt and is insensitive to changes occurring with much longer or much shorter horizons. To achieve a measure that simultaneously considers a wide range of horizons, we introduce a weighted average of several $X_{\text{eff, ann}}$ computed with n different time horizons Δt_i, and thus take advantage of the fact that annualized $X_{\text{eff, ann}}$ can be directly compared:

$$X_{\text{eff}} = \frac{\sum_{i=1}^{n} w_i X_{\text{eff, ann}, \Delta t_i}}{\sum_{i=1}^{n} w_i} \tag{13}$$

where the weights w_i can be chosen according to the relative importance of the time horizons Δt_i and may differ for trading models with different trading frequencies. Substituting $X_{\text{eff, ann}}$ by its expression (equation 12), X_{eff} becomes

$$X_{\text{eff}} = \bar{X} - \frac{C}{2} \frac{\sum_{i=1}^{n} w_i (A_i \sigma_i^2 / \Delta t_i)}{\sum_{i=1}^{n} w_i} \tag{14}$$

where the variance σ_i^2 is computed with equation (11) for the time horizon Δt_i, and A_i is the corresponding annualization factor ($= 1 \text{ year}/\Delta t_i$). Because $\sigma_i^2 \geq 0$, we have $X_{\text{eff}} \leq \bar{X}$. By empirically balancing risk and return of some test trading models, we found values between 0.08 and 0.15 to be reasonable for C.

By adopting this new measure, we depart from the formal utility function theory defined in Keeney and Raiffa (1976). This theory is based on the additivity of utilities, but in equation (13) we average effective returns, which are nonlinear functions of utilities. Nevertheless, we chose this definition because we do not see the utility of each horizon as a component of a meta-utility but rather as representing a typical segment of the market. If one of these segments endures a bad phase, its influence on the overall outcome need not be overproportional, which would be the case if we kept the formalism of additive utilities.

In the discussion of equation (12), we showed that the risk aversion C has no systematic dependence on the horizon Δt_i. Different dealers using a trading model might perceive the risks of various time horizons differently.

We might introduce special C values for individual horizons according to their trading preferences. However, we can achieve an equivalent effect by changing the weights w_i, which are already differentiated for each horizon. These weights reflect the importance of the horizons in terms of the risk sensitivity associated with each horizon.

Specifically, in our performance measure we use a standard weighting function that determines the weights w_i and thus the relative importance of the different time horizons.

$$w(\Delta t) = \frac{1}{2 + (\log(\Delta t/90 \text{ days}))^2} \qquad (15)$$

The weight maximum is set to the 90-day horizon in order to give sufficient importance to the short horizons in comparison with the long ones. This weighting function is designed to be applied to horizons Δt_i in a roughly geometric sequence.

An approximately geometric sequence of n horizons Δt_i is chosen with the following simple construction: once a testing period (full sample of size ΔT) has been established, it is divided by 4. If this division results in a time horizon longer than 2 years, the result is divided by 2. This is repeated until a horizon Δt_1 strictly shorter than 2 years is reached. We limit this longest horizon because dealers usually close their books after one year and are less sensitive to return clustering on longer horizons. The next horizon is obtained by dividing the previous one by 2. This is done until a last horizon between 5 and 10 days is reached. This shortest horizon is then forced to be $\Delta t_n = 7$ days. All time horizons are truncated to full days. If there is no integer multiple of a resulting Δt_i that exactly covers the full sample, the first interval analyzed at the start of the full sample is extended accordingly. The exact Δt_i values to be inserted in equations (14) and (15) are the results of equation (9).

To illustrate the effective return computation, Table 4.1 shows typical results for a USD–DEM trading model tested on six and a half years of high frequency data (March 1986 to September 1992). The analyzed time horizons Δt_i, the weights w_i, the standard deviations σ_i, the average returns $\bar{X}_{\Delta t_i}$, and the annualized effective returns $X_{\text{eff, ann}, \Delta t_i}$ (see equation (12)) are presented. The average yearly return of this run is $\bar{X} = 22.65\%$ and the effective yearly

Table 4.1 Typical results for the performance measure according to each horizon. The horizons Δt_i are given in days, the weights are normalized to one

Δt_i	594	297	148	74	37	18	7
w_i	0.086	0.139	0.212	0.234	0.171	0.104	0.056
σ_i	21.92%	11.80%	7.81%	5.37%	3.64%	2.41%	1.47%
$\bar{X}_{\Delta t_i}$	36.83%	18.42%	9.21%	4.60%	2.30%	1.12%	0.43%
$X_{\text{eff, ann}, \Delta t_i}$	7.88%	14.09%	15.15%	15.56%	16.12%	16.75%	16.99%

return (computed according to equation (14) with $C = 0.10$) is $X_{\text{eff}} = 14.91\%$. The yearly return is reduced by a 'risk premium' of about a third of the original value.

In the remainder of this study, most of the results are presented in terms of the risk-sensitive measure X_{eff}.

4.4 TRADING MODEL ALGORITHMS

The study was conducted using three different algorithms for taking positions (designated classes 40, 50 and 60), each working with eight rates: seven currencies against USD (USD–DEM, USD–CHF, GBP–USD, USD–JPY, USD–ITL, USD–FRF and USD–NLG) and one cross rate (DEM–JPY). The test period covers both the in and the out-of-sample period since we are not interested in the stability of the models but in their comparison.[3] A successful trading model can be viewed as a kind of filter of the price time series itself. It is, in some ways, a good simulation of the investment behavior of a particular market component. Since O&A trading models have proved to perform well during the past years, it is natural to use them to explore some of the properties of the FX markets. All models presented here model medium-term components of the market with one or two deals per week, often keeping their positions open overnight. We distinguish these medium-term components from the short-term components dealing a few times per day and staying neutral overnight as well as from the long-term components dealing once every month or less.

The class 40 models are basically trend-following and take positions when an indicator crosses a threshold. The indicator is a momentum based on specially weighted moving averages with repeated application of the EMA (Exponential Moving Average) operator (Pictet *et al.* 1992). In case of extreme FX-rate movements, however, the models adopt an overbought/oversold (contrarian) behavior and recommend taking a position against the current trend. The contrarian strategy is governed by rules that take the recent trading history of the model into account. The class 40 models go neutral only to save profits or when a stop-loss is reached. Their profit objective is typically at 3% (2.8% for some minor rates). When this objective is reached, a gliding stop-loss prevents the model from losing a large part of the profit already made by triggering its going neutral when the market reverses.

The class 50 models are based on the class 40 model algorithm, but they differ from the class 40 models in three main ways:

1. They have a much smaller profit objective (reduced from 3 to 1.2–1.5%).
2. They never take the same position twice in a row, that is, they stay neutral as long as there is no new signal in the opposite direction.

3. All other parameters common to the two model classes have been chosen to adopt a more conservative profile. In particular, the stop-loss is reduced from 3 to 2%.

While the class 40 and class 50 models rely on one indicator with one time horizon, the class 60 models use three different time horizons simultaneously to incorporate the views of three different market components. They construct their recommendations based on a combined view of all these components, each of which has its own indicator. The indicators are, in their structure, similar to that used by the class 40 models, but they are normalized with their long-term moving volatility (RMS (Room Mean Square) value). The signal of the component flips its sign when its indicator crosses a break level. The absolute value of the break level is then raised and fades with time until a minimum level is reached. The absolute value of the signal is defined to be high at fresh signals and low in overbought/oversold situations or close to a new break in the opposite direction. Additionally, the signal is modulated with a 'mood indicator'. The sum of the signals of the three components is the main trading indicator which can cause a deal when it crosses a certain level. Like the class 40 models, the class 60 models have a profit objective of 3%, but the stop-loss value (1.8%) and especially the moving loss limit (the moving stop-loss after reaching the profit objective, 0.1%) are smaller than those of the class 40 models. The dealing frequencies of the class 60 models are often higher than those of the class 40 and class 50 models (two or more deals per week in the long-term average), but the class 60 models are neutral more often than the class 40 models (somewhere in between the class 40 and the class 50 models). The class 60 models do not have contrarian strategy.

Table 4.2 shows the comparative performance of the class 40, class 50 and class 60 trading models over the full sample period (both in and out-of-sample) together with the performance of a simple 20-day moving average model tested with the same high frequency data and the same environment. The study presented here does not try to optimize the models in any way, so the distinction between in and out-of-sample is of little relevance. As the O&A trading models have shown consistent performance over the years, we chose to show the results on the full sample rather than only on the out-of-sample set in order to have a longer period.

All models produce a significant profit even when transaction costs are fully accounted for. However, they differ both in the size of the average profit and in the risk of temporary losses. The class 40 models have the highest average yearly returns but also the largest drawdowns on this sample. The class 50 models have the lowest returns and the smallest drawdowns. Even if the class 50 models present an average yearly return equal to that of the simple 20-day moving average model, their drawdown is three times smaller and the risk, therefore, much lower. The class 60 models have a performance somewhere

Table 4.2 Performance comparison between the O&A class 40, 50 and 60 trading models and a (benchmark) 20-day moving average model. The test was conducted from 03.03.86 to 01.03.93 for USD–DEM, USD–JPY, GBP–USD, USD–CHF and DEM–JPY, and from 01.12.86 to 01.03.93 for USD–FRF, USD–NLG and USD–ITL. The different performance measures displayed were explained in section 4.3

FX rate	Model	R (%)	X_{eff} (%)	D (%)	P/L	F
USD–DEM	MA(20)	5.5	−0.9	21.1	0.57	1.0
	Model 40	16.9	11.2	9.6	0.41	1.7
	Model 50	8.9	7.8	5.0	0.89	1.2
	Model 60	11.3	8.6	8.4	0.68	2.0
USD–JPY	MA(20)	6.6	0.6	21.3	0.53	0.9
	Model 40	9.6	4.2	10.9	0.59	1.5
	Model 50	4.8	2.7	11.2	0.81	2.0
	Model 60	6.0	3.5	9.6	0.45	1.9
GBP–USD	MA(20)	10.7	5.5	14.0	0.58	1.0
	Model 40	11.9	7.1	14.6	0.40	1.6
	Model 50	4.7	3.5	7.9	0.37	1.5
	Model 60	10.6	8.2	7.9	0.66	2.1
USD–CHF	MA(20)	8.0	0.9	19.2	0.59	1.1
	Model 40	11.6	6.1	14.5	0.55	1.3
	Model 50	8.3	7.1	6.7	0.68	1.3
	Model 60	14.0	10.1	16.9	0.65	1.9
USD–FRF	MA(20)	7.1	4.0	15.8	0.56	1.0
	Model 40	15.5	11.2	7.5	0.75	1.1
	Model 50	8.5	7.4	4.5	0.94	1.1
	Model 60	10.7	8.6	5.3	0.60	2.1
USD–NLG	MA(20)	7.5	3.3	16.6	0.55	1.0
	Model 40	16.4	10.9	8.7	0.50	1.7
	Model 50	8.1	6.9	5.3	0.89	1.0
	Model 60	14.0	11.2	7.4	0.69	2.1
USD–ITL	MA(20)	8.5	1.7	21.7	0.57	1.0
	Model 40	14.6	7.2	10.5	0.42	1.6
	Model 50	6.4	5.2	8.7	0.58	1.6
	Model 60	9.4	6.1	9.3	0.65	1.9
DEM–JPY	MA(20)	1.4	0.8	4.9	2.00	0.1
	Model 40	10.9	8.7	6.5	0.66	1.9
	Model 50	11.7	9.9	5.8	0.72	1.9
	Model 60	10.1	8.6	5.9	0.73	1.6
Average	MA(20)	7.7	2.2	18.5	0.56	1.0
	Model 40	13.4	8.3	10.4	0.54	1.6
	Model 50	7.7	6.3	6.9	0.73	1.4
	Model 60	10.8	8.1	8.8	0.64	2.0

between that of the class 40 and class 50 models, but they show a higher dealing frequency. As far as X_{eff} is concerned, the class 40 and the class 60 models achieve very close results even if the class 40 models have an average return that is 30% higher. This shows that, on average, the class 60 models present a good risk to return trade-off. The results displayed in Table 4.2 are a good illustration of the possibility of having diversified strategies that are all profitable but correspond to different risk profiles. This was formulated as the first conjecture in the Introduction (section 4.1).

4.5 TRADING MODELS WITH DIFFERENT GEOGRAPHICAL MARKETS

Although the FX market is a worldwide 24-hour market, each bid/ask price entered on the screen emanates from a particular location, and the subsequent deals, agreed over the telephone, are entered into dealers' books in particular centers. Realistic trading models should be configured for traders located in particular geographical locations. Our tick-by-tick data gives us the flexibility of configuring different opening hours for different markets. The results presented in the previous section and in Pictet *et al.* (1992) were computed for models running within the market constraints of Zurich. In this section we want to show how the effective return varies if the market constraints are changed. Six other markets are tested: Frankfurt, London, New York, Singapore, Tokyo and Vienna. They differ in their time zone, opening hours and local holidays. Table 4.3 shows the different parameters related to the active times of these markets.

The same eight FX rates used for the performance comparison in Table 4.2 were tested here. The test period was extended for the class 60 models (up to 4 June 1993), but the results are annualized. In Table 4.4, we present the average of X_{eff} over the eight FX rates for the seven markets and the corresponding mean dealing frequency. The bad results for Tokyo and Singapore are not surprising since these markets are the least liquid. Good

Table 4.3 Market business time constraints for tests of the trading models running for different geographical markets. The markets are listed in the order of their opening times in GMT

Market	Time zone	Opening time (local time)	Closing time (local time)	Holidays per year
Tokyo	JPT	09:00	18:00	15 days
Singapore	PRC	09:00	18:00	11 days
Frankfurt	MET	08:30	17:00	12 days
Vienna	MET	08:00	17:30	15 days
Zurich	MET	08:00	17:30	10 days
London	UKT	07:30	17:00	10 days
New York	EST	08:00	14:00	12 days

Table 4.4 The risk-adjusted return X_{eff} for the different markets is shown in percent; the dealing frequency F is given in number of deals per week. The sample starts on 3.3.86 for USD–DEM, USD–JPY, GBP–USD, USD–CHF and DEM–JPY, and on 1.12.86 for USD–FRF, USD–NLG and USD–ITL and runs up to 1.3.93 for the class 40 and class 50 models and up to 4.6.93 for the class 60 models. The markets are listed in the order of their opening times in GMT

Market	X_{eff}			F		
	40	50	60	40	50	60
Tokyo	−0.8	−0.9	1.6	1.3	1.3	1.4
Singapore	−0.4	−0.4	2.3	1.4	1.3	1.4
Frankfurt	7.5	5.7	6.7	1.5	1.4	1.8
Vienna	8.3	6.2	7.8	1.5	1.4	2.0
Zurich	8.3	6.3	7.7	1.6	1.5	2.0
London	8.6	6.4	8.2	1.6	1.5	2.0
New York	6.3	4.4	6.7	1.5	1.4	1.9

results in these markets are only obtained for USD–JPY and DEM–JPY. For the other five markets, X_{eff} generally does not vary much (within 1 to 2%), but it clearly peaks on the most active market (London) although the models were optimized for the Zurich market (in-sample: 3.3.86 to 1.3.89 for USD–DEM, USD–JPY, GBP–USD, USD–CHF and DEM–JPY, and 1.12.86 to 1.12.89 for USD–FRF, USD–NLG and USD–ITL). This presents first empirical evidence for our conjecture (conjecture 3 in section 4.1) that within the active times, the performance is not very sensitive to certain changing conditions.

The lowest X_{eff} values in this latter group of five are obtained for the New York market, whose business hours overlap with the other most liquid markets only in part (mainly in the morning). The afternoon in New York is still too early to catch the opening of the Tokyo market. It is also interesting to note that the dealing frequency varies from one market to the other and is, most of the time, positively correlated with the return. This correlation is not always true: we shall see the reverse effect in the next section. In this case, the models were optimized with a certain type of dealing frequency, and the fact that the frequency is reduced in certain markets only means that some good dealing opportunities were missed. One might argue that these findings are of limited value here since the models were only optimized for the Zurich market. We think that making better models for the New York, Tokyo and Singapore markets would be possible, but we can observe some particularly interesting behaviors when the models are used as they are. In the next section we shall see that a more extensive study confirms most of these first empirical results.

4.6 TRADING MODEL RESULTS AS FUNCTIONS OF THE BUSINESS HOURS

The different types of markets investigated above are not the only possible definitions of trading hours for the O&A trading models. We present another study here where we vary both the length and the starting point of the daily opening period. The main interest of this study is not to optimize specific model properties but to use realistic trading models to explore market structures. The study was conducted on all USD rates listed in Table 4.2. The three model classes were tested with daily working intervals of 1, 8, 9, 10, 11, 12, 13 and 24 hours, shifting the opening time in 30-minute steps from 0:00 to 24:00. The holidays were assumed to be those of Zurich in the whole study. The test period is a total of $5\frac{1}{2}$ years from 1 January 1987 to 1 July 1992 for all runs; the total number of test runs involved is above 5000.

In section 4.1, we introduced three conjectures, two of which are subjects of research: it is not favorable to extend the dealing period to more than the normal business hours or even to 24-hour trading for our model types (conjecture 2); and the most profitable dealing periods should be the most active and liquid ones (conjecture 3). To test these conjectures, two main questions were asked: is there an optimal daily business interval and do these optimal opening and closing hours differ for different rates?

Before detailing the results, let us first consider the outcome of such a study if the FX rates did follow a random walk. In this case, there should be no optimal daily business interval and the question of the opening and closing times should not matter. Independent of the location of the active interval during the day, it would not be possible (over a sufficiently long period) to make any profit out of FX deals. On the contrary, the models would lose money because of the transaction costs: the higher the dealing frequency, the more losses. However, as the empirical results show, there are optimal trading periods and optimal opening/closing times.

Table 4.5 shows the best X_{eff} values together with their corresponding working hours in Middle European Time (MET) for all rates and trading models used in this study. The models were optimized in-sample on $9\frac{1}{2}$ hours from 8:00 to 17:30. Some first remarks can be made by looking at the results: shorter time intervals (8–10 hours) are generally preferred to longer ones (11–13 hours), thus confirming conjecture 2. There is not much profit in long working time intervals; these only tend to increase the number of bad deals because the indicators are more sensitive to noise. In two cases (USD–CHF in class 40 and class 50), the 1-hour time interval is best, but the models still have significant peaks at the 9-hour interval for class 40 (from 8:30 to 17:30, 4.9%) and the 8-hour interval for class 50 (from 9:30 to 17:30, 3.6%). Yet, since longer time intervals cover a larger period, the X_{eff} values of longer time intervals are more stable against changing opening and

Table 4.5 The best X_{eff} in percent, as a function of the number of daily business hours and the opening and closing times in MET. The sixth column shows the X_{eff} reached when the models are allowed to trade 24 hours. The last column shows the hour that produces the best X_{eff} when only one hour per day is allowed for trading. These results are obtained for the period from 1.1.87 to 1.7.92

FX rate	Model	Best X_{eff}	Best interval size (hours)	Day time	X_{eff} (24h) (24-hour trading)	Best hour (1-hour trading)
USD–DEM	40	9.7	12	7:00–19:00	6.7	16:30–17:30
	50	8.5	9	8:30–17:30	7.9	09:30–10:30
	60	9.0	11	8:30–19:30	2.8	12:00–13:00
USD–JPY	40	4.3	9	8:30–17:30	−4.2	10:00–11:00
	50	5.2	11	5:30–16:30	−3.1	09:00–10:00
	60	7.6	9	3:00–12:00	0.5	17:00–18:00
GBP–USD	40	13.4	10	9:00–19:00	6.9	16:30–17:30
	50	8.1	8	4:00–12:00	5.2	06:00–07:00
	60	9.0	8	6:00–14:00	5.8	13:00–14:00
USD–CHF	40	7.4	1	16:30–17:30	−5.8	16:30–17:30
	50	4.8	1	10:30–11:30	−2.5	10:30–11:30
	60	5.1	8	9:30–17:30	−0.6	18:30–19:30
USD–FRF	40	11.2	8	11:00–19:00	0.5	17:00–18:00
	50	8.7	12	5:30–17:30	2.8	16:00–17:00
	60	9.4	9	8:00–17:00	1.6	16:00–17:00
USD–NLG	40	12.3	8	12:00–20:00	6.9	16:00–17:00
	50	6.2	13	10:30–23:30	4.8	03:00–04:00
	60	8.8	10	8:30–18:30	4.6	15:30–16:30
USD–ITL	40	9.2	9	12:00–21:00	0.3	16:30–17:30
	50	6.2	10	9:00–19:00	3.0	06:00–07:00
	60	6.6	8	11:00–19:00	1.3	13:00–14:00

closing hours, that is, their variance is clearly smaller than that of shorter intervals.

Further evidence in support of conjecture 2 of section 4.1 is given by the sixth column in Table 4.5 listing the X_{eff} values for 24-hour trading for comparison with the best X_{eff} values attained for shorter trading intervals. The X_{eff} (24-hour) values are much lower than the best X_{eff} values for almost all rates and models. This failure of 24-hour trading can be interpreted as an insufficiency of the models to deal with short-term price movements, in particular the disruptive market behaviors arising when the main dealing activity shifts from one geographical location to another (with a different time zone). A 24-hour trading interval leads to a dealing frequency higher than that of a 12-hour interval (a factor ~ 1.2 with the class 40 and class 50 models and ~ 1.5 with the class 60 models), although our trading algorithms consider medium-term time horizons, that is, horizons much longer than 12 hours. The additional trades originating from an increased daily trading period are mostly bad ones; 24-hour trading may become successful only if a new model explicitly treats the geographical components of a market, perhaps with a weighting scheme for information related to the time of day. Contrary to the 24-hour trading interval, the best 1-hour intervals that coincide with the most active times of the day are seldom significantly worse than the rest of the intervals tested.

In Table 4.5 there are also indications that conjecture 3 of section 4.1 is valid. The USD–JPY models show a strong tendency toward favoring opening hours early in the European morning (or closing times early in the afternoon), while GBP–USD and USD–ITL prefer opening times in the late morning. These results are in line with the time zones of the home markets of the currencies and must be related to market liquidity. For JPY, better results are obtained when its main market (Far East) is active, for GBP and ITL, when London (1 hour behind the Zurich market) is active (ITL is traded more in London than in Milan). The results for the class 40 and class 50 USD–NLG models seem to contradict this conjecture, but they should be qualified. For the class 40 model, there is, in fact, another peak with an X_{eff} of 11.3% at a 12-hour trading interval from 7:30 to 19:30, and for the class 50 model there is also a relative maximum with an X_{eff} of 6.0% at a 8-hour trading interval from 9:00 to 17:00.

The last column in Table 4.5 shows clearly that, if the models are only allowed to trade during one hour every working day, they will produce the best results when this hour is chosen during the period of the most active market.[4] The only exception is the maximum of the class 50 USD–NLG model at 3:00–4:00 (2.4%), but there are, in fact, other local maxima at 9:30–10:30 (1.2%) and 12:00–13:00 (1.2%) which lie in the active time of Europe (and, in the second case, also America). There is yet another plausible explanation for this exception: the main currency traded against NLG is not USD but DEM, so some discrepancies can occur on this market due to the fact that it is not very liquid in any case. Similar, although less pronounced effects are found with the USD–ITL and USD–FRF rates.

Figure 4.2 shows two-dimensional plots of X_{eff} as a function of the opening (x-axis) and the closing hours (y-axis) for two FX rates (USD–DEM and USD–FRF). Two salient features emerge from these plots, again confirming conjecture 3. First, the good performance of the models is concentrated on the times when their active hours overlap with those of the main active markets. This is true independent of the trading model under consideration. Second, the intervals that close at the same hour have more similar X_{eff} values than those with the same opening hour (especially during liquid market times). This is also true for rates not shown in Figure 4.2 as, for example, GBP–USD and illustrated in Figure 4.2 by the horizontal band structures. Therefore, the last possibility to trade has a stronger effect on the overall performance of these models than the first (opening hour). The closing hours in the evening in

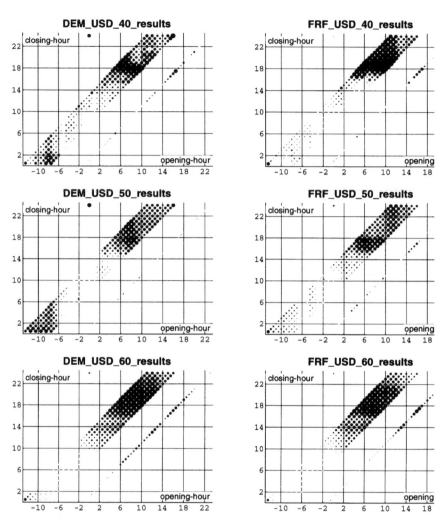

Figure 4.2 Two-dimensional plots of X_{eff} as a function of the opening hours (x variable) and the closing hours (y variable). The larger the black circle the larger the value of X_{eff}. The white circles indicate a negative value of X_{eff}. The time is given in MET. The sample is the same as for Table 4.5

Europe are very important because the European intra-day traders must close their positions while the New York market is fully active. This is again a hint that the liquidity of the market is an important factor.

There is also some kind of an 'edge structure' distinguishable in these graphs, that is, horizontal and vertical edges between different X_{eff} levels may

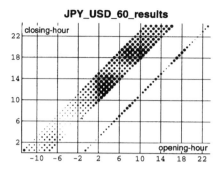 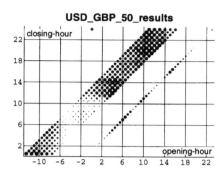

Figure 4.3 Two examples of the edge structure in two-dimensional plots of X_{eff} as a function of the opening hours (x-axis) and the closing hours (y-axis). The larger the black circle the larger the value of X_{eff}. The white circles indicate a negative value of X_{eff}. The time is given in MET. The sample is the same as for Table 4.5

be found. Figure 4.3 shows two such examples (USD–JPY class 60 and GBP–USD class 50). These structures are, in fact, related to the market activity and can be explained as follows for the two examples shown in Figure 4.3:

1. In the plot for the class 60 USD–JPY model,
   (a) a vertical line is well defined for an opening hour at 02:00, indicating the opening of the Japanese market and, therefore, the beginning of the most liquid time for this model; see also Dacorogna *et al.* (1993);
   (b) the horizontal line for a closing hour at 15:00 is slightly less clear, but around this time the European and the American markets jointly cause a high peak in the activity.
2. In the plot for the class 50 GBP–USD model,
   (a) the vertical line for an opening hour at 18:00 (-6 on the x-axis of Figure 4.3) is due to the fact that the model completely misses the European market after this time;
   (b) the horizontal line for a closing hour at 11:00 is due to the fact that the model misses the American market if it stops trading before this time.

Similar structures may be seen in most graphs independent of the model. For all FX rates traded in Europe there is a clear-cut drop in the X_{eff} values when the models open after 18:00.

4.7 CONCLUSION

We have presented a set of successful trading models that are used to study inherent market properties. Models with very different behaviors and risk profiles can be profitable even when transaction costs are accounted for. This fact illustrates and reinforces the hypothesis suggested in an earlier paper (Müller *et al.* 1993) of a market with *heterogeneous* trading behaviors. The different market participants have different time horizons for their analysis of past events and news and for their trading objectives. The market is driven by the combined actions of all these different types of traders or *components*. Each component has its own frame of reference just as each of the trading models presented here has its own history and decision process. Although different geographical locations have different business hours, it is possible to develop profitable trading strategies for them as long as their business hours significantly overlap with the most active periods of the FX market.

The systematic analysis of the influence of the trading hours on these models reveals some important facts. First of all, if we regard our model classes as representing medium-term components in the market, we see that it is not useful to stay active 24 hours a day. Without a much more sophisticated treatment of the intra-day movements, it does not pay for a medium-term trader to be active all the time. Second, it shows that, contrary to assumptions based on the classical efficient market hypothesis, a trading model is profitable when its active hours correspond to the most active hours of one of the main geographical components of the market. It is essential that the models execute their deals when the market is most liquid. This fact is illustrated by three empirical findings:

1. The maxima of performance are clustered around opening hours when the main markets are active;
2. The best active times are shifted for certain currencies to accommodate their main markets (Japan for JPY, London for GBP or ITL);
3. If the models are only allowed to trade for one hour, the best choice of this hour is usually around the peaks in the daily activity of the market.

The systematic variation of the business hours of the trading models again reveals the geographical structure of the FX market and its daily seasonality by the most profitable trading times being concentrated where the market is most liquid.

This study shows that developing trading models for the FX market also leads to a better understanding of the behavior of this market. Further developments in trading model technology should allow more refined studies of the FX market.

ENDNOTES

1. The abbreviations used here are defined by the International Organization for Standardization (code 4217).

2. In this chapter, we speak of a trading model 'dealing' or 'entering a position' although, as noted before, our models do not deal directly but instead instruct a human dealer to make trades. In our pursuit of realism, however, we consider the decisions made by our models as valid as any made by a 'real-life' dealer. In this respect we are deliberately loose in our phraseology.
3. The out-of-sample performance of these models is quite close to the in-sample performance and documented in Pictet *et al.* (1992) and Olsen & Associates (1993a, b, 1994)
4. For the most active times, the reader is referred to Müller *et al.* (1990) and to Dacorogna *et al.* (1993).

REFERENCES

Acar, E., Bertin, C. and Lequeux, P. (1993), 'Efficacité des moyennes mobiles à gérer le risque de change', Presentation at the XXXIXth International AEA Conference on Real Time Econometrics, 14–15 October 1993 in Luxembourg.

Brock, W., Lakonishok, J. and LeBaron, B. (1992), 'Simple Technical Trading Rules and the Stochastic Properties of Stock Returns', *The Journal of Finance*, **47**(5), 1731–1764.

Burke, G. (1993), 'Analyzing Trading Performance with Excel', *Futures*, **22**(9), 48–49.

Dacorogna, M.M., Müller, U.A., Nagler, R.J., Olsen, R.B. and Pictet, O.V. (1993), 'A Geographical Model for the Daily and Weekly Seasonal Volatility in the FX market', *Journal of International Money and Finance*, **12**(4), 413–438.

Keeney, R.L. and Raiffa, H. (1976), Decisions with Multiple Objectives: Preferences and Value Tradeoffs, John Wiley & Sons, New York.

LeBaron, B. (1992), 'Do Moving Average Trading Rule Results Imply Nonlinearities in Foreign Exchange Markets?', University of Wisconsin-Madison, Social Systems Research Institute, Working Paper No. 9222.

Levich, R.M. and Thomas, L.R. III (1993), 'The Significance of Technical Trading-rule Profits in the Foreign Exchange Market: a Bootstrap Approach', *Journal of International Money and Finance*, **12**(5), 451–474.

Müller, U.A., Dacorogna, M.M., Davé, R.D., Pictet, O.V., Olsen, R.B. and Ward, J.R. (1993), 'Fractals and Intrinsic Time—a Challenge to Econometricians', Invited presentation at the XXXIXth International AEA Conference on Real Time Econometrics, 14–15 Oct. 1993 in Luxembourg, and the 4th International PASE Workshop, 22–26 Nov 1993 in Ascona (Switzerland); also in 'Erfolgreiche Zinsprognose', ed. by B. Lüthje, Verband öffentlicher Banken, Bonn 1994, ISBN 3-927466-20-4; UAM.1993-08-16, Olsen & Associates, Seefeldstrasse 233, 8008 Zürich, Switzerland.

Müller, U.A., Dacorogna, M.M., Olsen, R.B., Pictet, O.V., Schwarz, M. and Morgenegg, C. (1990), 'Statistical Study of Foreign Exchange Rates, Empirical Evidence of a Price Change Scaling Law, and Intraday Analysis', *Journal of Banking and Finance*, **14**, 1189–1208.

Olsen & Associates (1993a), The O&A Class 40 Trading Models, a Performance Analysis, Release Documents, Olsen & Associates, Zurich.

Olsen & Associates (1993b), The O&A Class 50 Trading Models, a Performance Analysis, Release Documents, Olsen & Associates, Zurich.

Olsen & Associates (1994), The O&A Class 60 Trading Models, a Performance Analysis, Release Documents, Olsen & Associates, Zurich.

Pictet, O.V., Dacorogna, M.M., Müller, U.A., Olsen, R.B. and Ward, J.R. (1992), 'Real-time Trading Models for Foreign Exchange Rates', *Neural Network World*, **2**(6), 713–744.

Surajaras, P. and Sweeney, R.J. (1992), *Profit-making Speculation in Foreign Exchange Markets*, Westview Press, Boulder, Colo.

Taylor, M.P. and Allen, H. (1992), 'The Use of Technical Analysis in the Foreign Exchange Market', *Journal of International Money and Finance*, **11**, 304–314.

5
Dynamic Strategies: A Correlation Study

EMMANUEL ACAR and
PIERRE LEQUEUX

In recent years, and particularly for banking institutions involved with unstable financial markets, the need for worthwhile forecasts has been generally recognised by treasurers and academics alike. The choice of which dynamic strategy to follow depends upon the expectations about the stochastic process which drives prices. Many forecasting strategies can be used to predict future price movements from fundamental to technical indicators, as well as more advanced techniques such as neural networks and genetic algorithms. Unfortunately, the study of financial forecasts used for trading is relatively new. Many of the previous studies have used historical returns to exhibit the profitability of technical forecasts (Dacorogna *et al.* 1994, Dunis 1989, LeBaron 1991, 1992, Levich and Thomas 1993, Silber 1994, Surajaras and Sweeney 1992, Taylor 1986, 1990a, b, 1992). Only recent work by Neftçi (1991), Taylor (1994), Brock *et al.* (1992), Levich and Thomas (1993) and LeBaron (1991, 1992) has stressed the statistical properties of technical trading rules and the insight they might give us about the underlying process. Although Neftçi (1991) has examined the Markovian properties of trading strategies, the literature on their analytical properties remains relatively sparse.

This study is concerned with the forecasting of correlation between the rates of returns generated by dynamic strategies. In order to calculate the risk of a portfolio, a passive investor applying buy-and-hold strategies needs to

Forecasting Financial Markets: Exchange Rates, Interest Rates and Asset Management. Edited by
Christian Dunis. © 1996 John Wiley & Sons Ltd.

know how two underlying markets are related. This information is also necessary for an active investor, but is not by itself sufficient. The active investor also needs to know how two forecasting strategies she/he follows differ. Most investors initiate their positions during their time zone. Therefore, realistic trading models should be configured for traders located in particular centres. During a typical trading day, not all the times have the same informative value as input for forecasting. It is well known that financial markets, such as futures, are especially active at the opening and closing times. Lunchtimes can be remarkably quiet. Strategies based on daily data but triggered at particular times of the day may be an alternative to the use of high frequency data. This generates a non-synchronous trading problem which is dealt with in this study by establishing the correlation coefficient of dynamic trading strategies which may be triggered at particular times of the day.

Correlation coefficients are extensively used, especially in formulating hedging strategies. However, correlations are notoriously unstable, as many hedgers have found, and do not take into account the non-synchronous trading problem. In addition, most financial institutions follow between 150 and 250 assets and as many trading rules. It seems unlikely that analysts will be able to directly estimate correlation structures. Their ability to do so is severely limited by the vast number of correlation coefficients to be estimated. Recognition of this has motivated the search for development of formulae capable of describing and predicting the correlation structure between assets and strategies. The rationale of this study is that accurate measurement of correlation can be better achieved using stochastic modelling.

Establishing theoretical correlations between trading rules has been considered as an extremely difficult task (Brock *et al.* 1992). However, we show that exact analytical results can be obtained under the assumption that the forecast and the underlying process of price returns follow a bivariate normal random walk without drift. Examples are provided for technical indicators, although theoretical results are more general and only require that the underlying asset and forecast follow a bivariate normal law. Analytical formulae can therefore be applied to any forecasting system (fundamental, technical, neural network . . .) under these assumptions.

There are three reasons for investigating correlations between trading rules. First, trading rules correlations would provide a measure of similarity between trading systems. With the exception of Lukac *et al.* (1988), rules have been merely listed rather than classified on the basis of their properties. As a result, a multitude of forecasting systems has been proposed which are in fact extremely similar if not completely identical. Second, rules correlations would permit the construction of an efficient portfolio of rules. Until now such portfolios have been built empirically for given financial time series (Brorsen and Lukac 1990), but have never been established theoretically for given stochastic processes. Third, and perhaps more importantly, it would allow the joint profitability of a set of trading rules to be tested. Brock *et al.* (1992), and Surajaras and Sweeney (1992) and Prado (1992) have emphasised that such a test might have power, particularly against nonlinear alternatives. The resulting tests of non-zero profitability could then be more powerful than any single test.

Section 5.1 establishes the necessary preliminaries, trading rules correlations under the random walk assumption. Then, section 5.2 studies the effects of time of day and time aggregation. Finally, section 5.3 tests the adequacy of analytical formulae with empirical results observed for markets as different as spot foreign exchange, futures stock indices, bonds and commodities. Section 5.4 summarises our results and presents some conclusions.

5.1 TRADING RULES CORRELATIONS UNDER THE RANDOM WALK WITHOUT DRIFT ASSUMPTION

Section 5.1.1 defines our forecasting strategies and the rate of return they generate. Examples are given for some popular technical trading rules, although results can easily be extended to other forecasting strategies. Section 5.1.2 establishes the correlations between two trading rules applied to a bivariate random walk without drift.

5.1.1 Forecasting Strategies and Rule Returns

Suppose that on each day t, a decision rule is applied with the intention of achieving profitable trades. The price trend, based on market expectations, determines whether the asset is bought or sold. When the asset is bought, the position initiated in the market is said to be 'long'. When the asset is sold, the position initiated in the market is said to be 'short'. A forecasting technique is assessed as useful and will subsequently be used if it has economic value. In short, the forecast is seen as useful if in dealer terms, it can 'make money'. For achieving this purpose, market participants use price-based forecasts. Therefore, the predictor F_t is completely characterised by a mathematical function f of past prices $F_t = f\{P_t, P_{t-1}, P_{t-2} \ldots, P_0\}$.

The only crucial feature which is required from the forecasting technique is its ability to accurately predict the direction of the trend in order to generate profitable buy and sell signals. Trading signals, buy (+1) and sell (−1), can then be formalised by the binary stochastic process B_t:

$$\text{'Sell'} : B_t = -1 \quad \text{iff } F_t = f\{P_t, P_{t-1}, P_{t-2}, \ldots, P_0\} < 0$$

Notice that the signal of a trading rule is completely defined by the inequality giving a sell order, because if the position is not short, it is long. A particular class of forecasters are linear rules which can be expressed by a linear combination of logarithmic returns $X_t = \ln(P_t/P_{t-1})$:

$$F_t = \delta + \sum_{j=0}^{t} d_j X_{t-j} \tag{1}$$

with δ and the d_j being constants.

Only in the trivial case of a buy and hold strategy, the signal B_t is deterministic and is $+1$ irrespective of the underlying process. Otherwise, trading signals B_t are stochastic variables. By nature, the signal is a highly nonlinear function of the observed price series P_t (Neftçi and Policano 1984, Neftçi 1991), and therefore it can be highly dependent through time; B_t remains constant for a certain random period, then jumps to a new level as P_t behaves in a certain way. Trading in the asset occurs throughout the investment horizon at times that depend upon a fixed set of rules and future price changes. The most well-known example of a technical linear rule is provided by the simple moving average method[1] of order m for which

$$F_t = \sum_{j=1}^{m-1} (m-j) X_{t-j+1}$$

Returns at time t made by applying such a decision rule are called *rule returns*, denoted R_t. Their value can be expressed as

$$R_t = B_{t-1} X_t \Leftrightarrow \left\{ \begin{array}{l} R_t = -X_t \text{ if } B_{t-1} = -1 \\ R_t = +X_t \text{ if } B_{t-1} = +1 \end{array} \right\} \tag{2}$$

where B_{t-1} is the signal triggered by the trading rule at time $t-1$.

Two important remarks should be made. Rule returns are the product of a binary stochastic signal and a continuous returns random variable. Except in the trivial case of a buy and hold strategy, the signal B_t is a stochastic variable and so rule returns are conditional on the position taken in the market. This is the main feature of rule returns. In addition, our rule return definition clearly corresponds to an unrealised return. By 'unrealised' we mean that rule returns are recorded every day even if the position is neither closed nor reversed, but simply carries on.

5.1.2 Linear Rule Returns Correlation under the Random Walk Assumption

We now assume that two financial series, with underlying returns $X_{1,t}$ and $X_{2,t}$, follow a centred bivariate normal law with variances σ_1^2 and σ_2^2 and correlation coefficient ρ_x. Then two unbiased linear trading rules (similar or different) $F_{1, t}$ and $F_{2, t}$ are respectively applied to the two processes $\{X_{1, t}\}$ and $\{X_{2, t}\}$.

$$F_{1, t} = \sum_{i=0}^{m_1-2} d_{1, i} X_{1, t-i} \tag{3}$$

$$F_{2, t} = \sum_{i=0}^{m_2-2} d_{2, i} X_{2, t-i} \tag{4}$$

where m_1 and m_2 are the orders or lengths of the trading rules.

The linear rule $F_{i, t-1}$ generates signal $B_{i, t-1}$ and return $R_{i, t}$ from the underlying process $\{X_{i, t}\}$, given by $R_{i, t} = B_{i, t-1} X_{i, t}$. Precise theoretical correlations are now being established for any linear rules without a constant and highlighted, for the sake of clarity, by the popular technical linear rule, the simple moving average method.

5.1.2.1 Proposition 1[2]

Assuming that two underlying time series, $X_{1, t}$ and $X_{2, t}$, follow a centred bivariate normal law with underlying correlation ρ_x, then linear rule returns, $R_{1, t}$ and $R_{2, t}$ exhibit linear correlation coefficient ρ_R, given by

$$\rho_R = \rho(R_{1, t}, R_{2, t}) = \frac{2}{\pi} \rho_x \arcsin (\rho_x \rho_F) \tag{5}$$

where ρ_F is the correlation between two different forecasts applied to the same underlying process. We call it systems correlation. It is given by

$$\rho_F = \sum_{i=0}^{\mathrm{Min}\,(m_1, m_2)-2} d_{1, i} d_{2, i} \Bigg/ \left(\sqrt{\sum_{i=0}^{m_1-2} d_{1, i}^2} \sqrt{\sum_{i=0}^{m_2-2} d_{2, i}^2} \right) \tag{6}$$

In addition,

$$\rho(R_{1, t}, R_{2, t+h}) = \rho(R_{1, t+h}, R_{2, t}) = 0 \quad \text{for } h > 0. \tag{7}$$

Expression (5) suggests the following:

1. Rule returns correlation, ρ_R, is an even function of the underlying correlation ρ_x and an odd function of the systems correlation ρ_F. That means that rule returns will be negatively (positively) correlated if, and only if, the systems correlation is negative (positive).
2. Rule returns correlation is always lower in absolute value than the underlying correlation.

If one wants to minimise the risk of an investment, it turns out that diversifying trend-following systems between positively correlated assets can be beneficial beyond diversification of passive strategies, because the correlation between trading systems will be lower (property 1). However, this will be disadvantageous if the underlying assets are negatively correlated, because trading systems will be positively correlated (property 2).

For the remainder of this section we shall primarily focus our interest on returns rather than signals correlation since it has more implications within a portfolio context. We shall detail and interpret previous results by considering three cases from the simplest to the most general: (i) different rules applied to the same underlying process, (ii) the same rule applied to different underlying processes and (iii) different rules applied to different underlying processes.

5.1.2.2 Different rules applied to the same underlying process

When two different unbiased linear trading systems are applied to the same underlying process, $X_{1, t} = X_{2, t} = X_t$ and $\rho_x = 1$. In this case, correlations between rule returns, equation (5) becomes equal to

$$\rho_R = \frac{2}{\pi} \arc \sin (\rho_F) \qquad (8)$$

Table 5.1 shows correlations between various systems. For instance, $\rho[S(5), S(10)]$ means the rule returns correlation between the simple moving average of order 5 and the simple moving average of order 10, is equal to 0.666. Figure 5.1 illustrates correlations between rule returns as a function of correlations between forecasts.

Instead of listing differences between systems and orders which could be endless due to the infinite number of linear rules, it is worth emphasising two points. First, trend-following systems are positively correlated. Zero or negative correlation obviously requires the combination of trading rules of a different nature such as trend-following and contrarian strategies. Second, buy and sell signals, as well as returns of technical systems, are not independent

Table 5.1 Rule returns correlations

ρ	$S(2)$	$S(3)$	$S(5)$	$S(10)$	$S(20)$	$S(40)$	$S(80)$
$S(2)$	1	0.705	0.521	0.358	0.25	0.175	0.124
$S(3)$		1	0.71	0.484	0.336	0.236	0.166
$S(5)$			1	0.666	0.460	0.322	0.226
$S(10)$				1	0.680	0.472	0.331
$S(20)$					1	0.685	0.478
$S(40)$						1	0.688
$S(80)$							1

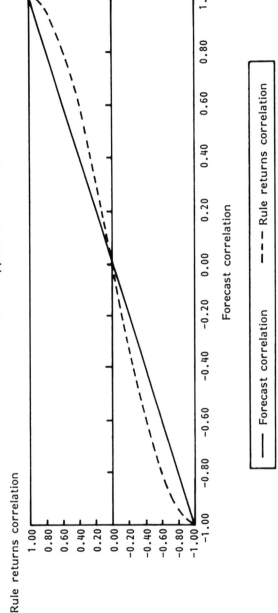
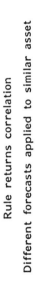

Figure 5.1 Rule returns correlation as a function of the forecast correlation

over time under the random walk assumption. Related findings are attributable to Working (1960). This research established that if in a time series constructed from independent increments, the individuals items are replaced, say, by monthly averages, spurious correlation is introduced between successive first differences of the averages. However, correlation between trading signals would contradict the hypothesis of Lukac *et al.* (1988) who considered, as an approximation, that buy and sell signals of systems are independent over time. They then concluded that all systems are on the same side of the market (significantly more than might randomly be expected) and that monthly returns are positively correlated. Our results show that it is not absolutely certain that the similarities between systems that Lukac *et al.* (1988) found are nothing more than would be expected from a random process.

5.1.2.3 *Same rule applied to different underlying processes*

When the same linear rule (non-deterministic, and so excluding buy and hold, or sell and hold strategies) is applied simultaneously to two assets, $\rho_F = 1$ and equation (5) becomes

$$\rho_R = \frac{2}{\pi} \rho_x \arcsin(\rho_x) \tag{9}$$

We can see two additional properties, when the same rule is applied to two different assets. First, rule returns correlations become independent of the rule itself and the sole function of the underlying correlation. Second, rule returns correlations are now an even function of the underlying correlation and thus are always positive. Figure 5.2 highlights formula (9) for some values of correlations of the underlying process.

5.1.2.4 *Different rules applied to different underlying processes*

Figure 5.3 examines the most general case where different rules are applied to different underlying processes. We use for this purpose different orders of simple moving averages. Having just proved that correlations between rule returns (when the same rule is applied to two different processes) do not depend on the rule itself, Table 5.2 exhibits constant diagonals.

Our results are consistent with Praetz (1979) but disagree with those of Sweeney (1986) and Surajaras and Sweeney (1992). On the one hand, Praetz (1979) noted that the results from both different securities and trading rules are likely to be positively correlated due to the presence of the market factor among security returns and due to the presence of many common rates in the

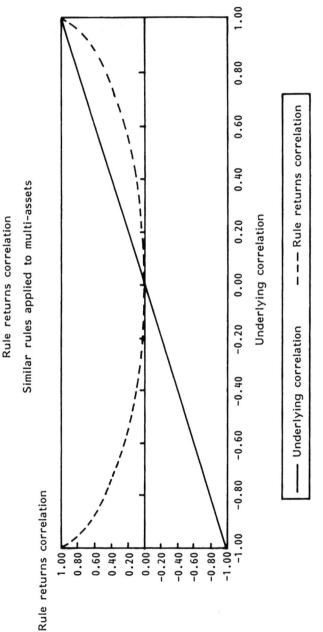

Figure 5.2 Rule returns correlation as a function of the underlying correlation

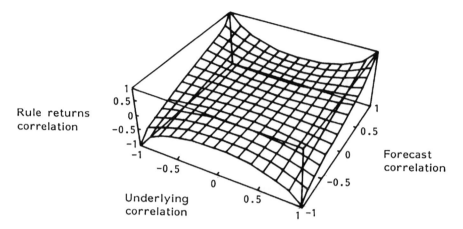

Rule returns correlation

Forecast correlation

Underlying correlation

Figure 5.3 Rule returns correlation as a function of the underlying correlation and forecast correlation

returns from short selling of similar trading rules. On the other hand, Sweeney (1986, p. 177) concluded that 'even if [exchange] rates are correlated, excess rates of return on trading strategies should be virtually uncorrelated because the signals are only randomly synchronised across currencies'. Surajaras and Sweeney (1992) assumed that on the one hand, under efficiency rules signals would be completely non-synchronised and, on the other hand, inefficiencies would create positive cross correlations. Our investigation leads to a different conclusion, i.e. even when underlying processes are correlated white noises, rules correlations although lower in absolute value cannot be zero. The presence of inefficiencies, more specifically positive autocorrelations, would even increase rules correlations. Our results clearly indicate that correlations between trading rules are strongly dependent on underlying correlations. This could explain why the correlations between trading rules can be low for equities (Sweeney 1988) and high for currencies (Surajaras and Sweeney

Table 5.2 Rule returns correlations ρ_R for underlying correlations $\rho_x = 0.85$

		Underlying correlation: $\rho_x = 0.85$			
ρ	$S(2)$	$S(5)$	$S(10)$	$S(20)$	$S(40)$
$S(2)$	0.55	0.362	0.254	0.179	0.126
$S(5)$		0.55	0.447	0.323	0.229
$S(10)$			0.55	0.455	0.331
$S(20)$				0.55	0.457
$S(40)$					0.55

1992). Accordingly, t-statistics can be highly sensitive to whether or not the covariance terms are included.

Overall, these results suggest that correlations between the same system applied to various assets can be much lower than correlations between various trend-following systems applied to the same asset. It seems that these results might hold empirically since diversification between assets has been found more beneficial than diversification between systems (Taylor 1990b, Brorsen and Boyd 1990).

5.2 TIMES EFFECTS ON TRADING RULE RETURNS

5.2.1 Time of the Day

In some cases, investors choose to take positions in a financial market at different times of the day. This is frequently the case with the 24-hour foreign exchange (FX) market. Most investors initiate their positions during their time zone. Geographical components related to the business hours of the different trading centres must be taken into account. Realistic trading models should be configured for traders located in particular centres. The European time zone is often perceived as the most important reason for the dominance of Europe as a currency centre. Most European trading desks come in towards the close of Tokyo trading and exit towards the middle of the New York trading day. Dacorogna *et al.* (1994) find that trading models work best for certain currencies at their most active times which are shifted to accommodate their main markets (Japan for the JPY, London for the GBP). The systematic variation of the business hours of the trading models reveals the geographical structure of the FX market and its daily seasonality by concentrating its most profitable trading times where the market is the most liquid.

In other cases, investors may be forced to take positions at different times of the day. This most often occurs when financial markets do not exhibit overlapping times. For instances, the Tokyo Stock Exchange approximately opens at 0.00 GMT to close at 6.00 GMT, whereas the New York Stock Exchange opens at 14.30 GMT to close at 21.00 GMT. This 'non-synchronous trading problem', or 'stale quote problem' may induce spurious lagged spillovers (see for instance Lin *et al.* 1994 and Aggarwal and Park 1994).

This section deals with the non-synchronous trading problem by establishing the correlation coefficient of trading strategies based on daily rates but applied at different times of the day. More specifically, let us assume that two trading rules are applied daily but at different times of the day. The first one is applied at time t and the second one at time $t^* = t - y$, where y is bounded between zero and one. A value of $y = n/24$ means that the second trading rule is applied n hours before the first one. For instance, a value of y equal to 0.25 means that the lag between the two trading rules is equal to 6 ($= 0.25 \times 24$) hours.

5.2.1.1 Proposition 2

Assuming that two underlying time series, $X_{1,t}$ and $X_{2,t}$ follow a centred bivariate normal law with underlying correlation ρ_x, then linear rule returns, $R_{1,t}$ and $R_{2,t}$ lagged y fraction of the unit time ($y = n/24$ for daily unit time and hourly lag n) exhibit a linear correlation coefficient ρ_R, given by

$$
\rho_R = (1-y)\frac{2}{\pi}\rho_x \arcsin\left(\rho_x \frac{(1-y)\displaystyle\sum_{i=0}^{\min(m_1,m_2)-2} d_{1,i}d_{2,i} + y\displaystyle\sum_{i=0}^{\min(m_1,m_2)-3} d_{1,i}d_{2,i+1}}{\sqrt{\displaystyle\sum_{i=0}^{m_1-2} d_{1,i}^2}\sqrt{\displaystyle\sum_{i=0}^{m_2-2} d_{2,i}^2}}\right)
$$

$$
+ y\frac{2}{\pi}\rho_x \arcsin\left(\rho_x \frac{y\displaystyle\sum_{i=0}^{\min(m_1,m_2)-2} d_{1,i}d_{2,i} + (1-y)\displaystyle\sum_{i=0}^{\min(m_1,m_2)-3} d_{1,i+1}d_{2,i}}{\sqrt{\displaystyle\sum_{i=0}^{m_1-2} d_{1,i}^2}\sqrt{\displaystyle\sum_{i=0}^{m_2-2} d_{2,i}^2}}\right)
$$

(10)

This formula suggests two important observations. Firstly, if $y = 0$ or 1, we obtain the correlation coefficient of two systems applied at the same time as stated in proposition 1. Secondly, the correlation coefficient is symmetrical around $y = 0.5$ ($n = 12$ hours). This means that a one-hour lag will produce the same correlation coefficient as a 23-hour lag.

Table 5.3 quantifies the correlation coefficient of a system applied to the same underlying market ($\rho_x = 1$) such that the time of the day effect is isolated. The systems we have considered are the simple moving averages of orders 2, 5, 10, 20, 40 and 80. For instance the correlation coefficient between the simple moving average of order 2 lagged 4 hours is equal to 0.540. Not surprisingly, the rows indicate that the correlation coefficient will be minimum if $y = 0.5$ (12 hours). The columns indicate that longer systems are associated with higher correlation coefficients, and as the order is lengthened, the time lag becomes less important. If we consider a simple moving average of order 40, the smallest coefficient correlation we can obtain using a different time of the day to trigger the position is 0.876. Therefore there can be some value in time diversification, but this must be for very short order systems (up to 5). As trading rules become increasingly short term in their focus, the 'time of the day' effect becomes more significant (Figure 5.4).

Formula (10) has many potential applications. Merely observing only rule return correlation does not provide insights on what contributes the most to the rule return correlation:

Table 5.3 Correlation $\mathrm{corr}(R_{1,t}, R_{1,t'})$ between a system applied at lagged times

System\LAG	0	1	2	3	4	5	6	7	8	9	10	11	12
S(2)	1	0.783	0.681	0.603	0.54	0.488	0.445	0.41	0.382	0.36	0.345	0.336	0.333
S(3)	1	0.833	0.756	0.697	0.65	0.61	0.578	0.551	0.53	0.514	0.503	0.496	0.494
S(5)	1	0.876	0.82	0.776	0.741	0.712	0.689	0.669	0.654	0.642	0.634	0.629	0.627
S(10)	1	0.915	0.876	0.847	0.823	0.803	0.787	0.774	0.763	0.755	0.75	0.746	0.745
S(20)	1	0.941	0.914	0.893	0.877	0.863	0.852	0.843	0.835	0.83	0.826	0.824	0.823
S(40)	1	0.958	0.94	0.925	0.914	0.904	0.896	0.89	0.885	0.881	0.878	0.876	0.876
S(80)	1	0.971	0.957	0.947	0.939	0.932	0.927	0.922	0.919	0.916	0.914	0.913	0.912

- the underlying correlation: ρ_x
- the systems correlation: product of linear coefficients $d_{1,i} d_{2,i}$
- the lagged time: y

On the other hand, the estimate of underlying correlation ρ_x between financial markets is sufficient to obtain an estimate of any linear rule returns correlations applied at different times of the day, which may not be observable at all. Indeed the systems correlation and the lagged time are constant, and so do not need to be estimated.

5.2.2 Time Aggregation

The key characteristics of financial markets are the different time horizons of their participants, some of whom trade short term, whereas others trade long term. In the FX market, market makers are at the short end of the scale while central banks can usually be characterised as long-term participants. For instance, to take advantage of the lag adjustment between interest rate and exchange rates moves, investors need to tie up their money for months or even years, a very long time for a forex trader. Some investors will thus tend to ignore these profit opportunities while others will decide to take a position. Even if investors choose similar strategies such as trend-following rules, their

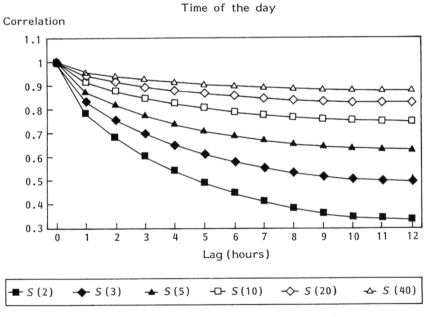

Figure 5.4 Rule returns correlation as a function of the lag

rates of return are likely to be different because of different holding periods. Long-term investors such as pension funds might want to consider only low frequency data (daily or weekly) whereas spot dealers will look at high frequency data (minute by minute). We present here another study where we vary the length of the period (daily, weekly) while keeping constant the point at which a new signal is triggered (close of the market).

For instance, let us assume that a pension fund follows a simple moving average of order 2, on weekly rates, when a trader applies the same system to daily rates. The aggregate time unit is here equal to 5 if we assume that a week includes five working days. Once again, the theoretical correlation between the returns generated by the two strategies can be worked out under the random walk assumption (see Appendix). This is equal to 0.059. This elementary example shows that time aggregation can differentiate trading rules as much, if not more, than different orders of trading rules applied to the same disaggregate series. Table 5.4 demonstrates that simple moving average methods applied every other day exhibit low positive correlations with systems applied daily. This effect is accentuated when the aggregation is done over a week (five working days, Table 5.5).

Table 5.4 Rule returns correlation under the random walk assumption

Aggregate(2) Disaggregate	S(2)	S(3)	S(5)	S(10)	S(20)	S(40)	S(80)
S(2)	0.250	0.218	0.173	0.123	0.087	0.062	0.044
S(3)	0.500	0.414	0.318	0.223	0.157	0.111	0.078
S(5)	0.583	0.658	0.520	0.365	0.256	0.181	0.128
S(10)	0.468	0.621	0.784	0.599	0.422	0.297	0.210
S(20)	0.342	0.461	0.626	0.858	0.641	0.452	0.318
S(40)	0.245	0.329	0.449	0.658	0.904	0.665	0.467
S(80)	0.174	0.233	0.318	0.467	0.674	0.934	0.677

Table 5.5 Rule returns correlation under the random walk assumption

Aggregate(5) Disaggregate	S(2)	S(3)	S(5)	S(10)	S(20)	S(40)	S(80)
S(2)	0.059	0.052	0.042	0.031	0.022	0.016	0.011
S(3)	0.108	0.095	0.076	0.055	0.039	0.028	0.020
S(5)	0.229	0.199	0.158	0.113	0.080	0.057	0.040
S(10)	0.483	0.470	0.377	0.262	0.187	0.133	0.095
S(20)	0.474	0.606	0.648	0.481	0.336	0.240	0.171
S(40)	0.368	0.492	0.656	0.740	0.542	0.380	0.271
S(80)	0.269	0.3661	0.492	0.712	0.798	0.577	0.407

5.3   TRADING RULE CORRELATIONS: AN EMPIRICAL STUDY

Having established expected correlations under the random walk assumption, we can now test whether correlations observed in financial markets are more likely to be generated from random walks than from inefficient markets. On the one hand, an excessively high correlation between trend-following strategies would mean that the trading rules are on the same side of the market significantly more than might be expected if the generating process were random. This would imply that the market exhibits trends and therefore positive autocorrelations. On the other hand, an excessively low correlation between trend-following strategies would suggest that the trading rules are on the opposite side of the market significantly more than might be expected from a random process. This could be explained by the presence of contrarian moves or negative autocorrelations.

5.3.1   Underlying Financial Markets

Various financial markets have been considered in this part of the study. They are:

1. Spot foreign exchange transactions: dollar against Deutsche Mark (USD/ DEM) and pound sterling against dollar (GBP/USD).
2. Futures contracts: CAC–Matif, FTSE–Liffe, German Government Bonds– Liffe (GGB), Gilts–Liffe, Cocoa–LCE (London Commodity Exchange), Coffee–LCE.

Our simulations roll forward each futures contract as it approaches the settlement date, just as a futures trader would. The futures contracts are the first future contract until the last trading day for Liffe and Matif contracts. For the London Commodity Exchange, contracts rollovers have occurred two weeks before the first trading day of the delivery month. For all futures contracts, a unique time series of logarithmic returns has been constructed as $X_t = \ln(P_t/P_{t-1})$. An example of rollovers is given in Table 5.6 for the Cocoa series. This particular time series is for the period 13–19 June 1990: $\{X_t\} = \{-3.05\%, 1.41\%, -0.62\%, -1\%\}$.

The times of the day investigated are specified in Table 5.7. Table 5.8 provides summary statistics including autocorrelations of order k, $r[k]$, for the closing time series. The assets investigated here include a wide range of volatilities, skewness, kurtosis and autocorrelations. The daily volatility varies

Table 5.6 Futures time series

Date	Delivery Month	Price (July 90)	Price (Sept. 90)	Logarithmic returns
13 June 1990	July 1990	800		
14 June 1990	July 1990	776		$-3.05\% = \ln(776/800)$
15 June 1990	July 1990	787	808	$1.41\% = \ln(787/776)$
18 June 1990	Sept 1990		803	$-0.62\% = \ln(803/808)$
19 June 1990	Sept 1990		795	$-1.00\% = \ln(795/803)$

Table 5.7 London times of price series

USD/ DEM	GBP/ USD	CAC	FTSE	Cocoa	Gilts	GGB
8.00	8.00	9.00 (open)	8.35 (open)	9.35 (open)	8.32 (open)	7.30 (open)
12.00						
16.00	16.00	16.00 (close)	16.10 (close)	16.45 (close)	16.15 (close)	16.15 (close)

from 0.343% for German Bonds to 1.641% for Cocoa. The sample is therefore considered representative of various market conditions.

5.3.2 Intra-market Correlations

The sample correlation between two times series x and y of length n has been estimated through the standard formula:

$$r(x, y) = \frac{1}{(n-1)} \sum_{i=1}^{n} (x_i - \bar{x})(y_i - \bar{y})$$

$$\times \left[\sqrt{\frac{1}{n-1} \sum_{i=1}^{n} (x_i - \bar{x})^2} \sqrt{\frac{1}{n-1} \sum_{i=1}^{n} (y_i - \bar{y})^2} \right]^{-1}$$

where

$$\bar{x} = \sum_{i=1}^{n} x_i \qquad \bar{y} = \sum_{i=1}^{n} y_i \qquad (11)$$

To determine the significance level, we use the fact that $z = \frac{1}{2}\log[(1+r)/(1-r)]$ is approximately normally distributed with mean $\mu_z = \frac{1}{2}\log[(1+\rho)/(1-\rho)]$ and variance $\sigma_z^2 = 1/(n-3)$ where ρ is the expected correlation

Table 5.8 Summary statistics, 3 January 1989–30 June 1994

	USD/DEM	GBP/USD	CAC	FTSE	Cocoa	Gilts	GGB
Sample size	1386	1386	1371	1388	1388	1409	1409
Average	-0.0073%	-0.0122%	-0.0073%	0.0119%	-0.0566%	-0.00219%	-0.00482%
Median	-0.0060%	0.0110%	0.0000%	0.0000%	-0.1250%	0.00000%	0.00000%
Variance	0.0052%	0.0052%	0.0154%	0.0100%	0.0269%	0.00299%	0.00118%
Standard deviation	0.7213%	0.7189%	1.2397%	0.9996%	1.6411%	0.54663%	0.34302%
Minimum	-3.4826%	-3.9481%	-7.6764%	-6.5567%	-6.6335%	-2.19125%	-1.94871%
Maximum	3.3418%	3.2609%	8.6266%	4.9636%	9.7672%	3.65441%	2.29646%
Skewness	0.202	-0.263	-0.113	-0.182	0.268	0.40092	0.00754
Standardised skewness	3.074	-3.992	-1.714	-2.776	4.079	6.14384	0.11551
Kurtosis	1.820	2.137	4.292	2.419	2.414	3.68470	5.31640
Standardised kurtosis	13.831	16.236	32.441	18.396	18.357	28.23270	40.73500
r[1]	0.04105	0.0967^a	-0.00127	-0.01158	0.05341^a	0.02931	0.03129
r[2]	-0.02201	0.0119	-0.01141	-0.02108	-0.05805^a	-0.00073	-0.04589
r[3]	-0.0284	-0.03141	-0.02096	-0.01793	-0.01594	-0.01067	0.03289
r[4]	0.04379	0.05231	0.05556^a	0.05513^a	0.06241^a	0.02160	0.05920^a
r[5]	0.03944	0.04713	-0.02782	0.01614	0.00842	0.02870	-0.01410
r[6]	-0.01555	-0.00583	-0.03244	-0.03038	-0.04939	-0.02543	-0.02962
r[7]	-0.03556	-0.04909	-0.01328	-0.05958^a	-0.00723	-0.04542	0.03844
r[8]	0.03418	0.02692	0.00563	0.05455^a	0.0214	0.05087	0.01079
r[9]	0.03075	0.02136	0.02034	0.00899	0.01909	0.01183	-0.06821^a
r[10]	-0.00938	0.03993	0.05751^a	0.0214	0.05255	0.04389	-0.04472
r[11]	-0.03833	-0.03366	-0.01163	-0.01585	-0.02881	0.02396	0.04210
r[12]	0.00652	0.02144	0.01643	0.0166	-0.06949^a	-0.02716	0.02780
r[13]	-0.00143	0.00008	-0.01608	0.02979	-0.0063	0.03072	0.00849
r[14]	0.02758	0.01933	-0.03982	0.02634	0.01728	-0.01409	0.04395
r[15]	-0.00148	0.02189	0.00466	-0.01437	0.02667	-0.04923	0.03625
r[16]	-0.03074	0.01143	-0.01201	0.00178	-0.03237	-0.01963	-0.02450
r[17]	-0.02052	-0.03533	-0.00998	-0.03766	-0.02405	0.02636	0.00353
r[18]	-0.032	-0.03969	-0.00082	0.01577	0.05286	-0.00957	-0.00431
r[19]	0.05988^a	0.00061	-0.05745^a	-0.00804	0.04603	-0.02314	0.06408^a
r[20]	0.03875	0.01422	0.01593	0.00051	0.00719	0.03362	-0.05739^a

^{a}Significant at the critical level of 5%.

coefficient. More details concerning this test can be found in Johnson and Wichern (1982).

Overall, theoretical correlations between trading systems applied to the same market (Table 5.1) closely estimate the observed correlations (Table 5.9 and Figure 5.5). The most significant departures occur, by decreasing order, for Cocoa, FTSE, Gilts and CAC. This may mean that the random walk assumption is less appropriate for these contracts and more acceptable for the USD/DEM, GBP/USD and German Government Bonds. In all cases, theoretical correlations are good ex-ante estimates since there are almost as

Table 5.9 Empirical correlations from time series at market close

USD/DEM	S(2)	S(3)	S(5)	S(10)	S(20)	S(40)	S(80)
S(2)	1	0.729	0.502	0.359	0.223	0.183	0.229[a]
S(3)		1	0.699	0.482	0.304	0.216	0.231[a]
S(5)			1	0.694	0.472	0.281	0.261
S(10)				1	0.630[a]	0.359[a]	0.266[a]
S(20)					1	0.628[a]	0.454
S(40)						1	0.663
S(80)							1
GBP/USD							
S(2)	1	0.714	0.539	0.339	0.251	0.210	0.188[a]
S(3)		1	0.699	0.474	0.319	0.224	0.172
S(5)			1	0.718[a]	0.525[a]	0.374[a]	0.244
S(10)				1	0.739[a]	0.496	0.337
S(20)					1	0.693	0.478
S(40)						1	0.664
S(80)							1
CAC							
S(2)	1	0.618[a]	0.530	0.339	0.239	0.174	0.146
S(3)		1	0.646[a]	0.350[a]	0.270[a]	0.188	0.161
S(5)			1	0.648	0.493	0.396[a]	0.300[a]
S(10)				1	0.678	0.532[a]	0.402[a]
S(20)					1	0.779[a]	0.621[a]
S(40)						1	0.734[a]
S(80)							1
FTSE							
S(2)	1	0.636[a]	0.462[a]	0.253[a]	0.109[a]	0.057[a]	−0.048[a]
S(3)		1	0.704	0.403[a]	0.279[a]	0.204	0.218
S(5)			1	0.630[a]	0.415[a]	0.260[a]	0.129[a]
S(10)				1	0.639[a]	0.481	0.326
S(20)					1	0.747[a]	0.509
S(40)						1	0.731[a]
S(80)							1

continued overleaf

Table 5.9 (*continued*)

USD/DEM	S(2)	S(3)	S(5)	S(10)	S(20)	S(40)	S(80)
Cocoa	1	0.636[a]	0.466[a]	0.288[a]	0.164[a]	0.181	0.108
S(2)							
S(3)		1	0.769[a]	0.528[a]	0.331	0.315[a]	0.281[a]
S(5)			1	0.706[a]	0.475	0.377[a]	0.318[a]
S(10)				1	0.617[a]	0.404[a]	0.331
S(20)					1	0.724[a]	0.547[a]
S(40)						1	0.746[a]
S(80)							1
German Government Bond							
S(2)	1	0.715	0.508	0.373	0.261	0.159	0.134
S(3)		1	0.732	0.513	0.372	0.285	0.261[a]
S(5)			1	0.658	0.437	0.346	0.244
S(10)				1	0.657	0.485	0.333
S(20)					1	0.765[a]	0.552[a]
S(40)						1	0.725[a]
S(80)							1
Gilts							
S(2)	1	0.724	0.551	0.375	0.227	0.090[a]	0.014[a]
S(3)		1	0.696	0.489	0.295	0.095[a]	−0.009[a]
S(5)			1	0.603[a]	0.405[a]	0.189[a]	0.088[a]
S(10)				1	0.700	0.396[a]	0.223[a]
S(20)					1	0.643[a]	0.422[a]
S(40)						1	0.722[a]
S(80)							1

[a]Significantly different from ρ_0 at the critical level of 5%.

many statistically significant overestimations of correlations (29) than underestimations (30).

5.3.3 Inter-markets Correlations

The correlations between similar trading rules applied to different underlying markets has been studied, but only for time series for which the closing times are strictly identical. They are the USD/DEM, GBP/USD and CAC at 16.00, and the gilts and government bonds at 16.15. Underlying market correlations have been estimated here using equation (11). Then expected correlations between similar trading rules applied to different markets have been worked out assuming the underlying correlation to be known through the use of formula (9). Again, observed correlations do not significantly deviate from their theoretical expectations (Table 5.10). There are, however, significant

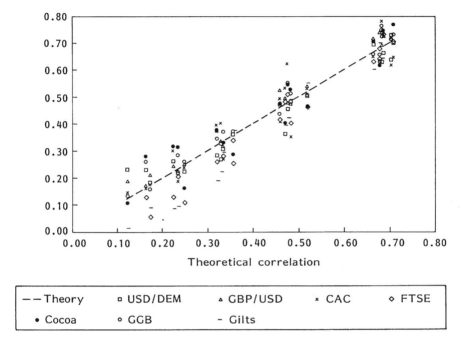

Figure 5.5 Rules returns correlation: intra-markets

Table 5.10 Inter-market correlations

Assets	USD/DEM, GBP/USD	USD/DEM, CAC	GBP/USD, CAC	GGB, Gilts
Underlying correlation ρ_x	−0.841	−0.101	0.085	0.450
Expected correlation of identical rule applied to both assets $\rho_0 = (2/\pi)\rho_x \arcsin(\rho_x)$	0.535	0.007	0.005	0.134
$S(2)$	0.554	0.017	−0.003	0.234[a]
$S(3)$	0.558	0.057	0.010	0.200[a]
$S(5)$	0.557	0.073[a]	−0.004	0.182
$S(10)$	0.558	0.029	−0.030	0.174
$S(20)$	0.479[a]	0.140[a]	0.009	0.288[a]
$S(40)$	0.603[a]	0.118[a]	0.067[a]	0.308[a]
$S(80)$	0.588[a]	0.098[a]	0.064[a]	0.313[a]

[a] Significantly different from ρ_0 at the critical level of 5%.

departures between the gilts and the GGB, especially for long-term orders trading rules. Gilts and GGB seem to be more correlated over long-term periods than indicated by the underlying correlation.

5.3.4 Correlations Between Close to Close Trading Rules with Open to Open Trading Rules

The time of the day effect has been investigated by comparing positions triggered by a similar trading rule at the opening time and positions triggered at closing times of the futures contract. For the spot foreign exchange, the opening and closing times have been respectively fixed at 8.00 and 16.00 London time.

Observed correlations are slightly below their expected values for the CAC, FTSE and above for the gilts, Cocoa and GBP/USD (Table 5.11 and Figure 5.6). For instance, the correlation between the simple moving average of order 2 triggered at opening time and at closing time for the CAC is equal to 0.303 which is about 25% less than the value (0.410) which would be expected from a seven-hour lagged random walk.

In the case of GGB, observed correlations are close to their expected values, suggesting that it may follow a random walk. For the USD/DEM, correlations between close and open rules are slightly above their expectations for short order systems and slightly below for long order ones. The time of the day effect been investigated further for the USD/DEM by additionally considering positions triggered at 12.00 London time (Table 5.12). This is just before the announcement of major news and might therefore signify a split between morning and afternoon activities. The results are in this case quite spectacular. All the correlations between midday and open rules are largely above their expectations, whereas most of the correlations between close and midday rules are below. The explanation for this may well lie in the presence of respectively positive/negative autocorrelations.

Table 5.11 Correlations between identical trading rules triggered on close and on open

	Theory 7h	CAC	Theory 7h45	FTSE	Gilts	Theory 7h10	Cocoa	Theory 8h45	GGB
$S(2)$	0.410	0.303[a]	0.388	0.304[a]	0.448[a]	0.405	0.503[a]	0.365	0.345
$S(3)$	0.551	0.500[a]	0.535	0.502	0.628[a]	0.547	0.571	0.518	0.514
$S(5)$	0.669	0.665	0.657	0.569[a]	0.723[a]	0.666	0.651	0.645	0.654
$S(10)$	0.774	0.716[a]	0.766	0.715[a]	0.773	0.772	0.765	0.757	0.786[a]
$S(20)$	0.843	0.845	0.837	0.753[a]	0.809[a]	0.841	0.860[a]	0.831	0.803
$S(40)$	0.89	0.881	0.886	0.837[a]	0.889	0.889	0.923[a]	0.882	0.840[a]
$S(80)$	0.922	0.891[a]	0.919	0.918	0.853[a]	0.922	0.931[a]	0.917	0.926[a]

[a]Significantly different from ρ_0 at the critical level of 5%.

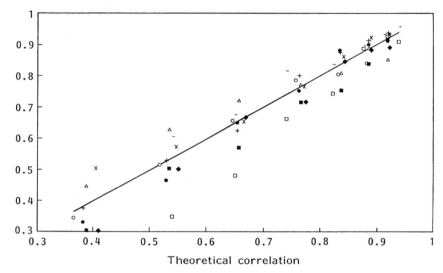

Rule returns correlation

Same rule, same asset, lagged positions close/open

◆ Cac	■ Ftse	▵ Gilts	× Cocoa	○ GGB	• $/Dem	+ Gbp/$
- $/Dem (12/8)		□ $/Dem (16/12)		— Theoretical		

Figure 5.6 Rule returns correlation: Lagged positions

Table 5.12 USD/DEM and GBP/USD: Correlations between close and open rules

	Theory 8h	USD/DEM Close/open	GBP/USD Close/open	Theory 4h	USD/DEM Midday/open	USD/DEM Close/ midday
$S(2)$	0.382	0.332[a]	0.376	0.540	0.605[a]	0.349[a]
$S(3)$	0.53	0.466[a]	0.528	0.650	0.674	0.480[a]
$S(5)$	0.654	0.649	0.623	0.741	0.815[a]	0.660[a]
$S(10)$	0.763	0.752	0.800[a]	0.823	0.835	0.743[a]
$S(20)$	0.835	0.880[a]	0.874[a]	0.877	0.897[a]	0.886
$S(40)$	0.885	0.900[a]	0.913[a]	0.914	0.937[a]	0.932[a]
$S(80)$	0.919	0.911	0.936[a]	0.939	0.957[a]	0.907[a]

[a]Significantly different from ρ_0 at the critical level of 5%.

5.3.4 Time Aggregation

Theoretical correlations are good *ex-ante* estimates of observed correlations (Table 5.13). The GGB exhibit the most significant departures. Overall there are slightly more observations above their expected values (15) than below (9). This would favour the hypothesis of trends over long-term intervals.

5.4 CONCLUSIONS

Correlations between trading rules applied to a same asset are non-zero, and may even be highly positive for trend-following systems. Correlations between the same trading rule applied to multiple assets are positive but lower in absolute value than correlations between underlying markets.

On the one hand, theoretical correlations between trading rules applied to the same underlying market do not depend on the market itself but only on the rules. This is equivalent to the assumption that the past correlation matrix contains information about what the rules correlation will be in the future but no information about the market. This assumes that there is a common mean correlation between rules irrespective of the markets.

On the other hand, theoretical correlations between the same trading rule applied to different underlying markets do not depend on the rule itself but only on the underlying markets. This assumes that there is a common mean correlation between underlying markets irrespective of the dynamic trading rules.

The time of the day effect is measured by establishing the correlation between identical daily trading rules applied to the same underlying market but lagged a few hours. The correlation is a negative function of the lag up to 12 hours. This increases when the order of the rule increases. A portfolio including different daily strategies applied at particular times of the day may well be an alternative to high frequency trading rules. Indeed such strategies may re-tain the specificity of each centre by focusing on a given time of the day while filtering other times which may present different patterns or even induce noise.

The success of theoretical correlations in forecasting observed trading rule correlations should not be surprising. Indeed, Elton and Gruber (1973) and Elton *et al.* (1978) have demonstrated the usefulness of averaging (smoothing) some of the data in the historical correlation matrix for forecasting purposes. The knowledge of theoretical trading rule correlations has many potential app-lications, including the construction of an efficient portfolio as well as the identification of a random walk from the joint profitability of technical trading rules.

Table 5.13 Correlations between daily and each two daily trading rules

Disaggregate\aggregate(2)	Theory	USD/DEM	GBP/USD	FTSE	CAC	Cocoa	GGB	Gilt
S(2)	0.250	0.253	0.363[a]	0.191[a]	0.202	0.331[a]	0.176[a]	0.297
S(3)	0.414	0.362[a]	0.462[a]	0.408	0.346[a]	0.379	0.415	0.403
S(5)	0.520	0.559[a]	0.588[a]	0.478[a]	0.529	0.485	0.510	0.475[a]
S(10)	0.599	0.552[a]	0.678[a]	0.570	0.622	0.617	0.633[a]	0.645[a]
S(20)	0.641	0.628	0.629	0.697[a]	0.742[a]	0.711[a]	0.748[a]	0.585[a]
S(40)	0.665	0.671	0.667	0.699[a]	0.711[a]	0.596[a]	0.752[a]	0.650

[a]Significantly different from ρ_0 at the critical level of 5%.

APPENDIX

Proofs of Propositions

Proposition 1

By assumption, $X_{1,t}$ and $X_{2,t}$ are normally distributed with

$$E(X_{1,t}) = 0 \qquad E(X_{2,t}) = 0 \qquad \text{var}(X_{1,t}) = \sigma_1^2 \qquad \text{var}(X_{2,t}) = \sigma_2^2$$

That implies that $F_{1,t}$ and $F_{2,t}$ are normally distributed with

$$E(F_{1,t}) = 0 \quad E(F_{2,t}) = 0 \quad \text{var}(F_{1,t}) = \sigma_1^2 \sum_{i=0}^{m_1-2} d_{1,i}^2 \quad \text{var}(F_{2,t}) = \sigma_2^2 \sum_{i=0}^{m_2-2} d_{2,i}^2$$

$$\text{cov}(F_{1,t}, F_{2,t}) = E(F_{1,t}, F_{2,t}) = \sigma_1 \sigma_2 \rho_x \sum_{i=0}^{\min(m_1, m_2)-2} d_{1,i} d_{2,i}$$

$$\Rightarrow \text{corr}(F_{1,t}, F_{2,t}) = \rho_{F_{1,2}} = \rho_x \rho_F \quad \text{where } \rho_F = \frac{\displaystyle\sum_{i=0}^{\min(m_1, m_2)-2} d_{1,i} d_{2,i}}{\sqrt{\displaystyle\sum_{i=0}^{m_1-2} d_{1,i}^2} \sqrt{\displaystyle\sum_{i=0}^{m_2-2} d_{2,i}^2}}$$

$$E(B_{1,t}) = \Pr(F_{1,t} > 0) - \Pr(F_{1,t} < 0) = 1 - 2 \cdot \Pr(F_{1,t} < 0) = 0$$

That is due to the fact that the distribution of the linear unbiased forecaster, $F_{1,t}$, is symmetrical around zero, as for the underlying returns X_t. It follows that similarly, $E(B_{2,t}) = 0$.

$$E(B_{1,t}^2) = E(B_{2,t}^2) = 1 \Rightarrow \text{var}(B_{1,t}) = \text{var}(B_{2,t}) = 1$$

$$\Rightarrow \rho(B_{1,t}, B_{2,t}) = \text{cov}(B_{1,t}, B_{2,t}) = E(B_{1,t}, B_{2,t})$$

$$= \Pr(F_{1,t} > 0, F_{2,t} > 0) + \Pr(F_{1,t} < 0, F_{2,t} < 0)$$

$$- \Pr(F_{1,t} > 0, F_{2,t} < 0) - \Pr(F_{1,t} < 0, F_{2,t} > 0)$$

$$= 2\{\Pr(F_{1,t} > 0, F_{2,t} > 0) - \Pr(F_{1,t} > 0, F_{2,t} < 0)\} \quad \text{(by symmetry)}$$

$$= 2\{[0, 0](\rho_{F_{1,2}}) - [0, 0](-\rho_{F_{1,2}})\}$$

where $\rho_{F_{1,2}}$ is as defined above and $[0, 0]$ is the bivariate truncated probability given by Johnson and Kotz (1972):

$$\rho_B = \rho(B_{1,t}, B_{2,t}) = \frac{2}{\pi} \text{arc} \sin(\rho_x \rho_F)$$

Acar (1993, Chapter 3) has shown that if the underlying time series X_t are independent identically normally distributed without drift and variance σ^2, linear rule returns R_t are independent normally identically distributed without drift and variance σ^2.

Applying this result, it follows that rule returns $R_{1,t}$ and $R_{2,t}$ are normally distributed with

$$E(R_{1,t}) = 0 \qquad E(R_{2,t}) = 0 \quad \text{and} \quad \text{cov}(R_{1,t}, R_{1,t+h}) = 0$$

$$\text{var}(R_{1,t}) = \sigma_1^2 \qquad \text{var}(R_{2,t}) = \sigma_2^2 \quad \text{and} \quad \text{cov}(R_{2,t}, R_{2,t+h}) = 0.$$

Covariances between trading rules are deduced from

$$\text{cov}(R_{1,t}, R_{2,t}) = E(R_{1,t} R_{2,t}) = E(B_{1,t-1} B_{2,t-1} X_{1,t} X_{2,t}) = E(B_{1,t-1} B_{2,t-1}) E(X_{1,t} X_{2,t})$$

We have just shown that:

$$E(B_{1,t-1} B_{2,t-1}) = \rho(B_{1,t-1}, B_{2,t-1}) = \frac{2}{\pi} \arcsin(\rho_x \rho_F)$$

Since by assumption $E(X_{1,t} X_{2,t}) = \sigma_1 \sigma_2 \rho_x$, it follows that

$$\text{cov}(R_{1,t}, R_{2,t}) = \sigma_1 \sigma_2 \rho_x \frac{2}{\pi} \arcsin(\rho_x \rho_F),$$

and then

$$\rho(R_{1,t}, R_{2,t}) = \frac{E(R_{1,t} R_{2,t})}{\sqrt{\text{var}(R_{1,t}) \text{var}(R_{2,t})}} = \frac{\sigma_1 \sigma_2 \rho_x (2/\pi) \arcsin(\rho_x \rho_F)}{\sigma_1 \sigma_2}$$

$$\Rightarrow \rho_R = \rho(R_{1,t}, R_{2,t}) = \frac{2}{\pi} \rho_x \arcsin(\rho_x \rho_F) \qquad (5)$$

In addition,

$$\rho(R_{1,t}, R_{2,t+h}) = \rho(R_{1,t+h}, R_{2,t}) = 0 \text{ for } h > 0$$

This result follows by noting that

$$\text{cov}(R_{1,t}, R_{2,t+h}) = E(B_{1,t-1} B_{2,t+h-1} X_{1,t} X_{2,t+h}) = E(B_{1,t-1} B_{2,t+h-1} X_{1,t}) E(X_{2,t+h}) = 0$$

$$\text{cov}(R_{1,t+h}, R_{2,t}) = E(B_{1,t+h-1} B_{2,t-1} X_{1,t+h} X_{2,t}) = E(B_{1,t+h-1} B_{2,t-1} X_{2,t}) E(X_{1,t+h}) = 0$$

Proposition 2: Times of the Day

Let us denote $P_{i,t}$ as the daily price of asset i $\{i = 1, 2\}$, at closing time t. The opening time is noted t^*, such that $t^* = t - y$ where $y = n/24$ and n is the number of hours separating the opening from closing time. Values of y are bounded between 0 and 1.

$$X_{i,t} = \ln(P_{i,t}/P_{i,t-1}), \text{ the underlying close to close return}$$

$$X_{i,t^*} = \ln(P_{i,t^*}/P_{i,t^*-1}), \text{ the underlying open to open return}$$

The first trading rule is applied to asset 1 from close to close and the second one to asset 2 from open to open. The close and open are lagged n hours ($y = n/24$ daily fraction). The rules we apply are linear and can be expressed as follows:

$$F_{1,\,t} = \sum_{j=0}^{m_1-1} d_{1,\,j} X_{1,\,t-j}$$

$$F_{2,\,t^*} = \sum_{j=0}^{m_2-1} d_{2,\,j} X_{2,\,t^*-j}$$

To establish the correlation coefficient, we must therefore evaluate rates of return over the same period, let us say from close to close. Then, adopting the notation used previously:

$$R_{1,\,t} = B_{1,\,t-1} \ln (P_{1,\,t}/P_{1,\,t-1}) = B_{1,\,t-1} \ln (P_{1,\,t^*}/P_{1,\,t-1}) + B_{1,\,t-1} \ln (P_{1,\,t}/P_{1,\,t^*})$$

$$R_{2,\,t} = B_{2,\,t^*-1} \ln (P_{2,\,t^*}/P_{2,\,t-1}) + B_{2,\,t^*} \ln (P_{2,\,t}/P_{2,\,t^*})$$

We now assume that the underlying assets follow a continuous bivariate normal random walk with

$$E(X_{1,\,t}) = 0 \qquad E(X_{2,\,t}) = 0 \quad \text{ar}\,(X_{1,\,t}) = \sigma_1^2 \qquad \text{var}\,(X_{2,\,t}) = \sigma_2^2 \quad \text{and}$$

$$E(X_{1,\,t} X_{2,\,t}) = \rho_x \sigma_1 \sigma_2$$

Then

$$E(R_{1,\,t} R_{2,\,t}) = E(B_{1,\,t-1} B_{2,\,t^*-1})(1-y)\rho_x \sigma_1 \sigma_2 + E(B_{1,\,t-1} B_{2,\,t^*})y\rho_x \sigma_1 \sigma_2$$

Using the results of proposition 1 and after rearrangements of terms, it is straightforward to show that

$$E(B_{1,\,t-1} B_{2,\,t^*-1}) = \frac{2}{\pi} \arcsin \left(\rho_x \frac{(1-y)\displaystyle\sum_{i=0}^{\min\,(m_1,\,m_2)-2} d_{1,\,i} d_{2,\,i} + y \displaystyle\sum_{i=0}^{\min\,(m_1,\,m_2)-3} d_{1,\,i} d_{2,\,i+1}}{\sqrt{\displaystyle\sum_{i=0}^{m_1-2} d_{1,\,i}^2} \sqrt{\displaystyle\sum_{i=0}^{m_2-2} d_{2,\,i}^2}} \right)$$

$$E(B_{1,\,t-1} B_{2,\,t^*}) = \frac{2}{\pi} \arcsin \left(\rho_x \frac{y\displaystyle\sum_{i=0}^{\min\,(m_1,\,m_2)-2} d_{1,\,i} d_{2,\,i} + (1-y) \displaystyle\sum_{i=0}^{\min\,(m_1,\,m_2)-3} d_{1,\,i+1} d_{2,\,i}}{\sqrt{\displaystyle\sum_{i=0}^{m_1-2} d_{1,\,i}^2} \sqrt{\displaystyle\sum_{i=0}^{m_2-2} d_{2,\,i}^2}} \right)$$

Since $\text{var}\,(R_{1,\,t}) = \sigma_1^2$, $\text{var}\,(R_{2,\,t}) = \sigma_2^2$, we have

$$\rho_R = (1-y)\frac{2}{\pi}\rho_x \arcsin \left(\rho_x \frac{(1-y)\displaystyle\sum_{i=0}^{\min\,(m_1,\,m_2)-2} d_{1,\,i} d_{2,\,i} + y \displaystyle\sum_{i=0}^{\min\,(m_1,\,m_2)-3} d_{1,\,i} d_{2,\,i+1}}{\sqrt{\displaystyle\sum_{i=0}^{m_1-2} d_{1,\,i}^2} \sqrt{\displaystyle\sum_{i=0}^{m_2-2} d_{2,\,i}^2}} \right)$$

$$+ y\frac{2}{\pi}\rho_x \text{ arc sin} \left(\rho_x \frac{y\displaystyle\sum_{i=0}^{\min(m_1,m_2)-2} d_{1,i}d_{2,i} + (1-y)\displaystyle\sum_{i=0}^{\min(m_1,m_2)-3} d_{1,i+1}d_{2,i}}{\sqrt{\displaystyle\sum_{i=0}^{m_1-2} d_{1,i}^2}\sqrt{\displaystyle\sum_{i=0}^{m_2-2} d_{2,i}^2}} \right) \tag{10}$$

Proposition 3: Time Aggregation

Let us denote X_t^* the underlying return over n days:

$$X_t^* = X_t + X_{t-1} + \ldots + X_{t-n+1}$$

We assume that a first trading rule is applied to daily rates of return. The forecast is defined as

$$F_{1,t} = \sum_{i=0}^{m_1-1} \lambda_i X_{t-i}$$

Then a second trading rule is applied to aggregated rates of return. The forecast is defined as

$$F_{2,t} = \sum_{i=0}^{m_2-1} \gamma_i X_{t-i}^* = \sum_{i=0}^{m_2-1} \gamma_i \left(\sum_{j=i}^{i+n-1} X_{t-j} \right)$$

The rates of return generated by both strategies are over a period of n days:

$$R_{1,n} = B_{1,t}X_{t+1} + B_{1,t+1}X_{t+2} + \ldots + B_{1,t+n-1}X_{t+n}$$
$$R_{2,n} = B_{2,t}X_{t+1} + B_{2,t}X_{t+2} + \ldots + B_{2,t}X_{t+n}$$

We can now calculate the correlation coefficient between the two returns. Since

$$E(R_{1,n}) = E(R_{2,n}) = 0$$

$$V(R_{1,n}) = V(R_{2,n}) = n\sigma^2$$

$$E(R_{1,n}R_{2,n}) = \{E(B_{1,t}B_{2,t}) + E(B_{1,t+1}B_{2,t}) + \ldots + E(B_{1,t+n-1}B_{2,t})\}\sigma^2$$

where

$$E(B_{1,t}B_{2,t+k}) = \frac{2}{\pi} \text{ arc sin} (\rho_{t+k})$$

where

$$\rho_{t+k} = \frac{E(F_{1,t}F_{2,t+k})}{\sqrt{\text{var}(F_{1,t})\text{var}(F_{2,t})}} k = 0, n-1$$

(see proposition 1). Then

$$\text{corr}(R_{1,n}R_{2,n}) = \frac{E(B_{1,t}B_{2,t}) + E(B_{1,t+1}B_{2,t}) + \ldots + E(B_{1,t+n-1}B_{2,t})}{n}$$

END NOTES

1. See Acar (1993) for a detailed discussion on the stochastic properties of the simple moving average method.
2. Proofs of propositions are given in the Appendix.

REFERENCES

Acar, E. (1993), 'Economic Evaluation of Financial Forecasting', Ph.D Thesis, City University London.

Aggarwal, R. and Park, Y.S. (1994), 'The Relationships between Daily US and Japanese Equity Prices: Evidence from Spot Versus Futures Markets', *Journal of Banking and Finance*, **18**, 757–773.

Brock, W., Lakonishok, J. and LeBaron, B. (1992), 'Simple Technical Rules and the Stochastic Properties of Stock Returns', *Journal of Finance*, **47**, 1731–1764.

Brorsen, B.W. and Boyd, M.S. (1990), 'Reducing Profit Variability from Technical Trading systems', *Technical Analysis of Stocks and Commodities*, March, 23–32.

Brorsen, B.W. and Lukac, L.P. (1990), 'Optimal Portfolios for Commodity Futures Funds', *Journal of Futures Markets*, **10**(3), 247–258.

Dacorogna, M.M., Müller, U.A., Jost, C., Pictet, O.V., Olsen R.B., and Ward, J.R. (1994), 'Heterogeneous Real-time Trading Strategies in the Foreign Exchange Market', *Presentation at the International Conference on Forecasting Financial Markets: New Advances for Exchange Rates and Stock Prices*, 2–4 February 1994, in London.

Dunis, C. (1989), 'Computerised Technical Systems and Exchange Rate Movements', in Dunis, C. and Feeny, M. (eds), *Exchange Rate Forecasting*, Woodhead-Faulkner, Cambridge, pp. 165–205.

Elton, E.J. and Gruber, M.J. (1973), 'Estimating the Dependence Structure of Share Prices—Implications for Portfolio Selection', *Journal of Finance*, **8**(5), 1203–1232.

Elton, E.J., Gruber, M.J. and Urich, T. (1978), 'Are Betas Best?', *Journal of Finance*, **23**(5), 1375–1384.

Johnson, N.L. and Kotz, S. (1972), *Distributions in Statistics: Continuous Multivariate Distributions*, John Wiley & Sons, New York.

Johnson, R.A. and Wichern, D.W. (1982), *Applied Multivariate Statistical Analysis*, Prentice Hall, New Jersey.

LeBaron, B. (1991), 'Technical Trading Rules and Regime Shifts in Foreign Exchange', University of Wisconsin, Social Science Research, Working Paper 9118.

LeBaron, B. (1992), 'Do Moving Average Trading Rule Results Imply Nonlinearities in Foreign Exchange Markets', University of Wisconsin, Social Science Research, Working Paper 9222.

Levich, R.M. and Thomas, L.R. (1993), 'The Significance of Technical Trading-Rule Profits in the Foreign Exchange Market: a Bootstrap Approach', *Journal of International Money and Finance*, **12**, 451–474.

Lin, W.L., Engle, R.F. and Ito, T. (1994), 'Do Bull and Bears Move Across Borders? International Transmission of Stock Returns and Volatility', *The Review of Financial Studies*, **7**(3), 507–538.

Lukac, L.P., Brorsen, B.W. and Irwin, S.H. (1988), 'Similarity of Computer Guided Technical Trading Systems', *Journal of Futures Markets*, **8**(1), 1–13.

Neftçi, S.N. (1991), 'Naive Trading Rules in Financial Markets and Wiener-Kolmogorov Prediction Theory: A Study of "Technical Analysis"', *Journal of Business*, **64**, 549–571.

Neftçi, S.N. and Policano, A.J. (1984), 'Can Chartists Outperform the Market? Market Efficiency Tests for "Technical Analysis"', *Journal of Futures Markets*, **4**(4), 465–478.

Prado, R. (1992), *Design, Testing, and Optimization of Trading Systems*, John Wiley & Sons, New York.

Praetz, P.D. (1979), 'A General Test of a Filter Effect', *Journal of Financial and Quantitative Analysis*, **14**, 385–394.

Silber, W. (1994), 'Technical Trading: When it Works and When it Doesn't', *The Journal of Derivatives*, Spring, 39–44.

Surajaras, P. and Sweeney, R.J. (1992), *Profit-making Speculation in Foreign Exchange Markets* The Political Economy of Global Interdependence, Westview Press, Boulder, Colo.

Sweeney, R.J. (1986), 'Beating the Foreign Exchange Market', *Journal of Finance*, **41**, 163–182.

Sweeney, R.J. (1988), 'Some New Filter Rule Tests: Method and Results', *Journal of Financial and Quantitative Analysis*, **23**, 285–300.

Taylor, S.J. (1986), *Modelling Financial Time Series*, John Wiley & Sons, Chichester.

Taylor, S.J. (1990a), 'Reward Available to Currency Futures Speculators: Compensation for Risk or Evidence of Inefficient Pricing?', *Economic Record (Supplement)*, **68**, 105–116.

Taylor, S.J. (1990b), 'Profitable Currency Futures Trading: A Comparison of Technical and Time-Series Trading Rules', in Thomas, L.R. (ed.), *The Currency Hedging Debate*, IFR Publishing, London, pp. 203–239.

Taylor, S.J. (1992), 'Efficiency of the Yen Futures Market at the Chicago Mercantile Exchange', in Goss, B.A. (ed.), *Rational Expectations and Efficiency in Futures Markets*, Routledge, London, pp. 109–128.

Taylor, S.J. (1994), 'Trading Futures Using the Channel Rule: A Study of the Predictive Power of Technical Analysis with Currency Examples', *Journal of Futures Markets*, **14**(2), 215–235.

Working, H. (1960), 'Note on the Correlation of First Differences Averages in a Random Chain', *Econometrica*, **28**, 916–918.

PART II
The Informational Content of
Volatility Markets

Using Option Prices to Estimate Realignment Probabilities in the European Monetary System

———— ALLAN M. MALZ ————

6.1 INTRODUCTION

The use of derivatives prices to draw conclusions about future asset prices is common. The forward exchange rate can be interpreted as the market's point estimate of the future spot exchange rate. Analogously, implied volatilities calculated from foreign currency options have been interpreted as the market's estimate of actual future volatility. In the same spirit, the prices of certain combinations of options can be interpreted as the market's best guess as to the skewness in the distribution of future exchange rates.

Options are frequently sold in combinations. Among the most common in the currency option markets is the *risk reversal*, consisting of an out-of-the-money call and out-of-the-money put. The exercise price of the call component is higher than the current forward exchange rate, and the exercise price of the put is lower. Risk reversals trade as a standard instrument in over-the-counter currency option markets, with prices expressed as the difference between the prices of the constituent put and call. This chapter describes a procedure for estimating the market's perceived probability distribution of future exchange rates from the prices of risk reversals and other currency

Forecasting Financial Markets: Exchange Rates, Interest Rates and Asset Management. Edited by Christian Dunis. © 1996 John Wiley & Sons Ltd.

options. It then uses this procedure to estimate the probability of a realignment of the French franc and pound sterling in the European Monetary System (EMS).

In academic studies, option prices have been interpreted as the market's forecast of the second moment of daily changes in the underlying asset price over the life of the option; when combined with a point estimate of the future asset price, they provide a picture of the probability distribution of the asset price at maturity. Some researchers, however, have attempted to extract information about higher moments of asset price distributions from options prices. Bates (1988a, 1991, 1993) uses prices of exchange-traded options to extract information about the third and fourth moments of asset price changes to form a more exact picture of the terminal distribution. The model described here is similar, but uses a simpler procedure made possible with risk reversal data to estimate the realignment probability of the French franc and pound sterling. In contrast to previous studies of Exchange Rate Mechanism (ERM) exchange rates, it is possible with this procedure to identify both the ex-ante probability and the magnitude of a realignment.[1]

6.2   INSTITUTIONAL FEATURES OF THE EMS[2]

The ERM began operations on 12 March 1979; it consists of (i) a grid of bilateral central parities; (ii) rates for compulsory intervention, or fluctuation limits, set until 2 August 1993, at 2.25% or 6% above and below the parities; and (iii) the obligation of central banks on both sides of a currency pair to purchase or sell unlimited amounts of currency at the fluctuation limits. Bundesbank concerns about the potential for the ERM to undermine its control of the German money supply were addressed by a public commitment from the German government to shield it from a potential conflict between the intervention obligations and monetary stability either by means of a realignment or by a temporary suspension of the intervention obligations. The unilateral Bundesbank reservation has remained in effect throughout the existence of the ERM (see Emminger 1986, pp. 361f.).

Until 1987, realignments in the ERM were frequent, and the system relied heavily on capital controls to counter selling pressures on weak currencies. From 1987 until 1992, there were no realignments in the EMS[3]. This period also witnessed a burst of political activity aimed at establishing a full-fledged currency union, the European Monetary Union (EMU), by the end of the 1990s; several European countries outside the ERM pegged their currencies to the German mark or to the European Currency Unit. Investors began to pour funds into assets denominated in European currencies other than the mark with the conviction that further realignments were unlikely. The persistent, but diminishing, interest rate differentials *vis-à-vis* mark-denominated assets were seen as more than adequate compensation for the dwindling exchange rate risk.

In 1991 and early 1992, 'convergence trading' was undermined by economic and political shocks.[4] German unification was financed by borrowing from the public. The Bundesbank tightened monetary policy to thwart the perceived threat to monetary stability. Two-thirds of the DM108 billion swing in the 1991 current account was financed by short-term funds attracted to mark deposits by rising interest rates. The difficult Maastricht summit in December 1991 and the Danish public's rejection of the draft Treaty on European Union on 2 June 1992, highlighted the obstacles to EMU.

Investors saw that the costs to politicians of participating in EMU—enduring the Bundesbank's tight-money regime—were increasing, while the prospective benefits were becoming more uncertain. Interest rate differentials *vis-à-vis* the mark had diminished; as a result, the buffer which might have absorbed part of the Bundesbank's interest rate hikes was thinner, and the return for bearing realignment risk had fallen. By late August 1992, positions in nonmark European assets were being liquidated on a large scale.

The lira devaluation on 13 September 1992, brought no end to the run on the lira and sterling; on 16 September 1992, after an attempt to combat selling pressure through interest rate hikes, Italy and the United Kingdom withdrew from the ERM. Other currencies were devalued once or several times over the next eight months. By mid-1993, calm appeared to have returned. Abruptly, in July 1993, provoked by an aggressive attempt by the Banque de France to cut interest rates to sub-German levels, the crisis flared again. On 1–2 August 1993, the fluctuation margins for all currency pairs other than mark/Dutch guilder were widened to ±15%, but the parities were left unchanged.

6.3   MEASURING THE CREDIBILITY OF ERM PARITIES

6.3.1   Inferences on Ex Ante Realignment Probabilities from Interest Rate Differentials

Empirical assessments of the credibility of ERM exchange rates have hitherto relied almost exclusively on interest rate differentials and the assumption of open interest parity. In the ERM context, realignment can be treated as a potential regime change that significantly affects the anticipated exchange rate. Forecasts of logarithmic changes in the exchange rate in n periods can be written as a probability-weighted average of forecasts conditioned on both current information and the occurrence of a realignment. Under open interest parity, the expected depreciation $E[s_{t+n} - s_t | \Theta_t]$ is equal to the forward premium of the mark *vis-à-vis* the domestic currency:

$$E[s_{t+n} - s_t | \Theta_t] = \pi_t^n E[s_{t+n} - s_t | \Theta_t, \text{realignment}]$$

$$+ (1 - \pi_t^n) E[s_{t+n} - s_t | \Theta_t, \text{no realignment}], \qquad (1)$$

where s_t is the logarithm of the exchange rate (domestic currency units per German mark), π_t^n is the subjective probability of a realignment, and Θ_t is the information set at time t.[5]

Equation (1) assumes that only zero or one realignment can occur between times t and $t + n$, corresponding to the infrequent changes in ERM parities prior to September 1992. The withdrawal of sterling and the lira from the ERM, the repeated devaluations of the peseta and escudo, and the widening of the bands were unprecedented. The zero–one realignment model is none-theless a valid approximation for the one-month maturities we will focus on here, since these were discrete events resulting in immediate, large changes in exchange rates.

Estimates of π_t^n based on this model agree in treating $E[s_{t+n} - s_t | \Theta_t,$ realignment], the anticipated exchange rate change in the event of a realignment, as a known constant. The procedure using option prices we present here, in contrast, identifies both π_t^n and $E[s_{t+n} - s_t | \Theta_t,$ realignment].

In this framework, Collins (1985, 1992) treats $E[s_{t+n} - s_t | \Theta_t,$ no realign-ment], the anticipated exchange rate change in the absence of a realignment, as an i.i.d. normal variate. The probability π_t^n is assumed to be determined by the shock of foreign exchange reserves held by the non-German central bank and the domestic interest rate.

More recent work has been done using target zone models incorporating realignment risk that interpret $E[s_{t+n} - s_t | \Theta_t,$ no realignment] as the exchange rate movement within the fluctuation limits. This component of expected exchange rate changes is mean-reverting and of significant magnitude relative to the interest rate differential.[6] Rose and Svensson (1991) and Rose (1993a,b) estimate the probability of realignment for the French franc and pound sterling using a fixed realignment size. Chen and Giovannini (1992, 1993) estimate projections of the expected value of devaluation $\pi_t^n E[s_{t+n} - s_t | \Theta_t,$ realignment] on fundamentals.

6.3.2   Inferences on Exchange Rate Credibility from Option Prices

Recently, attempts have been made to establish theoretical option values for exchange rates in a target zone. Dumas *et al.* (1993b) present a model of option values in a credible target zone. One implication of the model, directly related to the finding that mean reversion in a target zone is stronger, the longer the time horizon, is that the term structure of implied volatilities is downward sloping. Campa and Chang (1994) test this feature of the model on sterling/dollar option prices and find evidence against credibility of the target zone. Dumas *et al.* (1993a) study option valuation in target zones with realignments.

6.4   THE STOCHASTIC BEHAVIOR OF NOMINAL EXCHANGE RATES

The Black–Scholes model, the benchmark model for pricing and managing the risks of options, is based on the assumption that nominal exchange rate returns follow a random walk. To extract information about realignment expectations from option prices, we use an alternative model of option values based on an alternative specification of the stochastic behavior of exchange rate changes. Following is an outline of what is known about the statistical properties of exchange rates (see Boothe and Glassman (1987), Hsieh (1988), Baillie and McMahon (1989), and de Vries (1994) for surveys).

6.4.1   Stylized Facts Concerning Flexible Exchange Rates

Floating exchange rates, it is generally agreed, are unit root processes. There is less agreement on the behavior of the log price relatives or nominal returns $s_t - s_{t-1}$. Most investigations find these to be stationary and serially uncorrelated, but beyond that the results are less conclusive, in part because of the wide range of hypotheses about the process the price relatives follow.

The hypothesis that the log price relatives are nominal i.i.d. has been in doubt since the advent of floating exchange rates in the 1970s. The distribution of $s_t - s_{t-1}$ violates normality in three crucial respects. First, it is leptokurtotic or 'fat-tailed', that is, large values occur too frequently to be consistent with normality. Second, the distribution appears to be skewed, so positive and negative returns of a given size are not equally likely. Finally, the variance of the price relatives appears to be time varying. The lack of autocorrelation in $s_t - s_{t-1}$ indicates that its variance rather than its mean varies; it has long been noted that the volatility of asset price relatives clusters, that is, large absolute values of $s_t - s_{t-1}$ tend to be followed by large values. Thus, nominal returns are not both i.i.d. and normally distributed, suggesting two approaches to characterizing nominal exchange rate returns: nonnormal distributions and time-varying distribution parameters.

There is strong evidence that flexible exchange rate returns follow jump-diffusions, that is, a sum of i.i.d. normal and Poisson-distributed jump components, which can account both for the kurtosis and the skew in nominal returns (see Akgiray and Booth 1988, Tucker and Pond 1988, Jorion 1988). If jumps in either direction are equally likely, then the frequency of large changes will be greater than is consistent with normality, but no skew will be apparent. If jumps in one direction are larger or more frequent, the distribution will be skewed.

Time-varying parameters can be represented by autoregressive conditional heteroscedasticity (ARCH) models, which can account for kurtosis as well as for the time variation of volatility (see Hsieh 1988, 1989, and Baillie and Bollerslev 1989 for applications to currencies).

6.4.2 Stylized Facts Concerning Exchange Rates in a Target Zone

There are reasons to expect ERM currencies to display different stochastic properties. Models of credible target zones as well as target zones with realignment risk imply that the exchange rate is mean-reverting, tending to return to the central parity. Target zone models with realignment risk imply that exchange rates should show evidence of jumps.

Nieuwland *et al.* (1991, 1993) find no evidence of mean reversion but cite strong evidence of jumps in ERM exchange rates. Ball and Roma (1993) find that processes incorporating both jumps and mean reversion fit ERM currencies well. They combine Poisson-distributed jumps with a diffusion component that is Ornstein–Uhlenbeck or geometric Brownian with reflecting barriers. The reflecting-barrier process, in which mean reversion is driven by proximity to the fluctuation margins, worked best in earlier years of the ERM, while the Ornstein–Uhlenbeck process, in which mean reversion is driven by distance from the central parity, best describes the ERM in later years.

6.5 THE BLACK–SCHOLES IMPLIED VOLATILITY

Although option dealers are well aware that exchange rate behavior does not conform precisely to the assumptions of the Black–Scholes model, they use the model as a benchmark for option valuation and draw from it the terminology and metrics used by the option markets. The key assumption of the Black–Scholes foreign exchange option pricing model is that the logarithm of the forward exchange rate follows a geometric Brownian motion, that is

$$S_T = S_0 + (\alpha - r^*)\int_0^T S_t \, dt + \sigma \int_0^T S_t \, dW_t, \tag{2}$$

where W_t denotes a standard Brownian motion, S_t the level of the exchange rate, σ the variance rate or volatility, α the expected rate of return on the currency, and r^* the foreign risk-free interest rate; α, σ and r^* are assumed constant.[7] The model results in the Black–Scholes formulas for the values of options on foreign exchange. The value of a call is

$$v(S_t, \tau; X, \sigma, r, r^*) = S_t e^{-r^*\tau}\Phi(d + \sigma\sqrt{\tau}) - X e^{-r\tau}\Phi(d), \qquad (3)$$

and the value of a put is

$$w(S_t, \tau; X, \sigma, r, r^*) = X e^{-r\tau}\Phi(-d) - S_t e^{-r^*\tau}\Phi(-d - \sigma\sqrt{\tau}), \qquad (4)$$

where $\Phi(\cdot)$ represents the cumulative normal distribution, and

$$d = \frac{\ln(S_t/X) + (r - r^* - \sigma^2/2)\tau}{\sigma\sqrt{\tau}}, \qquad (5)$$

where $\tau \equiv T - t$. The volatility σ is not observable and must be estimated to calculate the option value.

If S_t is measured in units of domestic currency per foreign currency units, the Black–Scholes formulas are also expressed in domestic currency units. Exchange-traded currency options are usually defined this way. Alternatively, one can replace the Black–Scholes option value on the left-hand side of equations (3) or (4) with an observed option price v_t and interpret the formula as returning the volatility as an implicit function of v_t, the variables S_t and τ, and the parameters, X, r and r^*. Treated this way, the volatility is called the Black–Scholes implied volatility. The Black–Scholes formula increases monotonically in σ, so the implied volatility is a unique inverse function of $v(S_t, \tau; X, \sigma, r, r^*)$.[8]

Although option dealers are well aware that exchange rates do not conform precisely to the assumptions of the Black–Scholes model, they use the model as a benchmark for option valuation and draw the option markets' terminology from it. Rather than quoting option prices, dealers quote implied volatilities, or 'vols'.[9] If a dealer is asked to quote a one-month call option on mark-Paris (value of the mark in French francs), he might answer 'one-month-at-the-money forward calls are three at four', meaning that he buys a one-month at-the-money mark-Paris call option with an exercise price equal to the current forward exchange rate for three volatility points (three vols) and sells them for four. The value in francs is then calculated from the Black–Scholes formula.[10]

6.6 INFORMATION CONTENT OF RISK REVERSAL PRICES

6.6.1 Kurtosis, Skew and Option Prices

The Black–Scholes model of option values has motivated two lines of empirical research. One examines how closely the market prices of options correspond to their theoretical values. The other seeks to extract information about the probability distribution of the underlying asset from option prices. These agendas are closely related, because to translate option prices into accurate information about the underlying distribution, a correct option valuation model is required. A correct option pricing model, in turn, can be derived only from a correct characterization of the statistical properties of the underlying asset prices.

The Black–Scholes model implies that all options on the same asset have identical implied volatilities, regardless of time to maturity and moneyness. However, options with the same strike but different maturities, options with the same maturity but different strikes, and puts and calls with the same maturity and strike often have different implied volatilities. These biases offer tests of the Black–Scholes model and suggest alternative option pricing models.[11]

Out-of-the money options on currencies with flexible exchange rates often have higher implied volatilities than at-the-money options. This bias, called the volatility smile, is evidence that market participants view exchange rates as kurtotic. Out-of-the money call options on a currency often have implied volatilities that differ from those of equally out-of-the money puts. The bias, called skew, can be so strong as to offset or exceed the smile: the out-of-the-money put or call then has an implied volatility that is less than or equal to that of the at-the-money options. Option skew indicates that the market perceives directional bias in exchange rates. Cookson (1993, pp. 24ff) discusses the option smile and skew.

The Black–Scholes implied volatility has been interpreted as the market-adjusted certainty equivalent of the second moment of asset price returns over the life of the option.[12] The evidence from option prices on skew and kurtosis in expected future asset prices suggests that one might improve the Black–Scholes estimate of the perceived probability distribution using simultaneous observations of option prices with different strike prices. Breeden and Litzenberger (1978) showed that, given the probability distribution of the underlying asset price, the second derivative of the corresponding European call option formula with respect to the exercise price, evaluated at a particular level X^0, is the probability of the time T asset price being X^0 or higher. The Breeden–Litzenberger result has motivated attempts to numerically reconstruct a probability distribution consistent with a set of observed option prices.[13] Alternatively, one can postulate an alternative distribution to the normal i.i.d. Bates (1988a, 1991) fits option prices with varying exercise prices to a jump-diffusion option pricing formula to estimate the parameters of the jump-diffusion. This is essentially the method I employ below.

6.6.2 Risk Reversal Price Quotes

The over-the-counter currency option market convention for quoting risk reversal prices, like those for standard option price quotes, are based on the Black–Scholes implied volatility. A risk reversal consists of an out-of-the-money put and call. The dealer exchanges one of the options for the other with the counterparty. Because the put and call are generally not of equal value, the dealer pays or receives a premium for exchanging the options. This premium is expressed as the difference between the implied volatilities of the put and the call.

In order to quote risk reversal prices, dealers need a convention for expressing the degree to which the component put and call are out-of-the-money. Over-the-counter options markets have adopted the option delta, the rate of change of the Black–Scholes option value with respect to the spot rate, as a metric for moneyness. The delta of a currency call can be written

$$\delta_v(S_t, \tau; X, \sigma, r, r^*) \equiv \frac{\partial v(\cdot;\cdot)}{\partial S_t} = e^{-r^*\tau}\Phi(d + \sigma\sqrt{\tau}), \tag{6}$$

while that of currency put is

$$\delta_w(S_t, \tau; X, \sigma, r, r^*) \equiv \frac{\partial w(\cdot;\cdot)}{\partial S_t} = 1 - \delta_v(S_t, \tau; X, \sigma, r, r^*). \tag{7}$$

This metric is closely related to the probability distribution of logarithmic changes in the exchange rate, given that geometric Brownian motion is the true process. The probability distribution of the logarithmic change in the spot rate is simply $\Phi(d)$. Since $N(d + \sigma\sqrt{\tau})$ is a probability, for any positive S_t, σ, and τ, $0 < \delta_v < 1$.

Risk reversals are usually standardized as a combination of a 25-delta call and a 25-delta put. The dealer quotes the implied volatility differential at which he is prepared to exchange a 25-delta call for a 25-delta put. For example, if the mark-Paris rate is strongly expected to rise (French franc depreciation), an options dealer might quote mark-Paris risk reversals as follows: 'one-month 25-delta risk reversals are 1.5 and 3.0 mark calls over'. This means he stands ready to pay a net premium of 1.5 volatility points to buy a 25-delta mark call and sell a 25-delta mark put against the French franc, and charges a net premium of 3.0 volatility points to sell a 25-delta mark call and buy a 25-delta mark put.

6.6.3 A First Look at the Information Content of Risk Reversal Prices

The most direct way of accessing the information content of risk reversal prices is to recall the definition of an option: an option pays off if the exchange rate ends higher than the exercise price. The option price thus reflects the likelihood that it will end in-the-money. The constituent options in a risk reversal are equally out-of-the-money in delta terms. They would have the same price, and the risk reversal price would equal zero, if the market believed that the tails of the density function of percent changes in the forward rate were symmetrical, that is, increases or decreases in the forward rate of a given magnitude are equally likely. Directional biases are thus clearly revealed by the prices of risk reversals. If an out-of-the-money call on a currency is more valuable than an equally out-of-the-money put, this reflects a market consensus that, loosely speaking, the call is more likely to pay off, that is, the currency is more likely to appreciate than depreciate.[14]

Consider, for example, the mark-Paris risk reversal displayed in the top panel of Figure 6.1 as a long mark call/short mark put position. On 16 September 1992, mark calls were more expensive than puts. The strike price of the mark call component was FF3.4692 and that of the mark put FF3.3717. The risk reversal price indicates that the market considered the expected value of exchange rate realizations on 16 October in excess of FF3.4692 to be greater than that of realizations below FF3.3717. The data on market sentiment on future spot rates are independent of those contained in the current spot or forward exchange rates.

The risk reversal thus gives an indication of the relative likelihood, as perceived by the market, of a large appreciation or depreciation of the franc. In other words, it is a measure of the tail probabilities. The procedure outlined below for extracting the probability distribution of the exchange rate from risk reversal data can be thought of as a way of transforming, via the jump-diffusion model, the information on the expected values of currency moves embedded in option prices into a statement about probabilities.

Using volatilities as a metric for the option value and delta as a metric for moneyness leads to a reformulation of Bates' (1988a, 1991) option-based measure of asymmetry in the asset-price distribution, the crash premium. In the metrics here, the cash premium may be defined as the risk reversal price itself. In the Black–Scholes model, the risk reversal price is zero. If risk reversal prices deviate from zero, there is *ipso facto* a crash premium.

6.7 CURRENCY OPTION PRICES IN THE PRESENCE OF REALIGNMENT RISK

The prices of risk reversals indicate skew in the perceived distribution of the mark-Paris exchange rate. Following Bates (1988a, 1991), I explain the option price skew using an asymmetric jump-diffusion model of the stochastic process for the exchange rate, which can be written

$$S_T = S_0 + \int_0^T (\alpha - r^* - \lambda E[k]) S_t \, dt + \int_0^T \sigma_w S_t \, dW_t + \int_0^T S_t k \, dq_{t,\,T}, \qquad (8)$$

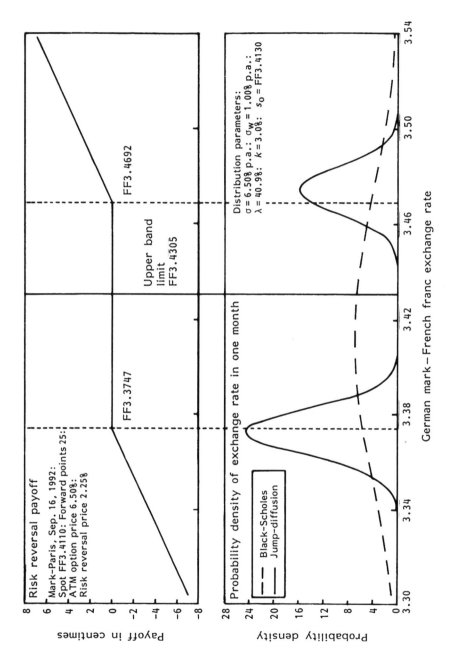

Figure 6.1 Risk reversals and the probability density function

where σ_w denotes the diffusion volatility of the exchange rate, $q_{t,T}$ is a Poisson counter over the interval (t, T) with average rate of occurrence of jumps λ, and k is the possibly random jump size.

The option pricing formula is derived by Merton (1976) and Bates (1988b, 1991; see also Ball and Torous 1983, 1985 and Jarrow and Rudd 1983, pp. 164ff.). An important point in deriving the option price is that the risk to a seller of options of an increase in the option price following a jump in the asset price cannot be managed by a continuous-adjustment hedging strategy. The option might jump further in-the-money, in which case the writer will be underhedged. If he attempts to hedge in advance of jumps, he will be overhedged unless a jump occurs. Therefore, in contrast to the Black–Scholes model, the jump-diffusion model does not permit risk-neutral pricing techniques without additional assumptions. The estimated parameters are the risk-neutral parameters and are not in general equal to the true parameters.[15]

For the mark cross rates in the ERM, it seems more appropriate to employ a simpler version of the jump-diffusion model, in which k is nonstochastic and there is either zero or one jump in the exchange rate over the life of the option. Ball and Torous (1983, 1985) and Bates (1988a) refer to this as the Bernoulli distribution version of the model. The formula for a call becomes

$$
\begin{aligned}
c(S_t, &\ \tau; X, \sigma_w, r, r^*, \lambda, k) \\
&= (1 - \lambda\tau)[S_t e^{-(r^*+\lambda k)\tau}\Phi(d_0 + \sigma_w\sqrt{\tau}) - X e^{-r\tau}\Phi(d_0)] \\
&\quad + \lambda\tau[S_t e^{-(r^*+\lambda k)\tau}(1 + k)\Phi(d_1 + \sigma_w\sqrt{\tau}) - X e^{-r\tau}\Phi(d_1)] \\
&= (1 - \lambda\tau)\nu(S_t e^{\lambda k\tau}, \tau; X, \sigma_w, r, r^*) + \lambda\tau\nu[S_t e^{\lambda k\tau}(1 + k), \tau; X, \sigma_w, r, r^*],
\end{aligned}
\tag{9}
$$

where

$$
d_0 = \frac{\ln(S_t/X) + (r - r^* - \lambda k - \sigma_w^2/2)\tau}{\sigma_w\sqrt{\tau}}
\tag{10}
$$

and

$$
d_1 = \frac{\ln(S_t/X) + \ln(1 + k) + (r - r^* - \lambda k - \sigma_w^2/2)\tau}{\sigma_w\sqrt{\tau}}.
\tag{11}
$$

The value of a European put option under jump-diffusion can be derived by invoking put–call parity:

$$
\begin{aligned}
p(S_t, &\ \tau; X, \sigma_w, r, r^*, \lambda, k) \\
&= (1 - \lambda\tau)[X e^{-r\tau}\Phi(-d_0) - S_t e^{-(r^*+\lambda k)\tau}\Phi(-d_0 - \sigma_w\sqrt{\tau})] \\
&\quad + \lambda\tau[Xe^{-r\tau}(1 + k)\Phi(-d_1) - S_t e^{-(r^*+\lambda k)\tau}\Phi(-d_1 - \sigma_w\sqrt{\tau})] \\
&= (1 - \lambda\tau)w(S_t e^{\lambda k\tau}, \tau; X, \sigma_w, r, r^*) + \lambda\tau w[S_t e^{\lambda k\tau}(1 + k), \tau; X, \sigma_w, r, r^*],
\end{aligned}
\tag{12}
$$

where d_0 and d_1 are as defined in equations (11) and (12).

The Bernoulli version of the jump-diffusion model captures the widespread, but not unanimous, market view that the risk for sterling or the franc was that a realignment or a collapse of the system would bring about a single sharp change in the currency's value, but that repeated realignments within a month's time were unlikely. Each formula is an average of the Black–Scholes option value given a jump, weighted by the probability of a jump, and the Black–Scholes value absent of a jump, weighted by the probability of no jump.

The expected value of a jump, λk, is added to the return on a foreign currency deposit r^* in the formulas. Intuitively, the current exchange rate must already have depreciated by, say, 5%, to reflect a jump with an expected value of 5%. Otherwise, the weighted average of the zero-jump and one-jump future spot rates would not equal the current forward rate. The λk term implies that if there is no jump, the exchange rate will appreciate by λk; if there is a jump, the exchange rate will depreciate by approximately $1 + k - \lambda k$, not including the forward points $S_t[e^{(r-r^*)\tau} - 1]$.

6.8 ESTIMATES OF REALIGNMENT PROBABILITIES USING OPTION PRICES

6.8.1 Normalized Black–Scholes and Jump-diffusion Option Price Formulas

Over-the-counter options and risk reversals are quoted in implied volatilities for options of a specified delta. This permits a simplification of the price formulas needed in estimating the jump-diffusion parameters from Black–Scholes prices. Data on the spot exchange rate, the foreign and domestic interest rates, and the exercise prices of the options are not needed.[16]

The data pertain to one-month options, so τ can be set to unity throughout. The volatilities are then converted from the standard annual basis on which they are quoted to a monthly basis by dividing by $\sqrt{12}$. To avoid clutter, I do not incorporate this change of units in the notation, but take it into account in estimation. The jump parameter λ, however, is a monthly rate.

Dividing equation (3) through by $X_t e^{-r}$ yields

$$v(R_t, \sigma) \equiv e^r v(R_t, 1; 1, \sigma, 0, 0) = R_t \Phi(d + \sigma) - \Phi(d), \qquad (13)$$

where $R_t \equiv F_{t, t+1}/X$, $F_{t, t+1} = S_t e^{r-r^*}$, and

$$d = \frac{\ln(R_t)}{\sigma} - \frac{\sigma}{2}. \qquad (14)$$

The simplified Black–Scholes formula for a currency put is

$$w(R_t, \sigma) \equiv e^r w(R_t, 1; 1, \sigma, 0, 0) = \Phi(-d) - R_t \Phi(-d - \sigma). \qquad (15)$$

The jump-diffusion formulas can be similarly normalized. The formula for a call is

$$c(R_t, \sigma_w, \lambda, k)$$

$$\equiv e^r c(R_t, 1; 1, \sigma_w, 0, 0, \lambda, k)$$

$$= e^r[(1 - \lambda)v(R_t e^{-\lambda k}, 1; 1, \sigma_w, 0, 0) + \lambda v(R_t(1 + k) e^{-\lambda k}, 1; 1, \sigma_w, 0, 0)]$$

$$= (1 - \lambda)v(R_t e^{-\lambda k}, \sigma_w) + \lambda v[R_t(1 + k) e^{-\lambda k}, \sigma_w],$$

(16)

and for a put

$$p(R_t, \sigma_w, \lambda, k) \equiv e^r p(R_t, 1; 1, \sigma_w, 0, 0, \lambda, k)$$

$$= (1 - \lambda)w(R_t e^{-\lambda k}, \sigma_w) + \lambda w[R_t(1 + k) e^{-\lambda k}, \sigma_w].$$

(17)

6.8.2 Estimation Procedure

The task is to estimate the three parameters σ_w, λ and k in the jump-diffusion formula. The data are the prices, in volatilities, of at-the-money forward one-month options and one-month 25-delta risk reversals. The jump-diffusion model, like the Black–Scholes model, postulates that the parameters are constants. In extracting the parameters from daily option prices for evidence on the market view of the future exchange rate distribution on that day, I implicitly permitted them to vary over time.

It is difficult to estimate all three parameters from daily data. If σ_w in the jump-diffusion formula is set at a value close to σ in the Black–Scholes formula, the option values the two formulas grind out will be so close to one another that it is hard to estimate the parameters λ and k reliably. In order for the jump parameters to have a role in explaining observed option prices, σ_w must have a value well below the observed at-the-money forward volatility. We assume that σ_w is constant over long periods and is equal to the implied volatility of mark-Paris options during periods when λ can be assumed close to zero. Increases in implied volatility are then due to increases in λ and k. The assumed values of 0.01 and 0.03 per annum are approximately equal to the observed implied volatility of mark-Paris and sterling–mark options, respectively, prior to the 1992 ERM crisis. Some experimentation indicates that the results are not sensitive to the assumed value for σ_w, as long as it is a small number. At somewhat higher values of σ_w, the estimated values of λ are somewhat lower.

The assumption that the Brownian component of the exchange rate's motion will not change in the event of a realignment implies that the alternative to no realignment is a realignment plus preservation of the previous band width. However, the experience of the ERM crisis shows that the alternative may be suspension of participation in the target zone or no realignment plus widening of the band. To the extent that the public believes in these latter alternatives, the assumption that the Brownian motion volatility is constant is implausible.

As a check on robustness, we estimate the parameters of the model for the French franc on the alternative assumption that, in the event of a realignment, the Brownian motion volatility, too, jumps, from 0.01 to 0.03%. The effect is limited: the estimated realignment probability increases slightly compared with the constant-volatility estimates.

As a further check of robustness, we estimated both λ and k jointly, and λ alone, with k set to an assumed value. The assumed values of k are 0.03 for the franc and 0.10 for sterling, approximately equal to the maximum depreciation these currencies experienced in the month after the widening of the ERM bands or the suspension of participation in the ERM. The French franc closed at a low of FF3.5453 against the mark on 16 August 1993, 3.2% below its floor of FF3.4305. The pound closed at a low of DM2.4301 on 5 October 1992, or about 12.5% below its floor of DM2.7780.

The mechanism estimation procedure is as follows. We first calculate the option prices in francs or sterling from the at-the-money volatilities and risk reversal prices expressed in vols. To do so:

1. We transform the risk reversal prices into levels of implied volatility for the one-month 25-delta puts and calls. The 25-delta mark call volatility is set equal to the at-the-money volatility plus 0.75 times the risk reversal price. The 25-delta mark put volatility is set equal to the at-the-money volatility minus 0.25 times the risk reversal price. This assignment, based on the suggestions of market participants in ERM, produces a lopsided smile, that is, the volatility of the put is lower than that of at-the-money volatilities.[17]
2. Next, we use these volatilities and equation (6) or (7) to solve for the forward rate/exercise price ratio at which the option delta is 25, 50, or 75%.
3. With both the implied volatility and the forward rate/exercise price ratio, we can transform the volatilities into option prices using the normalized Black–Scholes formula. These prices are expressed in percent of the exercise price, exponentiated up to time T values. The differences between the spot exchange rates and the exercise prices are small and the maturity short, so the prices are also expressed, approximately, as a percent of the spot rate.

Then we solve

$$\min_{\{\lambda_t, \, k_t\}} \sum_{i=1}^{3} (u_t^i)^2 \quad \text{or} \quad \min_{\{\lambda_t\}} \sum_{i=1}^{3} (u_t^i)^2,$$

with the u_t^i defined by

$$v(R_t^{25\delta}, \sigma_t^{25\delta}) = c(R_t^{25\delta}, \sigma_w, \lambda_t, k_t) + u_t^1$$
$$v(R_t^{50\delta}, \sigma_t^{50}) = c(R_t^{50\delta}, \sigma_w, \lambda_t, k_t) + u_t^2 \qquad (18)$$
$$w(R_t^{75\delta}, \sigma_t^{75}) = p(R_t^{75\delta}, \sigma_w, \lambda_t, k_t) + u_t^3,$$

where $R_t^{25\delta}$, $R_t^{50\delta}$ and $R_t^{75\delta}$ refer to the forward rate/exercise price ratio corresponding to the delta in the superscript, and $\sigma_t^{25\delta}$, $\sigma_t^{50\delta}$ and $\sigma_t^{75\delta}$ refer to the observed implied volatilities on the 25-delta call, the 50-delta call, and the 25-delta put, respectively. This step is carried out by nonlinear least squares.[18]

6.8.3   Data

While options on currencies and currency futures are traded on several exchanges, liquidity in currency option trading is centered in the over-the-counter market. The most important differences between over-the-counter and public currency option markets for the purposes of this chapter are:

1. Only American options are traded on the exchanges, while primarily European options are traded over-the-counter. Closed form solutions exist only for European options, making them simpler to evaluate.
2. Contract maturities on exchanges are fixed dates, so that option prices on successive days pertain to options of different maturities. In over-the-counter markets, a fresh option for standard maturities (1 week, and 1, 2, 3, 6 and 12 months) can be purchased each day, so that a series of prices for options of like maturity can be constructed.
3. Data on exchange-traded European cross-rate options are largely unavailable. The only European cross-rate option contract currently trading is the Philadelphia Stock Exchange's mark/sterling contract, which was introduced on 25 September 1992.

   Data on European cross-rate options are difficult to obtain. The difficulty is compounded by the illiquidity of the options markets during the crises of September 1992 and July 1993. Price data for the same instrument from different sources were therefore occasionally quite different. No dealers have systematic records of European cross-currency risk reversal prices during 1992 and 1993. Risk reversal price data for mark-Paris and sterling–mark for particular days were assembled by interviewing traders at several firms. Some traders had personal notes made at the time, including data on risk reversal prices, while others drew on memory. Two sources appeared particularly reliable and were able to provide risk reversal price data for the same dates for mark-Paris. We identify these as data sets I and II. Only one of these sources had data on sterling–mark risk reversals. The data should be considered indicative; they are not drawn from any firm's internal record of prices quoted at the time.[19]

6.8.4 The Implied Distribution of Future Exchange Rates and Realignment Probabilities

If the exchange rate follows the geometric Brownian process represented in equation (2), as assumed by the Black–Scholes model, the logarithm of its time T value is distributed normally:

$$\ln (S_T) \sim \Phi \left[\ln (S_t) + \left(r - r^* - \frac{\sigma^2}{2} \right) \tau, \sigma^2 \tau \right], \tag{19}$$

where r replaces α in the risk-neutral distribution. In consequence, the variable

$$z' = \frac{\ln (S_T) - \ln (S_t) + r - r^* + (\sigma^2/2)(T - T)}{\sigma(T - t)} \tag{20}$$

is a standard normal variate.

If the exchange rate follows the jump-diffusion process represented in equation (9), the risk-neutral distribution of the logarithm of the terminal exchange rate is

$$\ln (S_T) \sim \Phi \left[\ln (S_t) + \left(r - r^* - \lambda k - \frac{\sigma_w^2}{2} \right) \tau + q_{t, T} \ln (1 + k), \sigma_w^2 \tau \right]. \tag{21}$$

and the variate

$$z = \ln \left(\frac{S_T}{S_t} \right) - q_{t, T} \ln (1 + k) - \left(r - r^* - \lambda k - \frac{\sigma_w^2}{2} \right) \tau (\sigma_w \sqrt{\tau})^{-1} \tag{22}$$

is standard normal. In the Bernoulli distribution model, the Poisson counter $q_{t, T}$ takes on the value zero with probability $(1 - \lambda)$ and the value unity with probability λ. The terminal distribution function is thus a mixture of two normal distributions.

We use the parameter estimates, together with the forward rate, to calculate the probability distribution of the future exchange rate. The realignment probability is the likelihood that $S_T \leqslant \bar{S}$, where $\bar{S}$ denotes the upper fluctuation limit (francs or pounds per mark). Setting $\tau = 1$ and substituting $F_{t, t+1} = S_t e^{r - r^*}$, we calculate the probability as

$$\pi_t \equiv \text{prob}\{S_T \leqslant \bar{S}\} = (1 - \lambda)\Phi \left[\frac{\ln (\bar{S}/F_{t, t+1}) + \lambda k + \sigma_w^2/2}{\sigma_w} \right]$$

$$+ \lambda\Phi \left[\frac{\ln (\bar{S}/F_{t, t+1}) - \ln (1 + k) + \lambda k + \sigma_w^2/2}{\sigma_w} \right]. \tag{23}$$

Table 6.1 Market data used in estimating realignment probabilities: French franc

| Date | Exchange rates[a] | | Option prices[b] | | | | | |
| | S_t | $F_{t, t+1}$ | Data set *I* | | | Data set *II* | | |
			25δ call	50δ call	25δ put	25δ call	50δ call	25δ put
31 Jan 92	3.4075	3.4087	0.0547	0.1379	0.0509	0.0846	0.2009	0.0726
19 May 92	3.3617	3.3619	0.0723	0.1551	0.0536	0.0920	0.2295	0.0846
27 Jul 92	3.3761	3.3773	0.0723	0.1551	0.0536	0.1058	0.2581	0.0945
21 Aug 92	3.3943	3.3949	0.0893	0.2009	0.0710	0.1132	0.2866	0.1065
11 Sep 92	3.4040	3.4054	0.2223	0.4290	0.1417	0.1690	0.4290	0.1604
14 Sep 92	3.3912	3.3930	0.2223	0.4290	0.1417	0.2145	0.5140	0.1887
15 Sep 92	3.3945	3.3963	0.3431	0.7398	0.2612	0.2160	0.5140	0.1881
16 Sep 92	3.4112	3.4134	0.3431	0.7398	0.2612	0.3048	0.7398	0.2752
17 Sep 92	3.4206	3.4271	0.3151	0.6835	0.2416	0.3919	0.9638	0.3629
25 Sep 92	3.3856	3.3952	0.3151	0.6835	0.2416	0.4211	1.0195	0.3823
30 Sep 92	3.3794	3.4045	0.2946	0.6271	0.2193	0.4411	1.0751	0.4051
6 Jan 93	3.4065	3.4181	0.2869	0.6271	0.2220	0.1889	0.4574	0.1682
19 May 93	3.3722	3.3725	0.1069	0.2866	0.1087	0.0952	0.2295	0.0835
28 Jul 93	3.4098	3.4187	0.2894	0.6553	0.2360	0.2352	0.5706	0.2109
30 Jul 93	3.4299	3.4441	0.4710	1.0751	0.3937	0.2368	0.5706	0.2103

[a] Spot rates are from official fixings against the dollar. Forward rates are calculated from spot rates and one-month Eurocurrency deposit rates.
[b] The options are defined as puts and calls on the German mark in terms of the French franc. The prices are calculated from market implied volatilities using the Black–Scholes formula by a method described in the text and are expressed, approximately, in percent of the value, in francs, of the mark.

The probability that the exchange rate will exceed the weak intervention limit is displayed in Tables 6.2 and 6.3 and Figure 6.2 for the French franc and Table 6.5 and Figure 6.3 for sterling.

The implied density function for mark-Paris 16 September 1992, is displayed in the lower panel of Figure 6.1 and compared with the density implied by the Black–Scholes model, with the skew and kurtosis ignored. The jump-diffusion model may be thought of as a vehicle for transforming the expected values contained in risk reversal prices into probabilities.

The implied density function is bimodal because σ_w is small. It can be interpreted as saying that the franc will follow a low-volatility random walk with the starting point either at its no-realignment rate or its post-realignment rate. The forward rate on 16 September was FF3.4135. If there is no realignment, the exchange rate strengthens by λk (1.23%) to FF3.3720 and drifts with a volatility of 1% per annum. If there is a realignment, the exchange rate jumps to FF3.4730 and drifts with a volatility of 1%. With a higher σ_w, say, above 5%, and λ and k still equal to 0.41 and 0.03, the distribution would be unimodal, centered at FF3.4135 but skewed to the right.

Table 6.2 Realignment probability estimates: French franc. Data set I

| | Both λ and k estimated | | | | | | Only λ estimated; $k = 0.03$ | | | | |
| | Option prices[a] | | | Parameters | | | Option prices[a] | | | Parameters | |
Date	25δ call	50δ call	25δ put	λ_t	k_t	π_t	25δ call	50δ call	25δ put	λ_t	π_t
31 Jan 92	0.0543	0.1391	0.0497	0.1786	0.0052	0.0467	0.0596	0.1341	0.0442	0.0133	0.0227
19 May 92	0.0722	0.1558	0.0526	0.0702	0.0133	0.0002	0.0754	0.1526	0.0499	0.0252	0.0252
27 Jul 92	0.0722	0.1558	0.0526	0.0702	0.0133	0.0088	0.0754	0.1526	0.0499	0.0252	0.0252
21 Aug 92	0.0875	0.2077	0.0625	0.2501	0.0099	0.0358	0.1111	0.1840	0.0436	0.0441	0.0441
11 Sep 92	0.2110	0.4683	0.0863	0.2462	0.0254	0.2462	0.2549	0.4510	0.0673	0.1851	0.1851
14 Sep 92	0.2110	0.4683	0.0863	0.2462	0.0254	0.2454	0.2549	0.4510	0.0673	0.1851	0.1851
15 Sep 92	0.2938	0.8630	0.1668	0.3493	0.0389	0.3493	0.0724	0.7061	0.0970	0.4092	0.4068
16 Sep 92	0.2938	0.8630	0.1668	0.3493	0.0389	0.3493	0.0724	0.7061	0.0970	0.4092	0.4092
17 Sep 92	0.2712	0.7936	0.1536	0.3508	0.0356	0.3508	0.1278	0.6961	0.1088	0.3888	0.3888
25 Sep 92	0.2712	0.7936	0.1536	0.3508	0.0356	0.3508	0.1278	0.6961	0.1088	0.3888	0.3871
30 Sep 92	0.2582	0.7224	0.1342	0.3341	0.0331	0.3341	0.1775	0.6806	0.1225	0.3646	0.3646
6 Jan 93	0.2485	0.7238	0.1407	0.3522	0.0324	0.3522	0.1846	0.6883	0.1292	0.3754	0.3754
19 May 93	0.0928	0.3053	0.0958	0.4974	0.0123	0.0000	0.1701	0.2396	0.0269	0.0747	0.0747
28 Jul 93	0.2457	0.7594	0.1578	0.3777	0.0331	0.3777	0.1639	0.7032	0.1308	0.4005	0.4005
30 Jul 93	0.3867	1.2672	0.2827	0.3864	0.0556	0.3864	0.0000	0.7084	0.0024	0.4907	0.4907

[a]Option values are fitted using the jump-diffusion option pricing formula and the estimated parameter values.

Table 6.3 Realignment probability estimates: French franc. Data set II

| Date | Both λ and k estimated | | | | | | Only λ estimated; k = 0.03 | | | | |
| | Option prices[a] | | | Parameters | | | Option prices[a] | | | Parameters | |
	25δ call	50δ call	25δ put	λ_t	k_t	π_t	25δ call	50δ call	25 put	λ_t	π_t
31 Jan 92	0.0819	0.2087	0.0645	0.3133	0.0089	0.1444	0.1092	0.1812	0.0407	0.0425	0.0464
19 May 92	0.0857	0.2410	0.0736	0.4018	0.0098	0.0000	0.1300	0.1999	0.0355	0.0531	0.0529
27 Jul 92	0.0977	0.2745	0.0775	0.3856	0.0115	0.0005	0.1533	0.2239	0.0342	0.0663	0.0663
21 Aug 92	0.1011	0.3077	0.0878	0.5683	0.0125	0.0530	0.1732	0.2449	0.0300	0.0775	0.0775
11 Sep 92	0.1416	0.4797	0.1230	0.4473	0.0190	0.3931	0.2680	0.3961	0.0273	0.1554	0.1554
14 Sep 92	0.1819	0.5851	0.1329	0.4081	0.0247	0.3569	0.3034	0.5526	0.0577	0.2478	0.2478
15 Sep 92	0.1840	0.5852	0.1312	0.4027	0.0248	0.3787	0.3023	0.5549	0.0597	0.2494	0.2494
16 Sep 92	0.2498	0.8578	0.2038	0.4249	0.0362	0.4249	0.0992	0.7207	0.1142	0.4511	0.4511
17 Sep 92	0.3180	1.1210	0.2756	0.4301	0.0476	0.4301	0.0005	0.6857	0.0996	0.5902	0.5902
25 Sep 92	0.3416	1.1908	0.2895	0.4212	0.0509	0.4212	0.0001	0.6902	0.0695	0.5792	0.4281
30 Sep 92	0.3572	1.2548	0.3091	0.4239	0.0537	0.4239	0.0001	0.6986	0.0373	0.5581	0.5383
6 Jan 93	0.1611	0.5160	0.1208	0.4120	0.0217	0.4116	0.2821	0.4460	0.0351	0.1824	0.1831
19 May 93	0.0897	0.2412	0.0711	0.3593	0.0101	0.0000	0.1314	0.2020	0.0373	0.0543	0.0543
28 Jul 93	0.1960	0.6541	0.1527	0.4208	0.0274	0.4208	0.2769	0.6894	0.1512	0.3757	0.3757
30 Jul 93	0.1979	0.6544	0.1509	0.4162	0.0275	0.4189	0.2751	0.6877	0.1494	0.3732	0.3770

[a]Option values are fitted using the jump-diffusion option pricing formula and the estimated parameter values.

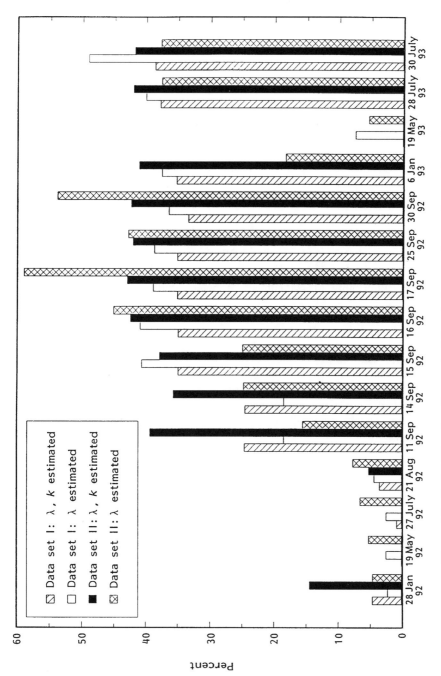

Figure 6.2 Probability of realignment of French franc: estimates from option prices

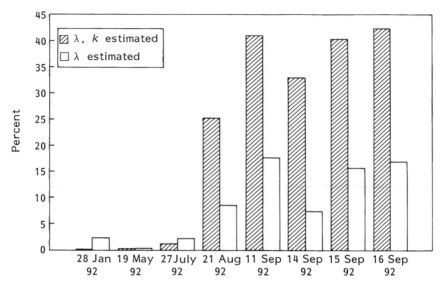

Figure 6.3 Probability of realignment of pound sterling: estimates from option prices

This approach employs the current forward rate as the market's point estimate of the future spot exchange rate, as dictated by the law of motion (9). However, one could also substitute for F_{t+1} any other point estimate of the future spot rate since the option prices inform us only about the shape of the distribution. The location of the distribution could be based, for example, on survey data.

6.8.5 Results

The data are displayed for the franc in Table 6.1 and for sterling in Table 6.4. The option price data are the output of the first step of the procedure and are shown in percent of the forward rate/exercise price ratio. We also report the estimated option values using the jump-diffusion formula, evaluated at the estimated values parameters. Comparison with the data indicates closeness of fit.

The results are displayed for the franc in Tables 6.2 and 6.3 and for sterling in Table 6.5. The estimates of λ_t are plausible, quite low before the onset of the crisis and during the period of quiescence for mark-Paris in spring of 1993, but rising at times of greater pressure. The estimates in which k is permitted to vary result for most days in a value not far from 0.03 for the

Table 6.4 Market data used in estimating realignment probabilities: pound sterling

Date	Exchange rates[a]		Option prices[b]		
	S_t	$F_{t,\,t+1}$	25δ call	50δ call	25δ put
31 Jan 92	2.8718	2.8745	0.1947	0.5027	0.1898
19 May 92	2.9264	2.9269	0.1386	0.3550	0.1329
27 Jul 92	2.8523	2.8535	0.1889	0.4914	0.1859
21 Aug 92	2.8072	2.8077	0.2171	0.5593	0.2115
11 Sep 92	2.7884	2.7894	0.3048	0.7735	0.2932
14 Sep 92	2.8110	2.8132	0.2987	0.7735	0.2955
15 Sep 92	2.7900	2.7920	0.3048	0.7735	0.2932
16 Sep 92	2.7781	2.7835	0.4461	1.1307	0.4338

[a]Spot rates are from official fixings against the dollar. Forward rates are calculated from spot rates and one-month Eurocurrency deposit rates.
[b]The options are defined as puts and calls on the German mark in terms of the pound sterling. The prices are calculated from market implied volatilities using the Black–Scholes formula by a method described in the text and are expressed, approximately, in percent of the value, in sterling, of the mark.

Table 6.5 Realignment probability estimates: pound sterling

	Both λ and k estimated					
	Option prices[a]			Parameters		
Date	25δ call	50δ call	25δ put	λ_t	k_t	π_t
31 Jan 92	0.1920	0.5240	0.1860	0.4010	0.0194	0.0007
19 May 92	0.1348	0.3561	0.1347	0.0210	0.0210	0.0000
27 Jul 92	0.1841	0.4992	0.1798	0.4033	0.0178	0.0119
21 Aug 92	0.2079	0.5745	0.1989	0.4107	0.0222	0.2521
11 Sep 92	0.2763	0.8222	0.2505	0.4169	0.0344	0.4105
14 Sep 92	0.2687	0.8204	0.2575	0.4406	0.0339	0.3300
15 Sep 92	0.2763	0.8222	0.2505	0.4169	0.0344	0.4041
16 Sep 92	0.3796	1.2524	0.3405	0.4239	0.0537	0.4248

	Only λ estimated; $k = 0.03$				
	Option prices[a]			Parameters	
Date	25δ call	50δ call	25δ put	λ_t	π_t
31 Jan 92	0.2445	0.4613	0.1229	0.0237	0.0237
19 May 92	0.1362	0.3572	0.1352	0.0029	0.0029
27 Jul 92	0.2356	0.4527	0.1232	0.0221	0.0224
21 Aug 92	0.2877	0.5004	0.1171	0.0309	0.0852
11 Sep 92	0.4565	0.6604	0.0982	0.0581	0.1762
14 Sep 92	0.4535	0.6558	0.0950	0.0574	0.0734
15 Sep 92	0.4565	0.6604	0.0982	0.0581	0.1566
16 Sep 92	0.7169	0.9997	0.0820	0.1105	0.1690

[a]Option values are fitted using the jump-diffusion option pricing formula and the estimated parameter values.

franc. For sterling, the estimated values of k are about 3 to 5% on the days of acute selling pressure, quite different from the assumed value of 0.10. These results suggest that the market was surprised by the extent, if not by the timing, of sterling's depreciation.

The estimated realignment probabilities conform closely to narrative versions of the ERM's unraveling. The probabilities were low at the beginning of 1992 for both sterling and the franc. By late August, they rose slightly for the franc but more sharply for sterling, consistent with sterling's role as the prime target of the speculative attack. The realignment probabilities continued to rise toward mid-September 1992 and peaked on 16 or 17 September for both currencies. Realignment probabilities for the franc remained high for the rest of 1992 and into early 1993 but declined as the ERM enjoyed a respite from pressure in the spring of 1993. In the last few days of the narrow-band ERM, the probability again returned to very high levels.

6.9   CONCLUSIONS

As shown in this chapter, option prices can be used to estimate the market's subjective probability distribution of future asset prices. Previous work on expectations of realignments in the ERM have focused on interest rate differentials as a raw indicator of these expectations. Figure 6.4 compares several such estimates for the French franc with those based on option prices.[20] Two generalizations emerge from a comparison of the option-based estimates with those based on the forward premium:

1. The option-based approach confirms the finding that the exchange markets did not price in a high probability of realignment until late August 1992.
2. During the periods of acutest pressure, the estimated probabilities of realignment using option prices are high compared with most estimates using forward premia.

The option-based estimates confirm the conclusion of other researchers that expectations were highly unstable during the ERM crisis: within a short space of time, the market consensus on the probability of a sharp depreciation of the franc changed dramatically (see for example Goldstein *et al.* 1993 and Eichengreen and Wyplosz 1993).

At the same time, there are significant differences between the probability estimates derived from forward premia and those derived from option prices. During early September, the options markets clearly reflect the intensity of the market's doubts about the French franc parity against the mark, while French interest rates do not. If we assume that the option prices provide the more

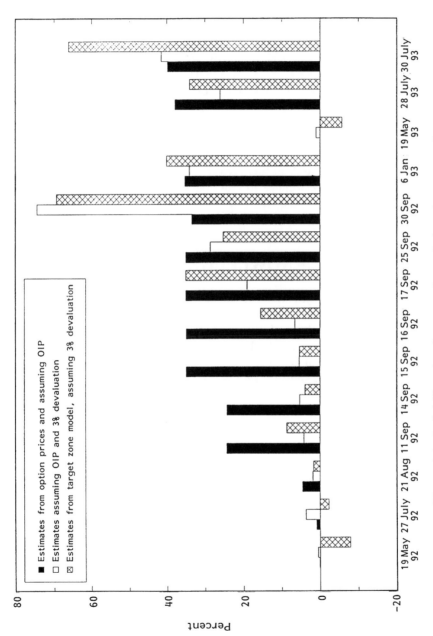

Figure 6.4 Probability of realignment of French franc in next month

accurate indicator of market sentiment, to what may we attribute the lag in the forward premium?

One explanation may be that in the short run, permitting money market rates to rise is only one possible central bank response to exchange rate pressures. Alternative and complementary responses include intervention in exchange markets, public declarations of resolve, and formal and informal attempts to curb speculative techniques. These responses may transitorily depress the money-market interest rates of currencies falling under selling pressure.

This chapter has shown the usefulness of drawing inferences on the perceived probability distribution of future exchange rates from other asset prices, such as options, rather than relying exclusively on interest rate differentials. Future research in this area should examine how the information contained in option prices relates to that contained in forward exchange rates, and whether indicators of skewness in the distribution of exchange rates can improve the forecasting ability of forward rates.

ACKNOWLEDGEMENTS

The author acknowledges helpful discussions with Richard Clarida of Columbia University; Peter Fisher and Tony Rodrigues of the Federal Reserve Bank of New York; Steve Depp and Brian Roseboro of Swiss Bank Corporation; Mark Spilker of Goldman, Sachs and Co.; and with participants in seminars at the Federal Reserve Bank of New York. A later version of this paper will appear in the *Journal of International Money and Finance*.

ENDNOTES

1. Malz (1995) presents a technique for extracting the risk-neutral probability density of the future exchange rate from option prices without assuming that the exchange rate follows a jump-diffusion and applies it to flexible exchange rates.
2. The history and institutions of the ERM are surveyed in Giavazzi and Giovannini (1989), Ungerer *et al.* (1990), and Gros and Thygesen (1992).
3. The 7 January 1990, realignment of the Italian lira was a technical step to ease its entry into narrow ±2.25 fluctuation bands around its central parities *vis-à-vis* the remaining narrow-band currencies.
4. The crisis of the ERM through early 1993 is reviewed by Eichengreen and Wyplosz (1993), Group of Ten (1993), and Goldstein *et al.* (1993).
5. This line of research is closely related to the 'peso problem' explanation of the prediction bias in forward foreign exchange rates. Its application to the ERM is surveyed in Neely (1994) and Malz (1994). The latter paper reestimates some of these models for the French franc and the pound sterling during the 1992–93 ERM crisis.
6. Krugman (1991) presents the credible target zone model. Bertola and Svensson

(1993) present a model of target zones with Poisson-distributed realignment probabilities. Svensson (1993) surveys models and empirical research on target zones.

7. The original exposition of the Black–Scholes model is Black and Scholes (1973). An identical model was developed independently and presented in Merton (1976). The application of the model to foreign currency options is also called the Garman–Kohlhagen model, after its publication by Garman and Kohlhagen (1983). See also Grabbe (1983). Merton (1982) provides an introduction to the properties of the two stochastic processes, geometric Brownian motion and jump-diffusion, on which this chapter focuses.

8. The notion of implied volatility was formalized by Latané and Rendleman (1976) and Schmalensee and Trippi (1978).

9. 'Vol' refers to both implied volatility and its unit of measure (percent per annum).

10. For example, a one-month call struck at-the-money forward with a domestic interest rate of 15% and a volatility of 6% would cost 2.3 centimes per mark of underlying. With a volatility of 10%, it would cost 3.9 centimes.

11. Tests have usually been carried out in terms of option values, using price data from option exchanges, but they can be translated into the implied volatility terms of the over-the-counter option markets. The Black–Scholes model was tested by MacBeth and Merville (1979) and Rubinstein (1985) for equity options, and by Bodurtha and Courtadon (1987) and Hsieh and Manas-Anton (1988) for exchange-traded currency options.

12. This research on implied volatility is analogous to that on the relationship of the forward exchange rate to market estimates of the first moment of the future spot rate. Lyons (1988) uses implied volatilities to test whether the forward exchange rate prediction bias can be explained by time-varying risk premiums based on a portfolio balance model of the exchange rate.

13. Shimko (1993) applies this finding to derive the implied probability distribution of the S&P 500 index. However, his method requires additional assumptions regarding the probability density above the highest and below the lowest exercise levels of traded option contracts. As shown in section 6.7, risk reversal data shed light primarily on these tail probabilities. Rubinstein (1994), Dupire (1994), and Derman and Kani (1994) also present numerical methods for recovering distributions from option prices.

14. Asymmetry in the tails is not, however, a sufficient condition for a nonzero risk reversal price. The expected value of exchange rate changes beyond the 25-delta points might be equal, even if the tails are not mirror images of one another.

15. The risk-neutral parameter λ might be greater than the 'true' subjective parameter if agents are risk-averse and are willing to pay a premium for, say, a mark-Paris call to protect themselves against a realignment. The risk-neutral parameter might be smaller, however, if agents can hedge partially by selling currency to the central bank, which then takes on part of the currency exposure.

16. The dimension reduction is similar to that of Merton (1973, p. 166). We both divide the current asset price by the exercise price to eliminate it as an argument and express the option price as a future value to eliminate the domestic interest rate. However, where Merton eliminates the volatility by combining it with the time to maturity, we set the time to maturity to unity. We also substitute the forward exchange rate for the spot rate in order to eliminate the foreign interest rate.

17. We estimated the parameters using other assignments, for example, by assigning all the risk reversal spread to the put or to the call, or splitting it evenly between the put and call. The parameter estimates were not sensitive to these changes.

18. This step is similar to the procedure outlined in Manaster and Rendleman (1982).

We carried out the estimation procedure using both Mathcad 5.0 and TSP 4.2. The numerical results were generally identical except for rounding errors.
19. The sources are Swiss Bank Corporation and Goldman Sachs.
20. The interest rate-based estimates are drawn from Malz (1994). The option-based estimates are the ones from data set I for which λ_t and k_t were estimated jointly.

REFERENCES

Akgiray, Vedat and Booth, G. Geoffrey (1988), 'Mixed Diffusion-Jump Process Modeling of Exchange Rate Movements', *Review of Economics and Statistics*, **70** (November), 631–637.

Baillie, Richard T. and Bollerslev, Tim (1989), 'The Message in Daily Exchange Rates: A Conditional-Variance Tale', *Journal of Business and Economic Statistics*, **7** (July), 297–305.

Baillie, Richard and McMahon, Patrick (1989), *The Foreign Exchange Market: Theory and Econometric Evidence*, Cambridge University Press, Cambridge.

Ball, Clifford A. and Roma, Antonio (1993), 'A Jump Diffusion Model for the European Monetary System', *Journal of International Money and Finance*, **12** (October), 475–492.

Ball, Clifford A. and Torous, Walter N. (1983), 'A Simplified Jump Process for Common Stock Returns', *Journal of Financial and Quantitative Analysis*, **18** (March), 53–65.

Ball, Clifford A. and Torous, Walter N. (1985), 'On Jumps in Common Stock Prices and Their Impact on Call Option Pricing', *Journal of Finance*, **40** (March), 155–173.

Bates, David S. (1988a), 'The Crash Premium: Option Pricing under Asymmetric Processes, with Applications to Options on Deutschemark Futures', University of Pennsylvania, Rodney L. White Center for Financial Research Working Paper no. 36–88, October.

Bates, David S. (1988b), 'Pricing Options on Jump-Diffusion Processes', University of Pennsylvania, Rodney L. White Center for Financial Research Working Paper no. 37–88, October.

Bates, David S. (1991), 'The Crash of '87: Was it Expected? The Evidence from Options Markets', *Journal of Finance*, **46** (July), 1009–1044.

Bates, David S. (1993), 'Jumps and Stochastic Volatility: Exchange Rate Processes Implicit in PHLX Deutschemark Options', NBER Working Paper no. 4596, December.

Bertola, Giuseppe and Svensson, Lars E.O. (1993), 'Stochastic Devaluation Risk and the Empirical Fit of Target Zone Models', *Review of Economic Studies*, **60** (July), 689–712.

Black, Fischer and Scholes, Myron (1973) 'The Pricing of Options and Corporate liabilities', *Journal of Political Economy*, **81** (May–June), 637–654.

Bodurtha, James N., Jr and Courtadon, Georges R. (1987) 'Tests of an American Option Pricing Model on the Foreign Currency Options Market', *Journal of Financial and Quantitative Analysis*, **22** (June), 153–167.

Boothe, Paul and Glassman, Debra (1987) 'The Statistical Distribution of Exchange Rates: Empirical Evidence and Economic Implications', *Journal of International Economics*, **22** (May), 297–319.

Breeden, Douglas T. and Litzenberger, Robert H. (1978) 'Prices of State-contingent Claims Implicit in Option Prices', *Journal of Business*, **51** (October), 621–651.

Campa, José M. and Kevin Chang, P.H. (1994), Assessing Realignment Risk in the Exchange Rate Mechanism Through Pound-Mark Cross-Rate Options', March, mimeo.

Chen, Zhaohui and Giovannini, Alberto (1992) 'Target Zones and the Distribution of Exchange Rates: An Estimation Method', *Economics Letters*, **40** (September), 83–89.

Chen, Zhaohui and Giovannini, Alberto (1993), 'The Determinants of Realignment Expectations under the EMS: Some Empirical Regularities', NBER Working Paper no. 4291, March.

Collins, Susan M. (1985), 'The Expected Timing of Devaluation: A Model of Realignments in the European Monetary System', Harvard University, October, mimeo.

Collins, Susan M. (1992), 'The Expected Timing of EMS Realignments: 1973–83', NBER Working Paper no. 4068, May.

Cookson, Richard (1993), 'Moving in the Right Direction', *Risk*, **6** (October), 22–26.

Derman, Emanuel and Kani, Iraj (1994), 'Riding on a Smile', *Risk*, **7** (February), 32–39.

Dumas, Bernard, Peter Jennergren, L. and Näslund, Bertil (1993a), 'Realignment Risk and Currency Option Pricing in Target Zones', NBER Working Paper no. 4458, September.

Dumas, Bernard, Peter Jennergren, L. and Näslund, Bertil (1993b), 'Currency Option Pricing in Credible Target Zones', NBER Working Paper no. 4522, November.

Dupire, Bruno (1994), 'Pricing with a Smile', *Risk*, **7** (January), 18–20.

Eichengreen, Barry, and Wyplosz, Charles (1993), 'The Unstable EMS', *Brookings Papers on Economic Activity*, **1**, 51–143.

Emminger, Otmar (1986), *D-mark, Dollar, Währungskrisen: Erinnerungen eines Ehemaligen Bundesbankpräsidenten*, Deutsche Verlags-Anstalt, Stuttgart.

Garman, Mark B. and Kohlhagen, Steven W. (1983), 'Foreign Currency Option Values', *Journal of International Money and Finance*, **2** (December): 231–237.

Giavazzi, Francesco and Giovannini, Alberto (1989), *Limiting Exchange Rate Flexibility: the European Monetary System*, MIT Press, Cambridge, Mass.

Goldstein, Morris, Folkerts-Landau, David, Garber, Peter, Rojas-Suárez, Liliana and Spencer, Michael (1993), *International Capital Markets: Part I. Exchange Rate Management and International Capital Flows*, International Monetary Fund, Washington.

Grabbe, J. Orlin (1983), 'The Pricing of Call and Put Options on Foreign Exchange', *Journal of International Money and Finance*, **2** (December), 239–253.

Gros, Daniel and Thygesen, Niels (1992), *European Monetary Integration*, Longman, London.

Group of Ten (1993), *International Capital Movements and Foreign Exchange Markets* [Dini Report].

Hsieh, David A. (1988), 'The Statistical Properties of Daily Foreign Exchange Rates: 1974–1983', *Journal of International Economics*, **24** (February), 129–145.

Hsieh, David A. (1989), 'Modeling Heteroscedasticity in Daily Foreign Exchange Rates: 1974–1983', *Journal of Business and Economic Statistics*, **7** (July), 307–317.

Hsieh, David A. and Manas-Anton, Luis (1988), 'Empirical Regularities in the Deutsche Mark Futures Options', *Advances in Futures and Options Research*, **3**, 183–208.

Jarrow, Robert A. and Rudd, Andrew (1983), *Option Pricing*, Irwin, Homewood, Ill.

Jorion, Philipe (1988), 'On Jump Processes in the Foreign Exchange and Stock Markets', *Review of Financial Studies*, **1** (Winter), 427–445.

Krugman, Paul R. (1991), 'Target Zones and Exchange Rate Dynamics', *Quarterly Journal of Economics*, **106** (August), 669–682.

Latané, Henry A. and Rendleman, Richard J. Jr (1976), 'Standard Deviations of Stock Price Relatives Implied in Option Prices', *Journal of Finance*, **31** (May), 369–381.

Lyons, Richard K. (1988), 'Tests of the Foreign Exchange Risk Premium Using the Expected Second Moments Implied by Option Pricing', *Journal of International Money and Finance*, **7** (March), 91–108.

Macbeth, James D. and Merville, Larry J. (1979), 'An Empirical Examination of the Black–Scholes Call Option Pricing Model', *Journal of Finance*, **34** (December), 1173–1186.

Malz, Allan M. (1994), 'Forward Premia and the Probability of Realignment: The Case of the ERM Crisis 1992–1993', Federal Reserve Bank of New York, October, mimeo.

Malz, Allan M. (1995), 'Recovering the Probability Distribution of Future Exchange Rates from Option Prices', Federal Reserve Bank of New York, July, mimeo.

Manaster, Steven and Rendleman, Richard J. Jr (1982), 'Option Prices as Predictors of Equilibrium Stock Prices', *Journal of Finance*, **37** (September), 1043–1057.

Merton, Robert C. (1973), 'The Theory of Rational Option Pricing', *Bell Journal of Economics and Management Science*, **4** (Spring), 141–183.

Merton, Robert C. (1976), 'Option Pricing When Underlying Stock Returns Are Discontinuous', *Journal of Financial Economics*, **3** (January–March), 125–144.

Merton, Robert C. (1982), 'On the Mathematics and Economics Assumptions of Continuous-Time Models', in Sharpe, William F. and Cootner, Cathryn M. (eds), *Financial Economics: Essays in Honor of Paul Cootner*, Prentice-Hall, Englewood Cliffs, N.J., 19–51.

Neely, Christopher J. (1994), 'Realignments of Target Zone Exchange Rate Systems: What Do We Know?', *Federal Reserve Bank of St. Louis Review*, **76** (September/October), 23–34.

Nieuwland, Fred G.M.C. Verschoor, Willem F.C. and Wolff, Christian C.P. (1991), 'EMS Exchange Rates', *Journal of International Financial Markets, Institutions and Money*, **1**, 21–42.

Nieuwland, Fred G.M.C. Verschoor, Willem F.C. and Wolff, Christian C.P. (1993), 'Stochastic Trends and Jumps in EMS Exchange Rates', July, mimeo.

Rose, Andrew K. (1993a) 'European Exchange Rate Credibility Before the Fall: The Case of Sterling', *Federal Reserve Bank of San Francisco Weekly Letter*, no. 93-18 (May 7).

Rose, Andrew K. (1993b), 'Sterling's ERM Credibility: Did the Dog Bark in the Night?' *Economics Letters*, **41**, 419–427.

Rose, Andrew K. and Svensson, Lars E.O. (1991), 'Expected and Predicted Realignments: The FF/DM Exchange Rate During the EMS', Board of Governors of the Federal Reserve System, International Finance Discussion Papers, no. 395, April.

Rubinstein, Mark (1985), 'Nonparametric Tests of Alternative Option Pricing Models Using All Reported Trades and Quotes on the 30 Most Active CBOE Option Classes from August 23, 1976 Through August 31, 1978', *Journal of Finance*, **40** (June), 455–480.

Rubinstein, Mark (1994), 'Implied Binomial Trees', *Journal of Finance*, **49** (July), 771–818.

Schmalensee, Richard and Trippi, Robert A. (1978), 'Common Stock Volatility Expectations Implied by Option Premia', *Journal of Finance*, **33** (March), 129–147.

Shimko, David (1993), 'Bounds of Probability', *Risk*, **6** (April), 33–37.

Svensson, Lars E.O. (1993), 'An Interpretation of Recent Research on Exchange Rate Target Zones', *Journal of Economic Perspectives*, **6** (Fall), 119–144.

Tucker, Alan L. and Pond, Lallon (1988), 'The Probability Distribution of Foreign Exchange Price Changes: Tests of Candidate Processes', *Review of Economics and Statistics*, **70** (November), 638–647.

Ungerer, Horst, Hauvonen, Jouko, J., Lopez-Claros, Augusto and Mayer, Thomas (1990), 'The European Monetary System: Developments and Perspectives', *Occasional Paper 73*, International Monetary Fund, Washington, DC.

Vries, Caspar G. de (1994), 'Stylized Facts of Nominal Exchange Rate Returns', in Frederick van der Ploeg (ed.), *The Handbook of International Macroeconomics*, Blackwell, Oxford and Cambridge, Mass, 348–389.

—— 7 ——

On the Term Structure of Interbank Interest Rates: Jump–diffusion Processes and Option Pricing

MANUEL MORENO and
J. IGNACIO PEÑA

7. INTRODUCTION

This chapter addresses the modeling of the term structure of interbank interest rates and the pricing of options on interest rate sensitive securities. Traditional (one or more factor) models have so far assumed that interest rates evolve over time in a continuous way, see Duffie (1992, pp. 129–139). But there are some circumstances where this may not be a reasonable assumption. One interesting case is domestic interbank markets which are subject to exogenous interventions by the monetary authorities in their attempts to control the money supply. In this case those interventions may cause jump-like behavior in observed interest rates. This idea is similar to Merton's (1976) analysis of stock option pricing. Merton suggested that bursts of information are better depicted in price behaviour as jumps. Thus, one may infer from Merton's suggestion that the unexpected interventions by the monetary authorities are a set of signals to the market which convey information on money supply.

Forecasting Financial Markets: Exchange Rates, Interest Rates and Asset Management. Edited by Christian Dunis. © 1996 John Wiley & Sons Ltd.

Of course many other reasons can affect interest rates in jump-like fashion, for instance supply or demand shocks and economic or political news. One of the targets of this chapter is to deal with all those possible influences under the same umbrella, by positing a general enough model that can cope with these kinds of effects. Note also that another practical advantage of employing diffusion processes with superimposed discrete jumps is that we can take into account the 'fat tails' usually found in the distribution of security prices.

The chapter is organized as follows. In section 7.2 we present the theoretical background. Section 7.3 describes the econometric approach. Section 7.4 addresses the basic characteristics of our data sample. The empirical analysis is presented in section 7.5. Section 7.6 analyzes the relationship between monetary authorities' interventions and the jump-like behavior of interest rates. Section 7.7 discusses the pricing of bonds and options. Finally, section 7.8 summarizes and concludes.

7.2 THEORETICAL BACKGROUND

The basic framework in this chapter is the single-factor model of interest rates, in the tradition of Vasicek (1977) and Cox et al. (1985a, b) among others. We generalize those models, following the suggestions by Das (1994a), who posits the addition of a jump component in the process followed by the state variable. The dynamics of the interest rate are given by the following jump–diffusion process:

$$dr = k(\theta - r)\,dt + \sigma r^\tau\,dz + J(\mu,\,\gamma^2)\,d\pi(h) \tag{1}$$

where, for the instantaneous riskless interest rate r, k is the coefficient of mean reversion, θ is the long run mean level of r, σ is the standard deviation of r, τ is the elasticity coefficient parameter, dz is a standard Gauss–Wiener process, J is the jump magnitude in r which has a normal distribution with mean μ and variance γ^2 and $d\pi(h)$ is a Poisson arrival process with a constant intensity parameter h. The jump and diffusion components on the interest rate process are assumed to be independent. Mean reversion ($k > 0$) ensures that r follows a stationary process.

Given the instantaneous interest rate r at period t, let $P[r, t, T]$ represent the price of a riskless pure discount bond maturing at period T. From Ito's lemma, the instantaneous rate of return on the bond is

$$dP = (P_r\,dr + 0.5P_{rr}(dr)^2 + P_t\,dt) \tag{2}$$

where subscripts denote partial derivatives. In perfect markets, the instantaneous expected rate of return for any asset can be written as the instantaneous riskless rate, r, plus a risk premium. Therefore, the risk-adjusted return on all zero coupon bonds must be the same. Assuming that the market price per unit of risk ($\lambda(.)$) for the bond is a general function that may depend on σ, r and τ, but not on $T - t$, and remembering that the jump and diffusion components in equation (1) are independent, the variance of changes in r is simply the sum of the variances of both components. The arbitrage-free pricing partial differential equation is as follows:

$$0 = (k(\theta - r) - \lambda(\sigma, r, \tau))P_r + P_t + 0.5\sigma^2 r^{2\tau} P_{rr} - rP + hE[P(r + J) - P(r)] \tag{3}$$

This is the fundamental equation for the price of any zero coupon bond which has a value that depends solely on the instantaneous rate, r, and the time to maturity, $T - t$. With the boundary condition,

$$P[r, T, T] = 1.0 \tag{4}$$

Analytical solutions of equation (3) (if available) are usually obtained by positing that the functional form of the bond price is given by

$$P[r, t, T] = A[t, T] \exp[-B[t, T]r] \tag{5}$$

where

$$A[t, T] = f_A(\Phi) \qquad B[t, T] = f_B(\Phi) \qquad \Phi = (T - t, k, \theta, \sigma, \tau, h, \mu, \gamma^2, \lambda) \tag{6}$$

If it is not possible to find an analytical solution, numerical procedures may be used to approximate equation (3).

Explicit expressions for $A[t, T]$ and $B[t, T]$ have been reported for some particular cases. Ahn and Thompson (1988) studied the case of $\tau = 0.5$ assuming a jump component equal to δdy where δ is a negative constant and the intensity of y is taken to be πr, i.e. the jump arrival rate is proportional to the level of interest rate. Das (1994a) studied the cases $\tau = 0.5$ and $\tau = 0.0$ and parameterized both the size and sign of the jump component. To our knowledge, expressions for $A[t, T]$ and $B[t, T]$ for general values of τ have not been reported.

The valuation framework presented above can be applied to other securities whose payoffs depend on interest rates, such as options and futures on bonds. Theoretical work on pricing interest rate sensitive securities for jump–diffusion processes include Ahn and Thompson (1988), Naik and Lee (1990), Das (1994a) and Naik and Lee (1995). In these papers analytic models for bond and option prices are given. However, none of these models permits the pricing of American options. This is unfortunate given that almost all traded interest sensitive securities have American features. Furthermore, the pricing of 'American-style' derivative securities usually requires numerical methods, either by binomial trees or by finite-differencing methods, see Duffie (1992, Ch. 10). Recently, applications of numerical methods to jump–diffusion processes have been reported by Amin (1993) for the binomial tree approach and by Das (1994b) for the finite-differencing approach. In this chapter we follow the latter approach, using the full implicit finite-differencing (FIFD) method for bond and option pricing.

We now develop the procedure to solve equation (3) using the FIFD method. When using this method, careful specification of the boundary conditions is required. Since the state variable, r, varies in the range $[0, \infty)$, and the process requires backward recursion in time on a discrete time grid of the state variable, it is hard to establish a grid over this support. To deal with this problem, we carry out the following transformation of variable

$$y = \frac{1}{1 + \beta r} \qquad \beta > 0 \tag{7}$$

The new state variable, y, varies in the range $(0, 1]$ and this makes the upper bound easy to establish. Using this transformation from r to y we obtain a transformed version of the partial differential equation (3):

$$0 = P_y \left[\sigma^2 \beta^{2-2\tau} y^{3-2\tau} (1-y)^{2\tau} - \beta y^2 \left(k \left(\theta - \frac{1-y}{\beta y} \right) - \lambda(\cdot) \right) \right]$$

$$+ P_{yy} \left[\tfrac{1}{2} \sigma^2 \beta^{2-2\tau} y^{4-2\tau} (1-y)^{2\beta} \right] + P_t - \left(\frac{1-y}{\beta y} \right) P \tag{8}$$

$$+ \left[EP \left(\frac{1-y}{\beta y} + J \right) - P \left(\frac{1-y}{\beta y} \right) \right] h$$

which can be written as

$$0 = P_y A + P_{yy} B + P_t - \left(\frac{1-y}{\beta y} \right) P + \left[EP \left(\frac{1-y}{\beta y} + J \right) - P \left(\frac{1-y}{\beta y} \right) \right] h \tag{9}$$

where

$$A = \left[\sigma^2 \beta^{2-2\tau} y^{3-2\tau} (1-y)^{2\tau} - \beta y^2 \left(k \left(\theta - \frac{1-y}{\beta y} \right) - \lambda(\cdot) \right) \right] \tag{10}$$

$$B = \left[\tfrac{1}{2} \sigma^2 \beta^{2-2\tau} y^{4-2\tau} (1-y)^{2\beta} \right]$$

The procedure to solve equation (8) using the FIFD method involves a two-dimensional grid where we have the (transformed) state variable (y) on one axis and time (t) on the other. Let the variable $i = 1, 2, \ldots N$ index the state variable axis and the variable $j = 1, 2, \ldots T$ index the time axis on the grid where N and T are the number of points on each axis. We denote the price of a bond on the grid as $P_{i,j}$ and the value of the state variable as $y_{i,j}$. The distance between adjacent nodes on the i-axis is equal to m, and that between adjacent nodes on the j-axis is equal to q. Using this notation, we can write the differential equation (8) in difference equation form as follows:

$$
0 = A_i \left[\frac{P_{i+1,j} - P_{i-1,j}}{2m} \right] + \left[\frac{P_{i,j+1} - P_{ij}}{q} \right] + B_i \left[\frac{P_{i+1,j} - 2P_{ij} + P_{i-1,j}}{m^2} \right]
$$

$$
+ h \sum_{n=1}^{N} P_{nj} \times \text{Prob} \left[\frac{1 - y_{nj}}{\beta y_{nj}} \middle| \frac{1 - y_{ij}}{\beta y_{ij}} \right] - h P_{ij} - \frac{1 - y}{\beta y} P_{ij} \tag{11}
$$

$$
i = 1, 2 \ldots N, j = 1, 2 \ldots T
$$

The boundary conditions for pricing the bonds at maturity are simply

$$
P\left(\frac{1 - y}{\beta y}, T, T \right) = 1.0 \tag{12}
$$

Rearranging equation (10) we can write

$$
- \frac{P_{i,j+1}}{q} = P_{i+1,j} a_i + P_{ij} b_i + P_{i-1,j} c_i + h \sum_{n=1}^{N} P_{n,j} \times \text{Prob} \left[\frac{1 - y_{n,j}}{\beta y_{n,j}} \middle| \frac{1 - y_{ij}}{\beta y_{ij}} \right] \tag{13}
$$

where

$$
a_i = \left[\frac{A_i}{2m} + \frac{B_i}{m^2} \right]
$$

$$
b_i = \left[-\frac{1}{q} - \frac{2B_i}{m^2} - \frac{1 - y}{\beta y} - h \right] \tag{14}
$$

$$
c_i = \left[-\frac{A_i}{2m} + \frac{B_i}{m^2} \right]
$$

This system of N equations is solved by backward recursion, given the boundary conditions for the bond. The $N \times T$ equations system in formulae (13) can be written in matrix form:

$$
P_{j+1} = XP_j \qquad j = T - 1, \ldots 1 \qquad X = -q(Q + Y) \tag{15}
$$

where Q is a $N \times N$ matrix containing the probabilities of jumping from any node P_{ij} to P_{nj}. P_{j+1} is an $N \times 1$ vector and Y is a tridiagonal matrix where each row contains the coefficients a_i, b_i and c_i. Backward recursion is performed by computing equation (15) from $j = T - 1$ to $j = 1$. For other interest rate derivative securities, which are functions of bond prices, appropriate boundary conditions can be imposed and the prices can be computed off the grid. This approach allows almost all forms of path-independent valuation.

7.3 ECONOMETRIC FRAMEWORK

The model to be estimated for the dynamics of the interest rate is the following jump–diffusion process:

$$dr = k(\theta - r)\,dt + \sigma r^\tau\,dz + J(\mu, \gamma^2)\,d\pi(h) \tag{16}$$

We follow a two-step procedure. First we estimate the pure diffusion part of the model, setting $h = 0$ in equation (16). Then we estimate both the jump's location and size using a likelihood ratio test-type statistic. Finally we estimate jointly the full diffusion–jump model.

The pure diffusion is estimated using the discrete time technology of Chan *et al.* (1992), based on an iterated version of Hansen's GMM (Generalized Method of Moments). The econometric specification is

$$r_t - r_{t-1} = a + br_{t-1} + \epsilon_t \qquad E[\epsilon_t] = 0 \qquad E[\epsilon_t^2] = \sigma^2 r_{t-1}^{2\tau} \tag{17}$$

so that

$$k = -b \qquad \theta = -\frac{a}{b} \tag{18}$$

Given the parameter vector $\Omega = (\alpha, \beta, \sigma, \tau)$ and the residuals ϵ_t in equation (17), let the moment vector $f_t(\Omega)$ be

$$f_t(\Omega) = \begin{bmatrix} \epsilon_t \\ \epsilon_t r_{t-1} \\ \epsilon_t^2 - \sigma^2 r_{t-1}^{2\tau} \\ (\epsilon_t^2 - \sigma^2 r_{t-1}^{2\tau})r_{t-1} \end{bmatrix} \tag{19}$$

Under the null hypothesis, if the restrictions implied by equation (16) are true, $E[f_t(\Omega)] = 0$. We replace $E[f_t(\Omega)]$ with its sample counterpart $g_T(\Omega)$, using T observations,

$$g_T(\Omega) = \frac{1}{T}\sum_{t=1}^{T} f_t(\Omega) \tag{20}$$

Then, the GMM estimator is

$$\Omega_0 = \operatorname{argmin} J_T(\Omega) \tag{21}$$

where

$$J_T(\Omega) = g_T(\Omega)' V g_T(\Omega) \tag{22}$$

and V is an appropriate weighting matrix. To deal with possible residual autocorrelation and heteroskedasticity we employ the Newey–West corrected covariance matrix for the GMM model and then iterate till convergence is achieved.

To test the overidentifying restrictions of the model, we use the chi-square test. The quantity $TJ_T(\Omega)$ is distributed χ^2 with degrees of freedom equal to the number of moment conditions less the number of parameters estimated.

Using the estimated values of the diffusion parameters, we estimate the jump locations using an approach based on the ideas of Aase and Guttorp (1987). Essentially the procedure is to compute a selected criterion function for each observation, assuming no jumps (restricted) and compare it with its value assuming one jump (unrestricted). In our case, the criterion function is the quadratic form $J_T(\Omega)$. We compute for each observation the test statistic

$$R = T[J_T(\Omega_0) - J_T(\Omega_1)] \qquad (23)$$

This test is asymptotically distributed χ^2 with one degree of freedom, and can be interpreted as the normalized difference of the restricted $J_T(\Omega_0)$ and unrestricted $J_T(\Omega_1)$ objective functions. This procedure provides the location and size of the jumps with their sign.

Therefore, at each point in time, we know whether or not, a jump occurred, as well as its sign. Thus, at each t, we can write the conditional expectation and variance of the change in the interest rate depending on the event at that time. Using a dummy variable D_i, $i = 1, 2 \ldots T$, which takes values $D_i = 1$ if there is a jump and $D_i = 0$ otherwise, we obtain the moments for the estimation as follows:

$$\epsilon_t = r_t - r_{t-1} - (a + br_{t-1}) - dD_t$$
$$E[\epsilon_t] = 0 \qquad (24)$$
$$E[\epsilon_t^2] - \sigma^2 r_{t-1} - (dD_t)^2 = 0$$

where we use as a starting point the parameters estimated for the pure diffusion process.

7.4 DATA CHARACTERISTICS

In this section, we address the basic characteristics of our data sample. The instantaneous riskless interest rate is approximated by daily overnight Spain interbank offer rates.[1] The data was obtained from the Research Department, Bank of Spain, and consists of annualized rates. Daily data spans the period from 1 January 1988 to 10 March 1994. The number of observations is 1534. Figure 7.1 shows the overnight rate. Note the periodic 'drops' in the overnight rate as well as the significant increase in the volatility associated with the turbulence in the European Monetary System. It is worth mentioning that in the period from September 1992 to May 1993 the peseta was devalued three times.

Table 7.1 provides summary statistics of the interest rate (r) as well as the changes in interest rate (dr). The unconditional average interest rate is 13%

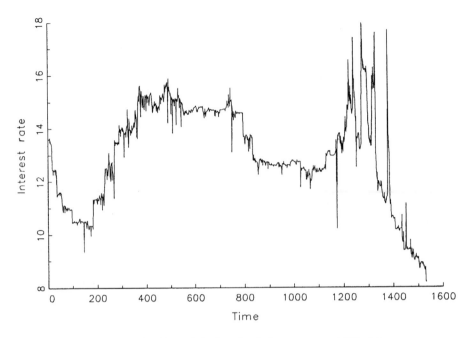

Figure 7.1 Overnight interbank interest rate 1988–94

and its standard deviation is around 180 basis points. The mean change in interest rates is slightly negative and its volatility is about 33 basis points. The excess kurtosis in the distribution of changes in interest rates indicates the presence of fat tails in the interest rate distribution. The autocorrelation coefficients of the interest rate (see Table 7.2) are close to unity and decay quite slowly. The autocorrelation coefficients of the changes in interest rate are small and negative. Therefore, mean reversion in interest rate is suggested in our sample.

Table 7.1 Interest rates: descriptive statistics

Variables	Number of observations	Mean	Standard deviation	Skewness coefficient	Excess kurtosis
r_t	1534	13.003	1.8363	−0.424	−0.496
$r_t - r_{t-1}$	1533	−0.0035	0.3368	3.0023	98.507

Note: This table provides summary statistics of the overnight Spain interbank interest rate (r_t) as well as the changes in this interest rate ($r_t - r_{t-1}$). Means, standard deviations, skewness coefficients and excess kurtosis are computed from January 1988 through March 1994. Raw data is in percentage terms.

Table 7.2 Interest rates: correlation structure

Variables	N	ρ_1	ρ_2	ρ_3	ρ_4	ρ_5	ρ_6
r_t	1534	0.9809	0.9656	0.9542	0.9450	0.9366	0.9287
$r_t - r_{t-1}$	1533	−0.113	−0.114	−0.067	−0.009	−0.013	0.052

Note: This table shows correlation coefficients of order j, denoted by ρ_j, of the overnight Spain interbank interest rate (r_t) as well as the changes in this interest rate ($r_t - r_{t-1}$). These coefficients are computed from January 1988 through March 1994. N denotes the number of observations. Raw data is in percentage terms.

7.5 EMPIRICAL ANALYSIS

This section presents the estimation of equation (17). First we estimate the pure diffusion model, which nests eight interest rate models (see Table 7.3) derived from the restrictions on the parameters a, b and τ in equation (17). In a second stage, we use the estimated values of the diffusion parameters to obtain the location, size and sign of the jumps.

7.5.1 Modelling Pure Diffusion Processes

Table 7.4 presents the estimation results obtained for the pure diffusion processes. We estimate the unrestricted diffusion process derived from equation (16) as well as eight restricted models derived through restrictions on the parameters of this model. The χ^2 tests for goodness-of-fit indicate that the Brennan–Schwartz (1980), Cox *et al.* (1985b) and Vasicek (1977)

Table 7.3 Alternative pure diffusion processes

Model	a	b	τ
Merton (1973)	—	0	0
Vasicek (1977)	—	—	0
Cox *et al.* (1985b)	—	—	0.5
Dothan (1978)	0	0	1
Black and Scholes (1973)	0	—	1
Brennan–Schwartz (1980)	—	—	1
Cox *et al.* (1980)	0	0	1.5
Cox (1975)	0	—	—
Unrestricted	—	—	—

Note: This table shows the alternative pure diffusion models that reflect the dynamics of the interest rate. These processes derive from restrictions on the parameters a, b and τ in the system of equations

$$r_t - r_{t-1} = a + br_{t-1} + \epsilon_t \qquad E[\epsilon_t] = 0 \qquad E[\epsilon_t^2] = \sigma^2 r_{t-1}^{2\tau} \qquad (17)$$

Table 7.4 Estimates of the alternative pure diffusion models

Model	a	b	σ^2	τ	χ^2	d.f.	R_1^2	R_2^2
Merton (1973)	0.00119 (0.181)	0	0.06304 (2.98)	0	5.30 (0.0706)	2	−0.0002	0
Vasicek (1977)	0.1721 (2.15)	−0.0132 (−2.15)	0.1113 (3.5)	0	0.7911 (0.3737)	1	0.0062	0
Cox et al. (1985b)	0.1834 (2.26)	−0.0145 (−2.28)	0.000001 (5.6)	0.5	0.3161 (0.5739)	1	0.0063	0.0009
Dothan (1978)	0	0	0.000452 (6.43)	1	5.23 (0.1557)	3	−0.0001	0.0006
Black and Scholes (1973)	0	−0.00008 (−0.18)	0.00044 (5.8)	1	5.216 (0.0736)	2	0.0	0.0007
Brennan–Schwartz (1980)	0.1874 (2.3)	−0.0146 (−2.3)	0.000657 (3.72)	1	0.0068 (0.9342)	1	0.0064	0.0014
Cox et al. (1980)	0	0	0.00957 (5.04)	1.5	5.308 (0.1506)	3	0.0	0.0006
Cox (1975)	0	−0.0001 (−0.17)	0.0016 (0.09)	0.85 (0.73)	5.213 (0.0224)	1	0.0	0.0009
Unrestricted	0.1874 (2.2)	−0.014 (−2.3)	0.000911 (3.4)	0.96 (29)	—	—	0.0064	0.0014

Note: This table provides the parameter estimates (with t-statistics in parentheses) of unrestricted and restricted alternative pure diffusion models for Spain interbank interest rates. GMM minimized criterion (χ^2) values, with p-values in parentheses and associated degrees of freedom (d.f.) are also reported. The sample period is from January 1988 to March 1994. The R_j^2 statistics are computed as the proportion of the total variation of the actual interest rate changes ($j = 1$) and their volatility ($j = 2$) explained by the respective predictive values for each model. The parameters are estimated by means of the generalized method of moments applied to the estimation of equation (16).

models exhibit the closest to zero GMM minimized criterion values. The lowest χ^2 value corresponds to the Brennan–Schwartz model, which assume the highest value for τ among these, and all three models have χ^2 values smaller than 0.8. In these models a single parameter, τ, is restricted. As no restrictions are imposed on the parameters a and b, all of them show mean reversion. The Dothan (1978) and Cox et al. (1980) models which assume that the parameters a and b are null, fit the data less well but none can be rejected at the 90% confidence level. The Black–Scholes (1973) and Merton (1973) models have χ^2 values in excess of 5 and can be rejected at the 90% confidence level. The Cox model, which assumes that the parameter a is equal to zero, can be rejected at the 95% confidence level.

Note that models which imply mean reversion have the lowest GMM criterion χ^2 values. On the other hand, models which assume that the parameters a and/or b are null—that is, there is no mean reversion in interest rates—have high χ^2 values and are therefore not acceptable.

The parameters' estimates of the unconstrained model, which are very similar to the estimates of the Brennan–Schwartz model, show that the parameters a and b are different from zero and, hence, there is evidence of mean reversion in interest rates. Another feature of this model is that the estimated value for the parameter τ is 0.96. Therefore, the conditional volatility of the process is very sensitive to the level of the interest rate. This value is higher than the values assumed by the most common models as the Vasicek or Cox et al. (1985b) models.

To obtain more information on the performance of the alternative pure diffusion models, we test their in-sample forecasting power in relation to the level and volatility of interest rates. First, we use the fitted values for equation (17) to compute the time series of conditional expected interest rate changes and conditional variances for the unrestricted and the eight restricted models. Then, we compute the $R_j^2(j = 1, 2)$ statistics. These two values are reported in the two last columns of Table 7.4 and show (for each model) the proportion of the total variation in the ex post interest rate changes or squared interest rate changes that can be explained by the conditional expected interest rate changes and conditional volatility measures, respectively.

The R_1^2 value is the measure related to the actual interest rate changes. The unrestricted and Brennan–Schwartz models have the best explanatory performance and are closely followed by the Cox et al. (1985b) and Vasicek models. The remaining models have no explanatory power. In the case of the R_2^2 statistic, which measures the degree of the model's explanatory power of the volatility of the interest rate changes, the highest value corresponds also to the unconstrained and the Brennan–Schwartz models, which are followed by the Cox et al. (1985b), Cox (1975) and Black–Scholes models. Therefore, these two measures, which indicate the predictive power of the models, provide a classification of the alternative models which is very similar to that obtained when parameters of the pure diffusion models were estimated. Given the previous results, we choose the Brennan–Schwartz process as a tentative model for the pure diffusion part of the Interbank interest rate.

7.5.2 Modelling Jumps

Once we have estimated the pure diffusion models, we use those results to estimate the location of the jumps. After applying the econometric procedure described in section 7.3, we find 77 jumps in the sample. Figure 7.2 plots the time series of the interest rate and the location of the jumps. The summary statistics of the jumps are reported in Table 7.5. The mean jump size is about 7 basis points and its volatility (measured by the standard deviation) is around 140 basis points. The arrival frequency of the jumps is 5.02% and, therefore, there is approximately one jump per month. The distribution of jump sizes is shown in Figures 7.3 and 7.4. Separating the jumps by their sign, there are 37 positive jumps while the remaining 40 are negative. The mean of the negative jumps is 100 basis points and the mean of the positive jumps is 123 basis points. The distribution of the negative jumps has a lower variance than the distribution of the positive jumps.

Once the location of the jumps is known, we are able to include this information in our model by means of dummy variables. This is done by estimating the two models in equations (25) through (28).

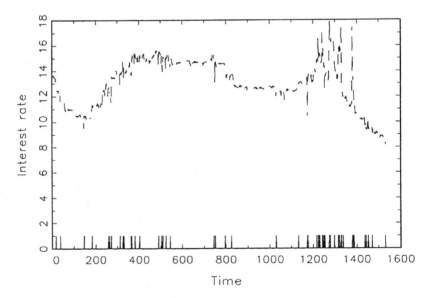

Figure 7.2 Jumps indicator and interest rate 1988–94

Table 7.5 Jumps size: descriptive statistics

Variables	Number of jumps	Mean	Standard deviation	Skewness coefficient	Excess kurtosis
$JUMP_t$	77	0.07037	1.392555	0.7515	3.90682
$JUMPPOS_t$	37	1.2313	0.985046	3.4132	14.3367
$JUMPNEG_t$	40	-1.00348	0.659994	-3.59903	16.5665

Note: This table provides summary statistics of the jumps located in the interest rates series from January 1988 through March 1994. We report statistics for the following variables: $JUMP_t$, which denotes jumps size, $JUMPPOS_t$, which includes the size of positive jumps, and $JUMPNEG_t$, which includes the size of negative jumps. N denotes, for each type, the number of located jumps.

The first model includes one dummy variable that indicates the moment when a jump occurred:

$$r_t - r_{t-1} = a + br_{t-1} + dD_t + \epsilon_t$$
$$E[\epsilon_t] = 0 \quad E[\epsilon_t^2] = \sigma^2 r_{t-1}^2$$
(25)

where

$$D_t = \begin{cases} 1 & \text{if there is a jump} \\ 0 & \text{otherwise} \end{cases}$$
(26)

We also estimate a second model with two dummy variables which distinguish between positive and negative jumps:

$$r_t - r_{t-1} = a + br_{t-1} + d^+D_t^+ + d^-D_t^- + \epsilon_t$$
$$E[\epsilon_t] = 0 \quad E[\epsilon_t^2] = \sigma^2 r_{t-1}^2$$
(27)

where

$$D_t^+ = \begin{cases} 1 & \text{if there is a positive jump} \\ 0 & \text{otherwise} \end{cases}$$
$$D_t^- = \begin{cases} 1 & \text{if there is a negative jump} \\ 0 & \text{otherwise} \end{cases}$$
(28)

The parameter estimates for the two-jump-Brennan–Schwartz models are shown in Table 7.6.

The a and b coefficients are both significantly different from zero, pointing out that mean reversion is present in our sample, even after taking account of jumps. The coefficient associated with the jump dummy variable is not different from zero. When different effects are allowed for positive and negative jumps the coefficients are statistically significant. The degree of fit of the model with jumps is similar to the model without jumps, as measured by the R^2. However, when separate variables are included for positive and

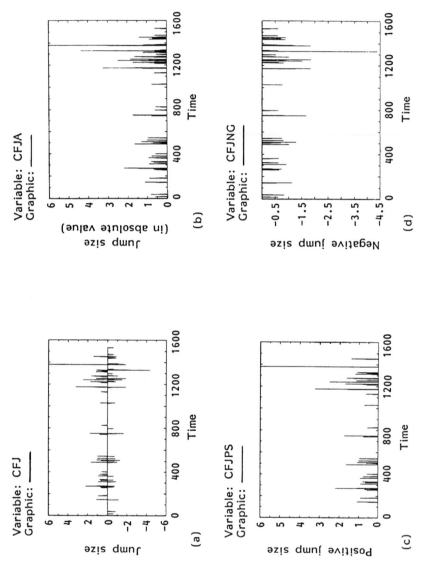

Figure 7.3 (a) Jump size; (b) jump size in absolute value; (c) positive jump size; (d) negative jump size

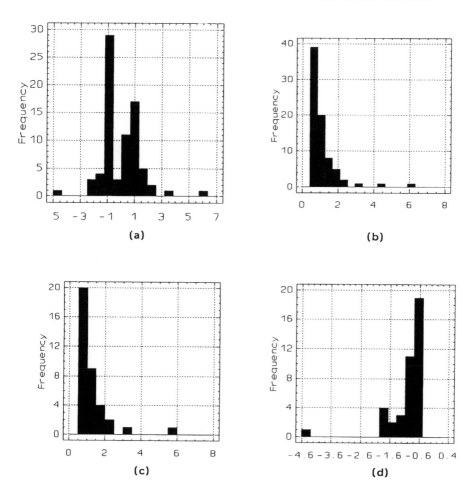

Figure 7.4 Distribution of: (a) jumps' size; (b) absolute jumps' size; (c) positive jumps' size; (d) negative jumps' size

negative jumps the degree of fit increases substantially. Therefore, we conclude that taking into account the presence of a jump process increases the model's explanatory power.

7.6 INTERVENTIONS BY MONETARY AUTHORITIES

In this section we investigate the extent to which interventions by the Bank of Spain (Spain's monetary authority) are responsible for at least part of the

Table 7.6 Estimates of the jump–diffusion models

Model	a	b	σ^2	d	d^+	d^-	R^2
(25)–(26)	0.1490 (2.46)	−0.0082 (−1.77)	0.0088 (−43.74)	0.0113 (0.28)	—	—	0.0064
(27)–(28)	0.1248 (3.17)	−0.0070 (−2.33)	0.0030 (−46.27)	—	1.1533 (31.19)	−1.08 (29.84)	0.5441

Note: This table contains the parameter estimates (with *t*-statistics in parentheses) of the two alternative jump–diffusion models for Spain interbank interest rates. The sample period is from January 1988 to March 1994. The parameters are estimated by means of the generalized method of moments and they are obtained from equations (25)–(26) and (27)–(28).

jump-like behavior of interest rate time series. The Bank of Spain (BS) uses a 'target' interest rate (*tipo de intervencion*, TI henceforth) in open market transactions. Periodically, the BS intervenes in the interbank market, offering money for lending or borrowing at the TI rate. Data for the TI rate was obtained from the Research Department of the Bank of Spain. Short-term rates tend to track the TI rate rather closely. This can be noticed from the regression results in Table 7.7. The regression of the short rate on the contemporaneous TI rate is highly significant. Also, the TI one-day lag is found to be significant. This reflects the fact that BS sets the TI rate after the start of the interbank trading session. The results in Table 7.7 suggest that about 50% of the total variance in the short rate is explained by its relationship with the TI rate.

We compare a change in the BS target rate with the occurrence of a jump as derived in the jump–diffusion model. If both occur together, we assume that the jump was caused by the BS intervention. There were a total of 77 jumps in the interest rate and 160 BS target rate changes. Jumps and changes in the BS target rate coincide on 22 days. The summary statistics for these jumps and the associated changes in the BS target rate are reported in Table 7.8. The mean jump size is near zero and the volatility of the jumps, indicated by their standard deviation, is about 160 basis points. Therefore, this restricted

Table 7.7 The short rate and the TI rate

Variables	Constant	TI(t)	TI($t-1$)	Φ	Adjusted R^2	*DW*
Estimate	−0.122	0.882	0.146	0.827	0.472	2.10
t-stat	−0.301	15.53	2.57	53.19		

Note: This table provides regression results on the relationship between the short rate and the TI rate. The sample period is from January 1988 to March 1994. The regression is corrected for first-order autocorrelation (coefficient Φ) and is run on contemporaneous and one lagged values of the BS target rate TI. Robust standard errors are computed using the Newey–West covariance matrix estimator.

Table 7.8 Coincidence between jumps and BS actions. Jumps size: descriptive statistics

Variables	Number of jumps	Mean	Standard deviation	Skewness	Excess kurtosis
JUMPBS$_t$	22	0.01111	1.60083	−0.4879	1.6869
JUMPPSBS$_t$	10	1.3962	0.8150	1.4609	2.0053
JUMPNGBS$_t$	12	−1.1431	1.0729	−2.9163	9.0796

Note: This table provides summary statistics of the jumps that occur simultaneously with a change in the BS target rate. The sample period is from January 1988 through March 1994. We report these statistics for the following variables: JUMPBS$_t$, which denotes jumps size, JUMPPSBS$_t$, which includes the size of positive jumps, and JUMPNGBS$_t$, which shows the size of negative jumps. N denotes, for each type, the number of located jumps.

set of 22 jumps is more volatile than the whole set of 77 jumps. In a similar way to the whole set of jumps, the highest jump sizes occur in the last 20 months of our sample period.

In the 22 days where BS actions and jumps occurred together, there were 10 positive and 12 negative jumps. Therefore, in this restricted set of jumps, the proportion of positive and negative jumps is similar to the proportion we found in the whole sample. Their average, in the restricted set of jumps, is greater than the values obtained in the whole sample and, similarly, the mean value of the positive jumps is greater than the (absolute value of the) mean value of negative jumps, which is in excess of 110 basis points.

We build a window of five days around the BS target rate change in order to check if the market was able to anticipate (or reverse) a BS move. If we find that the change in the BS target rate is preceded by a jump in the market in the prior week, this may be interpreted as anticipation. The results are displayed graphically in Figure 7.5. In this figure, the x-axis represents the number of days by which the BS intervention precedes the jump (a negative value indicates the number of days between a jump and a posterior BS rate change). The highest peaks of this figure correspond to the central value (number of days in which a BS action and a jump occur simultaneously) and

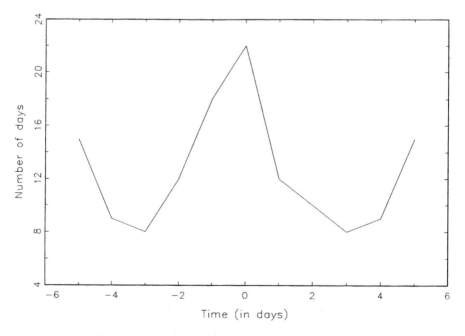

Figure 7.5 Relation between jumps and BS actions

to the extreme values (days in which a BS action and a jump are separated by five days). Another interesting feature of this figure is its symmetry.

Therefore, we may say that some, but not all, jumps are related to the monetary authorities' interventions, but perhaps there are also other factors (e.g. exchange rate shocks) that should be taken into account if we want to explain the occurrence of jumps in our sample. In conclusion, it seems that the analysis indicates that about one-third of jump-like shocks are coincident with BS actions. Moreover, it is not very clear whether the market was able to either anticipate or reverse a BS move systematically.

7.7 PRICING DERIVATIVES

For illustrative purposes, we implement the algorithm described in section 7.2 to price bonds with maturities of 3 months and 1 year and also a 3-month option on a 1-year bond.[2] The options, puts and calls, are priced under pure-diffusion and jump–diffusion assumptions. We price both European and American options. The following parameter values are used:

$$a = 0.149, \qquad b = -0.008, \qquad \sigma = 0.0088, \qquad \lambda(.) = 0 \tag{29}$$
$$\mu = 0, \qquad \gamma = 1.392, \qquad h = 12.3, \qquad \tau = 1.0$$

The strike price is 0.95. The parameters in equation (29) are those of the

Table 7.9 Examples of pricing bonds and options using the FIFD method

Security	$r = 0.08$	$r = 0.09$	$r = 0.10$	$r = 0.11$	$r = 0.12$
Diffusion					
Bond (3-month)	0.9791	0.9779	0.9756	0.9748	0.9722
Bond (1-year)	0.9295	0.9232	0.9176	0.9108	0.9042
Call	0.0087	0.0051	0.0022	0.0011	0.0003
Put(European)	0.0021	0.0051	0.0087	0.0116	0.0131
Put(American)	0.0097	0.0176	0.0192	0.0271	0.0342
Jump–diffusion					
Bond (3-month)	0.9794	0.9782	0.9758	0.9749	0.9725
Bond (1-year)	0.9297	0.9234	0.9177	0.9110	0.9046
Call	0.0091	0.0054	0.0026	0.0015	0.0008
Put(European)	0.0021	0.0051	0.0087	0.0116	0.0131
Put(American)	0.0097	0.0176	0.0190	0.0271	0.0340

Note: This table contains bond values for maturities of 3 months and 1 year at different values of the current overnight rate. Values are for zero-coupon bonds with face values of 1.0 and $r = 0.08$, 0.09, 0.10, 0.11, 0.12. The arrival rate is $h = 12.3$ jumps per year and the jumps are distributed $\sim N(0, 1.392)$. The other parameters are $a = 0.149$, $b = -0.008$, $\sigma = 0.0088$, $\lambda = 0.0$. Option prices are computed for the three-month option on the one-year discount bond. The strike price is 0.95. The pricing results are identical for European and American call options.

model estimated for the overnight interest rate which follows a jump-enhanced Brennan–Schwartz process.

Table 7.9 contains the results. Given that the pricing results for European and American call options are identical, we report both jointly. There are some interesting facts. The price of a one-year bond is higher under the jump–diffusion model. This is the well-known 'asymmetric' effect, caused by the asymmetry of the bond pricing function. This feature of high prices will increase with the duration of the bond. Also, options will increase in value because the jumps induce 'fat tails' into the distribution of bond prices. This is the 'time value' effect. In the case of calls, both effects, asymmetric and time value, result in the option increase in value. However, in the case of puts, the asymmetric effect reduces the option value whereas the time value effect increases its value. The trade-off between these two forces leaves the jump–diffusion value of the put indeterminate in comparison with the pure-diffusion case.

7.8 CONCLUSION

This chapter has presented a single-factor model for the term structure of the interbank interest rate, when the instantaneous rate follows a jump–diffusion process. The empirical implementation suggests that jump-diffusions better explain interest rate behaviour than pure-diffusion models. Some economic implications of jump activity are explored with an analysis of changes in the Bank of Spain target rate. As a result, some, but not all, jumps are found to be related to Central Bank interventions. Additionally, we price European-style and American-style interest rate contingent claims (bond and options) using the FIFD approach, enhanced to deal with partial differential equations derived in a jump–diffusion model. The existence of jumps affects bonds and call options very much as in the case of stocks. We find underpricing if the jumps are not taken into account. However, the put options pricing presents some indeterminacies.

ACKNOWLEDGEMENTS

The authors are grateful to the Bank of Spain who kindly provided some data. Partial financial support was provided by DGICYT grant PB93-0234. Michele Boldrin, Javier Estrada, Esther Ruiz, Christian Dunis and participants in the Second Chemical Bank–Imperial College International Conference provided helpful comments. The usual caveat applies.

ENDNOTES

1. The interest rate data is computed as the average rate for all transactions on a specified term in a given day.
2. Many other pricing simulations for bonds and options were performed. The bond pricing simulation was performed for maturities ranging from 1 year to 10 years. The option pricing simulation was performed for 3, 6 and 9 months' options on bonds of different maturities. Detailed results are available on request.

REFERENCES

Aase, K. and Guttorp, P. (1987), 'Estimation in Models for Security Prices', *Scandinavian Actuarial Journal*, **6**, 211–224.

Ahn, C.M. and Thompson, H.E. (1988), 'Jump–Diffusion Processes and Term Structure of Interest Rates', *Journal of Finance*, **43**, 155–174.

Amin, K. (1993), 'Jump–Diffusion Option Valuation in Discrete Time', *Journal of Finance*, **48**, 1833–1863.

Ball, C. and Torous, W.N. (1985), 'On Jumps in Common Stock Prices and Their Impact on Call Option Pricing', *Journal of Finance*, **40**, 155–173.

Black, F. and Scholes, M. (1973), 'The Pricing of Options and Corporate Liabilities', *Journal of Political Economy*, **81**, 637–654.

Brennan, M. and Schwartz, E.S. (1980), 'Analyzing Convertible Bonds', *Journal of Financial and Quantitative Analysis*, **15**, 907–929.

Chan, K.C., Karolyi, G.A., Longstaff, F.A. and Sanders, A.B. (1992), 'An Empirical Comparison of Alternative Models of the Short-Term Interest Rate', *Journal of Finance*, **47**, 1209–1228.

Cox, J.C. (1975), 'Notes on Option Pricing I: Constant Elasticity of Variance Diffusions', Working Paper, Stanford University.

Cox, J.C., Ingersoll, J.E. and Ross, S.A. (1980), 'An Analysis of Variable Rate Loan Contracts', *Journal of Finance*, **35**, 389–403.

Cox, J.C., Ingersoll, J.E. and Ross, S.A. (1985a), 'An Intertemporal General Equilibrium Model of Asset Prices', *Econometrica*, **53**, 363–384.

Cox, J.C., Ingersoll, J.E. and Ross, S.A. (1985b), 'A Theory of the Term Structure of Interest Rates', *Econometrica*, **53**, 385–407.

Das, S.R. (1993), 'Mean Rate Shifts and Alternative Models of the Interest Rate: Theory and Evidence', Working Paper, Stern School of Business, New York University.

Das, S.R. (1994a), 'Jump-Hunting Interest Rates', Working Paper, Stern School of Business, New York University.

Das, S.R. (1994b), 'Discrete-Time Bond and Option Pricing for Jump–Diffusion Process', Working Paper, Harvard Business School.

Dothan, U. (1978), 'On the Term Structure of Interest Rates', *Journal of Financial Economics*, **6**, 59–69.

Duffie, D. (1992), *Dynamic Asset Pricing Theory*, Princeton University Press, Princeton, NJ.

Merton, R.C. (1973), 'Theory of Rational Option Pricing', *Bell Journal of Economics and Management Science*, **4**, 141–183.

Merton, R.C. (1976), 'Option Pricing when Underlying Stock Returns are Discontinuous', *Journal of Financial Economics*, **3**, 125–144.

Naik, V. and Lee, M. (1990), 'General Equilibrium Pricing of Options on the Market Portfolio with Discontinuous Returns', *Review of Financial Studies*, **3**, 493–521.

Naik, V. and Lee, M. (1995), 'The Yield Curve and Bond Option Prices with Discrete Shifts in Economic Regimes', mimeo.

Vasicek, O. (1977), 'An Equilibrium Characterization of the Term Structure', *Journal of Financial Economics*, **5**, 177–188.

8

Conditional Volatility and Informational Efficiency of the PHLX Currency Options Market

XINZHONG XU and
STEPHEN J. TAYLOR

8.1 INTRODUCTION

Options markets are often viewed as markets for volatility trading. Options prices provide forecasts of the future average variance of returns from the underlying asset over the life of the option. The ability of the volatility forecast implied by options prices to predict future volatility is considered a measure of the information content of option prices (Day and Lewis 1992a). Until recently most research into information content has focused on relationships between implied volatility and measures of the subsequent realised volatility (Latane and Rendleman 1976, Chiras and Manaster 1978, Gemmill 1986, Shastri and Tandon 1986, Scott and Tucker 1989). This prior research concludes that volatility predictors calculated from option prices are better predictors of future volatility than standard deviations calculated from historical asset price data. However, Canina and Figlewski (1993) claim that neither implied volatilities nor historical volatilities have much predictive power for the S&P 100 index.

This chapter previously appeared under the same title in the *Journal of Banking and Finance*, September 1995, pp 803–821. © 1995 Journal of Banking and Finance. Reproduced by permission of Journal of Banking and Finance/Elsevier Science.

Day and Lewis (1992a) develop a new methodology based upon autoregressive conditional heteroskedastic (ARCH) models. They examine the information content of implied volatilities, obtained from call options on the S&P 100 index, relative to ARCH estimates of conditional volatility by adding the implied volatility to ARCH models as an exogenous variable. They find that both implied volatility and historical series of asset returns contain incremental information. The null hypothesis that returns contain no volatility information additional to that found in options prices is rejected. Likewise, the hypothesis that options prices have no additional information is rejected. These results imply that the US stock options market either does not use all publicly available information in setting options prices or that the dividend-adjusted version of the Black–Scholes formula used for computing implied volatility is misspecified. Similar results have been found by Day and Lewis (1992b) for the conditional volatility of oil futures and by Lamoureux and Lastrapes (1993) for the conditional volatility of individual stocks. However, it should be noted that these ARCH tests might be unreliable because the implied volatility variable used in the tests is not necessarily appropriate. The ARCH conditional volatility is always for the next period, typically the next day or week. As an implied volatility for the next period rarely exists, Day and Lewis (1992a) use implied volatilities obtained from options having short times to maturity, which range from 7 to 36 days. The implied volatilities used by Lamoureux and Lastrapes (1993) correspond to maturities of between 64 and 129 trading days. It is known that implied volatilities at any moment in time vary for different times to option expiry. This term structure of volatility expectations has been ignored in previous applications of ARCH methodology. This chapter includes an empirical evaluation of whether or not this methodological issue is important.

The relative importance of implied and historical volatility predictors is examined once more in this chapter using ARCH models, but we go one step further. The first implied predictor used here is an estimate of the volatility expectation for the next period calculated from the volatility term structure model developed in Xu and Taylor (1994). Results for this predictor are compared with results for a second predictor defined by short maturity implied volatilities. We study four exchange rate series and find that for three series the implied volatility information alone gives optimal predictions of one-period ahead conditional volatility. Consequently the volatility information provided by currency returns has no incremental predictive power. This is consistent with the informational efficiency of the Philadelphia currency options market. Out-of-sample forecast comparisons confirm this conclusion. The choice of implied volatility predictor (term structure or short maturity) does not affect the conclusions for our data.

The rest of the chapter is organised as follows. Section 8.2 describes the data and a method for estimating volatility expectations for any set of future periods. Exchange rates and options prices from January 1985 to February 1992 are analysed. Within-sample calculations are confined to the period until November 1989. The subsequent data are reserved for out-of-sample forecasting evaluations. Section 8.3 discusses briefly the definitions of ARCH models and the specifications of empirical tests of the informational efficiency of the options market. The empirical within-sample results are presented in section 8.4 followed by out-of-sample forecasting results in section 8.5. The chapter concludes with a summary in section 8.6.

8.2   DATA AND IMPLIED VOLATILITY METHODOLOGY

8.2.1   Datasets

The primary source database for the options prices is the transaction report compiled daily by the Philadelphia Stock Exchange (PHLX). Daily closing option prices and the simultaneous spot exchange rate quotes have been used for the British pound, Deutsche Mark, Japanese yen and Swiss franc quoted against the US dollar from 2 January 1985 to 8 January 1992. However, the transaction report is not available for some trading days. For some other days the report is not complete or in a few cases it is clearly erroneous. Prices have been collected manually from the *Wall Street Journal* (*WSJ*) whenever necessary. Approximately 10% of our implied volatilities are calculated from *WSJ* prices.[1]

Uninformative options records are removed from the database. Options which violate boundary conditions, or are either deep in- or out-of-the-money, or have time to expiry less than 10 calendar days are not considered. In addition, all implied volatilities more than five standard deviations distant from their sample mean are excluded.

The interest rates used are London Euro-currency rates, collected from Datastream. Daily closing prices for futures[2] contracts traded at the International Monetary Market (IMM) in Chicago are also collected from Datastream. Each futures contract is used for the three months prior to its expiration month. At the rollover date, the closing price of the new contract on the previous day before the rollover is used in the calculation of the relative price change. Results from estimating ARCH models show that the choice of method and timing for rolling over futures contracts has insignificant effects.

The IMM closes at 1.20 p.m. while the PHLX closes at 2.00 p.m., and this could lead to bias in favour of the informational efficiency of the options market. However, it has been checked that the conclusions presented in section 8.4 do not change even if we use the options estimate of volatility expectations from the previous day.

8.2.2 Computation of Implied Volatility

Implied volatilities have been calculated from American model prices, approximated by the very accurate functions derived in Barone-Adesi and Whaley (1987). The calculations use an interval subdivision method, which always converges to a unique solution.

All the implied volatilities are calculated for nearest-the-money options; the selected exercise price on a specific day for a specific maturity minimises $|S - X|$.[3] Nearest-the-money options are chosen for two reasons. First, given the widely reported 'strike bias' or 'smile effect' (Shastri and Wethyavivorn 1987, Sheikh 1991, Taylor and Xu 1994), including out-of-the-money and in-the-money options would introduce further noise into volatility expectation estimates. Second, the approximation that the implied volatility of a rationally priced option will equal the mean expected volatility over the time to expiry is generally considered more satisfactory for an at-the-money option than for all other options (Stein 1989, Day and Lewis 1992a, Heynen et al. 1994).

8.2.3 Estimating the Term Structure of Volatility Expectations

Implied volatilities have a term structure. One set of volatility expectations is obtained by estimating a time-varying term structure model for volatility expectations. Complete details are given in Xu and Taylor (1994).

Market agents will have expectations at time t about price volatility during future time periods. Suppose they form expectations of the quantities

$$\text{var}(R_{t+\tau}), \quad \text{with} \quad R_{t+\tau} = \ln P_{t+\tau} - \ln P_{t+\tau-1}, \quad \tau = 1, 2, 3, \ldots \quad (1)$$

where P refers to the price of the asset upon which options are traded.

The volatility term structure model involves two factors representing short-term ($\tau = 1$) and long-term ($\tau \to \infty$) annualised volatility expectations, denoted α_t and μ_t respectively. As the horizon τ increases, the volatility expectations are assumed to revert towards the long-term expectation and the rate of reversion, ϕ, is assumed to be the same for all t. Then the expected volatility at time t for an interval of general length T, from time t to time $t + T$, is the quantity v_T given by

$$v_T^2 = \mu_t^2 + \frac{1 - \phi^T}{T(1 - \phi)}(\alpha_t^2 - \mu_t^2) \quad (2)$$

providing it is assumed that subsequent asset prices, $\{P_{t+\tau}, \tau > 0\}$, follow a random walk.

Kalman filtering methodology applied to implied volatilities provides estimates for the term structure parameters, particularly ϕ, and also time series of short-term and long-term volatility expectation estimates, $\{\hat{\alpha}_t\}$ and $\{\hat{\mu}_t\}$.

8.3   ARCH METHODOLOGY

8.3.1   Specifications of ARCH Models Using Returns Information

The expected variance for the next time interval, $t + 1$, can be obtained from returns up to time t by using the conditional variance h_{t+1} from an ARCH model. In general:

$$h_{t+1} = \text{var}(R_{t+1}|I_t) \tag{3}$$

where I_t denotes the information set of all observed returns up to time t. The most successful and parsimonious models are the generalised autoregressive conditional heteroskedastic GARCH(1,1) model of Bollerslev (1986) and the exponential ARCH(1) model of Nelson (1991). These models have provided satisfactory descriptions of numerous financial time series (Bollerslev *et al.* 1992).

The GARCH(1,1) model defines the conditional variance recursively using residual terms, which are returns minus their conditional means, thus:

$$\varepsilon_t = R_t - E[R_t|I_{t-1}] \tag{4}$$

and

$$h_{t+1} = c + a\varepsilon_t^2 + bh_t. \tag{5}$$

A few examples of applications are Akgiray (1989), Baillie and Bollerslev (1989), Baillie and DeGennaro (1990) and Hsieh (1989).

Nelson (1991) introduces models whose conditional variances are an asymmetric function of the residuals ε_t. The exponential ARCH(1) model involves standardised residuals, z_t,

$$z_t = \varepsilon_t/h_t^{1/2}, \tag{6}$$

and an autoregressive AR(1) specification for $\ln(h_t)$:

$$\ln(h_{t+1}) - \lambda = \rho[\ln(h_t) - \lambda] + \theta z_t + \gamma(|z_t| - E[|z_t|]). \tag{7}$$

Examples of equity studies are Nelson (1991) and Poon and Taylor (1992).

8.3.2   Tests of the Informational Efficiency of the Options Market

As noted in section 8.2.3, an estimate $\hat{\alpha}_t^2$ of expected short-term squared volatility can also be obtained from a term structure model for option prices.

The estimate can be rescaled to give a variance estimate for one period rather than an annualised quantity. The estimate is then for the following unobservable conditional variance

$$\alpha_t^2 = \text{var}\,(R_{t+1}|M_t). \tag{8}$$

Here α_t is not an annualised figure and M_t is the information used by options market agents when they set prices at time t. The set M_t is presumed to include observed returns I_t. Day and Lewis (1992a) use implied volatility from short maturity options to approximate α_t. To evaluate their methodology, we use the implied volatility from an option with the least time to maturity but greater than nine calendar days.

Options prices will provide optimal predictions of volatility when options markets use information efficiently and the pricing model correctly specifies the relationship between prices and volatility expectations. Information other than options prices should not have incremental predictive power when this join hypothesis is true.

To test the hypothesis that options prices give optimal one-period ahead volatility predictions two ARCH models are estimated. The first model only uses options information, the second model also uses returns information. For a GARCH(1,1) specification the two models are

$$h_{t+1} = c + d\hat{\alpha}_t^2 \tag{9}$$

and

$$h_{t+1} = c + a\varepsilon_t^2 + bh_t + d\hat{\alpha}_t^2. \tag{10}$$

For the symmetric version of exponential ARCH(1,0) the models are

$$\ln\,(h_{t+1}) = \lambda + \delta \ln\,(\hat{\alpha}_t^2) \tag{11}$$

and

$$\ln\,(h_{t+1}) = \lambda(1-\rho) + \rho \ln\,(h_t) + \gamma(|z_t| - E[|z_t|]) + \delta \ln\,(\hat{\alpha}_t^2). \tag{12}$$

Likelihood ratio tests of the null hypothesis $a = b = 0$ or $\rho = \gamma = 0$ can be evaluated by comparing $LR = 2(L_1 - L_0)$ with χ_2^2, with L_0 and L_1 the maximum log-likelihoods either for equations (9) and (10) or (11) and (12). These tests make strong and possibly optimistic assumptions about the asymptotic distribution of the likelihood ratio.[4] The relative information content of the two sets of estimates for α_t^2 can be assessed by comparing their maximum values of the log-likelihood.

Estimates $\hat{\mu}_t^2$ of the squared long-term expectation should have no incremental power to predict short-term volatility if market expectations are rational. This hypothesis is tested by including an additional term $e\hat{\mu}_t^2$ in equations (9) and (10) and a term $\eta \ln\,(\hat{\mu}_t^2)$ in equations (11) and (12).

8.3.3 Seasonal Volatility Effects

It is known that returns measured over more than 24 hours often have higher variances than 24-hour returns. The equations for h_t require revisions to allow for this seasonality. It is assumed that equations (5), (7) and (9)–(12) all apply to a non-seasonal conditional variance h_{t+1}^* defined to be the conditional variance h_{t+1} divided by a seasonal term. We replace h_t, h_{t+1}, and ε_t by h_t^*, h_{t+1}^* and ε_t^* (where $\varepsilon_t^* = h_t^{*1/2} z_t$) and assume

$$h_t/h_t^* = \begin{cases} 1 & \text{if close } t \text{ is 24 hours after close } t - 1 \\ M & \text{if } t \text{ falls on a Monday and } t - 1 \text{ on a Friday} \\ H & \text{if a holiday occurs between close } t \text{ and close } t - 1. \end{cases} \tag{13}$$

ARCH models for h_t^* combined with equation (13) define appropriate models for h_t.

The options estimates $\hat{\alpha}_t^2$ and $\hat{\mu}_t^2$ need to reflect the seasonal effects measured by M and H. Annualised estimates $\hat{\alpha}_{A,t}^2$ have been converted into non-seasonal, daily estimates using appropriate calendar constants for currency markets, as follows:

$$\hat{\alpha}_t^2 = \hat{\alpha}_{A,t}^2 / (196 + 48M + 8H). \tag{14}$$

8.3.4 The Conditional Distribution

Empirical evidence decisively rejects the hypothesis that the distribution of a return R_t conditional upon the information set I_{t-1} of past returns is normal for high frequency data (Engle and Bollerslev 1986, Baillie and Bollerslev 1989, Taylor 1994). Two empirically better conditional distributions are the scaled t and the generalised error distribution (GED) (Taylor 1994). The shape of the conditional distribution z_t then depends on the degrees-of-freedom ω for the scaled t and the tail-thickness parameter ν for the GED. Normal distributions are given by $\omega \to \infty$ and $\nu = 2$.

8.3.5 Estimation

Model parameters occur in the definitions of the non-seasonal conditional variance, the seasonal multipliers and the conditional distribution. All of these parameters can be simultaneously estimated by maximising the likelihood function for a set of observed returns and volatility expectations implied by options prices. The likelihood function for a given parameter vector is calculated from the conditional variances and the standardised return residuals (Bollerslev et al. 1992, Taylor 1994).

8.4 EMPIRICAL RESULTS WITHIN-SAMPLE

All the results presented from estimating ARCH models are for the period from January 1985 to November 1989. Prices for 1990 and 1991 are used in section 8.5 for *ex ante* forecast evaluations.

8.4.1 ARCH Models That Only Use Returns Information

Initial comparisons are made between the GARCH(1,1) model and the symmetric exponential ARCH(1) model (i.e. $\theta = 0$ in equation (7)) and between the three most popular conditional distributions, the normal, the scaled-t and the GED. Comparisons are also made between two ways to define the conditional mean return: either always zero, which is reasonable for futures data, or the appropriate figure defined by five dummy variables, one for each day of the week. To maximise the log-likelihood an initial value for the conditional variance is required. Empirical evidence suggests that the choice of initial value does not matter much, and we report the results as if the initial value is an additional parameter.

The following conclusions are obtained for all models estimated. There is no significant increase in the maximum log-likelihood when dummy variables define the conditional mean, consequently it is assumed to be zero. There is no uniform statistical result across the currencies about the significance of the variance dummy variables, but all the point estimates are well above one. Consequently these dummy variables are included in all the models discussed here.

The results presented in Table 8.1 reflect the above conclusions. The results for the scaled-t distribution are not reported to save space because the GED distribution is always slightly superior to the scaled-t distribution. The differences in maximum log-likelihoods between the GED and the normal conditional distribution all exceed 20 for the GARCH(1,1) and symmetric exponential ARCH(1) models. As the normal distribution is the GED with $\nu = 2$, doubling log-likelihood differences and comparing test values with χ_1^2 shows they are all statistically significant at the 0.1% significance level. A fat-tailed, non-normal conditional distribution enhances the descriptive accuracy of the model. Comparing the log-likelihoods for GARCH(1,1) and symmetric exponential ARCH(1,0) reveals very small differences. The differences between GARCH and exponential ARCH are 1.01 for the pound, -1.87 for the Mark, 1.12 for the yen and -2.47 for the franc when the conditional distribution is GED. There is thus no clear-cut difference between the two models.

Now we consider more general ARCH models with the GED conditional distribution. First, consider the asymmetric specification for the volatility response in the exponential ARCH(1) model. The increases in maximum log-likelihoods are less than 0.7 for all four currencies; the hypothesis $\theta = 0$ cannot be rejected at the 10% significance level. As noted by Taylor (1994),

Table 8.1 Parameter estimates for GARCH(1,1) and exponential ARCH(1) models

GARCH(1,1)

$$h_t = h_t^*, \; Mh_t^*, \; Hh_t^*, \; \text{and} \; h_{t+1}^* = c + a\varepsilon_t^2(h_t^*/h_t) + bh_t^*$$

	$10^5 c/(1 - a - b)$	a	$a + b$	ν	$\ln(L)$
BP	6.0576	0.0466	0.9839	2	4254.01
	5.9589	0.0391	0.9877	1.1854	4297.04
DM	6.1391	0.0837	0.9569	2	4292.89
	6.0004	0.0738	0.9583	1.2528	4327.31
JY	4.9830	0.1012	0.8712	2	4391.42
	5.1111	0.0960	0.9189	1.0336	4478.84
SF	7.4797	0.0642	0.9617	2	4152.34
	7.3561	0.0599	0.9611	1.3778	4173.67

Exponential ARCH(1)

$$h_t = h_t^*, \; Mh_t^*, \; Hh_t^*, \; \text{and} \; \ln(h_{t+1}^*) = (1 - \rho)\lambda + \rho \ln(h_t^*) + \gamma(|z_t| - E[|z_t|])$$

	λ	γ	ρ	ν	$\ln(L)$
BP	−9.4316	0.1206	0.9795	2	4251.67
	−9.8054	0.1095	0.9835	1.1802	4296.03
DM	−9.5816	0.1708	0.9594	2	4295.11
	−9.8108	0.1574	0.9617	1.2571	4329.18
JY	−9.8369	0.2155	0.8604	2	4388.97
	−9.9819	0.2089	0.9117	1.0299	4477.72
SF	−9.3939	0.1347	0.9689	2	4155.43
	−9.5704	0.1260	0.9687	1.3855	4176.14

Note: Maximum likelihood estimates and the maxima of the log-likelihood function for ARCH models fitted to daily BP/$, DM/$, JY/$ and SF/$ exchange rates between January 1985 and November 1989. The ARCH models contain seasonal dummy variables M and H for Mondays and holidays, and the estimates of these parameters are not given here. The conditional distribution is GED with tail-thickness parameter ν. The special case $\nu = 2$ defines a normal distribution. The conditional mean is equal to zero.

there are plausible theories for a negative θ in stock models but none for a non-zero θ in a currency model. Price and volatility innovations can therefore be assumed independent when pricing currency options.

Second, consider higher-order ARCH models. Results not reported here show such models have nothing extra to offer. Results for the tests of the informational efficiency of the currency options market are reported later for GARCH(1,1) and symmetric exponential ARCH(1) models with the GED conditional distribution. However, not unexpectedly, all the conclusions also stand for other distributions and higher-order ARCH models.

8.4.2 Informational Efficiency of the Currency Options Market

Tables 8.2 and 8.3 present the model estimates used for tests of informational efficiency. Table 8.2 uses market volatility expectations for the next period

Table 8.2 Parameter estimates for GARCH(1,1) models including the term structure volatility expectations, with GED conditional distributions

Panel A: British pound

$10^5 \times c$	a	b	d	e	v	$\ln(L)$
0.0735	0.0391	0.9485			1.1854	4297.04
(3.81)	(2.56)	(108.35)			(17.73)	
			1.0000		1.2297	4300.23
					(20.57)	
1.2065			0.8459		1.2307	4312.17
(3.53)			(9.19)		(17.74)	
1.1858	0.0297	0.0000	0.8276		1.2313	4312.41
(3.22)	(0.64)		(8.07)		(17.75)	
0.5960			0.7538	0.1771	1.2344	4313.02
(0.81)			(6.21)	(1.22)	(17.73)	
0.6152	0.0138	0.0000	0.7456	0.1682	1.2347	4313.11
(1.01)	(0.43)		(6.11)	(1.15)	(17.73)	

Panel B: Deutsche Mark

$10^5 \times c$	a	b	d	e	v	$\ln(L)$
0.2500	0.0738	0.8846			1.2528	4327.31
(6.02)	(3.81)	(52.78)			(17.62)	
			1.0000		1.2494	4328.74
					(20.77)	
1.1266			0.7941		1.3289	4349.69
(3.84)			(10.23)		(17.51)	
1.1260	0.0000	0.0000	0.7943		1.3282	4349.69
(3.84)			(10.24)		(17.51)	
1.1262			0.7945	0.0000	1.3285	4349.69
(3.84)			(10.24)		(17.51)	
1.1265	0.0000	0.0000	0.7944	0.0000	1.3285	4349.69
(3.84)			(10.23)		(17.51)	

Panel C: Japanese yen

$10^5 \times c$	a	b	d	e	v	$\ln(L)$
0.4147	0.0960	0.8229			1.0366	4478.84
(6.39)	(3.13)	(26.41)			(18.87)	
			1.0000		0.9982	4442.75
					(24.57)	
1.6907			0.7139		1.0278	4480.48
(4.83)			(6.82)		(19.15)	
1.5515	0.1252	0.0000	0.6185		1.0419	4485.21
(4.40)	(2.28)		(5.77)		(19.03)	
1.6854			0.7151	0.0000	1.0278	4480.48
(4.51)			(6.37)		(19.18)	
1.5476	0.1255	0.0000	0.6185	0.0000	1.0462	4485.21
(4.40)	(2.29)		(5.78)		(19.03)	

continued overleaf

Table 8.2   *(continued)*

Panel D: Swiss franc

$10^5 \times c$	a	b	d	e	v	$\ln(L)$
0.2860	0.0570	0.9041			1.3777	4173.67
(7.42)	(3.52)	(56.60)			(17.42)	
			1.0000		1.4512	4181.43
					(19.40)	
1.3539			0.8864		1.4519	4192.13
(2.83)			(8.98)		(17.12)	
1.3537	0.000	0.0000	0.8864		1.4519	4192.13
(2.83)			(8.98)		(17.12)	
1.3533			0.8864	0.0000	1.4519	4192.13
(2.83)			(8.98)		(17.12)	
1.3536	0.0000	0.0000	0.8864	0.0000	1.4519	4192.13
(2.83)			(8.98)		(17.12)	

Notes: The terms $\hat{\alpha}_t$ and $\hat{\mu}_t$ are respectively short- and long-term volatility expectations obtained from a term structure model

$$h_t = h_t^*, \ Mh_t^*, \ Hh_t^*,$$

and

$$h_{t+1}^* = c + a\varepsilon_t^2(h_t^*/h_t) + bh_t^* + d\hat{\alpha}_t^2 + e\hat{\mu}_t^2.$$

The numbers in parentheses are *t*-statistics estimated using the hessian and numerical second derivatives. All parameters are constrained to be non-negative. When a parameter estimate is zero or smaller than 10^{-6} then no estimated standard error is reported.

Table 8.3   Parameter estimates for GARCH(1,1) models including short maturity implied volatilities, with GED conditional distributions

Panel A: British pound

$10^5 \times c$	a	b	d	v	$\ln(L)$
0.0735	0.0391	0.9485		1.1854	4297.04
(3.81)	(2.56)	(108.3)		(17.73)	
			1.0000	1.2632	4315.33
				(18.75)	
0.0000			1.0313	1.2524	4315.49
			(18.75)	(17.76)	
0.0000	0.0061	0.0000	1.0250	1.2524	4315.51
	(0.19)		(15.74)	(17.75)	

continued overleaf

Table 8.3   *(continued)*

Panel B: Deutsche Mark

$10^5 \times c$	a	b	d	v	$\ln(L)$
0.2500	0.0738	0.8846		1.2528	4327.31
(6.02)	(3.81)	(52.78)		(17.62)	
			1.0000	1.3196	4349.49
				(17.85)	
0.0000			0.9719	1.3320	4349.64
			(19.42)	(17.42)	
0.0000	0.0000	0.0429	0.9295	1.3321	4349.65
		(1.43)	(3.11)	(17.40)	

Panel C: Japanese yen

$10^5 \times c$	a	b	d	v	$\ln(L)$
0.4147	0.0960	0.8299		1.0336	4478.84
(6.39)	(3.13)	(26.41)		(18.87)	
			1.0000	1.0470	4473.03
				(22.11)	
0.9941			0.8698	1.0245	4478.53
(2.08)			(6.02)	(19.13)	
0.6033	0.1202	0.4017	0.3922	1.0420	4483.78
(1.72)	(2.58)	(1.56)	(1.64)	(18.98)	

Panel D: Swiss franc

$10^5 \times c$	a	b	d	v	$\ln(L)$
0.2860	0.0570	0.9041		1.3777	4173.67
(7.42)	(3.52)	(56.00)		(17.42)	
			1.0000	1.4669	4187.16
				(18.56)	
0.5761			0.9993	1.4480	4190.66
(1.22)			(10.23)	(17.09)	
0.2339	0.0000	0.2144	0.8211	1.4515	4191.03
(0.47)		(0.80)	(3.08)	(17.05)	

Notes: The term $\hat{\alpha}_t$ is the implied volatility for the shortest maturity option with more than nine calendar days to expiry

$$h_t = h_t^*, \, Mh_t^*, \, Hh_t^*,$$

and

$$h_{t+1}^* = c + a\varepsilon_t^2(h_t^*/h_t) + bh_t^* + d\hat{\alpha}_t^2$$

The numbers in parentheses are t-statistics estimated using the hessian and numerical second derivatives. All parameters are constrained to be non-negative. When a parameter estimate is zero or smaller then 10^{-6} then no estimated standard error is reported.

given by the term structure model outlined in section 8.2.3. Table 8.3 uses the short maturity implied volatility.

Equation (10) includes options market volatility information as an exogenous variable in the GARCH(1,1) model for the conditional volatility. The increases in maximum log-likelihoods compared with those from the standard GARCH(1,1) model, i.e. equation (5), are as follows:

	Pound	Mark	Yen	Franc
Table 8.2	15.37	22.38	6.37	18.37
Table 8.3	18.47	22.34	4.94	17.36

Doubling these increases and comparing these test values with χ_1^2 shows clearly that the hypothesis that the options prices have no incremental information content can be rejected at the 0.5% significance level for each currency.

The more important question is whether options market volatility information is sufficient for predicting the next day's conditional volatility. As equation (9) only includes options market volatility information in the conditional variance equation, it is nested within equation (10). Thus a likelihood ratio test can again be used. The decreases in maximum log-likelihoods are as follows:

	Pound	Mark	Yen	Franc
Table 8.2	0.24	0.00	4.73	0.00
Table 8.3	0.02	0.01	5.25	0.37

Doubling these numbers and comparing these test values with χ_2^2 shows that the null hypothesis that returns contain no volatility information in addition to that already conveyed by options prices cannot be rejected for any currency at the 0.5% significance level. The null can be rejected at the 1% level for the yen. To conclude, the options market was informationally efficient for the three European currencies, the pound, the Mark and the franc, from 1985 to 1989; however, no such firm conclusion can apply to the yen.

When the options market forms rational volatility expectations, long-term expectations have no incremental power to predict short-term conditional volatility. This null hypothesis is tested by evaluating the increases in maximum log-likelihood when the term structure estimate of long-term volatility is an additional variable in equations (9) and (10). The results in Table 8.2 show the null hypothesis must be accepted.

The hypothesis that market expectations from option prices are unbiased estimates for one-period ahead future volatility implies $c = 0$ and $d = 1$ in equation (9). Likelihood ratio tests are once more appropriate. The results in Table 8.2 reject the hypothesis at the 0.5% level for all four currencies. The results in Table 8.3 show much less evidence for bias. The term structure expectations for the next day are extrapolations and this can explain the bias identified by Table 8.2.

The maximum log-likelihoods in Tables 8.2 and 8.3 are very similar for our preferred model (equation (9), so $a = b = 0$). The higher values are in Table 8.2 for three currencies and in Table 8.3 for the pound.

Tests of the informational efficiency of the options market using the symmetric exponential ARCH(1) specification lead to the same conclusions as those reported above for the GARCH(1,1) specification.

8.5   OUT-OF-SAMPLE VOLATILITY FORECASTING

The tests in section 8.4 characterise within-sample properties of volatility information because the likelihoods of both the ARCH and term structure models are maximised over the complete sample period. The direction of any within-sample biases is unknown (Day and Lewis 1992a). In this section we compare the *ex ante* forecasting ability of historical volatility predictors, forecasts from standard ARCH models and options market forecasts over a longer time horizon than considered in section 8.4.

The data cover seven years and we require a large sample to estimate the parameters in both the ARCH models and the volatility term structure model. Less than two and a half years of data remain after using five years to select and estimate the ARCH and term structure models. A four-week forecast horizon allows us to evaluate 30 non-overlapping, four-week ahead forecasts for the period from 18 October 1989 to 4 February 1992.

The non-seasonal, realised volatility is calculated *ex post* as follows:

$$V_{R,t} = \sqrt{\frac{1}{N} \sum_{i=1}^{N} \varepsilon_{t+i}^{*2}}, \tag{15}$$

where N is the number of trading periods in some four-week interval. Note that the non-seasonal quantity ε_t^{*2} is one of R_t^2, R_t^2/M or R_t^2/H, with the choice determined by equation (13). The benchmark forecast is the simple historical volatility over the last four weeks, i.e.

$$V_{H,t} = \sqrt{\frac{1}{N} \sum_{i=0}^{N-1} \varepsilon_{t-i}^{*2}} = V_{R,t-N}. \tag{16}$$

The ARCH forecast for the realised volatility of the returns over N future periods can be obtained from N single period forecasts all made at the same time. In the case of the GARCH(1,1) model, the volatility forecast can be calculated by

$$V_{G,t} = \sqrt{\frac{1}{N}\sum_{i=1}^{N}\hat{h}_{t+i}}, \tag{17}$$

where

$$h_{t+1}^{*} = c + a\varepsilon_t^{*2} + bh_t^{*}$$

and

$$\hat{h}_{t+i} = \frac{c}{1-a-b} + (a+b)^{i-1}\left(h_{t+1}^{*} - \frac{c}{1-a-b}\right), \quad i = 1, 2, 3, \ldots.$$

All of the preceding volatility measures are annualised by multiplying by $(196 + 48M + 8H)^{1/2}$.

Forecasts can be derived from option prices, both from the term structure model and from a matched maturity option. The forecasts from the term structure model, $V_{TS,t}$, can be calculated from equation (2) with T equal to 28 calendar days. The matched forecast at time t is the implied volatility for an option whose time to maturity is nearest to 28 calendar days, denoted $V_{M,t}$.

The parameters in both the GARCH model and the term structure model of implied volatility are re-estimated as new observations come in on a rolling basis. We use a constant sample size of 250 weeks of daily data by adding the latest four weeks of observations and deleting the first four weeks of observations in the previous sample.[5]

Forecasting performance is initially evaluated using the mean forecast error (ME), the mean absolute error (MAE) and the root mean square error (RMSE), calculated from forecasts $V_{F,t}$ given by one of the five methods above and realised figures $V_{R,t}$ as follows:

$$\text{ME} = \frac{1}{n}\sum_{t\in S}(V_{F,t} - V_{R,t})$$

$$\text{MAE} = \frac{1}{n}\sum_{t\in S}|V_{F,t} - V_{R,t}|$$

$$\text{RMSE} = \left[\frac{1}{n}\sum_{t\in S}(V_{F,t} - V_{R,t})^2\right]^{1/2}$$

Here S indicates the set of times at which *ex ante* forecasts are produced and n denotes the number of forecasts made using each method.[6] For this study, $n = 30$.

The results, listed in Table 8.4, clearly demonstrate the superiority of the two volatility forecasts computed from options prices.[7] The smallest RMSE is

Table 8.4 Comparisons of alternative out-of-sample volatility forecasts.

Panel A: British pound (average realised volatility = 0.11433)

	Historical volatility	GARCH(1,1)		Implied volatility	
		Normal	GED	Term structure	Matched
ME	−0.001038	0.001737	0.002015	0.005234	0.004447
MAE	0.033370	0.029240	0.029384	0.028412	0.029083
RMSE	0.041493	0.036214	0.036531	0.032527	0.033399

Panel B: Deutsche Mark (average realised volatility = 0.12121)

	Historical volatility	GARCH(1,1)		Implied volatility	
		Normal	GED	Term structure	Matched
ME	−0.001736	0.001095	−0.000083	0.000788	0.000279
MAE	0.032874	0.032247	0.031692	0.025364	0.025945
RMSE	0.040840	0.040525	0.039836	0.032931	0.034312

Panel C: Japanese yen (average realised volatility = 0.10585)

	Historical volatility	GARCH(1,1)		Implied volatility	
		Normal	GED	Term structure	Matched
ME	−0.000217	0.007983	0.008441	0.000469	−0.000369
MAE	0.037799	0.030106	0.030415	0.025612	0.025727
RMSE	0.045695	0.034854	0.035267	0.030865	0.030763

Panel D: Swiss franc (average realised volatility = 0.12789)

	Historical volatility	GARCH(1,1)		Implied volatility	
		Normal	GED	Term structure	Matched
ME	−0.001915	0.000674	0.000355	−0.001246	−0.002130
MAE	0.028903	0.023740	0.023654	0.024342	0.023883
RMSE	0.034371	0.029103	0.029066	0.028720	0.028315

Note: The implied forecasts are estimates of the market's volatility expectation for the next 28 days obtained either from a term structure model or the option with maturity closest to 28 days.
The numbers tabulated are mean forecast errors (ME), mean absolute errors (MAE) and root mean square errors (RMSE).

obtained by the options forecasts for each currency. The differences in Table 8.4 between the two options forecasts are minimal. The options forecasts also have the smallest MAE for the pound, the Mark and the yen while the GARCH forecast with the GED conditional distribution achieves the smallest MAE for the franc.[8] The ME values for both options forecasts are very small (less than 1% of the average volatility) for the Mark, the yen and the franc and are not statistically different from zero at the 5% level, although the ME nearest zero is obtained by the historical volatility forecast for the pound and the yen and by the GARCH forecast for the Mark and the franc.

The forecasts from the GARCH model offer a marked improvement over naïve historical volatility forecasts for all four currencies. The GARCH forecasts have up to 20% smaller MAEs and RMSEs than naïve historical volatility forecasts. Comparing the GARCH forecasts with different conditional distributions reveals that forecasts from non-normal modes do not convincingly outperform forecasts from normal models. Some caution should be exercised in interpreting these results as we only predict 30 four-week realised volatilities.

Lamoureux and Lastrapes (1993) perform encompassing regressions of the realised volatility on their three alternative out-of-sample forecasts and argue that the regressions provide further insight into the nature of the different forecast models. Like them, we are interested in the incremental predictive power of the forecasts. Care is required because all forecasts are highly correlated. We apply the stepwise regression technique to select statistically significant regressors from the forecasts. The only forecast selected for the pound, the Mark and the yen is the term structure implied predictor (5% significance level, F-test). This implies no bivariate predictor is significantly more accurate than the term structure predictor. A similar conclusion has been obtained by Day and Lewis (1992b) for oil futures. However, no forecast is significant for the Swiss franc. The poor performance in the case of the Swiss franc could well be due to the block of inferior data mentioned in note 1. The within-sample and out-of-sample methodologies give the same conclusion that the volatility forecast obtained from option prices is optimal: returns from the underlying asset do not contain significant incremental information for predicting future volatility.

Finally, we perform the test of the null hypothesis that the volatility forecast from option prices is an unbiased estimate for the four-week-ahead realised volatility. We run regressions of the realised volatility on the term structure forecast with and without a constant term. The results show that the unbiased hypothesis cannot be rejected. The slope coefficients are all very close to 1 when the constant term is suppressed.

8.6 SUMMARY

This chapter examines the informational efficiency of the currency options market at the PLHX using an ARCH methodology. By using likelihood ratio tests, we find that volatility forecasts estimated from call and put options prices contain incremental information relative to standard ARCH specifications for conditional volatility which only use the information in past returns. This is found for all four currencies. Furthermore, when predicting one-period ahead volatility, the hypothesis that past returns have no incremental information content in addition to the information conveyed by the options market cannot be rejected for the pound, the Mark and the franc, and is only marginally rejected for the yen. We also find that market agents are rational in forming their expectations about future volatility, as the long-term expected volatility has no extra power when predicting short-term volatility.

The out-of-sample volatility forecasts confirm the above results. The two implied volatility forecasts markedly outperform the forecasts from past returns (the historical volatility forecast and forecasts from ARCH models) when predicting four-week ahead realised volatility. Further tests support the hypothesis that the options market's volatility expectations are unbiased predictions of future volatility.

These results suggest that the Philadelphia currency options market is informationally efficient in setting prices and the volatility expectations in option prices provide superior predictors of both one-period ahead and longer horizon (i.e. four weeks) conditional volatilities. This conclusion contrasts with the lack of informational efficiency identified for US stock options markets by Day and Lewis (1992a), Lamoureux and Lastrapes (1993) and Canina and Figlewski (1993). The superior informational efficiency of the currency options market is consistent with the arguments developed in the final section of Canina and Figlewski (1993): they expect efficiency to be enhanced in an environment which permits low cost arbitrage trading.

The ultimate efficiency test is whether excessive profits can be made by some trading strategy. As Harvey and Whaley (1992) find, even if superior forecasts of future volatility are made then abnormal returns are not necessarily possible when transaction costs are taken into account. This issue will be explored in future research.

ACKNOWLEDGEMENTS

X. Xu was at the Financial Options Research Centre, University of Warwick, when the chapter was written and revised. We thank two anonymous referees, Stewart Hodges, Michael Selby, Martin Walker and participants at the 1993 meeting of the European Finance Association for their helpful comments and advice. We thank the Philadelphia Stock Exchange for providing their currency options data.

ENDNOTES

1. For the period from 18 December 1990 to 15 March 1991 there are no data for the Swiss franc in the PHLX database and the *WSJ* did not list the closing SF/$ spot exchange rate, so spot rates were collected from Datastream while option prices were collected from the *WSJ*. This affects the accuracy of implied volatilities calculated from option prices and in turn affects the performance of implied volatility forecasts, and thus the results for the Swiss franc in section 8.5 should be interpreted with some caution.

2. The volatility of currency futures prices is identical to the volatility of spot exchange rates if domestic and foreign interest rates are non-stochastic. Differences between spot and futures volatilities will be minimal as the futures maturities are always less than four months. Future prices, rather than spot prices, were available to us from Datastream for the whole period under study.
3. Equal forward and exercise prices define the at-the-money option in theoretical arguments, but these arguments are usually developed for European options.
4. We recognise that asymptotic theory for ARCH models is difficult (Bollerslev *et al.* 1992, section 8.2.6) and sometimes unreliable (Lumsdaine 1995), consequently we use very small nominal significance levels.
5. We also estimated parameters and forecast the volatility on a continual updating basis, which only adds new observations. The results, not reported here in detail, are not very different from the results based on the rolling method; the only significant result, which is rather data related, is reported in note 8. Our results differ from the finding of Lamoureux and Lastrapes (1993); however, the underlying assets, the number of observations in the rolling samples, and the forecasting horizon are all different.
6. Note that an optimal forecast will not have MAE = RMSE = 0 because $V_{R,t}$ is only a point estimate of the asset's price volatility which is unobservable.
7. Replacing $V_{F,t}$ and $V_{R,t}$ by $V_{F,t}^2$ and $V_{R,t}^2$ in the definition of ME, MAE and RMSE provides identical conclusions to those presented in the text.
8. Using the updating method to re-estimate parameters reduces the effect of the inferior data for the Swiss franc (note 1) and then the implied volatility forecast also has the smallest MAE.

REFERENCES

Akgiray, V. (1989), 'Conditional Heteroscedasticity in Time Series of Stock Returns: Evidence and Forecasts', *Journal of Business*, **62**, 55–80.
Baillie, R.T. and Bollerslev, T. (1989), 'The Message in Daily Exchange Rates: a Conditional-Variance Tale', *Journal of Business and Economic Statistics*, **7**, 297–305.
Baillie, R.T. and DeGennaro, R.P. (1990), 'Stock Returns and Volatility', *Journal of Financial and Quantitative Analysis*, **25**, 203–214.
Barone-Adesi, G. and Whaley, R.E. (1987), 'Efficient Analytic Approximation of American Option Values', *Journal of Finance*, **42**, 301–320.
Bollerslev, T. (1986), 'Generalised Autoregressive Conditional Heteroscedasticity', *Journal of Econometrics*, **31**, 307–327.
Bollerslev, T., Chou, R.Y. and Kroner, K.F. (1992), 'ARCH Modeling in Finance: A Review of the Theory and Empirical Evidence', *Journal of Econometrics*, **52**, 5–59.
Canina, L. and Figlewski, S. (1993), 'The Informational Content of Implied Volatility', *Review of Financial Studies*, **6**, 659–681.
Chiras, D.P. and Manaster, S. (1978), The Information Content of Option Prices and a Test of Market Efficiency, *Journal of Financial Economics*, **6**, 213–234.
Day, T.E. and Lewis, C.M. (1992a), 'Stock Market Volatility and the Information Content of Stock Index Options', *Journal of Econometrics*, **52**, 289–311.
Day, T.E. and Lewis, C.M. (1992b), 'Initial Margin Policy and Volatility in the Crude Oil Future Market', *Proceedings of the Options Conference*, FORC, Warwick University.

Engle, R. and Bollerslev, T. (1986), 'Modelling the Persistence of Conditional Variances', *Econometric Review*, **5**, 1–50.

Gemmill, G. T. (1986), 'The Forecasting Performance of Stock Options on the London Traded Options Market', *Journal of Business Finance and Accounting*, **13**, 535–546.

Harvey, C.R. and Whaley, R.E. (1992), 'Market Volatility Prediction and the Efficiency of the S&P 100 Index Option Market', *Journal of Financial Economics*, **31**, 43–73.

Heynen, R, Kemna, A.G.Z. and Vorst, T. (1994), 'Analysis of the Term Structure of Implied Volatilities', *Journal of Financial and Quantitative Analysis*, **29**, 31–56.

Hsieh, D.A. (1989), 'Modelling Heteroscedasticity in Daily Foreign-exchange Rates', *Journal of Business and Economic Statistics*, **7**, 307–317.

Lamoureux, C.B. and Lastrapes, W.D. (1993), 'Forecasting Stock Return Variance: Toward an Understanding of Stochastic Implied Volatilities', *Review of Financial Studies*, **6**, 293–326.

Latane, H. and Rendleman, R.J. (1976), 'Standard Deviation of Stock Price Ratios Implied by Option Premia', *Journal of Finance*, **31**, 369–382.

Lumsdaine, R.L. (1995), 'Finite Sample Properties of the Maximum Likelihood Estimator in GARCH(1,1) and IGARCH(1,1) Models: a Monte Carlo Investigation, *Journal of Business and Economic Statistics*, **13**, 1–10.

Nelson, D.B. (1991), 'Conditional Heteroscedasticity in Asset Returns: A New Approach', *Econometrica*, **59**, 347–370.

Poon, S. and Taylor, S.J. (1992), Stock Returns and Volatility: An Empirical Study of the UK Stock Market, *Journal of Banking and Finance*, **16**, 37–59.

Scott, E. and Tucker, A. L. (1989), 'Predicting Currency Return Volatility', *Journal of Banking and Finance*, **13**, 839–851.

Shastri, K. and Tandon, K. (1986), 'An Empirical Test of a Valuation Model for American Options on Futures Contracts', *Journal of Financial and Quantitative Analysis*, **10**, 377–392.

Shastri, K. and Wethyavivorn, K. (1987), 'The Valuation of Currency Options for Alternate Stochastic Processes', *Journal of Financial Research*, **10** (2), 283–293.

Sheikh, A. M. (1991), 'Transaction Data Tests of S&P 100 Call Option Pricing', *Journal of Financial and Quantitative Analysis*, **26**, 459–475.

Stein, J.C. (1989), 'Overreactions in the Options Market', *Journal of Finance*, **44**, 1011–1023.

Taylor, S.J. (1994), 'Modelling Stochastic Volatility', *Mathematical Finance*, **4**, 183–204.

Taylor, S.J. and Xu, X. (1994), 'The Magnitude of Implied Volatility Smiles: Theory and Empirical Evidence for Exchange Rates', *The Review of Futures Markets*, **13**, 355–380.

Xu, X. and Taylor, S.J. (1994), 'The Term Structure of Volatility Implied by Foreign Exchange Options', *Journal of Financial and Quantitative Analysis*, **29**, 57–74.

9
Efficiency Tests with Overlapping Data: An Application to the Currency Options Market

CHRISTIAN DUNIS and ANDRÉ KELLER

9.1 INTRODUCTION

This study applies usual efficiency tests to the currency options market. According to the efficient markets hypothesis, the markets-derived forecast of volatility, universally known as the 'implied volatility', should be an unbiased predictor of future empirical volatility, known as the 'historical volatility'. We test this hypothesis for six major currencies: the Deutsche Mark, sterling, the Swiss franc and the Japanese yen quoted against the US dollar (we use the notation of the International Organization for Standardization, respectively USD/DEM, GBP/USD, USD/CHF and USD/JPY), and sterling and the yen quoted against the Deutsche Mark (respectively GBP/DEM and DEM/JPY).

Our approach which extends a simple model often applied to the spot and forward markets for foreign exchange (see, amongst others, Frenkel 1976, Levich 1989 and MacDonald and Taylor 1992), has two significant originalities: the first one is to use *market volatility data* to test directly for currency options market efficiency as volatility has now become an

This chapter previously appeared under the same title in *Working Papers in Financial Economics*, No. 2, July 1994, pp 1–9. © 1994 Chemical Bank. Reproduced with permission.

observable and traded quantity in financial markets; the second innovation is the use of *panel regression* (see, for instance, Chamberlain 1982, 1985, Hsiao 1986, Greene 1991 and Mátyás and Sevestre 1992), an econometric technique that allows for the technical problems that arise when using overlapping data in financial time series analysis.

Our study uses daily data from the Chemical Bank over-the-counter (OTC) volatility database. For the four rates quoted against the USD the study period is 11/09/1989 to 03/09/1993. For the two rates quoted against the DEM, it is 09/11/1989 to 03/09/1993.

The structure of the chapter is as follows. First, we present our methodology for testing the efficiency of the currency options market. Second, we show our estimation procedure for panel data, a methodology we chose for its simplicity which, in our view, makes it a much less cumbersome and thus a preferable alternative to the approach proposed by Hansen and Hodrick (1980). Finally, we discuss the empirical results we have obtained: if overall they show much better technical properties than those reached with overlapping data, they also go a long way towards rejecting the efficient market hypothesis for curency options as it can be safely rejected in over 91% of the cases we studied. In other words, implied volatility is not in general an optimal forecast of future exchange rate volatility.

9.2 MARKET EFFICIENCY AND CURRENCY OPTIONS

Dealing in currency options has probably been one of the fastest growth areas in the foreign exchange market over the last decade. But, whereas economic research in the field of forex markets largely focused on devising structural models of exchange rate determination and the issue of efficiency, most of the literature on options has concentrated on improving the basic Black–Scholes formula and only a few articles have so far addressed the issue of the efficiency of the currency options market.

Klemkosky and Resnick (1979) sought to demonstrate market efficiency by an empirical validation of the put–call parity theorem.[1] However, like Galai (1977), Chiras and Manaster (1978) and Harvey and Whaley (1992), they used data from listed options on exchanges, rather than OTC data.

Xu and Taylor (1994) also use data from the Philadelphia exchange for their study on the efficiency of the currency options market. The problem in using exchange data is that only call and put prices are available for given strike levels. The corresponding implied volatility series must therefore be *backed out* using a specific option pricing model. This procedure generates two sorts of potential biases: material errors or mismatches can affect the variables that are needed for the solving of the pricing model, e.g. the forward points or the spot rate, and, more importantly, the very specification of the pricing model that is chosen can have a crucial impact on the final 'backed out' implied volatility series.

In this chapter, we use *data directly available from the marketplace*. This original approach seems further warranted by current market practice whereby brokers and market makers in currency options deal in fact *in volatility terms* and no longer in option prices terms.[2]

Accordingly, following earlier work by Dunis (1993) and extending it by addressing the problem of overlapping data, we attempt to test *directly* the efficiency of the currency options market, using Chemical Bank's data bank on *market quoted implied volatilities* and thus avoiding the possible biases that we just mentioned. We carry out efficiency tests based on those described in the economic literature on the efficiency of the foreign exchange market. Specifically, if economic agents are assumed to be risk neutral, the forward rate should be an *unbiased* predictor of the future spot rate (see, for instance, MacDonald and Taylor 1992, particularly pp. 28–34).

For the currency options market, the efficient markets hypothesis should entail that the volatility quoted today for, say, the next 3-month period is an unbiased predictor of the empirical exchange rate volatility that will occur over that 3-month period (i.e. the *ex post* 3-month historical volatility as recorded in $t + 3$ for the 3-month period from t to $t + 3$): true, a systematic bias would see option traders systematically buy or sell implied volatility by buying or selling straddles which eventually would make the above inefficiency disappear.

9.2.1 The Efficient Markets Model

Let $VI_{3, t}$ and $VH_{3, t}$ be respectively the 3-month implied volatility quoted at t for the next 3-month period, and the historical 3-month volatility recorded at t for the previous 3-month period.

The usual condition for $VI_{3, t}$ to be an unbiased predictor of the future historical volatility $VH_{3, t+3}$ is the equation

$$VH_{3, t+3} = \alpha + \beta VI_{3, t} + \varepsilon_t \qquad (1)$$

in conjunction with the null hypothesis H_0: $\alpha = 0$, $\beta = 1$ and the error terms $\{\varepsilon_t\}$ are independently and identically normally distributed (i.i.d.).[3] In other words, the expectation is that the constant term should be equal to zero, the slope coefficient should not differ significantly from unity and, last not least, the error term should not be serially correlated. The satisfaction of these conditions implies the acceptance of what is known as the 'weak efficiency hypothesis'.

Furthermore, if the currency options market is efficient, then the information contained in $VI_{3,t}$ should summarize all the information at time t that is relevant to the determination at t of $VH_{3,t+3}$. In particular, the addition of part of the information stock available at time $t-1$, namely $VI_{3,t-1}$, should not add anything new to the information content already in $VI_{3,t}$. Specifically, the inclusion of $VI_{3,t-1}$ as a further explanatory variable to the right-hand side of equation (1) should change nothing: it should not significantly affect the coefficient of determination $\bar{R}^2$ and $VI_{3,t-1}$ should have a coefficient not statistically different from zero.

Thus, a further and even more demanding test of market efficiency, i.e. the 'strong efficiency hypothesis', will be given by equation (2):

$$VH_{3,t+3} = \alpha + \beta VI_{3,t} + \gamma VI_{3,t-1} + \varepsilon_t \qquad (2)$$

where the same constraints apply to α, β and ε_t as in equation (1) and where the null hypothesis further requires that $\gamma = 0$.

9.2.2 The Data Bank

The data source was Chemical Bank's data bank for implied volatilities for the six following exchange rates: USD/DEM, GBP/USD, USD/CHF, USD/JPY, GBP/DEM and DEM/JPY. These *at-the-money forward, market-quoted volatilities* were obtained from brokers via Reuters on a daily basis, at the close of business in London.

Historical volatilities were computed as the annualised root mean square variation (RMSV) of the former exchange rates which were downloaded from Reuters via a data feed on a daily basis at 4.50 p.m. London time.

In the circumstances, equations (1) and (2) were tested on daily data for the six exchange rate volatilities mentioned above, both for one-month and three-month time horizons, over the period 11/09/1989 to 03/09/1993 (the starting date was in fact 09/11/1989 for both GBP/DEM and DEM/JPY).

Both implied and historical volatility series for the six exchange rates studied are shown, for both the one- and three-month horizons, in the graphs of Figure 9.1.

9.3 ESTIMATION PROCEDURE WITH OVERLAPPING DATA

9.3.1 The Use of Panel Data

A problem with the estimation of β in equation (1) is the fact that the data are overlapping, which leads to a dependence between observations.

In our case, we aim to see whether, for instance, the one-month implied volatility recorded on the first day of the month is a 'good' predictor of the

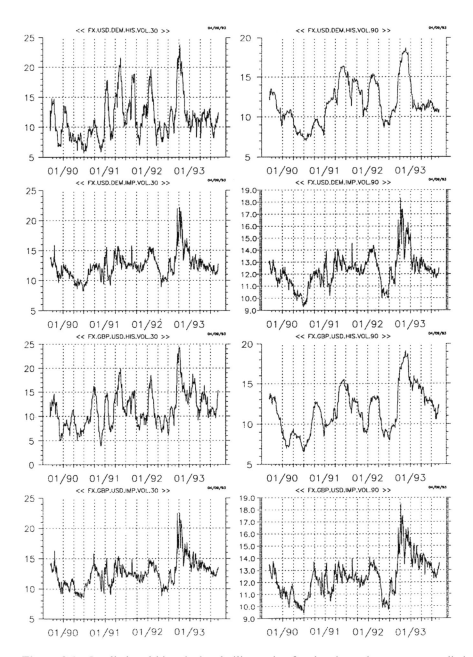

Figure 9.1 Implied and historical volatility series for the six exchange rates studied for both one- and three-month horizons

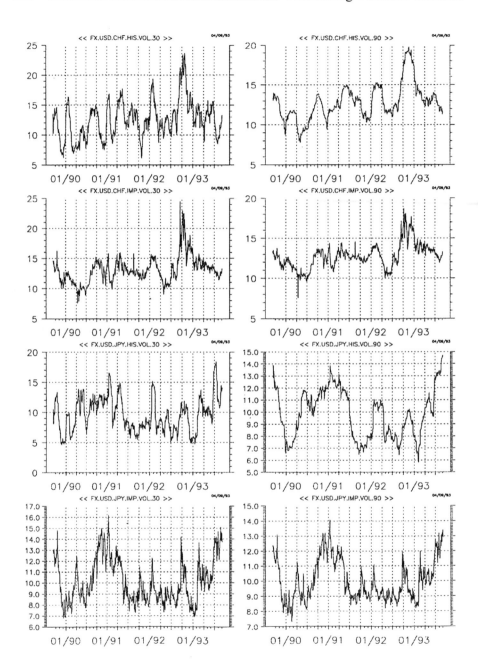

Figure 9.1 (*continued*)

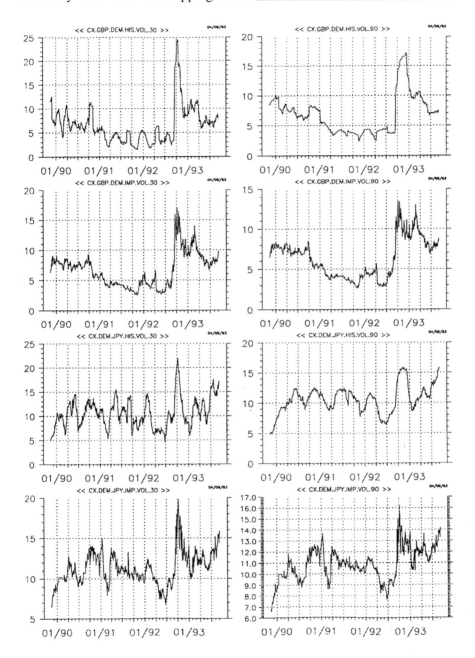

Figure 9.1 (*continued*)

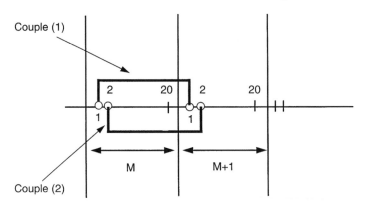

Figure 9.2 Overlapping data. This chart illustrates how observation couples overlap over two months, M and M + 1. One aim to see if, on day 1 of month M, the 'market' forecast is a 'good' predictor of what will happen between that day and day 1 of month M + 1. And so on for day 2, day 3, . . .

one-month historical volatility recorded on the first day of the following month. Reasoning in the same way for each following day until the last day of the month will inevitably lead to an overlapping of data that is inherent to this type of relationship (see Figure 9.2).

In the general case, one observes the data point pairs (x_t, y_{t+1}), x_t being the one-month market 'forecast' and y_{t+1} the spot rate (here, the realised exchange rate volatility) one month after.

It is easy to see the econometric consequences of such non-independence of the data. Most notably, an *under-estimation of the calculated variances of the estimators* occurs as a result of the strong autocorrelation of the residuals.

In the circumstances, it seems preferable to replace the variables current index (t) by the double index (i, t): this allows us to identify in (i) the index of the day that is considered and in (t) the index of the month considered. To restore data independence, our study considers each day as a distinct individual which is observed over a certain number of months (or quarters in the case of the three-month horizon). Such a presentation is equivalent to *panelising* our observation sample. The obvious method to apply to this sort of problem is therefore that of *panel econometrics* (see, amongst others, Chamberlain 1982, 1985, Hsiao 1986, Greene 1991 and Mátyás and Sevestre 1992).

9.3.2 The Econometric Model on Panel Data

Our weak efficiency test relates implied volatility (VI) and historical volatility (VH) according to a relationship similar to equation (1). The linear econometric model on panel data takes the following standard form:

$$VH_{i,t} = \alpha + \beta VI_{i, t-n} + \eta_{i, t} \tag{3}$$

with $i = 1, 2, \ldots, n$ and $t = 1, 2, \ldots, T$ and the disturbances $\eta_{i, t}$ are a random variable. In our study, we have the number of individuals n equal to 20 or 60, depending on the maturity under consideration, i.e. 1 or 3 months (respectively 20 or 60 trading days).

The stronger version of the efficiency test derives in the same way from equation (2) and its econometric testing takes the following standard form:

$$VH_{i,t} = \alpha + \beta VI_{i, t-n} + \gamma VI_{i, t-2n} + \eta_{i, t} \tag{4}$$

As there might be a systematic tendency for $\eta_{i, t}$ to be higher for some individuals than for others (the so-called 'individual' effect) and/or for some time periods than for others (the so-called 'time' effect), the error terms are decomposed as follows:

$$\eta_{i, t} = \delta_i + \lambda_t + v_{i, t} \tag{5}$$

where δ_i represents the 'individual' effect and λ_t the 'time' effect. As usual, the random component is supposed to be i.i.d. with a zero mean and a constant variance. In particular, δ_i accounts for variables which are assumed to reflect individual differences and affect the observations for a given individual, whereas λ_t accounts for explanatory variables that are specific to a given time period but are identical for most individuals.

For simplicity and because λ_t accounts for potentially omitted variables that are identical for most individuals, the composite error model chosen in this study is limited to the following formulation:

$$VH_{i,t} = \alpha + \beta VI_{i, t-n} + \eta_{i, t} \tag{3}$$

$$\eta_{i, t} = \delta_i + v_{i, t} \tag{6}$$

The estimators that can be calculated by regression analysis are the following:[4]

1. β_{OLS} is an ordinary least squares (OLS) estimator on the original non-overlapping data $VI_{i, t-n}$, $VH_{i, t}$.
2. β_W is a 'within' estimator on the *centred* non-overlapping data, $VI_{i, t-n} - VI_{i.}$ and $VH_{i, t} - VH_{i.}$ where we have

$$VI_{i.} = 1/T \cdot \Sigma VI_{i, t-n}$$

and

$$VH_{i.} = 1/T \cdot \Sigma VH_{i, t}$$

The 'within' estimator reflects the correlation between observations for a given 'individual', i.e. a given trading day. In the presence of seasonality, the observations for a particular trading day should be correlated with other observations for that day.

3. β_B is a 'between' estimator on 'individual' data that have been aggregated over time ($VI_{i.}$, $VH_{i.}$). The 'between' estimator reflects the correlation between different trading days of a month (or a quarter). A zero correlation will then reflect independence between those trading days.

Over the period 11/09/1989 to 03/09/1993, we have 1040 data points in total with 67 missing data (i.e. London bank holidays) and a 1-point lag per month: the number of usable data is therefore restricted to 972.

The number of observation periods t is either 52 when one considers the 1-month maturity or 17 when one considers the 3-month maturity (49 and 16 respectively for GBP/DEM and DEM/JPY).

For the 1-month time horizon, the total number of data must be split between 20 'individuals' (i.e. the days of the month) studied over a period of 52 months (i.e. our time period). In the circumstances, we were lucky to have an integer number of periods, so the end of our estimation period corresponded to that of our data bank, i.e. 03/09/1993.

For the GBP/DEM and the DEM/JPY volatilities, the original observation period is 09/11/1989 to 03/09/1993: it comprises 20 'individuals' over a 49-month period (still for the 1-month time horizon) and the end of our estimation period in both these cases had to be brought back to 12/08/1993. For the 3-month time horizon, we have 60 'individuals' (i.e. the days of the quarter) observed over 16 quarters and our estimation period in this case had to be brought back to 15/07/1993.

The use of non-overlapping data leads to significant technical improvements when one compares these results with those obtained with overlapping data as already shown in Dunis and Keller (1993). Specifically, such a treatment of the data reduces very significantly the autocorrelation that affected the original overlapping daily volatilities.

This can be illustrated with the USD/DEM one-month volatility by looking at the Durbin–Watson statistics. True, with overlapping data we have the following OLS estimators (T-statistics are shown in parentheses):

$$VH_t = 1.31 + 0.82VI_{t-1} \quad \text{with } R^2 = 0.22 \text{ and } DW = 0.07.$$
$$\quad\quad (2.1) \quad (16.5)$$

With non-overlapping data using panel regression and the OLS technique, the Durbin–Watson statistic improves sharply:

$$VH_{i,t} = 1.73 + 0.80VI_{i,t-1} \quad \text{with } R^2 = 0.20 \text{ and } DW = 1.65.$$
$$\quad\quad (2.7) \quad (15.6)$$

Thus, our study confirms the results of recent econometric research which has shown the incidence of overlapping data on the serial correlation of the error term (see, amongst others, Cumby *et al*. 1983, Hansen 1982, Hansen and Hodrick 1980, Levich 1989 and MacDonald and Taylor 1989).

Finally, the use of *panel regression* that we suggest appears to be a much less burdensome alternative to the approach followed by Hansen and Hodrick (1980) which implies the construction of an appropriate variance/covariance matrix. True, a thorough comparison of both methods has yet to be done but the simplicity of our approach makes it quite appealing.

9.4 EMPIRICAL RESULTS

Tables 9.1 to 9.6 present the detailed results of the efficiency tests we carried out on non-overlapping data.

For each daily currency volatility studied, the efficiency of the currency options market is tested at the one-month and the three-month maturities.

For each maturity, we test the intensity of the link between *realized* (i.e. historical) volatility and the *market view* (i.e. implied volatility). The question of whether implied volatility is an unbiased predictor of empirical exchange rate volatility is investigated by tests of increasing stringency. The weak efficiency hypothesis implies a relationship between historical volatility and the implied volatility prevailing in the previous period, whether it be one or three months. The stronger version of market efficiency adds one further lag to implied volatility, the assumption being that this should not bring in extra information, i.e. the coefficient for that lagged variable should not be statistically different from zero.

As described above, we calculated two different estimators for our non-overlapping data sample: the least squares 'OLS' estimator and the 'within' estimator in order to assess *potential individual disparities*, i.e. potential *intra-month and/or intra-quarter seasonalities*.

From this point of view, if the use of non-overlapping data allows us to correct the effects of autocorrelation and improves the overall quality and reliability of our results, it does not lead to any particular findings in terms of seasonality of exchange rate volatility. True, as can be seen in Tables 9.1 to 9.6, the multiple correlation coefficient adjusted for degrees of freedom $\bar{R}^2$ for the 'within' regression is relatively low. Consequently, any seasonal effect of the day of the month and/or the quarter is only marginal.

Furthermore, the results obtained with the 'OLS' and the 'within' estimators are very close which implies a very weak inter-individual disparity and a quasi-perfect overlapping of the data points sets. As the total variance is accounted for mostly by the 'within' variance, the variance due to the 'between' estimator is negligible. This implies a rather weak dependence between the different trading days.

The usual econometric results are given for both equations, both estimation

Table 9.1 Empirical results of efficiency tests from panel regressions for USD/DEM at one and three-month horizons[a] (11 September 1989–3 September 1993)

Dependent variable VH	Independent variables			Statistics					F-test		
1-month	Constant	$VI_{(1, t-1)}$	$VI_{(1, t-2)}$	$\bar{R}^2$	SSR	DW	Q(df)	NT	α	β	γ
USD/DEM (OLS)	1.73 (2.7)	0.80 (15.6)	—	0.20	10226.4	1.65	1753.6 (93)	972	7.3	16.1	—
USD/DEM (W)	—	0.80 (15.4)	—	0.20	10224.8	1.65	1770.0 (93)	972	—	15.8	—
USD/DEM (OLS)	4.11 (5.7)	1.03 (16.3)	−0.40 (−6.7)	0.23	9515.0	1.78	1530.0 (90)	938	33.1	0.2 (**)	45.1
USD/DEM (W)	—	1.03 (16.1)	−0.40 (−6.7)	0.23	9510.5	1.78	1543.1 (90)	938	—	0.2 (**)	44.2
3-month	Constant	$VI_{(3, t-1)}$	$VI_{(3, t-2)}$	$\bar{R}^2$	SSR	DW	Q(df)	NT	α	β	γ
USD/DEM (OLS)	4.90 (6.2)	0.58 (9.0)	—	0.08	7175.5	1.96	5046.8 (90)	954	38.0	43.5	—
USD/DEM (W)	—	0.57 (8.5)	—	0.08	7140.2	1.97	5072.1 (90)	954	—	42.0	—
USD/DEM (OLS)	6.44 (6.4)	0.61 (9.1)	−0.16 (−2.4)	0.08	6788.7	1.89	4418.1 (90)	920	40.6	33.4	5.8 (*)
USD/DEM (W)	—	0.61 (8.7)	−0.17 (−2.4)	0.08	6743.8	1.90	4437.9 (90)	920	—	32.1	5.6 (*)

[a]OLS is the ordinary least squares estimator and W is the 'within' estimator.
T-statisitcs are shown in parentheses below each variable's coefficient.
$\bar{R}^2$ is the coefficient of determination adjusted for degrees of freedom.
SSR is the sum of squared residuals. DW is the Durbin–Watson statistic. Q is the Box–Pierce test for white noise.
df indicates the degrees of freedom. NT is the number of usable observations.
F-test is the Fisher test of coefficient restrictions against the null hypothesis where $\alpha = 0$, $\beta = 1$ and $\gamma = 0$.
(Critical values are 3.84 and the 5% significance level (**) and 6.64 at the 1% significance level (*)).

Table 9.2 Empirical results of efficiency tests from panel regressions for GBP/USD at one and three-month horizons[a] (11 September 1989–3 September 1993)

Dependent variable VH	Independent variables			Statistics					F-test		
1-month	Constant	$VI_{(1,t-1)}$	$VI_{(1,t-2)}$	$\bar{R}^2$	SSR	DW	Q(df)	NT	α	β	γ
GBP/USD (OLS)	0.41 (0.7)	0.88 (19.0)	—	0.27	9656.1	1.89	1622.4 (93)	972	0.5 (**)	6.5 (*)	—
GBP/USD (W)	—	0.88 (18.8)		0.27	9648.1	1.89	1632.2 (93)	972	—	6.4 (*)	—
GBP/USD (OLS)	1.88 (2.8)	1.03 (17.0)	−0.26 (−4.4)	0.27	9248.7	1.97	1454.1 (90)	938	8.1	0.2 (**)	19.1
GBP/USD (W)	—	1.03 (16.8)	−0.26 (−4.3)	0.27	9243.5	1.97	1467.0 (90)	938	—	0.2 (**)	18.6
3-month	Constant	$VI_{(3,t-1)}$	$VI_{(3,t-2)}$	$\bar{R}^2$	SSR	DW	Q(df)	NT	α	β	γ
GBP/USD (OLS)	1.63 (2.3)	0.83 (14.6)		0.18	6861.3	2.26	5685.5 (90)	954	5.3 (*)	9.1	—
GBP/USD (W)	—	0.83 (14.1)		0.18	6839.2	2.27	5721.1 (90)	954	—	8.7	—
GBP/USD (OLS)	3.10 (3.6)	0.91 (14.9)	−0.20 (−3.3)	0.20	6427.2	2.21	4860.6 (90)	920	13.1	2.1 (**)	10.9
GBP/USD (W)	—	0.91 (14.5)	−0.20 (−3.2)	0.20	6393.7	2.22	4884.2 (90)	920	—	2.0 (**)	10.1

[a]See notes at bottom of Table 9.1.

Table 9.3 Empirical results of efficiency tests from panel regressions for USD/CHF at one and three-month horizons[a] (11 September 1989–3 September 1993)

Dependent variable VH	Independent variables			Statistics					F-test		
1-month	Constant	$VI_{(1,t-1)}$	$VI_{(1,t-2)}$	$\bar{R}^2$	SSR	DW	Q(df)	NT	α	β	γ
USD/CHF (OLS)	4.49 (8.0)	0.63 (14.7)		0.18	8068.5	1.78	2226.0 (93)	972	63.8	76.6	—
USD/CHF (W)	—	0.63 (14.5)		0.18	8069.3	1.78	2251.5 (93)	972	—	74.9	—
USD/CHF (OLS)	6.17 (9.9)	0.80 (14.6)	−0.30 (−5.4)	0.20	7564.3	1.93	1871.7 (90)	938	98.2	13.9	29.6
USD/CHF (W)	—	0.80 (14.4)	−0.30 (−5.4)	0.20	7562.4	1.94	1892.0 (90)	938	—	13.6	29.0
3-month	Constant	$VI_{(3,t-1)}$	$VI_{(3,t-2)}$	$\bar{R}^2$	SSR	DW	Q(df)	NT	α	β	γ
USD/CHF (OLS)	6.74 (11.1)	0.49 (10.4)		0.10	4738.6	2.13	6353.5 (90)	954	123.1	114.9	—
USD/CHF (W)	—	0.49 (10.0)		0.10	4716.2	2.14	6388.4 (90)	954	—	109.5	—
USD/CHF (OLS)	8.61 (11.5)	0.57 (11.5)	−0.23 (−4.5)	0.12	4412.8	2.04	5403.3 (90)	920	132.7	73.4	20.5
USD/CHF (W)	—	0.57 (11.0)	−0.23 (−4.4)	0.12	4391.0	2.05	5424.6 (90)	920	—	69.9	19.3

[a]See notes at bottom of Table 9.1.

Table 9.4 Empirical results of efficiency tests from panel regressions for USD/JPY at one and three-month horizons[a] (11 September 1989–3 September 1993)

Dependent variable VH	Independent variables			Statistics					F-test		
1-month	Constant	$VI_{(1,t-1)}$	$VI_{(1,t-2)}$	$\bar{R}^2$	SSR	DW	Q(df)	NT	α	β	γ
USD/JPY (OLS)	2.20 (5.3)	0.74 (18.3)		0.25	6132.4	2.10	1508.0 (93)	972	27.6	40.6	—
USD/JPY (W)	—	0.74 (18.0)		0.25	6134.4	2.10	1508.2 (93)	972	—	40.1	—
USD/JPY (OLS)	2.36 (5.1)	0.81 (15.2)	−0.08 (−1.5)	0.27	5827.1	2.15	1376.6 (90)	938	25.7	12.7	2.4 (**)
USD/JPY (W)	—	0.81 (15.1)	−0.08 (−1.5)	0.27	5823.3	2.15	1378.8 (90)	938	—	12.4	2.4 (**)
3-month	Constant	$VI_{(3,t-1)}$	$VI_{(3,t-2)}$	$\bar{R}^2$	SSR	DW	Q(df)	NT	α	β	γ
USD/JPY (OLS)	3.18 (6.6)	0.67 (14.0)		0.17	3658.2	1.94	5281.1 (90)	954	43.1	46.2	—
USD/JPY (W)	—	0.67 (13.5)		0.17	3644.7	1.95	5324.9 (90)	954	—	44.1	—
USD/JPY (OLS)	5.81 (9.8)	0.78 (15.6)	−0.37 (−7.6)	0.22	3361.8	2.14	4194.8 (90)	920	96.1	19.9	57.3
USD/JPY (W)	—	0.77 (15.0)	−0.38 (−7.4)	0.22	3346.9	2.15	4216.4 (90)	920	—	19.2	54.3

[a]See notes at bottom of Table 9.1.

Table 9.5 Empirical results of efficiency tests from panel regressions for GBP/DEM at one and three-month horizons[a] (9 November 1989–3 September 1993)

Dependent variable VH	Independent variables			Statistics					F-test		
1-month	Constant	$VI_{(1, t-1)}$	$VI_{(1, t-2)}$	$\bar{R}^2$	SSR	DW	Q(df)	NT	α	β	γ
GBP/DEM (OLS)	0.09 (0.4)	0.97 (28.7)	—	0.47	7367.9	1.84	1699.2 (90)	914	0.1 (**)	0.8 (**)	—
GBP/DEM (W)	—	0.97 (28.4)		0.47	7367.2	1.84	1694.8 (90)	914	—	0.8 (**)	—
GBP/DEM (OLS)	1.02 (4.3)	1.57 (28.4)	−0.74 (−13.3)	0.56	5983.2	2.14	1175.9 (87)	881	18.8	106.3	177.1
GBP/DEM (W)	—	1.57 (28.1)	−0.74 (−13.2)	0.56	5983.9	2.14	1175.3 (87)	881	—	104.0	173.0
3-month	Constant	$VI_{(3, t-1)}$	$VI_{(3, t-2)}$	$\bar{R}^2$	SSR	DW	Q(df)	NT	α	β	γ
GBP/DEM (OLS)	1.92 (7.4)	0.79 (20.3)		0.32	7025.2	1.96	4487.0 (87)	894	54.6	29.1	—
GBP/DEM (W)	—	0.79 (19.5)		0.31	7030.7	1.96	4471.2 (87)	894	—	27.2	—
GBP/DEM (OLS)	2.43 (8.7)	0.99 (19.6)	−0.29 (−5.6)	0.35	6364.7	2.13	3784.0 (87)	860	75.9	0.1 (**)	31.7
GBP/DEM (W)	—	0.99 (19.0)	−0.29 (−5.4)	0.35	6353.4	2.14	3778.2 (87)	860	—	0.1 (**)	29.4

[a]See notes at bottom of Table 9.1.

Table 9.6 Empirical results of efficiency tests from panel regressions for DEM/JPY at one and three-month horizons[a] (9 November 1989–3 September 1993)

Dependent variable VH	Independent variables			Statistics					F-test		
1-month	Constant	$VI_{(1, t-1)}$	$VI_{(1, t-2)}$	$\bar{R}^2$	SSR	DW	Q(df)	NT	α	β	γ
DEM/JPY (OLS)	5.56 (10.1)	0.44 (9.1)	—	0.08	7321.9	1.85	1994.7 (90)	914	102.7	135.8	—
DEM/JPY (W)	—	0.44 (8.9)	—	0.08	7307.7	1.85	2006.5 (90)	914	—	134.6	—
DEM/JPY (OLS)	8.52 (13.8)	0.68 (12.4)	−0.50 (−9.2)	0.16	6489.8	2.07	1394.1 (87)	881	191.3	35.3	84.4
DEM/JPY (W)	—	0.67 (12.1)	−0.50 (−9.1)	0.16	6470.9	2.07	1404.7 (87)	881	—	35.6	82.9
3-month	Constant	$VI_{(3, t-1)}$	$VI_{(3, t-2)}$	$\bar{R}^2$	SSR	DW	Q(df)	NT	α	β	γ
DEM/JPY (OLS)	12.23 (22.7)	−0.17 (−3.4)	—	0.01	3953.6	2.28	6869.6 (87)	894	513.5	553.1	—
DEM/JPY (W)	—	−0.18 (−3.4)	—	0.01	3919.5	2.29	6931.9 (87)	894	—	523.6	—
DEM/JPY (OLS)	16.60 (23.0)	−0.14 (−2.8)	−0.44 (−9.1)	0.10	3444.1	2.37	5099.3 (87)	860	526.9	549.5	82.2
DEM/JPY (W)	—	−0.14 (−2.8)	−0.45 (−8.9)	0.10	3413.4	2.38	5182.9 (87)	860	—	518.2	79.6

[a] See notes at bottom of Table 9.1.

procedures and both time horizons: estimators and their T-statistics, the multiple correlation coefficient adjusted for degrees of freedom $\bar{R}^2$ and residual variance. As can be seen from the tables, the efficient markets model accounts for only a small part of the variance of historical volatilities, generally less than 30% except for the GBP/DEM volatility where it explains 56% of the variance at the one-month horizon for equation (4).

Other statistics make it possible to assess the quality of the properties of our regressions. Concerning the residuals, the Durbin–Watson statistic is always close to 2 which allows us to reject first-order serial correlation. Nevertheless, the Box–Pierce test for white noise is always in the critical region, well above the theoretical value derived from a reduced normal law, which leads to a rejection of the null hypothesis of white noise residuals in all cases.

We further conducted separate Fisher tests of coefficient restrictions on the parameters α, β and γ, testing for the values $\alpha = 0$, $\beta = 1$ and $\gamma = 0$.[5] These tests make it possible to answer our initial question about the efficiency of the currency options market.

Table 9.7 summarizes the results of our efficiency tests on the six daily exchange rate volatilities. For each currency volatility studied, it reports the results of both equations (3) and (4) at the one-month and the three-month horizons in terms of our 'efficiency criteria', i.e. whether for equation (3), we have $\alpha = 0$, $\beta = 1$ and the error terms are i.i.d., and, for equation (4), we also have $\gamma = 0$.

The interpretation rests on the separate tests on the coefficients α, β and γ (we also computed joint tests which are more restrictive and then the null hypothesis is rejected in all cases but one, i.e. equation (3) for the one-month GBP/DEM volatility).

Still, even when one uses the separate tests and despite the fact that some efficiency criteria may be satisfied, the *joint hypothesis* that the slope coefficient does not differ significantly from unity, the constant term is equal to zero and the error term is not serially correlated must be rejected. Hence implied volatility should not be considered as an unbiased predictor of future exchange rate volatility.

As Table 9.7 shows, we were not able to find a single case where efficiency could be safely assumed. At best, an assumption of 'semi-efficiency' can be made for those cases where, out of the three 'efficiency criteria' in equation (3), two were satisfied, e.g. for the GBP/USD or the GBP/DEM volatility at the one-month time horizon (but one must remember that the case for efficiency rests on the *joint* satisfaction of all three criteria).

The same would apply to equation (4), when three out of four of our 'efficiency criteria' were met. Even then, as summarized in Table 9.7, the 'semi-efficiency' we have just defined is rejected in close to 92% of all the cases we examined: true, we can only accept it for the GBP/USD and GBP/

Table 9.7 Summary of results of efficiency tests with non-overlapping data

		$\alpha = 0$	$\beta = 1$	$\gamma = 0$	White noise	Conclusion[a]
USD/DEM	Equation (3)	No	No	n.a.	No	Efficiency rejected
(1-month)	Equation (4)	No	Yes	No	No	Efficiency rejected
USD/DEM	Equation (3)	No	No	n.a.	No	Efficiency rejected
(3-month)	Equation (4)	No	No	Yes	No	Efficiency rejected
GBP/USD	Equation (3)	Yes	Yes	n.a.	No	Semi-efficiency
(1-month)	Equation (4)	No	Yes	No	No	Efficiency rejected
GBP/USD	Equation (3)	Yes	No	n.a.	No	Efficiency rejected
(3-month)	Equation (4)	No	Yes	No	No	Efficiency rejected
USD/CHF	Equation (3)	No	No	n.a.	No	Efficiency rejected
(1-month)	Equation (4)	No	No	No	No	Efficiency rejected
USD/CHF	Equation (3)	No	No	n.a.	No	Efficiency rejected
(3-month)	Equation (4)	No	No	No	No	Efficiency rejected
USD/JPY	Equation (3)	No	No	n.a.	No	Efficiency rejected
(1-month)	Equation (4)	No	No	Yes	No	Efficiency rejected
USD/JPY	Equation (3)	No	No	n.a.	No	Efficiency rejected
(3-month)	Equation (4)	No	No	No	No	Efficiency rejected
GBP/DEM	Equation (3)	Yes	Yes	n.a.	No	Semi-efficiency
(1-month)	Equation (4)	No	No	No	No	Efficiency rejected
GBP/DEM	Equation (3)	No	No	n.a.	No	Efficiency rejected
(3-month)	Equation (4)	No	Yes	No	No	Efficiency rejected
DEM/JPY	Equation (3)	No	No	n.a.	No	Efficiency rejected
(1-month)	Equation (4)	No	No	No	No	Efficiency rejected
DEM/JPY	Equation (3)	No	No	n.a.	No	Efficiency rejected
(3-month)	Equation (4)	No	No	No	No	Efficiency rejected

[a] 'Semi-efficiency' is defined in this table as resulting from the satisfaction of two out of three, for equation (3), or three out of four, for equation (4), of our efficiency criteria (i.e. $\alpha = 0$, $\beta = 1$, $\gamma = 0$ and the error terms are i.i.d.).

DEM volatilities (and still, only in two cases out of the eight covered for these two currencies). Restricting our analysis to the sole examination of the slope coefficient, the condition that it is equal to unity is met in only six occasions overall, i.e. only 25% of the time.

On the whole, the empirical results we present do not support the view of an efficient market for currency options. This contrasts with the conclusions reached by Xu and Taylor (1994) on the informational efficiency of the Philadelphia currency options market for the GBP/USD, DEM/USD, CHF/USD and JPY/USD exchange rates (these are all quoted in US dollar terms on the Philadelphia exchange).

In practical terms, our findings imply that at least part of the information stock available at time t remains *unexploited*, which means that the implied volatility forecast of future exchange rate volatility may be beaten for a profit by those operators who are capable of spotting and using successfully that extra information neglected by the rest of the market.

9.5 SUMMARY AND CONCLUSION

In this chapter, we have used the markets-derived forecast of volatility, i.e. implied volatilities directly quoted by currency option market makers and brokers, to test directly for the efficiency of the currency options market. By so doing, we have deliberately avoided the potential bias introduced by the use of a specific option pricing model to 'back out' the implied volatility series from exchange quoted prices for puts and calls.

We have also proposed an original application of a method for dealing with the technical problems that arise when using overlapping data in financial time series analysis, such as the first-order autocorrelation of the residuals and its mechanical consequences on the reliability of the estimators.

Concerning the treatment of overlapping data, the use of panel regression that we suggest appears to be a much less burdensome alternative to the approach followed by Hansen and Hodrick (1980).

The use of two different estimators leads us to reject any intra-month and/or intra-quarter seasonality in currency volatilities and to conclude that there is no obvious seasonality in the currency options market.

Still, if our study confirms the results of recent econometric research which has shown the incidence of overlapping data on the serial correlation of the error term, the use of non-overlapping data does not lead to the acceptance of the efficient market hypothesis.

True, our empirical results lead us to reject the efficient market hypothesis for currency options as it can be safely rejected in over 91% of the cases we studied. Although the case for using implied volatility as the *optimal predictor* of future exchange rate volatility has a strong intuitive appeal, the empirical evidence we have produced for the period end-1989 to mid-1993 does not support this view. Except in the two cases of the GBP/USD and the GBP/DEM, implied volatility is neither an unbiased predictor nor the best possible forecast of future exchange rate volatility.

This suggests that it should not be used without modification in any forecasting and/or option pricing exercise. The models presented in this chapter could be a way of producing revised forecasts although their statistical fit, as one might expect, is relatively low.

In the circumstances, the issue of how to improve on this predictor's performance remains open for further research. Along these lines, Vasilellis and Meade (1994) suggest combining volatility forecasts, with quite good results for the stock market. However, preliminary work on currencies by

Atekpe (1994) using almost exactly the same data bank used for this chapter proved disappointing. In other words, the implied volatility forecast may not be the best predictor around, but it is still a difficult one to beat consistently. A better specification of the GARCH-generated forecasts, using an MA(1)–GARCH(1,1) model to take account of the weak serial dependence in the mean as proposed by Bollerslev *et al.* (1993) and/or the use of stochastic volatility forecasts as suggested by Taylor (1994) could nevertheless probably improve the overall combination process, with potentially significant payoffs in terms of forecasting accuracy.

ENDNOTES

1. The put–call forward parity (PCFP) states that, for any exercise price E, the difference between a put and a call, $P_{(E)} - C_{(E)}$, equals the difference between E and the forward rate F, discounted to the present at the interest rate r:

$$C_{(E)} - P_{(E)} = (F - E)/(1 + r)^t \qquad (7)$$

Buying the call and selling the put at the given exercise price E is equivalent to a 'long' forward contract at price E. The total cost of this 'synthetic' forward contract must include the difference between the cost of the call and the proceeds from the put. Since this difference is paid (or received) in advance, it must be discounted at the interest rate r:

$$F = E + ((C_{(E)} - P_{(E)}) \cdot (1 + r)^t) \qquad (8)$$

In an efficient market, buying the currency forward 'synthetically' at price E and then selling it at the prevailing forward price F should produce a zero profit, since this is a *risk-free arbitrage*.

   It also follows from equation (7) that, in the case where the exercise price is equal to the forward rate, i.e. $E = F$, then $C_{(F)} = P_{(F)}$, i.e. the price of the call and of the put are equal. For more details on currency options relationships, see Giddy (1983) and Derosa (1992).

2. The market data we used were *at-the-money forward volatilities*, as the use of either in-the-money or out-of-the-money volatilities would have introduced a significant bias in our analysis due to the so-called 'smile effect', i.e. the fact that volatility is 'priced' higher for strike levels which are not at-the-money.

3. Note that the specification of a model for testing weak efficiency in the form of unbiased predictions is not unique and the 'usual' assumptions are made to allow the use of estimation procedures based on least squares. Alternative efficiency tests include *orthogonality tests of forecast errors* which can be implemented by estimating an equation of the form:

$$VH_{3,\,t+3} - VI_{3,\,t} = \mathbf{G}\mathbf{X}_t + \varepsilon_t \qquad (9)$$

where $\mathbf{X}_t$ is a vector of variables part of the stock of information available at time t, $\mathbf{G}$ is a vector of parameters and ε_t is the error term. The null hypothesis requires that $\mathbf{G}$ should be the null vector so that the 'forecasting errors' are orthogonal to the set of information available at time t. For more details, see, for instance, Hansen and Hodrick (1980) and MacDonald and Taylor (1991).

4. For a more detailed presentation of panel methodology, see Hsiao (1986, pp. 25–70) and Mátyás (1992, pp. 46–71). The estimators formulae can be found in Hsiao (1986, pp. 32–38).
5. As the Fisher test is used here to check for specific values of the coefficients and not to reject the null hypothesis as usual, the readings for the test are inverted, i.e. the 5% significance level is more restrictive than the 1% level.

REFERENCES

Atekpe, R. (1994), 'Forecasting Volatility and Correlations between Foreign Exchange Rates', Presentation to the Forecasting Financial Markets Conference organized by Chemical Bank and Imperial College, London, 2–4 February.

Bollerslev, T., Engle, R.F. and Nelson, D.B. (1993), 'ARCH Models', unpublished manuscript, Discussion Paper 93–49, November, Department of Economics, UCSD.

Chamberlain, G. (1982), 'Multivariate Regression Models for Panel Data', *Journal of Econometrics*, **18**, 5–46.

Chamberlain, G. (1985), 'Panel Data', in Griliches, Z. and Intriligator, M.D. (eds), *Handbook of Econometrics*, Volume II, North-Holland, Amsterdam, 1247–1318.

Chiras, D.P. and Manaster, S. (1978), 'The Information Content of Options Prices and a Test of Market Efficiency', *Journal of Financial Economics*, **6**, 213–234.

Cumby, R.E., Huizinga, J. and Obstfeld, M. (1983), 'Two-step Two-stage Least Squares Estimation in Models with Rational Expectations', *Journal of Econometrics*, **21**, 333–355.

Derosa, D.F. (1992), *Options on Foreign Exchange*, Probus, Chicago.

Dunis, C. (1993), 'Implied versus Historical Volatility: An Empirical Test of the Efficiency of the Currency Options Market', in Motamen-Scobie, H. (ed.), *The European Single Market: Monetary and Fiscal Policy Harmonization*, Chapman & Hall, London, 165–180.

Dunis, C. and Keller, A. (1993), 'Implied versus Historical Volatility: An Empirical Test of the Efficiency of the Currency Options Market Using Non-Overlapping Data', Presentation to the Financial Markets Dynamics and Forecasting Conference organized by Caisse des Dépôts et Consignations, Paris, 2–4 September.

Frenkel, J.A. (1976), 'A Monetary Approach to the Exchange Rate: Doctrinal Aspects and Empirical Evidence', *Scandinavian Journal of Economics*, **78**, 200–224.

Galai, D. (1977), 'A Test of Market Efficiency of the Chicago Board Options Exchange', *Journal of Business*, **50**, 167–197.

Giddy, I.H. (1983), 'Foreign Exchange Options', *Journal of Futures Markets*, **2**, 143–166.

Greene, W.H. (1991), *Econometric Analysis*, Maxwell MacMillan International, New York.

Hansen, L.P. (1982), 'Large Sample Properties of Generalized Method of Moments Estimators', *Econometrica*, **50**, 1029–1054.

Hansen, L.P. and Hodrick, R.J. (1980), 'Forward Exchange Rates as Optimal Predictors of Future Spot Exchange Rate: an Econometric Analysis', *Journal of Political Economy*, **88**, 829–853.

Harvey, C.R. and Whaley, R.E. (1992), 'Market Volatility Prediction and the Efficiency of the S&P 100 Option Market', *Journal of Financial Economics*, **31**, 43–73.

Hsiao, C. (1986), *Analysis of Panel*, Econometric Society Monographs, 11, Cambridge University Press, Cambridge.

Klemkosky, R.C. and Resnick, B.G. (1979), 'Put–Call Parity and Market Efficiency', *Journal of Finance*, **34**, 1141–1155.

Levich, R.M. (1989), 'Forward Rates as the Optimal Future Spot Rate Forecast', in Dunis, C. and Feeny, M. (eds), *Exchange Rate Forecasting*, Woodhead-Faulkner, Cambridge, 75–98.

MacDonald, R. and Taylor, M.P. (1989), 'Foreign Exchange Market Efficiency and Cointegration: Some Evidence from the Recent Float', *Economics Letters*, **1**, 63–68.

MacDonald, R. and Taylor, M.P. (1991), 'Risk, Efficiency and Speculation in the 1920s Foreign Exchange Market: an Overlapping Data Analysis', *Weltwirtschaftliches Archiv*, **3**, 500–523.

MacDonald, R. and Taylor, M.P. (1992), 'Exchange Rate Economics: A Survey', *IMF Staff Papers*, **39**, 1–57.

Mátyás, L. (1992), 'Error Components Models', in Mátyás, L. and Sevestre, P. (1992) (eds), *The Econometrics of Panel Data*, Kluwer, Dordrecht, 46–71.

Mátyás, L. and Sevestre, P. (1992) (eds), *The Econometrics of Panel Data*, Kluwer, Dordrecht.

Taylor, S.J. (1994), 'Modelling Stochastic Volatility', *Mathematical Finance*, **4**, 183–204.

Vasilellis, G. and Meade, N. (1994), 'Forecasting Volatility for Portfolio Selection', Presentation to the Forecasting Financial Conference organized by Chemical Bank and Imperial College, London, 2–4 February.

Xu, X. and Taylor, S.J. (1994), 'Conditional Volatility and the Informational Efficiency of the PHLX Currency Options Market', Presentation to the 'Forecasting Financial Markets' Conference organized by Chemical Bank and Imperial College, London, 2–4 February. Reprinted in this book as Chapter 8, 181–200.

PART III
Applications of Neural Networks and Genetic Algorithms

10
Leading Edge Forecasting Techniques for Exchange Rate Prediction

IAN NABNEY, CHRISTIAN DUNIS,
RICHARD DALLAWAY, SWEE LEONG
and WENDY REDSHAW

10.1 INTRODUCTION AND SUMMARY

This chapter describes how modern machine learning techniques can be used in conjunction with statistical methods to forecast short-term movements in exchange rates, producing models suitable for use in trading. It compares the results achieved by two different techniques and shows how they can be used in a complementary fashion.

The two techniques used were rule induction, which is a method of extracting classification rules from data, and neural networks, which afford powerful and general methods for nonlinear function modelling.

The chapter contains four further sections. In section 10.2 there is a brief description of the modelling techniques used in our work.

The third section shows how the methods were applied to build inter-day forecasting models for three different markets. This earlier work, carried out by Logica, showed how existing expertise can be used to develop better forecasting models.

The fourth section describes recent work carried out with Chemical Bank which looked at intra-day forecasting models for two markets. All the results were assessed both in terms of forecasting accuracy and with a number of measures supplied by Chemical Bank's QRT group. These measures are those generally used in a trading environment and reflect traders' perceptions of the key performance parameters of a position in the currency markets. The final models also took into account 'slippage', i.e. the price difference between when the model is run and when a subsequent order is executed, to give a more realistic assessment of their likely performance in practice. Using neural networks, an annualised return of over 35% was achieved in both markets on independent test data (by comparison, the 'risk-free' interest rates during the test period were ranging between 3.1 and 7.9% per annum for the underlying markets). A foreign exchange trading system partly based on the modelling techniques used in this study was subsequently developed by Chemical Bank's QRT group.

Finally, section 10.5 draws some conclusions from the work described in the chapter, and suggests some future directions for the use of machine learning techniques in this area.

10.2   FORECASTING TECHNIQUES

This section gives a brief introduction to the two forecasting techniques whose application to exchange rate prediction is described in this chapter. Both techniques allow the detection and modelling of nonlinear effects in data, whereas the majority of conventional statistical methods build linear models (see Chatfield and Collins 1986).

10.2.1   Rule Induction and DATAMARINER

Rule induction is a technique for identifying patterns and relationships in data and expressing them as rules. A rule induction system is given a set of historical examples in each of which a number of attributes are measured and the class or outcome recorded. From these examples the system identifies what the examples in each class have in common; generally the aim is to find the simplest rules that can distinguish between examples from distinct classes. The effectiveness of the rule induction approach is dependent on the quality of the attributes used to discriminate between classes. The rules can be interpreted either as a causal relationship or as a description of the examples in a particular class. They can then be used to classify new examples (see, for instance, Nabney and Jenkins 1992, Quinlan 1986 and Race 1988).

As an example we consider how rule induction may be applied to forecasting exchange rates with a 24-hour horizon. Each close of day represents an 'example'; its class could be the direction of the price change 24 hours after the time of forecast. The attributes used in the rules could be technical indicators extracted from the time series data, together with useful external indicators (such as secondary market information). So if there were four indicators for detecting trends and four indicators for detecting a ranging market a rule for predicting the direction of price movement could have the following form:

IF

> range_4 $>=$ 0.01
> range_1 $>=$ 1.0
> trend_2 $>=$ 0.0005
> trend_3 $<=$ 0.02

THEN

> price_movement = up (0.75)
> price_movement = down (0.25)

This rule has isolated circumstances when there is a 75% chance that the exchange rate tomorrow will be higher than today. If the indicators are chosen so that they are familiar to traders or analysts, then these rules can be related to their own experience. Results expressed as descriptive rules are usually easier for most users to interpret. For example, the usefulness, or otherwise, of attributes can easily be assessed by the frequency with which they are used in the rules.

There are a number of rule induction packages currently available. However, these have several drawbacks. First, they are usually based on a particular algorithm, called ID3 (see Quinlan 1986), which has a number of limitations: for example, it produces a decision tree, which tends to be more difficult to interpret than modular rules. Second, the tools are generally aimed at supporting the analysis of small amounts of data when applications in finance generally imply the analysis of large data sets. Most seriously of all, there is often a limited range of support tools; unfortunately, rule induction by itself is often not powerful enough to extract all the knowledge from data.

To overcome the drawbacks summarised above, we have used the DATAMARINER software which is described in Nabney and Jenkins (1992); this is a set of closely integrated analytical tools with an easy to use graphical interface. At the heart of the data exploration toolkit is a novel rule induction algorithm, designed to overcome some of the drawbacks of ID3 and other techniques (see Nabney and Jenkins 1992). This algorithm works on a rules-per-class basis, i.e. for each class in turn, rules are induced to separate examples in that class from examples in all the remaining classes. This produces structured rules directly rather than a decision tree. There are three advantages that follow from this:

1. The rules are in a suitable form for understanding a classification; namely a description of each class in the simplest way that enables it to be distinguished from the other classes.
2. The rule set is structured in a more modular fashion which enables the user to focus on a single rule at a time to a large extent. As noted by Cendrowska (1988), decision trees can be hard to understand, particularly when the number of nodes is large.
3. Empirical results gathered from a number of studies carried out by Logica have shown that DATAMARINER generates many fewer rules than the ID3 algorithm, without loss of accuracy.[1]

Many of the other tools in DATAMARINER are standard statistical analysis; however, the results of any analysis are always expressed in the form of rules. The most important features of DATAMARINER for the purposes of this chapter are:

• the formation of new attributes: ratios and simple linear combinations of existing numeric attributes can be constructed using statistical techniques;
• the pruning of rules: to allow rules to generalise well to new data, they can be pruned using a statistically well-founded technique. This prevents the rules from tracking noise in the data they were generated from, a problem called *over-training*, i.e. the equivalent to model overfitting in econometrics.

10.2.2 Neural Networks

Neural networks are a powerful method of modelling complex nonlinear relationships. Like rule induction, a neural network is *trained* on a set of data and the performance of the trained model is evaluated by testing it on previously unseen data.

There are a large number of different neural network models. The most commonly used is the multi-layer perceptron (MLP) which feeds its inputs along a series of weighted connections and applies nonlinear functions at the nodes (for more details on the MLP and the workings of a neural network model, see, for instance, Pao 1989, Rumelhart and McClelland 1986 and, for an application to exchange rates, Dunis 1995).

An MLP, like rule induction, requires a set of examples for each of which a number of attributes are measured and some outcome is recorded. However, unlike rule induction, this outcome does not need to be a discrete classification. In fact, neural networks process numeric values, and an MLP can be used to model multiple numeric outputs.

This greater capability gives more choice in how neural networks may be applied to the problem of forecasting exchange rates. At each prediction, the forecast could be either the direction of the price movement (encoded as +1.0 for up, 0.0 for no change and −1.0 for down) or the new price.

There are powerful theoretical results that state that an MLP, if it is sufficiently large, can approximate any continuous deterministic function (see, for instance, Cybenko 1989, Funahashi 1989 and Hornik *et al.* 1989). Thus, if we can select the correct inputs for a network, it should be able to model whatever function is required. This implies that provided that a neural network is presented with a sufficiently large time window of previous data, it should be able to extract any 'derived attributes' that are required.

There are two caveats to apply to this, arising from the need to keep the number of inputs reasonably small. First, it may not be feasible to use only a contiguous window of data, since the model may need isolated inputs with very large delays. (For example, the hourly sales forecasts for a retailer will be heavily dependent on the day of the week, which could be represented by the sales from 168 hours earlier.) Second, the system may not be of finite order, which means that to make a prediction, knowledge of all its previous states is needed.

In addition to the above considerations, this capability of approximating any continuous function can be problematic as the underlying behaviour that the network is supposed to learn may change over time. More importantly, the model thus created is a deterministic functional map, hence it is not able to learn patterns arising from truly random perturbations. In fact, when a deterministic process is 'contaminated' by a stochastic perturbation, the neural network will try to learn from spurious relationships arising purely from noise in addition to the 'true' underlying process, which raises the issue of over-training or noise fitting. It will then only learn the mean of the target data, which may not prove useful when there are outliers in the data.

A technique commonly used to prevent over training is the use of a third set of data, the validation set, which is independent of both training and test data. Periodically during training, the error of the neural network on the validation set is measured. The network is trained until this error goes up significantly, and the final network is the one with the lowest error on the validation set. This technique plays the same role as pruning does for rule induction.

The powerful approximation capability of neural networks does have a price. A trained MLP represents a complex mathematical function and it is very difficult to understand in detail the operation of even very small networks. Hence the results are more difficult to interpret than those arising from rule induction.

10.3 INTER-DAY TRADING MODELS

In a former study, Logica analysed historical data on the close of day prices of three different exchange rates over the same time period (respectively the US dollar/Deutsche Mark, the US dollar/Japanese yen and the British pound/US dollar rates), together with attributes, or 'technical indicators' (such as median prices over a time window, relative strength indices, . . .), which were believed by the client to have good forecasting ability. The objective was to predict the direction of the next price movement based on these attributes.

On presentation to the rule induction system, the class was the direction of the price movement the following day. Of the 1500 examples in each data set, half were used for training, and half for testing.

The rule induction system achieved an accuracy of between 64 and 69% on this data. A neural network approach using a standard MLP with the same inputs as for rule induction achieved an accuracy of between 60 and 65%. By way of comparison, when the linear technique of Kalman filtering was applied to this data, the accuracy was in the range 55–60%.[2]

The quality of these results was slightly surprising since all the attributes were numeric, and rule induction has principally been used in domains where there are some discrete attributes. We concluded that this study showed the power of the DATAMARINER approach where rule induction is combined with statistical techniques. The capability of forming linear combinations and ratios of existing attributes during the induction process itself was essential for achieving a high accuracy. Because the data was extremely noisy, the ability to prune the rules at a variety of different levels also improved performance dramatically: pruning was done by assessing the statistical significance of each condition in a rule and then removing those conditions that were likely to have occurred by chance.[3] It seems likely that another reason for the good performance of rule induction was the use of highly predictive technical indicators as inputs to the modelling technique.

Another advantage of rule induction over other techniques on this problem was the extra information that was easily accessible from the rules about the data. For example, the newly constructed attributes for two of the markets were very similar, suggesting a similarity in the underlying mechanisms affecting prices in those two markets. The usage of attributes in the rule conditions was also interesting: for example, certain attributes were used very frequently, while others were hardly used at all, and could perhaps be replaced by different attributes derived from pre-processing techniques. Finally, some of the attributes constructed as ratio attributes could be used as extra inputs for other techniques, such as neural networks.

10.4   INTRA-DAY TRADING MODELS

The aim of this study was to determine the potential of machine learning techniques for modelling intra-day movements in exchange rates.

10.4.1   Analysis Procedure

Two markets were studied: US dollar/Swiss franc (USD/CHF), and Deutsche Mark/French franc (DEM/FRF). These currencies were chosen because the USD/CHF market has a high volatility, while the DEM/FRF market had relatively low volatility up until the ERM crisis in August 1993. In each case tick data was supplied for the primary currency pair and, in addition, a secondary time series representing the USD/DEM rate current at the time of the trade in the primary currency. The data was collected from the year 1 October 1992 to 1 October 1993. Each data file was approximately 50 Mb in size, which meant that extracting indicators often took several hours.

In addition to prediction accuracy, we specified a detailed set of measures to evaluate the trading performance of the models (see Tables 10.1 and 10.2).

The first set of experiments involved the use of DATAMARINER to make 20 minute-ahead predictions. Training data was taken from 11 January 1993 to 9 March 1993 and test data was from 9 March 1993 to 26 April 1993. The trading day was assumed to last from 08:00 to 18:00. Weekends and UK holidays were ignored. The output was a simple prediction that the price movement would be 'up', 'down', or 'no change'. After determining the best algorithm parameters, good results were achieved on USD/CHF (at best, about 50% annual return), and poorer results on DEM/FRF (at best, about 12% annual return).

At this point we decided to make the evaluation criteria more realistic by introducing a slippage of 20 basis points for each position (40 points when squaring off a position).

The existing models were evaluated with this new cost and performed poorly, trading at a loss. This was mainly because they took positions too often (they were being used to take a decision every 10 minutes). It was therefore decided to use a 60-minute predictive horizon. It was also decided to evaluate the performance of neural networks in order to obtain some comparative results.

With a one-hour horizon, it becomes more important to make good use of the available data. It was split into three sets (our standard practice when using neural networks): the training set was from 8 October 1992 to 15 March

1993 (120 days), the validation set from 15 March 1993 to 3 May 1993 (50 days), and the test set from 3 May 1993 to the end of the data (80 days). Data was used from 00:00 to 21:00 (i.e. from the opening of Tokyo to the close of New York).

Because neural networks are general function modellers, there is more latitude over the selection of inputs from the time series for good performance. Information from the secondary price time series was not included, as the work with DATAMARINER had shown that it was of limited use in forecasting movements in the primary series. The output of the neural network was the forecast price one hour on from the current time.

All the neural networks used in this project were MLPs. Systematic experiments were performed to determine a suitable neural network structure and training algorithm parameters (cf. the initial work with DATAMARINER). Once the best values had been determined, the network was trained until a minimum in the error was attained. When using the resulting model for trading, the price prediction was banded into five classes: 'large up', 'small up', 'no change', 'small down', and 'large down', as shown in Figure 10.1.

The 'change threshold' which defined the boundary between small and large movements was generally chosen to be the same as the slippage (0.002). The trading technique that was used is shown in Figure 10.2. Here the boxes denote the 'current position' (the model starts square), and the arrows denote the transitions which are carried out when the model makes the prediction given by the attached label.

The use of neural networks immediately led to improved performance on USD/CHF: there was a 55% annualised return on the test data. The performance on DEM/FRF was less good: 23% on the full test data, where most of the profit was made at the ERM crisis. (The annualised gain on the test data before the crisis was 3%.)

To improve the DEM/FRF results, changes were made to the input attributes; in particular further indicators were added to the inputs. This improved results on the test data to 37%. Some further experiments with DATAMARINER with a one-hour prediction horizon and five classes (as shown in Figure 10.1) were carried out; these achieved a 9% annualised return on test data.

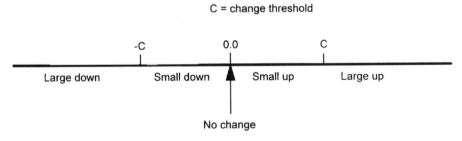

Figure 10.1   Prediction classes

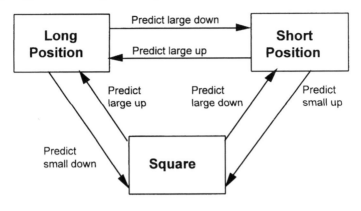

Figure 10.2   Trading with a model

10.4.2   Results

10.4.2.1   Rule Induction

The performance of the rules induced by DATAMARINER was disappointing. For example, the 'best' set of rules on DEM/FRF produced an annualised return of 9.31%, hardly more than the 'risk-free' rate of interest on the French franc or on the Deutsche Mark over the same period, i.e. respectively 7.88 and 7.69%.

The probable reason for this was that in a short study it was not possible to find the best indicators to derive from the raw price series data. This point is considered further in section 10.5.

It was found that the correlation of attributes with the classification and their usage in the rules was different for the two markets. For USD/CHF, traditional technical indicators and their ratios were the best predictors for a 20-minute horizon. For DEM/FRF, it was found that volume data was important: this was probably because all the training data came from before the ERM crisis, when large movements were scarce and volume was correlated with a change/no change classification.

10.4.2.2   Neural Networks

The good results achieved with neural networks showed the power of the technique in modelling complex time series data.

Tables 10.1 and 10.2 document the results of our USD/CHF and DEM/FRF models. They both detail the number of days for the test period, the average holding period of each position, the standard deviation of the series of gains and losses, the maximum gain, the number of winning trades, the average gain, the percentage of winning trades, the cumulative gain per USD or per

Table 10.1 Neural network results on USD/CHF

No. days	41	No. positions	25
Mean time in pos.	28.10 hours	Correct direction	52.5%
StdDev (Gain/Loss)	0.012	StdDev (%ChgFX)	0.165
MaxPosGain	0.046	MaxPosLoss	−0.020
NumGainPos	17	NumLossPos	8
AvgGain	0.0102	AvgLoss	−0.0047
%GainPos	68	%LossPos	32
CumGain	0.1395	%CumGain	9.032
Annual %CumGain	55.07	GainLossRatio	4.61
RMS error	0.00286	Sharpe ratio	4.60
Prob. of losing 100 pips	19.90	MaxDrawdown	0.020
			(1 position)

Table 10.2 Neural network results on DEM/FRF

No. days	71	No. positions	55
Mean time in pos.	15.71 hours	Correct direction	54.5%
StdDev(Gain/Loss)	0.0187	StdDev (%ChgFX)	0.0766
MaxPosGain	0.095	MaxPosLoss	−0.034
NumGainPos	41	NumLossPos	14
AvgGain	0.0103	AvgLoss	−0.0049
%GainPos	74.5	%LossPos	25.5
CumGain	0.3544	%CumGain	10.52
Annual %CumGain	37.05	GainLossRatio	6.13
RMS error	0.00068	Sharpe ratio	6.672
Prob. of losing 100 pips	15.63	MaxDrawdown	0.0455
			(3 positions)

DEM, the annualised percentage gain, the root mean squared error, the probability of losing 0.01 CHF per USD traded (or 0.01 FRF per DEM traded), the number of positions taken, the percentage of correct directional forecasts by the models, the standard deviation of the underlying exchange rate, the maximum loss, the number of losing trades, the average loss, the percentage of losing trades, the percentage gain over the test period, the gain-to-loss ratio (i.e. the ratio of the average gain weighted by the percentage of winning trades over the average loss weighted by the percentage of losing trades), the Sharpe ratio (a measure of profitability adjusted for risk commonly used by fund managers) and the maximum drawdown of each model (i.e. the largest cumulative loss recorded over the test period).

Table 10.1 shows the results achieved on USD/CHF with the original set of inputs and a 60-minute forecast horizon. Note that the error on the validation set increased rapidly, so that training finished after about 15 000 epochs. This was probably caused by significant differences between training and validation sets, suggesting the desirability of using more data for training, either by using more historical data or by oversampling.[4]

Still, with high Sharpe and gain-to-loss ratios, a low probability of losing 0.01 CHF per USD traded and a high annualised return, our USD/CHF trading model appears quite satisfactory.

The graph in Figure 10.3 shows the training, validation and test sets for USD/CHF while the graph in Figure 10.4 displays the evolution of the trading performance of the neural network model over the test period.

The results achieved on the whole of the DEM/FRF test data follow in Table 10.2. These used further technical indicators as additional inputs. Here too the performance sensitivities of our DEM/FRF trading model are quite satisfactory although the maximum drawdown is about 10 times the average loss. This occurs during the period of high volatility following the ERM crisis. The graph in Figure 10.5 shows the training, validation, and test sets for DEM/FRF. The cumulative gain chart for the test data (Figure 10.6) shows how the return becomes much more volatile after the ERM crisis. Even in the period following the large jump in the exchange rate, however, the model gives good returns. In the period before the crisis, the cumulative gain is about 0.1, which is an annual rate of about 15.7%.

Encouraging as these results are, there are still improvements that could be made to the forecasting accuracy of the model. It is noticeable that while the errors on the training data are symmetrically distributed about a near-zero mean (see Figure 10.7), the errors on the test data are biased, with a non-zero mean (see Figure 10.8).

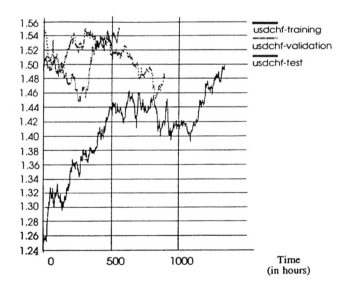

Figure 10.3 USD/CHF data sets

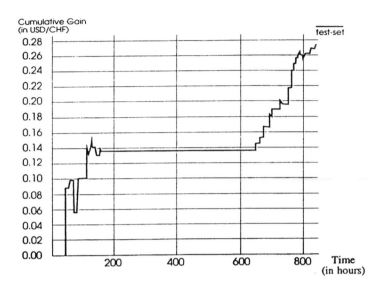

Figure 10.4 USD/CHF cumulative gain

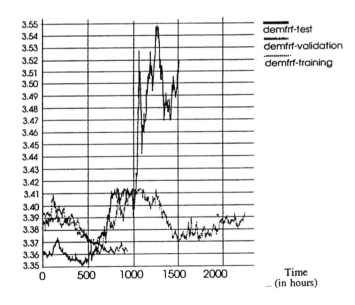

Figure 10.5 DEM/FRF data sets

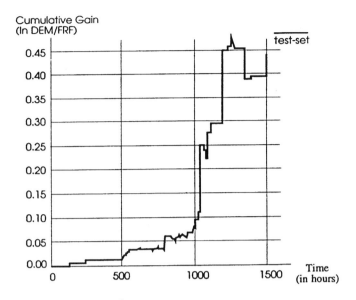

Figure 10.6 DEM/FRF cumulative gain

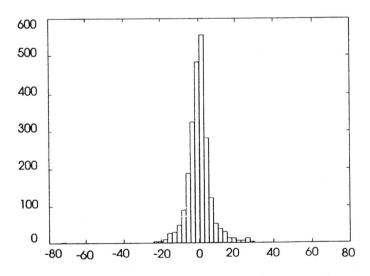

Figure 10.7 DEM/FRF neural network error histogram for training data (in pips)

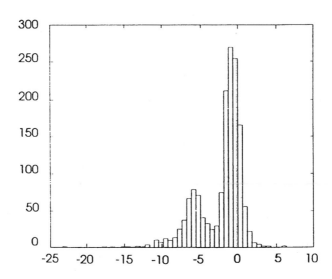

Figure 10.8   DEM/FRF neural network error histogram for test data (in pips)

Given that trading performance is the main means of evaluating models, it may be useful to modify the error function used during training to take into account the eventual classification of the network prediction. (So that output errors that lead to an incorrect classification are penalised more heavily than those that do not.) Although this is attractive, it would reduce the flexibility of using the neural model.

10.5   CONCLUSIONS

The study carried out on inter-day trading showed that when good indicators are available, rule induction can give results as accurate as other techniques. In addition, the clarity of the rules gave interesting insights into the data, allowing comparisons between the different markets to be drawn.

On our intra-day study, although work remains to be done to improve the models, the neural network approach appeared to offer significantly better performance. The return achieved with the best neural models was very encouraging. Chemical Bank's QRT group is currently developing a trading system which uses neural models partially based on techniques similar to those used in this study.

One of the most important lessons to be learned from the study was that the way a model is evaluated affects its construction. The current method of trading with the model during evaluation is very simple and inflexible compared to the way that human traders work. It is important to evaluate models in a way that is as similar as possible to the way in which they will be used, whether that is for trading directly or to advise human traders.

DATAMARINER did not achieve as good results as the neural network approach. The most likely reason for this was that the indicators used during the project were suboptimal, since the results improved with the use of different technical indicators.

Although the neural network approach was successful, there are a number of issues that were raised which could be investigated further.

1. *Network architecture.* The work in this project used a simple MLP with a single hidden layer. The largest network performed best, and so it would be advisable to consider larger networks, and also networks with more hidden layers to see if performance could be improved.
2. *Input features.* Although the precise form of the features input to a neural network is not as crucial as for rule induction, considerable improvements in accuracy can be achieved by using inputs that contain more information. The improvement achieved on the DEM/FRF results by using additional inputs suggests that there is more that can be done with this data. An alternative is to use recurrent networks, which have an internal memory, so as to avoid having to determine the precise window of past data required to model the system.
3. *Confidence intervals.* It would clearly be useful to have error bounds on exchange rate forecasts. There are techniques for estimating confidence intervals on neural network outputs; the most principled of these depend on training the network in a Bayesian framework, as in Williams *et al.* (1995).
4. *On-line learning.* The work in this study has built a single model that is then fixed and evaluated on test data. There are neural network models that can be trained on-line, so that changes in the underlying system are tracked. This might be an attractive approach for this application, provided that a suitable validation scheme was developed. A fixed model can be validated by evaluating its performance on recent out-of-sample data; this is not possible if the most recent data is used for adjusting the model on-line.

In both studies, all the training and testing of models was carried out on 'dead' data; using such models in a real-time system presents a number of additional problems. During the studies, all the models were developed and tested with data extracts on a stand-alone machine. The intra-day trading system currently being developed takes a live data feed and is integrated with other trading floor systems. In addition, spurious prices are removed and the models have to produce their predictions in real time. The response of the neural networks described in this chapter is sufficiently fast for this not to be a problem.

ENDNOTES

1. A comparative evaluation of DATAMARINER was carried out on a range of databases from the repository of machine learning databases maintained at the University of California at Irvine by D. Aha. These databases are drawn from commercial, medical and scientific fields. In nearly every case, the accuracy of the rules generated by Logica's algorithm was as good as or better than the figures quoted in the literature for other rule induction algorithms (see Nabney and Grasl 1991).
2. For more details on the use of Kalman filtering, see, amongst others, Harvey (1981, pp. 101–119), and Kalman (1960).
3. In practice, clauses were pruned from a rule starting from the last condition. The Fisher one-tailed probability distribution was used to decide if an individual clause provided a statistically significant increase in discrimination between classes.
4. In this context, oversampling refers to the technique of generating further time series which overlap with the original one. For example, if the original data was generated every hour on the hour, another time series could be generated every hour on the half hour. As such, this technique is similar to the analysis of panel data (see, amongst others, Chamberlain 1985 and Mátyás and Sevestre 1992).

REFERENCES

Cendrowska, J. (1988), 'PRISM: An Algorithm for Inducing Modular Rules', *International Journal of Man–Machine Studies*, **27**, 349–370.
Chatfield, C. and Collins, A.J. (1986), *Introduction to Multivariate Analysis*, Chapman & Hall, London.
Chamberlain, G. (1985), 'Panel Data', in Griliches, Z. and Intriligator, M.D. (eds), *Handbook of Econometrics*, Volume II, North-Holland, Amsterdam.
Cybenko, G. (1989), 'Approximation by Superposition of a Sigmoidal Function', *Math. Control, Signals and Systems*, **2**, 303–314.
Dunis, C. (1995), 'The Economic Value of Leading Edge Techniques for Exchange Rate Prediction', *Working Papers in Financial Economics*, **5**, 1–7.
Funahashi, K. (1989), 'On the Approximate Realization of Continuous Mapping by Neural Networks', *Neural Networks*, **2**, 183–192.
Harvey, A.C. (1981), *Time Series Models*, Philip Allen, London.
Hornik, K., Stinchcombe, M. and White, H. (1989), 'Multilayer Feedforward Networks Are Universal Approximators', *Neural Networks*, **2**, 359–366.
Kalman, R.E. (1960), 'A New Approach to Linear Filtering and Prediction Problems', *Journal of Basic Engineering*, **1**, 35–45.
Mátyás, L. and Sevestre, P. (1992) (eds), *The Econometrics of Panel Data*, Kluwer, Dordrecht.
Nabney, I.T. and Grasl, O. (1991), 'Rule Induction for Data Exploration', Avignon June '91 Conference on Expert Systems and their Applications, **1**, 329–341.
Nabney, I.T. and Jenkins, P.G. (1992), 'Rule Induction in Finance and Marketing', IBC Conference on Data Mining in Finance and Marketing, September.

Pao, Y.H. (1989), *Adaptive Pattern Recognition and Neural Networks*, Addison-Wesley, Reading, Mass.

Rumelhart, D.E. and McClelland, J.L. (eds) (1986), *Parallel Distributed Processing: Exploration in the Microstructure of Cognition*, MIT Press, Cambridge, Mass.

Quinlan, J.R. (1986), 'Induction of Decision Trees', *Machine Learning*, **1**, 81–106.

Race, P.R. (1988), 'Rule Induction in Investment Appraisal', *The Journal of the Operational Research Society*, **12**, 1113–1123.

Williams, C.K.I., Qazaz, C., Bishop, C.M. and Zhu, H. (1995), 'On the Relationship between Bayesian Error Bars and the Input Data Density', 4th IEE Conference on Artificial Neural Networks, Cambridge, 26–28 June, 160–165.

11

Market Inefficiencies, Technical Trading and Neural Networks

D. J. E. BAESTAENS,
W. M. VAN DEN BERGH
and H. VAUDREY

11.1 TECHNICAL ANALYSIS AND THE EFFICIENT MARKET HYPOTHESIS

Recently, the efficient market hypothesis has come under fire, somewhat surprisingly from the academic establishment (Kupiec 1993). The weak form of the hypothesis states that an investor cannot earn systematically excess returns (i.e. net of cost and compensation for the risk of the strategy) by developing trading rules based on historical data. However, it has become fashionable in academic literature to suggest that financial markets may after all display some signs of predictability (Ding *et al.* 1993; Peters 1994). Brock *et al.* (1992) have shown that some of the popular chartist techniques such as the *trading range break (TRB) rule* and the *moving average (MA) rule* may generate profitable trading rules under certain assumptions. The TRB rule states that you should sell when the price exceeds its last peak and buy when it drops below its last trough, while MA rules are based on the idea that you should buy when a short-term MA moves above (crosses) a long-term MA and sell when a short-term MA moves under a long-term MA. Several

Forecasting Financial Markets: Exchange Rates, Interest Rates and Asset Management. Edited by Christian Dunis. © 1996 John Wiley & Sons Ltd.

versions of these trading rules were tested on Dow Jones stock index data from 1897 to 1988 using simulated series from random walk and GARCH models as a benchmark. Both types of trading rules proved to generate significant returns: sell signals were followed by an average price fall of 9% and buy signals by an average rise of 12% on a yearly basis. None of the predictions of the benchmark models appeared to produce significant returns.

Unfortunately, the results of technical analysis stand or fall with the quality of the aforementioned optimization procedure. Setting the time span of a long moving average to say 125 days inevitably limits the scope of possible time series characteristics within the data set. It should be obvious that doing so without proper validation may result in overfitting and loss of generalization. What is more, many investors believe that the intuition of the analyst and not the application of a selection procedure or formula is the key to successful investment. Hawley *et al.* (1990) therefore assert that, while the pattern recognition capabilities of neural networks suggest possibilities for their use in technical analysis, the most beneficial applications are likely to be designed by the chartists themselves. Other arguments warn against too much preprocessing of the input data and as a result we refrained from over-optimizing the data. To preserve the statistical representativity of the data, we selected a weekly time span on which to train the neural network. For a 50–20–1 neural network, it roughly amounts to 10 input patterns per weight.

The computation of technical indicators such as moving averages or relative strength indices is to be viewed as a method of pattern recognition. Neural networks have in principle the capacity to classify these patterns and hence predict the corresponding return profile.

The structure of the chapter is the following. Section 11.2 addresses the Unilever data set and the derived trading rules in more detail. A neural net replication of the CMA rule is presented in section 11.3, while section 11.4 provides some results. Finally, section 11.5 offers some concluding remarks.

11.2 Data Collection and Rule Definition

From Datastream, we collected Unilever's daily stock price in Dutch guilders from January 1973 to March 1992 resulting in about 5000 records. We then divided this sample into two parts: the first 2500 records to be used as a training set for the neural network models, the following 2501 records used for testing purposes. Unilever, a large multinational, was chosen because its conservative and defensive character implies that its return pattern has not fundamentally altered over time as a result of major restructurings or acquisitions.

Table 11.1 Daily returns: descriptive statistics

Unilever Amsterdam daily returns

	Full sample	73–75	76–79	80–82	83–84	85–87	88–89	90–93
N	5292	782	1043	784	521	783	521	858
Mean	0.00037	−0.00025	−0.00005	0.00065	0.00091	0.00065	0.00087	0.00029
Std. Derivation	0.0123	0.0138	0.0084	0.0113	0.0105	0.0170	0.0153	0.0091
Skewness	−0.0300	−0.2733	−0.3725	0.1525	0.0374	−0.0104	0.1363	−0.1327
Kurtosis	21.85	6.36	4.14	5.00	2.85	25.10	21.45	2.83
$r(1)$	0.026	0.123	0.072	0.013	0.105	0.024	−0.166	0.065
$r(2)$	−0.045	−0.005	0.011	0.019	0.029	−0.140	−0.097	0.040
$r(3)$	−0.030	−0.029	0.007	0.014	0.064	−0.045	−0.123	−0.003
$r(4)$	0.036	−0.046	−0.027	−0.056	−0.001	0.084	0.215	0.034
$r(5)$	−0.006	0.066	−0.018	−0.011	−0.023	0.005	−0.051	−0.058
Bartlett std.	0.014	0.036	−0.031	0.036	0.044	0.036	0.044	0.034

While the full sample is not highly skewed, as can be seen in Table 11.1, both the training set and the test set display significant respectively negative and positive skewness. The daily return pattern is highly leptokurtic, especially during the last 10 years. Note the high (but gradually decreasing after 1987) volatility for the test set. Interestingly, the training set exhibits high positive (negative) correlation for the first (fourth) lag while the test set displays a high negative (positive) correlation for lag two (four).

To minimise optimization 'biases', we restricted our trading rule to the simple crossing-moving averages (CMA) rule advocated by Brock *et al.* (1992). This rule is unsophisticated in that it does not include Fibonacci numbers in the computation of the indicator! Importantly, technical analysis purports to forecast the direction of a price change (down, neutral, up) rather than its magnitude. The CMA rule then computes a fixed function f_{CMA}: $R^L \rightarrow \{-1, 0, +1\}$ where L (respectively l) is the length of the long-term (respectively short-term) moving average given by

$$f_{CMA}(p(t), p(t-1), \ldots, p(t-L+1)) = \text{sign}\left(\frac{1}{l}\sum_{j=0}^{l-1} p(t-j) - \frac{1}{L}\sum_{j=0}^{L-1} p(t-j)\right)$$

(1)

When using the band version of the rule parametrized with q:

$$f_{CMA}(p(t), p(t-1), \ldots, p(t-L+1), q) =$$

$$\begin{cases} 1 & \text{if } \frac{1}{l}\sum_{j=0}^{l-1} p(t-j) - (1+q)\frac{1}{L}\sum_{j=0}^{L-1} p(t-1) > 0 \\ -1 & \text{if } \frac{1}{l}\sum_{j=0}^{l-1} p(t-j) - (1-q)\frac{1}{L}\sum_{j=0}^{L-1} p(t-j) < 0 \\ 0 & \text{otherwise} \end{cases}$$

(2)

Viewed in the formalism of neural networks, this rule can be seen as a constrained weights network taking L past prices in its input layer with two hidden linear nodes computing the moving averages and a single threshold output node that produces the trading signal.

Note that in this formulation the band version of the rule can be easily implemented with extra threshold units operating on the two moving average nodes with appropriate weightings. Obviously, the CMA rule assumes the two moving averages contain information relevant to predict the direction of future returns.

Whatever the neural model specification, the question of how to choose the parameters L, l and q remains open. Again following Brock *et al.* (1992), L and l were set to respectively 50 and 1. We then investigated the sensitivity of the CMA rule to increasing values for q (with $0 \leq q \leq 0.5$). Table 11.2 shows the

Table 11.2 The CMA $L - l$ rule with $L = 50$ and $l = 1$

Period	Rule	N(buy)	N(sell)	Buy	Sell	Buy–sell	Buy > 0 (%)	Sell < 0 (%)	Good (%)
					Unilever daily-returns technical analysis results				
Training	(1, 50, 0)	1313	1137	0.00052 (1.150)	−0.00039 (−1.205)	0.00046 (2.031)	46.0	45.3	45.7
Test	(1, 50, 0)	1674	777	0.00074 (0.221)	0.00047 (−0.303)	0.00035 (0.447)	48.6	41.7	46.4
Training	(1, 50, 0.02)	783	656	0.00052 (0.964)	−0.00074 (−1.714)	0.00062 (2.167)	44.6	47.7	46.0
Test	(1, 50, 0.02)	1233	454	0.00073 (0.184)	0.00041 (−0.331)	0.00042 (0.424)	48.5	42.5	46.9
Training	(1, 50, 0.05)	262	285	0.00169 (2.251)	−0.00076 (−1.229)	0.00120 (2.605)	48.5	49.5	49.0
Test	(1, 50, 0.05)	577	191	0.00100 (0.573)	0.00086 (0.212)	0.00054 (0.126)	48.4	46.1	47.8

[a]Column 1 gives the set under study.
Column 2 gives the rule under study. The first (second) figure is the length of the short (long)-term moving average while the third one gives the band value.
Columns 3 and 4 the number of buy and sell signals generated.
Columns 5 and 6 the mean return on a buy (sell) signal with respective *t*-values.
Column 7 the differences between mean daily buy and sell returns and corresponding *t*-value.
Column 8, 9 and 10 summarizes the fraction of good buy, sell and buy-or-sell signals.

daily return on buy (sell) signal is positive (negative) but not significantly different from the unconditional mean return. Furthermore, the percentage of good predictions based on any signal (buy > 0 and sell < 0) always lies below 50%. However, even this bad score still produces positive cumulative returns as a result of skewness in the data. Interestingly, the 1–50 rule performs reasonably well on the training set but very badly on the out-of-sample test set. This finding casts serious doubts on the suitability of the CMA rule to predict Unilever's stock return. Since the two sets were treated completely independently, with no overlapping information, the number of trading signals always equals the set size minus the long-term moving average lag for $q = 0$.

We experimented with different values for L and l while holding q constant at 0. Unlike the results obtained by Brock *et al.* (1992), none of the calculated series yielded significant results.

Assuming the data are autocorrelated, scrambling the return series obviously would remove serial correlation. As the CMA rule appears to generate even worse results on the shuffled series, the original unscrambled data are conjectured to be autocorrelated to some extent. The CMA rule, however, does not appear to produce a sufficient number of correct signals to be considered as a reliable trading model even though the results are worse for the bootstrap alternative. It could mean that none of the moving averages used are good 'feature extractors' for the stock series under study (or simply that this lag value is not used by Unilever traders). Of course, we did not search exhaustively for appropriate lags nor did we attempt to apply another technical rule such as the TRB. Our aim is to investigate the degree to which neural networks represent a suitable approximation function to detect market inefficiencies.

11.3 NEURAL NETWORK REPLICATION OF THE CMA RULE

A static neural network model can be viewed as a generalization of the CMA rule except for the fact that the L, l and q parameter values are not preset. The neural network is assumed to identify the relevant indicator(s) and to estimate efficient values. As with the technical analysis framework, we look at the raw prices and issue a trading signal (buy, hold or sell) for every new point in the time series. Again, several choices with respect to the time window and the number of indicators have to be made.

To reduce the number of models, we limited the input window of historical prices to the last five trading days (week). This choice may be somewhat arbitrary, but ensures a reasonable amount of data points (2500 for training) relative to the number of weights even with a large number of hidden units (Bellmann 1961). Each record of five consecutive prices was rescaled to fall into the [0, 1] range. While the actual values are lost, the procedure forces every input pattern into the hypercube $[0, 1]^5$ whatever the price level, hereby guaranteeing an *invariance to translation* for a given pattern. In the presence of two input patterns i and j with j consisting of prices which are all equal to those of $i + f10$, both i and j display the same structure. This rescaling is not unreasonable since a human trader is likely to evaluate price series in comparable standardized ways. Figure 11.1 shows the impact of the transformation.

The direction of tomorrow's price, the sign of the return, stands for the target. The signal is coded as follows:

$\qquad$ 0 $\qquad$ for a sell signal

$\qquad$ 0.5 $\quad$ for a neutral signal and

$\qquad$ 1 $\qquad$ for a buy signal

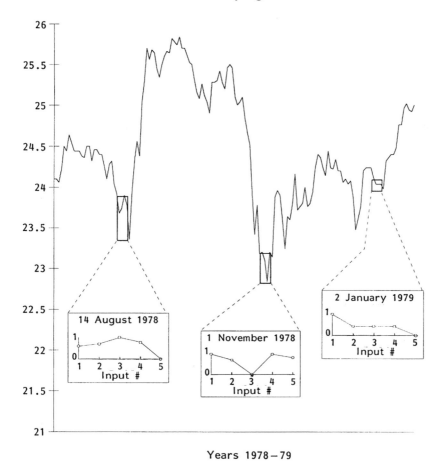

Years 1978−79

Figure 11.1 Rescaling of various input patterns

Remember the CMA rule yielded relatively better results for an unscrambled data set. We therefore implicitly assume the presence of some market inefficiency (and therefore predictability) as signalled by small deviations around the hyperplane $s = 0.5$ depicted in Figure 11.2. Efficient markets imply the probability of a buy (or sell) signal given past information equals 50% or 0.5. In this case, the decision surface in the lagged space (the input space for the network) coincides with the hyperplane $s = 0.5$. However, the presence of some degree of inefficiency causes some regions of the input space to correspond to values (slightly) different from 0.5 resulting in a decision surface exhibiting small *local* bumps around the hyperplane $s = 0.5$.

A neural network appears well suited to mapping this surface where data allows enough nonlinear resources (hidden units) to be used. The problem now resides in the fact that we obviously do not want the network to overfit the training set (the wavy light grey curve) since we defined inefficiencies as slight deviations from the 0.5 hyperplane. Technically, we are looking for a solution in the model space not too far from the 0.5 hyperplane (the thick solid curve), that is, a solution resulting in an RMSE close to 0.5 (assuming away neutral signals). Learning will be difficult to monitor with a validation set since the RMSE will already approximate 0.5 when starting with small random weights (the solid 0.5 line).

We are prevented from using a classical cross-validation procedure to halt training since the training procedure is likely to stop immediately once the learning algorithm runs (depending on the order of presentation of the learning set examples). We therefore used a regularization technique instead.

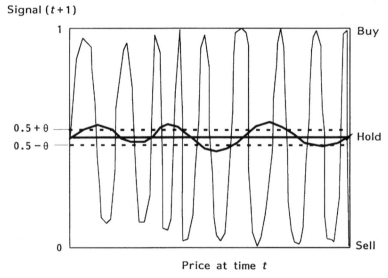

Figure 11.2 Concept of inefficiency—deviations from the hyperplane s

To prevent the network creating a too complex decision surface, a penalty term was added to the error criterion and the learning algorithm adapted accordingly. We are in fact minimizing the following error criterion with T_k the desired signal for pattern k and O_k the network's output signal:

$$\min \frac{1}{2} \sum_{k=1}^{p} \sum_{i=1}^{o} (T_k^o - O_k^o)^2 + \frac{\eta}{2} \sum_{i \to j} w_{ij}^2 \tag{3}$$

where η is a parameter included to prevent the weights from taking large values reducing the class of functions the network can realize.

Furthermore, the parameter θ has been introduced to reduce the number of trading signals given by the network for the obvious reason that transaction costs cap the number of daily trades. Since the network will never exactly generate 0.5, we treated the output signals falling within θ of 0.5 as equivalent to no trade signals.

Finally, to evaluate the network's performance, three benchmarks similar to the ones applied in Table 11.2 will be presented:

- $R(\text{buy})$ = The mean return per buy signal
- $R(\text{sell})$ = The mean return per sell signal
- $R(\text{buy or sell})$ = The mean return on any signal

11.4 NEURAL NETWORKS RESULTS

A 5–20–1 network was trained for 3000 epochs using Fahlman's quickprop learning algorithm that is faster than the standard back-propagation algorithm (Fahlman 1988). Using the partial second-order derivative of the overall error with respect to each weight, the learning procedure allows for taking large steps in weight space without overshooting the solution. These computations were carried out on a Sun workstation using the NevProp v1.16 program. The software is available on the Internet from the University of Nevada, Reno. A validation set was identified to enable the algorithm to adjust the network's weights with respect to a pseudo out-of-sample set that is not the actual test set. The network model therefore is not 'optimized' in function of the test data, thus minimizing the danger of overfitting.

The number of hidden units is arbitrary (and can be optimized using an appropriate information criterion) but is believed to provide enough machine resources to place sigmoids in hyperspace. The learning rate (ε) was set to 0.25 and the decay term (η) to 0.0005. Since the learning was stopped after a fixed number of epochs, one should not focus too much on the parameter values since there is no reason why convergence would have been reached. However, even early stopping as in this case still can result in models with

Table 11.3 Out-of-sample results

Theta	N(buy)	N(Sell)	Buy	Sell	Buy–sell	Buy > 0 (%)	Sell < 0 (%)	Good (%)
0	1227	1273	0.000202422 (−0.907)	0.001060779 (0.885)	−0.000855357 (−1.551)	49.71	43.91	46.76
0.05	579	505	0.001354794 (1.121)	0.000916909 (0.411)	0.000437885 (0.520)	52.33	43.56	48.25
0.075	352	280	0.001558538 (1.167)	0.000534146 (−0.121)	0.001024392 (0.925)	54.26	43.93	49.68
0.09	237	211	0.001486564 (0.901)	0.000369101 (−0.273)	0.001117463 (0.854)	53.16	45.97	49.78
0.1	167	172	0.002342778 (1.541)	−0.000277507 (−0.841)	0.002620284 (1.744)	56.29	49.42	52.80
0.105	143	155	0.001983581 (1.130)	−0.000890226 (−1.336)	0.002873807 (1.792)	54.55	50.97	52.68
0.11	125	142	0.002400483 (1.389)	−0.001244718 (−1.579)	0.003645201 (2.149)	56.00	50.70	53.18
0.115	113	124	0.0023238 (1.266)	−0.000669051 (−1.028)	0.002992851 (1.664)	53.98	49.19	51.48
0.12	93	113	0.001913469 (0.872)	−0.000995397 (−1.229)	0.002908866 (1.502)	54.84	50.44	52.43
0.125	79	106	0.001337069 (0.441)	−0.00110616 (−1.273)	0.002443229 (1.188)	56.96	51.89	54.05

interesting properties. Nevertheless, the arbitrary parameter setting that results proves a major drawback of the neural network approach.

Table 11.3 reports the out-of-sample performance of the trained network for different values of the rejection threshold. Again transaction costs are ignored. Interestingly, both the percentage of good buy and sell signals are increasing with the threshold, i.e. while reducing the number of transactions. Apparently, *inefficiencies* (defined as small deviations from the 0.5 line in Figure 11.2) occurring during the training period (1970s) seem to reaffirm themselves during the test period (1980s).

For $\theta = 0$, the percentage of good signals falls below 50% since every pattern is a buy or a sell signal while the target might be a hold signal in 10% of the cases. Figure 11.3 plots the return performance against increasing threshold values. The mean return per transaction (buy or sell) around 0.13% compares favourably with the unconditional mean return of 0.064% (for the highest value for θ).

The performance of the trading model peaks at around 250 transactions for the whole test set (equivalent to about 25 annual transactions). A further reduction in the number of transactions by increasing the threshold caused the mean return per transaction to decrease.

To improve our understanding of the drivers behind buy and sell signals, we plotted eight input patterns correctly generating a buy (respectively sell) signal in Figure 11.4. As we did not examine every single significant deviation (bump) from the 0.5 line, for instance by applying a clustering technique along the lines of the method of Gorman and Sejnowski (1988), the findings for the eight patterns cannot be generalized. Within each group though, patterns appear to share some commonalities indicating they correspond to similar regions in the input space.

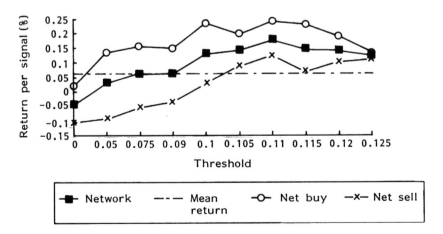

Figure 11.3   Conditional returns for increasing values of θ

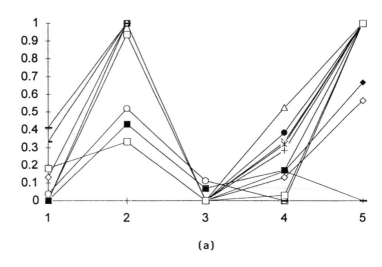

(a)

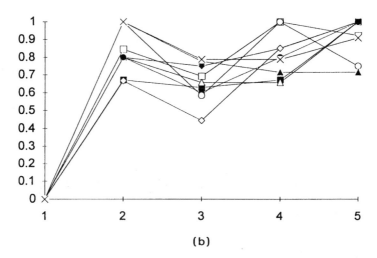

(b)

Figure 11.4 Activation patterns: (a) high positive output activation patterns (b) high negative output activation patterns

Finally, the model's contribution may be assessed by the amount of money it allows one to earn. Figure 11.5 shows the result obtained with $\theta = 0.15$ and where a buy (sell) signal prompts the trader to accumulate his one-day return positively (negatively). False signals cause the cumulative returns to drop. Neutral signals are ignored, that is the accumulated return is transferred to

Returns in Dutch guilders

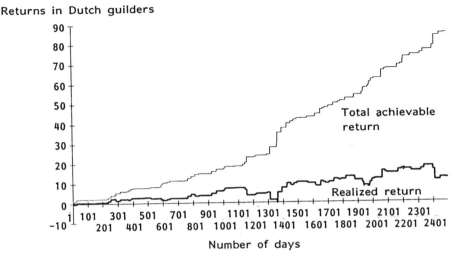

Figure 11.5 Paper trading profits

the next day. He will realize around 14% of the maximal achievable return (obtained by a system trading on the assumption that all signals are true). The system clearly displays an upward trend away from the zero profit line. However, no profits can be made once transaction costs are taken into account.

11.5   DISCUSSION

This neural network application has demonstrated that a static nonlinear system can be trained to perform technical analysis at a basic level. Our approach differs from others in the field in that we did not attempt to optimize the input set. Raw data series were presented to a network predicting the direction of future price levels. Furthermore, an original rescaling of the data ensured invariance in the input space. The network was then trained using a regularization penalty term to constrain the interpolated surface realized by the network. The model produced up to 54% correct signals. This result may be indicative of the presence of market inefficiencies (defined as small deviations from the 0.5 hyperplane) and of the adequacy of a neural network tool to reveal these. However, before such techniques could be implemented in the trading room, further research is required. The promising results have not yielded a profitable trading strategy. The following suggestions may contribute to identifying an improved trading strategy.

First, an enlarged database would enhance data representativity and increase the dimension of the input patterns. This could be achieved by including stocks similar to Unilever. The question of how to measure similarity remains open.

Second, the use of tick data would increase the data frequency and allow for the use of an economical (or operational) time-scale where time is compressed in low volume period and enlarged for high volume rather than a calendar time-scale. The inclusion of hints as suggested by Abu-Mostafa (1993) should not be underrated.

Third, a radial basis functions network allows a more localized mapping as compared to a classical sigmoidal network and may consequently lead to an improved detection of local 'inefficiencies' in the input space. Moreover, confidence intervals or error bars can be computed following procedures suggested by MacKay (1991) or Le Cun et al. (1990). Unfortunately, all these methods assume convergence of the learning algorithm.

Fourth, an alternative error criterion including transaction cost and accounting for both the direction and absolute value may lead to improvements. Alternatively, an additional output node denoting the absolute value of the return could be implemented.

Fifth, the model could be included in a multi-network decision environment and their combined power measured under a given decision rule (Würtz and de Groot 1992).

Finally, recurrent networks incorporating feedback mechanisms may add a more dynamic approach.

REFERENCES

Abu-Mostafa, Y.S. (1993) 'A Method for Learning from Hints', in Hanson, S., Cowan, J. and Giles, C. (eds), *Advances in Neural Information Processing Systems*, Vol. 5, pp. 73–80, Morgan-Kaufmann, San Diego.

Baestaens, D.J.E., van den Bergh, W.M. and Wood, D. (1994), *Neural Network Solutions for Trading in Financial Markets*, Pitman/Financial Times Publishing, London.

Bellman, R.E. (1961), *Adaptive Control Processes*, Princeton University Press, Princeton, NJ.

Brock, W.A., Lakonishok, J. and LeBaron, B. (1992), 'Simple Technical Trading Rules and the Stochastic Properties of Stock Returns', *Journal of Finance*, **27** (5), 1731–1764.

Ding, Z., Granger, C.W.J. and Engle, R.F. (1993), 'A Long Memory Property of Stock Market Returns and a New Model', *Journal of Empirical Finance*, **1** (1), 83–106.

The Economist (1993), 'The Mathematics of Markets, A Survey of the Frontiers of Finance, *The Economist*, October 9, 1–20.

Fahlman, S. (1988), 'An Empirical Study of Learning Speed in Back-Propagation Networks', *Technical Report CMU-CS-88-162*, CMU.

Gorman, R.P. and Sejnowski, T.J. (1988), 'Analysis of Hidden Units in a Layered Network Trained to Classify Sonar Targets', *Neural Networks*, **1**, 75–89.

Hawley, D.D., Johnson, J.D. and Raina, D. (1990), 'Artificial Neural Systems: a New Tool for Financial Decision-Making', *Financial Analysts Journal*, Nov./Dec. 1990, 63–72.

Kryzanowski, L., Galler, M. and Wright, D.W. (1993), 'Using Artificial Neural Networks to Pick Stocks', *Financial Analysts Journal*, 21–27.

Kupiec, P.H. (1993), 'Do Stock Prices Exhibit Excess Volatility, Frequently Deviate from Fundamental Values and Generally Behave Inefficiently?', *Financial Markets, Institutions & Instruments*, **2** (1), Blackwell, Cambridge, Mass.

Le Cun Y., Denker, J.S. and Solla S.A. (1990), 'Optimal Brain Damage', in Touretzky, D.S. (ed.), *Advances in Neural Information Processing Systems*, Vol. 2, Kaufman, San Mateo, Calif. pp. 598–605.

MacKay, D.J.C. (1991), 'A Practical Bayesian Framework for Backprop Networks', submitted to *Neural Computation*.

Peters, E.E. (1991a), *Chaos and Order in the Capital Markets, A New View of Cycles, Prices and Market Volatility*, John Wiley, New York.

Peters, E.E. (1991b), 'A Chaotic Attractor for the S&P 500', *Financial Analysts Journal*, March–April, 55–62.

Peters, E.E. (1994), *Fractal Market Analysis*, John Wiley, New York.

Ripley, B.D. (1993), 'Statistical Aspects of Neural Networks', in Barndorff-Nielsen, O.E., Jensen, J.L. and Kendall, W.S. (eds), *Networks and Chaos: Statistical and Probabilistic Aspects*, Chapman & Hall, London, pp. 40–123.

White, H. (1988), 'Economic Prediction Using Neural Networks: The Case of IBM Daily Stock Returns', in Trippi, R.R. and Turban, E. (1993), *Neural Networks in Finance and Investing*, Probus, Chicago, Ill. pp. 315–329.

Würtz, D. and de Groot, C. (1992), 'Forecasting Time Series with Connectionist Networks: Applications in Statistics, Signal Processing and Economics', in Belli, F. and Radermacher, F.J. (eds), *Lecture Notes in Artificial Intelligence*, 604, Springer-Verlag, Heidelberg, 175–199.

12

The Use of Error Feedback Terms in Neural Network Modelling of Financial Time Series

A. N. BURGESS
and
A. N. REFENES

12.1 INTRODUCTION: CORRELATED RESIDUALS AND NON-STATIONARITY

When modelling financial time series it is often found that the error at a given time-step is related in some way to the errors at previous and successive time-steps. In linear time series modelling this phenomenon of 'serial correlation' is usually taken as an indication that a model is poorly specified (i.e. there is some structure in the actual data series which is not being captured by the model). Such misspecification could be due either to missing variables or to nonlinearities in the data. However, serial correlation can also be exhibited if a data series is non-stationary (i.e. its statistical properties change over time).

This is easy to illustrate by considering, for example, a system which exhibits random shifts in its mean value from time to time but which in all other respects is stationary. A model fitted to data from a given period will

---

Forecasting Financial Markets: Exchange Rates, Interest Rates and Asset Management. Edited by Christian Dunis. © 1996 John Wiley & Sons Ltd.

'learn' the overall mean of the in-sample data, and will also 'learn' to predict the systematic element of the variations around this mean value. Consider the effect that future changes in the mean level will have on the errors made by the system: if the mean level shifts upwards the model will consistently underestimate the true value; if the mean level drops then the model will consistently overestimate; residuals (errors) for successive periods will be related in that they will have the same average value. A very simple example of this type is presented in Figure 12.1.

The fact that non-stationarity can manifest itself as a systematic relationship between successive residuals raises the possibility that the effects of non-stationarity can be reduced by using previous residuals as inputs to the model. Thus, the model can be improved by eliminating that proportion of the systematic error which is predictable from previous residuals. In the simple example above, this would be 100% of the total error, except for the period in which the 'shock' occurs. For real financial data series we would expect, at best, only to be able to reduce the error rather than to eliminate it, but in the knowledge that even small improvements in performance can be very significant in terms of providing a competitive advantage in making investment decisions.

The structure of the chapter is as follows. In section 12.2, we present the definitional framework for moving average and autoregressive processes. In section 12.3, we discuss different modelling approaches for moving average processes. In section 12.4, we present simulation results for alternative modelling approaches while, in section 12.5, we show empirical results for the modelling of the DAX futures contract in terms of its relationship to the CAC40 contract. Section 12.6 gives some concluding remarks.

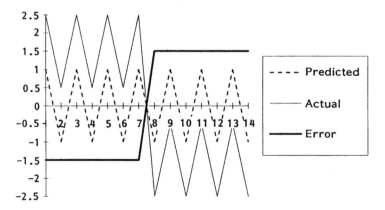

Figure 12.1   Relationship between non-stationarity and correlated residuals

12.2 MOVING AVERAGE VERSUS AUTOREGRESSIVE PROCESSES

Consider a time series $y(t)$ which consists of a systematic component, which can in principle be predicted, and a purely random set of innovations, or 'shocks', $\varepsilon(t)$. Then an *autoregressive* (AR) series is one in which the systematic component is a function of previous values of the time series, i.e.:

$$y(t + 1) = f(y(t), y(t - 1), y(t - 2) \ldots) + \varepsilon(t + 1)$$

A *moving average* (MA) process, on the other hand, is one in which the systematic component is a function of past innovations, i.e.:

$$y(t + 1) = f(\varepsilon(t), \varepsilon(t - 1), \varepsilon(t - 2) \ldots) + \varepsilon(t + 1)$$

In fact, there are strong intuitive grounds for using MA processes to model financial time series. For instance, whilst the initial impact of an unpredictable 'shock', such as the unexpected announcement of an interest rate cut, cannot be accounted for, in practice the effects of the shock will not all be immediate but will instead be spread out over a period of time. Moving average models are ideally suited to modelling this type of behaviour.

The linear time series analysis literature considers models which incorporate both autoregressive and moving average elements, the so-called ARMA and ARIMA models (see, amongst others, Box and Jenkins 1976 and Harvey 1981). The modelling of financial time series using neural networks, however, has been almost exclusively limited to a purely AR approach (see, for instance, Weigend *et al.* 1991 and Kingdon 1993).

12.3 MODELLING MOVING AVERAGE PROCESSES

Autoregressive modelling is popular amongst neural network researchers because the input values for an AR model can be easily identified: they are simply the lagged values of the time series itself. In contrast, the external shocks, or innovations, in a time series cannot be observed directly and modelling MA processes is consequently more complicated.

Whereas the past values of a time series are directly measurable, the innovations are more difficult to identify, even after the event. This is because the true innovation is that part of the observed value which could not have been anticipated. Thus, in practice, an innovation can only be identified relative to a particular model of expectations and the true innovations could only be known if expectations could be modelled with complete accuracy.

Below, we discuss three approaches which have been adopted to circumvent the difficulties of modelling MA processes: AR approximation, two-stage modelling and recurrent networks. We argue that whilst these approaches do have some merits, they also suffer from serious limitations. We suggest that a more natural approach to modelling MA processes is to use a novel type of recurrent network in which the errors from previous time-steps are used as inputs to the network.

12.3.1 Autoregressive Approximation

Any MA process can in fact be represented in autoregressive form. Consider the first-order MA process:

$$y_t = \theta \cdot \varepsilon_{t-1} + \varepsilon_t$$

which gives

$$\varepsilon_t = y_t - \theta \cdot \varepsilon_{t-1}$$

By repeated substitution we obtain

$$y_t = \theta(y_{t-1} - \theta(y_{t-2} - \theta(y_{t-3} - \theta(\ldots)))) + \varepsilon_t$$

or

$$y_t = \theta y_{t-1} - \theta^2 y_{t-2} + \theta^3 y_{t-3} - \theta^4 y_{t-4} + \ldots + \varepsilon_t$$

Thus in order to completely represent even a first-order MA process an infinite number of AR terms is required. This in fact overstates the problem because if the system is stable, then $|\theta| < 1$ and θ^n tends to 0 as n tends to infinity. Beyond the first few lags the predictive power of the lagged terms is small and the process can be approximated to a high degree using a relatively small number of lags.

Even so, this approach increases the number of variables within the model. This is particularly problematical when building neural models due to the high variance caused by fitting models containing large numbers of free parameters. Table 12.1 shows the number of AR terms which are required to

Table 12.1 Number of lagged terms required to approximate a moving average process

Coefficient θ	R^2 of MA model (%)	Number of AR terms
0.1	1	1
0.2	4	1
0.3	9	1
0.4	16	2
0.5	25	2
0.6	36	3
0.7	49	4
0.8	64	6
0.9	81	11

model a first-order MA process to 90% accuracy, as a function of the coefficient θ.

For weak models, which explain 25% or less of the variance of the target series, an AR model requires only one or two terms to approximate the MA. However, it is precisely for those cases where the model could potentially be very powerful that the AR approximation requires a large number of lagged terms and greatly increases the overfitting risk due to model variance.

12.3.2 Two-stage Modelling

However, we can consider the error of any model as consisting of two components—one due to modelling error and the other due to innovations. The residuals of an unbiased model will be unbiased estimates of the innovations. A first improvement over a purely AR approach is to exploit this relationship by building a secondary model of the residual errors; an example in which an AR neural network model is combined with a linear error model is reported in Ginzburg and Horn (1993). The initial model is built exactly as if no MA component existed. A separate model of the time series of residuals is then built from the first model. The combined prediction is then the prediction of the first model plus the predicted residual.

This multi-stage modelling methodology has the advantage of using standard modelling techniques and thus of being relatively straightforward to implement. Conceptually, however, it is far from transparent. This is because the two models are integrated only at the time of making the final prediction. The error model is not a true MA model because the residuals of the first model are clearly not the best estimates of the true innovations (a better estimate would be the residuals of the combined model). Trying to interpret the combined models and to identify the existence of an MA component is almost impossible under these circumstances. In spite of this, it is likely that in the presence of an MA component this methodology would outperform a purely AR approach. At worst, the error model would add nothing to the predictive power of the system without significantly degrading the performance of the initial model.

12.3.3 Recurrent Networks

Perhaps the most promising approach to modelling MA processes is to attempt to capture the feedback element in the system by using neural networks with recurrent connections. Many types of recurrent network have been developed (see, for instance, Elman 1990 and Werbos 1990). Whilst these networks are capable of modelling some of the dynamic aspects of a time series, they are not ideally suited to modelling financial time series which embody MA processes. This is because the 'feedback' in standard recurrent networks is purely a function of the internals of the network model, whereas the effect we wish to model is that of an *external shock* to the system. In fact, if lagged values of the time series are used in conjunction with recurrent connections, the network can in principle reconstruct the innovations. These are simply the difference between predicted and actual values.

So existing recurrent networks are capable of modelling MA processes but do so in an indirect and non-transparent manner. If the correct lagged values are matched with delayed recurrent connections then the innovations can be identified and the MA process indirectly modelled. This causes three potential problems: first, modelling the innovations is subject to estimation error; second, two input variables are required to model each innovation term; finally, the same input variables are used to model AR and MA components making it difficult to isolate the two effects and rendering the model even less transparent than neural networks are usually.

12.3.4 Error Feedback

We propose an alternative algorithm which addresses these weaknesses. The error modelling is directly integrated within the neural network learning procedure. The neural network inputs are augmented by q error feedback inputs, whose values are determined by the error made by the network during the q previous forecasts. As the neural network learns, the error feedback terms converge towards the true innovation terms. With p lagged values and q error feedback units a network has the potential to learn an arbitrary nonlinear function relating p AR and q MA terms to the next value of the series. This justifies calling such a model a *non-parametric nonlinear ARMA(p, q) model*. In cases where the underlying process contains MA elements the resulting model will typically be both more accurate and more transparent than is possible using either a purely AR approach, a two-stage approach or a standard recurrent network.

12.4 EXPERIMENTAL RESULTS

To illustrate the danger of adopting a purely AR approach to modelling time series which contain MA elements we first consider a synthetic problem. The aim of the experiment is to evaluate the performance of four different models on the benchmark: a linear autoregressive model, AR(L); a linear model with error feedback, MA(L); a neural network autoregressive model, AR(NN); and a neural network with error feedback, MA(NN).

In order to generate the benchmark series we use a random generator to produce a series of independent identically normally distributed (i.i.d.) innovation terms, $\varepsilon(t)$. From these we generate the series $y(t)$ such that

$$y(t) = 0.6\varepsilon(t - 1) + 0.5\varepsilon(t - 1) \cdot \varepsilon(t - 2) + \varepsilon(t)$$

Where $\varepsilon(-1)$ and $\varepsilon(-2)$ are taken as zero, then $y(0) = \varepsilon(0)$. Note that (i) the random $\varepsilon(t)$ term makes the series non-deterministic and (ii) the systematic element is partly linear and partly nonlinear (see Figure 12.2). In fact, if we treat the series as being analogous to price *changes* and integrate it over time, as shown in Figure 12.3, the resulting series has a similar appearance to many real financial time series.

Target

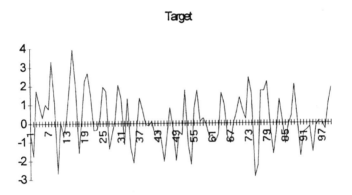

Figure 12.2 The benchmark series

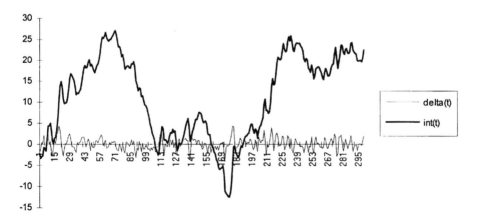

Figure 12.3 The benchmark viewed as price changes of a hypothetical asset

For simplicity, an iterative learning procedure (gradient descent) was used to train each model. For the AR(L) model, this procedure guarantees convergence to the same (optimal) solution that we would achieve by using linear regression. For the MA(L) model, the results obtained might be marginally worse than would be expected by using a full-blown maximum likelihood estimation of the parameters in the model.

Out of a total of 300 samples, the first 200 were used for training and the final 100 reserved for out-of-sample testing. Details of the model architectures and the out-of-sample results obtained are shown in Table 12.2.

We observe three points from a comparison of the results. First, the neural network models outperform their respective linear counterparts in each case. Second, each MA model outperforms its respective AR counterpart. This indicates that the error feedback terms allow the series to be more accurately modelled than is possible using a purely AR approach. Third, the MA(L) model outperforms the AR(NN) model, a warning that, even for nonlinear problems, a poorly specified neural network model can fail to beat a well-specified linear model.

In general, we note that the MA(NN) model achieves a performance which is 80% of the 'ideal' model, compared to the other three models which only achieve 20–30% of this 'ideal' performance. This shows that the error feedback method can extract a large part of the information which is contained in the directly unobservable innovation terms.

12.5 MODELLING CONCURRENT EQUITY INDEX FUTURES

We have applied the error feedback approach to a problem of modelling concurrent European index futures. In particular, the aim of our experiments was to model the German DAX index in terms of its relationship to the

Table 12.2 Results of different models on benchmark problem

| Model | Inputs | | Hidden units | MSE | Variance explained (R^2) (%) |
	Autoregressive	Error feedback			
AR(L)	2	—	—	1.63	10.9
MA(L)	—	2	—	1.58	13.6
AR(NN)	2	—	3	1.61	11.8
MA(NN)	—	2	3	1.21	34.0
Ideal	—	2[a]	—	1.00	45.0

[a]The 'ideal' model is the theoretically optimal model which could be constructed if it were possible to observe the innovation terms directly (rather than having to approximate them using error feedback).

French CAC40 index. The motivation for applying error feedback modelling to this problem was the hypothesis that the two indices would exhibit a degree of cointegration (see Granger 1981).

The phenomenon of cointegration has been widely studied in the statistics community, primarily using linear models but also through the use of parametric nonlinear models (see Granger 1995). In statistical terms, two time series are said to be cointegrated if they are individually non-stationary, but there is a linear combination of the two which is stationary. In practical terms, this implies that an equilibrium or 'fair value' relationship exists between the two time series and that whilst this may be distorted in the short term, the series will tend to move gradually back into line with each other. In cases where cointegration has been identified, the normal approach is to use changes in one series as an input when modelling changes in the other series.

However, this approach is not ideal because the model is still essentially one of *returns* (differences in prices) whilst the cointegration relationship itself is essentially between the actual price *levels*. Typically the restoration of the fair value relationship will not happen over a fixed time-scale. In fact, it might take hours, days, weeks or even months. Thus, if the problem is transformed from one of levels to one of returns (which must by definition be calculated over a given, and fixed, period) there is every reason to believe that information will be lost and the performance of the model will suffer as a result.

12.5.1 Modelling the Dynamics of Cointegration Using Error Feedback

The solution is to build a model which relates the level of one time series (in this case the DAX) to that of the other time series (the CAC40). Under these circumstances, a standard regression model will model the average or expected value of the DAX given the level of the CAC40. If the series are in fact cointegrated, such a model would give an indication of the fair value for the DAX, and by comparing this to the actual value we could determine if the DAX was in fact overvalued (and hence should be sold) or undervalued (and hence should be bought).

However, this approach does not enable us to model the *dynamics* by which the cointegrating mechanism operates. If the 'mispricing' time series exhibits trends or patterns of any sort then ideally these would be included within the model. In order to do this, it is necessary to model the DAX not merely in terms of the CAC40 but also in terms of the extent to which the underlying relationship is currently or has been distorted by temporary factors. In fact, these 'distortions' from the fair value are easy to identify because, by our definition of fair value, they are simply the residual errors of the original model.

Clearly, one approach would be to build two models, one of the fair value relationship and another for the dynamics of the cointegration. However, an alternative approach is to build a single model which employs error feedback terms. In this case, the fair value relationship and the cointegration dynamics are modelled by a single neural network. The AR inputs of Table 12.2 are used to model the DAX/CAC40 relationship and the error feedback inputs are used to model the distortion/restoration effect of the cointegration.

For a linear, or indeed any purely additive model, we would expect to obtain no significant advantage (except that of increased transparency) from building a combined model as opposed to using a two-stage modelling process. However, a key feature of neural networks is the capacity to model conditional relationships in which the influence of one variable can depend upon the value taken by other variables. In this case we could hypothesise that the cointegration dynamics might vary depending upon the relative levels of the two indices: in other words, the cointegrating relationship could be a nonlinear one, as argued in Burgess (1996).

12.5.2 Modelling Results

Table 12.3 shows the results of modelling the DAX in terms of the CAC40 using both linear and nonlinear models. In each case the expected value of the DAX is modelled as a function of the (contemporaneous) value of the CAC40 together with up to three error feedback terms. The error feedback terms are spaced at intervals of one week and thus represent the mispricing at one week, two weeks, etc., prior to the date of the prediction. The nonlinear model architecture is a standard feedforward neural network with a single hidden layer containing three units.

Table 12.3 Out-of-sample fits of different cointegration models

Type	Error feedback	Correlation of the residuals	R^2 (forecast/actual) (%)
Linear	0	0.92	73
	1	0.86	60
	2	0.85	64
	3	0.90	77
Nonlinear	0	0.91	50
	1	0.94	81
	2	0.95	88
	3	0.95	90

We used the Datastream data bank, taking daily data from 4 January 1987 to 30 September 1990 to estimate the model parameters. We left a further two and a half years for out-of-sample testing (1 October 1990 to 31 March 1992). Table 12.3 shows the degree to which the different models fit the data during the out-of-sample period.

For all but the simplest models the correlation and associated R^2 figures are very high. However, these figures cannot be used as the basis of any test of market efficiency because the models are concerned with the contemporaneous relationship between the CAC40 and the DAX and do not directly make any predictions about future values.

12.5.3 Scenario Analysis

In order to evaluate the models within the context of a simulated trading strategy, we use the models to make indirect forecasts about the DAX through a process of scenario analysis. The error feedback inputs, being lagged, are all available at least one week ahead of time making the future value of the CAC40 the only unknown. The historical volatility of the CAC40 was calculated and for each prediction five possible scenarios are considered in which the CAC40 remains at the same value, moves up by one or two standard deviations, and moves down by one or two standard deviations.

Empirical probabilities were assigned to each scenario and the relative return between the DAX and the CAC40 was estimated in each case, based on the modelled value of the DAX under each scenario. The predicted relative return was then calculated as a weighted average of the different outcomes. Under the null hypothesis of a linear cointegration effect, the expected relative return on the two indices should depend only on the current mispricing and hence should be the same under all scenarios. In fact, the results were found to be quite robust to assumptions about the probability distribution of price changes in the CAC40.

The simple trading strategy which we use to evaluate the performance of the models is to take a long position in one index and an offsetting short position in the other index. In this way the net profit is equal to the relative return between the two indices. The results for selected models are shown in Figure 12.4.

In order to illustrate that these results are due to the predictive power of the different models, rather than to the underlying trading strategy, we provide a statistical analysis of the trading results in Table 12.4.

The results shown in Figure 12.4 and Tables 12.3 and 12.4 clearly indicate that there is a certain degree of predictability in the relative returns of the two indices. The static linear model makes only limited trading profits in spite of the fact that two series do exhibit a degree of cointegration, which can be

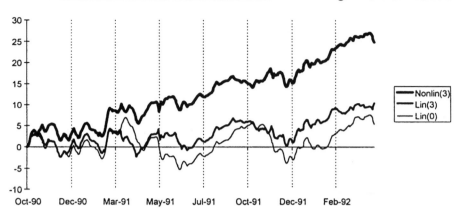

Figure 12.4 Out-of-sample trading performance of different models

Table 12.4 Statistical analysis of trading performance

Model	Correlation forecast/actual	Correct direction (%)	Risk/reward t-statistic[a]	Out-of-sample return (%)
Linear (0)	0.10	54	0.67	5.35
Linear (3)	0.13	55	1.32	10.40
Nonlinear (3)	0.22	57	3.18	24.79

[a]The risk/reward t-statistic is the ratio average return/standard deviation of returns adjusted for the sample size.

verified by a standard test such as the 'unit root' test (see Dickey and Fuller 1979). However, the addition of the error feedback terms can be seen not only to improve the quality of the contemporaneous model but also, through a scenario analysis, to improve profits during simulated trading. This indicates that there is a predictable element in the dynamics of the cointegration. Finally, and most interesting of all, the nonlinear model substantially outperforms the equivalent linear model, suggesting that the cointegration is actually nonlinear in nature.

12.6 SUMMARY

We have shown how the use of error feedback terms is theoretically motivated both as a possible means of reducing the effects of non-stationarity in a time series and also in order to model more accurately time series which are partially or wholly 'moving average' in nature.

By means of a benchmark time series (actually a nonlinear MA process) we show that the performance of both nonlinear and linear models is substantially improved by the use of error feedback terms. We also note that the linear model with error feedback terms outperforms the AR neural network, a warning that, even for nonlinear problems, a poorly specified neural network model might fail to beat a well-specified linear model. A promising result is that the neural network with error feedback terms achieves 80% of the performance of an 'ideal' model as opposed to the 20–30% achieved by the other models, which suggests that the error feedback method can extract the majority of the information which is contained in the directly unobservable innovation terms.

The error feedback neural network provides a natural method of modelling the dynamic effects of nonlinear cointegration. A set of linear and nonlinear models were compared, each relating the German DAX to the French CAC40 stock market index. The superior out-of-sample performance statistics for the neural network models suggest the presence of nonlinear effects.

In order to evaluate the models in the context of a simulated trading strategy, a scenario analysis approach was adopted under which the models were used to generate forecasts of the relative returns under scenarios of the CAC40 staying the same, moving up by one or two standard deviations, and moving down by one or two standard deviations. Using a simple long/short strategy in the out-of-sample period of two and a half years, the best performance was 25% and was achieved by the neural network model with three error feedback terms. This suggests that not only are the dynamics of cointegration an important consideration, but that there are significant nonlinear effects within the relationship between the two markets.

REFERENCES

Box, G.E.P. and Jenkins, G.M. (1976), *Time Series Analysis, Forecasting and Control*, revised edition, Holden-Day, San Francisco.

Burgess, A.N. (1996), 'Modelling Nonlinear Cointegration in International Equity Index Futures', in Refenes, A.N. *et al.*, *Proceedings of the 3rd International Conference on Neural Networks in the Capital Markets*, World Scientific, London (forthcoming).

Dickey, D.A. and Fuller, W.A. (1979), 'Distribution of the Estimators for Auto-regressive Time Series with a Unit Root', *Journal of the American Statistical Association*, **74**, 427–431.

Elman, J.L. (1990), 'Finding Structure in Time', *Cognitive Science*, **14**, 179–211.

Ginzburg, I. and Horn, D. (1993), 'Combined Neural Networks for Time Series Analysis', *Advances in Neural Information Processing Systems*, Vol. 6, Morgan-Kaufmann, San Francisco, 224–231.

Granger, C.W.J. (1981), 'Some Properties of Time Series Data and Their Use in Econometric Model Specification', *Journal of Econometrics*, **16**, 121–130.

Granger, C.W.J. (1995), 'Modelling Nonlinear Relationships between Extended-Memory Variables', *Econometrica*, **63**, 265–279.

Harvey, A.C. (1981), *The Econometric Analysis of Time Series Models*, John Wiley, New York.

Kingdon, J. (1993), 'Neural Nets for Time Series Forecasting: Criteria for Performance with an Application in Gilt Futures Pricing', in Refenes, A.N. (ed.), *Neural Networks in the Capital Markets*, John Wiley, Chichester, pp. 261–276.

Weigend, A.S., Rumelhart, D.E. and Huberman, B.A. (1991), 'Generalization by Weight Elimination with Application to Forecasting', *Proc. IJCNN 1991*, IEEE Press, Washington, 837–841.

Werbos, P.J. (1990), 'Backpropagation through Time: What it Does and How to Do it', *IEEE Transcripts on Neural Networks*, **78** (10), 261–277.

13

An Evolutionary Algorithm for Portfolio Selection Within a Downside Risk Framework

ANDREA LORASCHI and
ANDREA G. B. TETTAMANZI

13.1 INTRODUCTION

This chapter examines a financial application of evolutionary algorithms (Michalewicz 1992) to some issues raised by recent research in portfolio theory (PT) concerning the use of non-trivial indices of risk.

The central problem of PT concerns selecting the weights of assets in a portfolio which minimise a certain measure of risk for any given level of expected return. According to mainstream PT (Markowitz 1959), a meaningful measure of risk is given by the variance of the distribution of portfolio returns. However, while leading to elegant analytical results and easy practical implementation, this approach fails to capture what an investor perceives as the essence of risk, that is, the chance of incurring a loss.

In this respect, the economic literature has recently proposed alternative measures of risk. An interesting family of measures, defined as lower partial moments (Harlow 1991), refers to the downside part of the distribution of returns and has therefore become known under the name of downside risk.

A number of difficulties are encountered when trying to apply this new approach even to simple problems. First, the nature of these risk measures

---

prevents from devising general analytical solutions and quadratic optimisation techniques cannot by applied because the shape of the objective function is, in general, non-convex. Moreover, the typical sizes of real world portfolio selection problems are of the order of hundreds of assets. Thus, expected return and risk are calculated using historical series made up of hundreds of historical returns. Even the software packages that apply the conventional mean–variance approach through quadratic optimisation suffer limitations as the size of the problem grows beyond a certain threshold. Things become more elaborate as it is usual practice among fund managers to impose various constraints on their optimal portfolios.

The authors have carried out experiments applying evolutionary algorithms to the portfolio selection problem using the downside risk approach and obtained satisfactory results. Evolutionary algorithms appear to be well suited to the task of solving difficult problems in high dimensional spaces because they combine features from random search and Monte Carlo methods with some powerful heuristics borrowed from natural evolution. On the basis of this approach, the authors have developed a software decision support system for SIGE Consulenza SIM which has been named DRAGO (*downside risk asset allocation with genetic optimisation*). This tool has proved successful in devising portfolios where the optimised set of weights provides protection against potential under-performance of the portfolio with respect to a given benchmark.

Section 13.2 provides a critical overview of modern portfolio theory and discusses a family of downside risk indices. Section 13.3 presents a brief introduction to evolutionary algorithms. Portfolio optimisation is formulated as a two-objective convex optimisation problem in section 13.4 and an evolutionary algorithm to solve it (DRAGO) is described in section 13.5. A brief discussion of experiments and results is given in section 13.6.

13.2   PORTFOLIO OPTIMISATION

13.2.1   Modern Portfolio Theory

Choosing an optimal portfolio weighting of assets when their future rate of return is uncertain may be seen as a problem of minimising the uncertainty for a given level of the portfolio expected return. Modern portfolio theory (MPT) calls this *uncertainty* risk and measures it as the standard deviation or the variance of the probability distribution of future returns. Within this framework, portfolios are optimised through the use of quadratic programming methods.

Other more recent approaches that require less simplistic assumptions, such as those based on the idea of *downside* risk, are not very easy to deal with using deterministic combinatorial optimisation methods.

The notion of risk as the variance of returns is at the foundation of MPT. Yet, Markowitz (1959), acknowledged as one of the first developers of MPT, pointed out that variance 'often leads to unsatisfactory predictions of [investor] behaviour'. Realising that the investor perceives risk only on the downside part of the return distribution, he proposed the use of *semivariance*, defined as the weighted average of the squared distances of the returns below the mean of the distribution, as an index of risk. In mathematical notation:

$$\text{semivar} = \sum_{R_i < E[R]} p_i (R_i - E[R])^2$$

where R_i is one of the elements of the portfolio return distribution, p_i its attached probability and $E[R]$ the expected (mean) return. However, because of the inherent difficulties in carrying out the necessary calculations, he built his model based on the variance. Choosing an optimal portfolio, thus, became a question of variance minimisation for a given level of expected return. Markowitz showed that as the level of risk increases, the expected return attached to optimal portfolios draws a convex non-decreasing curve (efficient frontier). That is, to attain a greater expected return, an investor must accept a higher exposure to risk.

Minimising variance is equivalent to minimising semivariance *if the return distribution is symmetric around the mean*. Distributions of returns, though, are more often skewed than symmetric. If, for example, a distribution is highly skewed to the left, variance will greatly underestimate the risk of realising a return below the mean.

13.2.2 Drawbacks of Modern Portfolio Theory

Variance has the advantage of naturally lending itself to analytical treatment, but it shows serious drawbacks when used as an index of risk. As Domar and Musgrave (1944) remarked in a seminal article: 'Of all the possible questions which the investor may ask, the most important one, it appears to us, is concerned with the probability of a loss. This is the essence of risk' (p. 396). Therefore, semivariance might be regarded as an alternative candidate, but its reliance on the concept of distance from the mean since it varies from distribution to distribution may lead to the unwanted result of discarding an asset that should be preferred to others because it could offer *with certainty* higher realised returns even if it shows a relatively higher semivariance. For instance, Figure 13.1 shows two return distributions with same mean, but

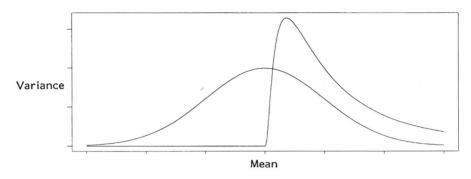

Figure 13.1   Different shapes of return distributions

different variances: intuitively, the higher variance distribution will be, in fact, regarded as less risky by an investor, contrary to what MPT would suggest.

13.2.3   Downside Risk Indices

A new approach, which only recently has been partially explored by the literature in the field, defines risk as a measure related to the part of a return distribution below a certain target of return. Adapting the formula of semivariance to the concept of subjective threshold below which the investor judges risky the investment, τ, leads to the *target semivariance* (TS) expression:

$$TS = \sum_{R_i < \tau} p_i(\tau - R_i)^2$$

This measure of *downside risk* (DSR) (Bawa 1975, Harlow 1991) is usefully generalised as:

$$DSR(\tau) = \sum_{R_i < \tau} p_i(\tau - R_i)^q$$

The parameter q may be seen as a coefficient of risk aversion in the sense that if:

$q = 0$, the above expression equals the probability of realising a return below the target (shortfall probability);

$q = 1$, it shows the expected value of the returns below the target (target shortfall);

$q = 2$, it is equivalent to the target semivariance;

$q > 2$, the formula attaches increasing weight to the returns below the target, i.e. the higher the parameter, the more the investor dislikes downside risk.

13.2.4 Implementation Issues

A straightforward substitution of DSR in place of variance within the MPT context raises computational problems. This formula does not lend itself to analytical treatment and the classic deterministic algorithms used for optimisation purposes are no longer suitable.

Figure 13.2 shows the downside risk surface for a simple problem involving only three assets. As can be seen, the surface is very rugged and there are many local optima. A gradient descent method could not handle such a situation in a satisfactory way. Moreover, as the number of dimensions increases, the computation effort required for calculating the gradient increases accordingly, and usual dimensions are in the order of the hundreds.

13.3 EVOLUTIONARY ALGORITHMS

The term 'evolutionary algorithms' encompasses a family of stochastic optimisation techniques based on the key concept of evolution.

The first proposals in this direction date back to the mid-1960s. John Holland, at the University of Michigan, introduced genetic algorithms (Holland

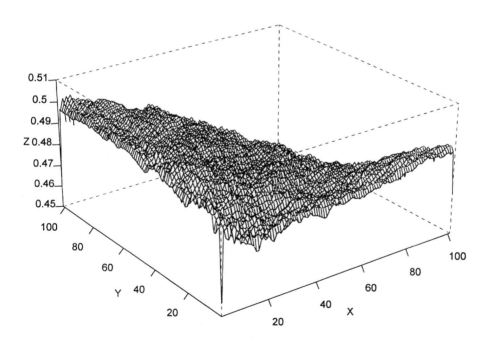

Figure 13.2 Downside risk surface

1975, Goldberg 1989, Davis 1991) and Lawrence Fogel, of the University of California at San Diego, came up with evolutionary programming (Fogel *et al.* 1966). In Europe, Ingo Rechenberg and Hans-Paul Schwefel, at the Technical University of Berlin, independently began to work on evolution strategies (Rechenberg 1973, Schwefel 1981). Their pioneering works eventually gave rise to a broad class of optimisation methods particularly well suited for hard problems where little is known about the underlying *search* space.

The latest development of this research thread is the so-called genetic programming, introduced by John Koza (1993), at Stanford University.

A recent work of reference and synthesis in the field of evolutionary algorithms is Michalewicz (1992).

An evolutionary algorithm maintains a population of candidate solutions for the problem at hand and makes it evolve by iteratively applying a (usually quite small) set of stochastic operators, known as *mutation, recombination, reproduction* and *selection*. Mutation randomly perturbs a candidate solution. Recombination decomposes two distinct solutions and then randomly mixes their parts to form a novel solution. Reproduction replicates the most successful solutions found in a population at a rate proportional to their relative goodness; while selection purges poor solutions from a population.

The initial population may be either a random sample of the *solution* space or may be seeded with solutions found by simple local search procedures, if these are available. The resulting process tends to find globally optimal solutions to the problem much in the same way as in nature, where populations of organisms tend to adapt to their surrounding environment.

13.4 PROBLEM FORMULATION

Portfolio optimisation can be viewed as a convex combination parametric programming problem (Steuer 1986), in that an investor wants to minimise risk while maximising expected return (on the efficient frontier a larger expected return corresponds to a greater risk). This can be expressed as a two-objective optimisation problem:

$$\min_{w} \{Risk(w)\}$$

$$\max_{w} \{Return(w)\}$$

subject to

$$\sum_i w_i = 1, \quad w_i \geq 0$$

These two objectives can be parametrised to yield a convex combination parametric programming problem with objective

$$\min_{w} \{\lambda Risk(w) - (1 - \lambda) Return(w)\}$$

where parameter λ is a trade-off coefficient ranging between 0 and 1. When $\lambda = 0$, the investor disregards risk and only seeks to maximise expected return. When $\lambda = 1$, the risk alone is being minimised, whatever the expected return.

Since there is no general way to tell which particular trade-off between risk and return is to be considered the best, optimising a portfolio means finding a whole range of optimal portfolios for all the possible values of the trade-off coefficient. The investors will, thus, be able to choose the one they believe appropriate for their requirements.

13.5   AN EVOLUTIONARY APPROACH

The structure of the portfolio optimisation problem itself suggests a global architecture for an evolutionary algorithm, many solutions being actually needed—one for each trade-off coefficient considered. A natural way to achieve that in an evolutionary setting is to have a number of distinct populations evolve in parallel with different trade-off coefficient values. The greater this number, the finer the resolution with which an investor will be able to examine the efficient frontier.

Because it is likely that slight variations in the trade-off coefficient do not significantly worsen a good solution, a natural way to sustain the evolutionary process is to allow *migration* or *cross-breeding* between individuals belonging to immediately neighbouring populations.

13.5.1   Algorithm Overview

This idea has been implemented by breaking up the population into several subpopulations, or *species*, one for each value of the trade-off coefficient. Individuals from a species are allowed to mate only with individuals from the same or an adjacent species. Furthermore, new individuals always replace the worst individual of their own species, so that the balance among species is always maintained.

The evolutionary algorithm implemented by the authors is based on a modified version of Darrel Whitley's GENITOR system (Whitley and Kauth 1988), which uses a *steady-state breeding* strategy and *elitist selection*.

The overall structure of the algorithm is as follows:

```
create initial population;
repeat
    select(γ);
    select(κ) such that |λκ − λγ| ⩽ 1;
    ζ := crossover(γ, κ);
    mutate(γ);
    replace(worst(λζ),ζ);
until termination condition.
```

13.5.2 Encoding and Fitness

As pointed out by Michalewicz and Janikow (1992), the most effective strategy for handling constraints in evolutionary algorithms consists, as long as this is feasible, in choosing an appropriate *encoding* and *reproduction* procedure such that illegal solutions are never generated or, even better, such that any possible chromosome encodes for a legal solution. This relieves the algorithm from having to check new individuals for constraint satisfaction.

The encoding that has been selected is intuitive and has the advantage that only legal solutions can be represented, i.e. the share of asset i is encoded in the genotype γ as an integer γ_i between 0 and a positive constant g_{max}. The actual weight w_i of that share is computed as the ratio of its encoded value to the total sum of all the encoded values in the chromosome,

$$w_i = \frac{\gamma_i}{\sum_j \gamma_j}$$

An additional integer γ_0 encodes the trade-off coefficient λ to be used to evaluate the objective function $z(\mathbf{w}; \lambda)$ for the corresponding portfolio $\mathbf{w}$.

The objective function is defined as

$$z(\mathbf{w}; \lambda) = (1 - \lambda)\, \text{Return}\,(\mathbf{w}) - \lambda \text{DSR}(\mathbf{w})$$

where the return and downside risk are appropriately scaled.

In GENITOR, a lower *fitness* value corresponds to a better solution. DRAGO scales fitness in such a way that the best individual of each species always has zero fitness. The fitness of individual γ, corresponding to portfolio $\mathbf{w}$, is calculated as

$$f(\gamma) = \frac{z_{max}(\lambda_\gamma) - z(\mathbf{w}; \lambda_\gamma)}{z_{max}(\lambda_\gamma) - z_{min}(\lambda_\gamma) + 1}$$

where $z_{max}(\lambda)$ and $z_{min}(\lambda)$ stand for the maximum and minimum values of the objective function for the best and worst individuals respectively in the species associated with the trade-off coefficient λ.

13.5.3 Genetic Operators

A variation of uniform crossover has been employed as a genetic re-combination operator suitable for the problem. Let δ and κ be two parent chromosomes and

$$\text{TOT}_\gamma = \sum_i \gamma_i, \qquad \text{TOT}_\kappa = \sum_i \kappa_i$$

Furthermore, suppose that the ith gene in γ, γ_i has been chosen to be passed on to the offspring. Then, the value of the ith gene in the offspring ζ is

$$\zeta_i = \min\left(g_{max}, \gamma_i \frac{\text{TOT}_\gamma + \text{TOT}_\kappa}{2\text{TOT}_\gamma}\right)$$

The *mutation* operator adopted by DRAGO alters a gene either by incrementing or decreasing it by one. This ensures that a chromosome undergoing mutation will not experience abrupt changes (mutation should not disrupt *schemata*).

While preserving schemata, this mutation strategy still involves a certain randomness, for it implies that a chromosome with a high total sum is less sensitive to mutations, whereas a chromosome with a small total sum feels the effect of a mutation more strongly.

13.6 EXPERIMENTS AND RESULTS

Since its implementation, DRAGO has undergone a comprehensive testing in the field, with portfolios ranging from a few dozens to hundreds of assets.

To demonstrate the typical working of the algorithm, Figure 13.3 shows snapshots of the evolution of a population of 200 individuals over 10 000 *generations* (here generation means the birth of a new individual and the death of the worst one). The population is segmented into 20 species, the mutation rate is set to 0.5 and the risk aversion coefficient q is set to 2, i.e. target semivariance is the index of risk.

Note that the space of risk and return is not the original problem space (which in this case has 15 dimensions), but only a convenient transformed space to view solutions. Therefore, although the initial population is uniformly distributed over the original problem space, it does not look so in the figure.

Execution times to obtain satisfactory solutions range between 5 minutes

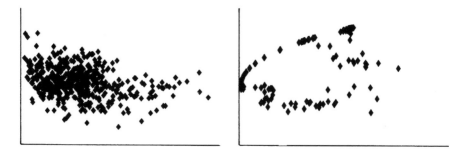

Figure 13.3   Initial and final populations

for the simplest problems and 10 hours for more complex cases on a quite ordinary 25 MHz 486DX-based personal computer.

13.7   CONCLUSIONS

Downside risk is a more reasonable measure of risk on which portfolios of assets should be optimised. With conventional methods such non-standard indices would hardly be available for optimisation.

The use of an evolutionary approach to portfolio optimisation has made it possible to employ in an operational setting meaningful indices of risk other than variance.

The resulting decision support system shows responses that are adequate for most practical uses. Speed is not a critical issue in this context because the average portfolio manager deals with typical investment horizons in the order of weeks or months.

REFERENCES

Bawa, V.S. (1975), 'Optimal Rules for Ordering Uncertain Prospects', *Journal of Financial Economics*, **2**, 95–121.

Davis, L. (1991), *Handbook of Genetic Algorithms*, VNR Computer Library, Van Nostrand Reinhold, New York.

Domar, E. and Musgrave, R.A. (1994), 'Proportional Income Taxation and Risk Trading', *Quarterly Journal of Economics*, **59**, 388–422.

Fogel, L.J., Owens, A.J. and Walsh, M.J. (1966), *Artificial Intelligence through Simulated Evolution*, John Wiley, New York.

Goldberg, D.E. (1989), *Genetic Algorithms in Search, Optimisation and Machine Learning*, Addison Wesley, Reading, Mass.

Harlow, H.V. (1991), 'Asset Allocation in a Downside Risk Framework', *Financial Analysts Journal*, September/October, 30–40.

Holland, J.H. (1975), *Adaptation in Natural and Artificial Systems*, MIT Press, Cambridge, Mass.

Koza, J.R. (1993), *Genetic Programming: On the Programming of Computers by Means of Natural Selection*, MIT Press, Cambridge, Mass.

Markowitz, H.M. (1959), *Portfolio Selection*, John Wiley, New York.

Michalewicz, Z. (1992), *Genetic Algorithms + Data Structures = Evolution Programs*, Springer-Verlag, Berlin, 151–157.

Michalewicz, Z. and Janikow, C.Z. (1991), 'Handling Constraints in Genetic Algorithms', in Belew, R.K. and Booker, L.B. (eds), *Proceedings of the Fourth International Conference on Genetic Algorithms*, Morgan Kaufmann, San Mateo, Calif.

Rechenberg, I. (1973), *Evolutionsstrategie: Optimierung technischer Systeme nach Prinzipien der biologischen Evolution*, Fromman-Holzboog Verlag, Stuttgart.

Schwefel, H.-P. (1981), *Numerical Optimisation of Computer Models*, John Wiley, New York.

Steuer, R.E. (1986), *Multiple Criteria Optimisation: Theory, Computation and Application*, John Wiley, New York.

Whitley, D. and Kauth, J. (1988), *GENITOR: A Different Genetic Algorithm*, Technical Report CS-88-101, Colorado State University, Fort Collins, Colo.

Index

Index compiled by Geoffrey C. Jones